# Emily Hobhouse and the British Concentration Camp Scandal

Emily Hobhouse

# Emily Hobhouse and the British Concentration Camp Scandal

An exposé of the treatment of Boer women
and children during the South African War
by one of its most vociferous opponents
ILLUSTRATED

Emily Hobhouse

**LEONAUR**

*Emily Hobhouse and the British Concentration Camp Scandal*
*An exposé of the treatment of Boer women and children during the South African War*
*by one of its most vociferous opponents*
ILLUSTRATED
by Emily Hobhouse

First published under the title
*The Brunt of the War and Where It Fell*

Leonaur is an imprint of Oakpast Ltd

Copyright in this form © 2017 Oakpast Ltd

ISBN: 978-1-78282-610-1 (hardcover)
ISBN: 978-1-78282-611-8 (softcover)

**http://www.leonaur.com**

# Contents

PREFACE FROM THE PAST (1587)

*Go little Booke, God graunt thou none offende,*
*For so meant hee which sought to set thee foorth,*
*And when thou commest where souldiours seem to wend.*
*Submit thyselfe as writte but little woorth:*
*Confesse withall, that thou hast bene too bolde,*
*To speake so plaine of Haughtie hartes in place.*
*And say that he which wrote thee coulde haue tolde*
*Full many a tale, of blouds that were not base.*

*My meaning is no more but to declare.*
*That Haughtie hartes do spend their time in vaine,*
*Which follow warres and bring themselues in snare*
*Of sundrie ylls, and many a pinching paine,*
*Whiles if they list to occupie their braine*
*In other feates with lesser toile ygot,*
*They might haue fame, whenas they haue it not.*

*As first (percase) you skipt Philosophie,*
*That noble skill which doth surmount the rest,*
*Wherto if you had tied your memorie,*
*Then bruntes of warre had never bruzde your brest.*
*Yet had our name bene blazde, and you bene blest.*
*Aske Aristotle if I speake amis,*
*Fewe souldiours' fame can greater be than his.*

To

THE WOMEN OF SOUTH AFRICA

WHOSE ENDURANCE OF HARDSHIP

RESIGNATION IN LOSS

INDEPENDENCE UNDER COERCION

DIGNITY IN HUMILIATION

PATIENCE THROUGH PAIN AND

TRANQUILITY AMIDST DEATH

KINDLED THE REVERENT APPRECIATION

OF THE WRITER, AND HAS EXCITED

THE SYMPATHY OF THE WORLD

## Some Articles of The Hague Convention

Art. XLIV.—Any compulsion of the population of occupied territory to take part in military operations against its own country is prohibited.

Art. XLV.—Any pressure on the population of occupied territory to take the oath to the hostile power is prohibited.

Art. XLVI.—Family honour and rights, individual lives and property, as well as religious convictions and liberty, must be respected. Private property cannot be confiscated.

Art. XLVII.—Pillage is formally prohibited.

Art. L.—No general penalty, pecuniary or otherwise, can be inflicted on the population, on account of the acts of individuals for which it cannot be regarded as collectively responsible.

## Manual of Military Law (1899)

As the object of war is confined to disabling the enemy, the infliction of any injuries beyond that which is required to produce disability is needless cruelty.

The general principle is that in the mode of carrying on war no greater harm shall be done to the enemy than necessity requires for the purpose of bringing him to terms. This principle excludes gratuitous barbarities, and every description of cruelty and insult, which serves only to exasperate the sufferings or to increase the hatred of the enemy without weakening his strength or tending to procure his submission.

# Introduction

This book is designed to give an outline of the recent war, from the standpoint of the women and children. There is no fear of aggravating a controversy amongst the Boers by its publication, for it will add nothing to their knowledge; these facts and many more are already well known in South Africa. But, so far, little has been heard in England of the farm-burning and the camps, from the side of those most concerned. The story is therefore largely told in the letters of women and in descriptions written by their friends.

On them fell the brunt of the war. More adult Boers perished in the camps than fell in the field of battle, and over four times as many children. A sketch is given of the history and extent of farm-burning, to demonstrate how wide was the eviction of families, and how powerless they were in the grasp of circumstances. The comments put forward by all parties on its policy and on that of concentration are recorded. My own connection with the movement is shortly described, as well as the opposition aroused by my efforts to lessen the hardships and save the lives of the women and

I take also this opportunity of publicly denying the accusation, so widely made in the Press and elsewhere, that I have slandered the British troops. No one has yet substantiated this accusation from my words or writings.

★★★★★★

See Blue Book, Cd. 1163, 1902. "Mr. G. H. Turvey expressed astonishment at persons like Sir H. Campbell Bannerman and Miss Hobhouse slandering without foundation, men fighting for the honour of old England."—Public Meeting at Ladybrand, "On Vile Fabrications and Slanders."

★★★★★★

I have, on the contrary, done my utmost to uphold the honour of the army. It is true that as long as war exists the honour of a country is confided to its soldiers, who will never cease to shield it; but is not the converse also true, and is it not often forgotten? *viz.* that the honour of the soldiers is confided to the country? If advantage is taken of the necessary obedience of soldiers to demand of them services outside the recognised rules of warfare, or in performance of which their moral duty must clash with their professional duty, the blame lies on the country and its government but not upon the army.

In these pages, it is no part of my object to cast blame on any individual, but I have striven simply to portray the sufferings of the weak and the young with truth and moderation.

To the plain man and woman, outside the political and military worlds, it seems as though in war an arbitrary line is drawn, one side of which is counted barbarism, the other civilisation. May it not be that, in reality, all war is barbarous, varying only in degree? History shows that as nations have advanced in civilisation this line has gradually been raised, and watchful care is needed lest it slip back. None of us can claim to be wholly civilised till we have drawn the line above war itself and established universal arbitration in place of universal armaments.

The deaths of the Boer children will not have been in vain if their blood shall prove to be the seed of this higher rule of nations. Their innocent histories ought to become fully known and widely understood, and so implant a hatred of war and a shrinking from its horrors, which shall issue in a ripened determination amongst the kingdoms of the world to settle future differences by methods more worthy of civilised men.

My thanks are due to Mr. Alfred Marks, for a detailed and careful compilation of the rates of mortality.

CHAPTER 1

# Homes Destroyed

*"The tramp of Power, and its long trail of pain."*—William Watson.

After Lord Roberts had arrived in South Africa and had assumed command, he issued early in February the well-known First Proclamation. The success of this document depended upon the power of the occupying army to hold and protect the country which it entered, and upon carefully distinguishing between the few individuals who abused its terms and the many who did not. It was a familiar topic in the Concentration Camps, where it was constantly quoted in a dreary, puzzled way by countless women, who, unconscious of having ever abused its leniency, could not understand why its promises were disregarded. The proclamation is given in full, as upon it hung so much for good or ill.

FIRST PROCLAMATION OF LORD ROBERTS TO BURGHERS OF
ORANGE FREE STATE.

Feb, 1900.

The British troops under my command having entered the Orange Free State, I feel it my duty to make known to all *Burghers* the cause of our coming, as well as to do all in my power to put an end to the devastation caused by this war, so that, should they continue the war, the inhabitants of the Orange Free State may not do so ignorantly, but with full knowledge of their responsibility before God for the lives lost in the campaign.

Before the war began the British Government, which had always desired and cultivated peace and friendship with the people of the Orange Free State, gave a solemn assurance to President Steyn that, if the Orange Free State remained neutral, its territory would not be invaded, and its independence would be at all times fully respected by Her Majesty's Government.

In spite of that declaration, the Government of the Orange Free State was guilty of a wanton and unjustifiable invasion of British territory.

The British Government believes that this act of aggression was not committed with the general approval and free will of a people with whom it has lived in complete amity for so many years. It believes that the responsibility rests wholly with the Government of the Orange Free State, acting, not in the interests of the country, but under mischievous influences from without. The British Government, therefore, wishes the people of the Orange Free State to understand that it bears them no ill-will, and, as far as is compatible with the successful conduct of the war, and the re-establishment of peace in South Africa, it is anxious to preserve them from the evils brought upon them by the wrongful action of their government

I therefore warn all *burghers* to desist from any further hostility towards Her Majesty's Government and the troops under my command, and I undertake that any of them who may so desist, and who are found staying in their homes and quietly pursuing their ordinary occupations, will not be made to suffer in their persons or property on account of their having taken up arms in obedience to the order of their government. Those, however, who oppose the forces under my command, or furnish the enemy with supplies or information, will be dealt with according to the customs of war.

Requisitions for food, forage, fuel, or shelter, made on the authority of the officers in command of Her Majesty's troops, must be at once complied with; but everything will be paid for on the spot, prices being regulated by the local market rates. If the inhabitants of any district refuse to comply with the demands made on them, the supplies will be taken by force, a full receipt being given.

Should any inhabitant of the country consider that he or any member of his household has been unjustly treated by any Officer, soldier, or civilian attached to the British Army, he should submit his complaint, either personally or in writing, to my headquarters or to the headquarters of the nearest general officer. Should the complaint, on inquiry, be substantiated, redress will be given.

Orders have been issued by me, prohibiting soldiers from entering private houses, or molesting the civil population on any pretext whatever, and every precaution has been taken against injury to property on the part of any person belonging to, or connected with, the army.

But already, it appears, complaints had been made that soldiers had entered private houses and molested the civil population. A month earlier a Reuter's telegram had stated that:

General Babington's party, in a short excursion of twelve miles into the Free State, came upon three Boer farmsteads, and these they destroyed with dynamite and fire. The homesteads on Zwiegler's Farm, and two belonging to Lubbe, the *commandant* of the local commando, were burnt, having been used as camps by the enemy.—Reuter's Special Service, Jan. 11, 1900. From *Pen Pictures of the War.*

Mr. Conan Doyle alluded to the same incident when he wrote:

Methuen's cavalry on January 9th made another raid over the Free State border, which is remarkable for the fact that, save in the case of Colonel Plumer's Rhodesian Force, it was the first time that the enemy's frontier had been violated. The expedition under Babington consisted of the same regiments and the same battery which had covered Pilcher's advance.... With the aid of a party of the Victorian Mounted Rifles, a considerable tract of country was overrun and some farmhouses destroyed. The latter extreme measure may have been taken as a warning to the Boers that such depredations as they had carried out in parts of Natal could not pass with impunity, but both the policy and the humanity of such a course appear to be open to question, and there was some cause for the remonstrance which President Kruger shortly after addressed to us upon the subject.—*Great Boer War,* also published by Leonaur.

This protest from the Presidents ran as follows:—

We learn from many sides that the British troops, contrary to the recognised usages of war, are guilty of the destruction by burning and blowing up with dynamite of farmhouses, of the devastation of farms and the goods therein, whereby unprotected women and children are often deprived of food and cover. This happens not only in the places where barbarians are encouraged by British officers, but even in the Cape Colony and in this State, where white brigands come out from the theatre of war with the evident intention of carrying out a general devastation, without any reason recognised by the customs of war, and without in any way furthering the operations.

We wish earnestly to protest against such acts.—Cd. 582, Bloemfontein, Feb. 3, 1900.

It was during the last days of December 1899 and the first of January 1900 that the burning of farms began, Lubbeshock, the residence of Commandant Lubbe, being one of the earliest destroyed. The commander-in-chief, who was still in Cape Town, and who had probably heard nothing of this preliminary destruction, replied two days later asking for particulars and referring to depredations in Cape Colony. In this despatch, he emphasises the principle that it is barbarous to attempt to force men to take sides against their own sovereign and country.

Cape Town, Feb, 5, 1900.

I beg to acknowledge your Honours' telegram charging the British troops with the destruction of property contrary to the recognised usages of war, and with brigandage and devastation. These charges are made in vague and general terms. No specific case is mentioned and no evidence given.

I have seen such charges made before now in the Press, but in no case which has come under my notice have they been substantiated. The most stringent instructions have been issued to the British troops to respect private property, as far as is compatible with the conduct of military operations. All wanton destruction or injury to peaceful inhabitants is contrary to British practice and tradition, and will if necessary be rigorously repressed by me.

I regret that your Honours should have seen fit to repeat the untrue statement that 'barbarians have been encouraged by British officers' to commit depredations. In the only case in which a raid has been perpetrated by native subjects of the queen, the act was contrary to the instructions of the British officer nearest to the spot, and entirely disconcerted his operations. The women and children taken prisoners by the natives were restored to their homes by the agency of the British officer in question.

I regret to say that it is the Republican forces which have in some cases been guilty of carrying on the war in a manner not in accordance with civilised usage. I refer especially to the expulsion of loyal subjects of Her Majesty from their homes in the invaded districts of this Colony, because they refused to be commandeered by the invader. It is barbarous to attempt to force men to take sides against their own sovereign and country by threats of spoliation and expulsion. Men, women, and children have had to leave their homes owing to such compulsion, and many of those who were formerly in comfortable circumstances are now being maintained by charity.

That a war should inflict hardships and injury on peaceful inhabitants is inevitable, but it is the desire of Her Majesty's Government, and it is my intention, to conduct this war with as little injury as possible to peaceable inhabitants and to private property, and I hope your Honours will exercise your authority to ensure its being conducted in a similar spirit on your side.

A few days later he added a postscript to this despatch—

Feb. 12.

In continuation of my telegram of the 5th February, I beg to call your Honours' attention to the wanton destruction of property by the Boer forces in Natal. They not only have helped themselves freely to the cattle and other property of farmers without payment, but they have utterly wrecked the contents of many farmhouses. As an instance, I would specify Mr. Theodore Wood's farm, 'Longwood,' near Springfield. I point out how very different is the conduct of the British troops. It is reported to me from Modder River that farms within the actual area of the British Camp have never even been entered, the occupants are unmolested, and their houses, gardens, and crops remain absolutely untouched.

In reply to these two telegrams a long despatch was sent by the Boer Presidents. For some reason, not explained, their telegram does not appear in the Blue Book from which the foregoing despatches are taken. (Cd. 582, 1901.)

I therefore give it in full. Specific cases asked for by Lord Roberts are given, and it deals with other matters closely connected with the fate of women and children.

From State President Orange Free State, and State President of the South African Republic. Sent from Bloemfontein at 9.20. p.m. 19th February 1900. To His Excellency Lord Roberts, Cape Town, t9th February. (Reply to Nos. 2 and 3 in Cd. 582, 1901, but not published there.) We have the honour to acknowledge the receipt of your Excellency's telegram of 5th inst. The specific cases of needless destruction of properties by British troops are so numerous that we consider, with all due deference, that on inquiry the accuracy of the complaint would at once become manifest.

To quote but a few cases out of many: several farmhouses have been destroyed near the Jacobsdal boundary, amongst others: Commandant Lubbe's residence on his farm Lubbeshock, and those of his brothers and brothers-in-law on Weltevreden, Karulaagte, du Toitsheuvel, and Badenhorstoest were totally destroyed by British patrols late in December. On the farm Greuspan of D. Combrink the furniture was destroyed and a part burnt, and the dwelling-house was practically blown up by dynamite on the 4th January.

Altogether we received official information during December and January of eighteen houses wholly or partially burnt or destroyed, in the Jacobsdal district alone. At Bloemdraai, on Orange River, the dwelling-house was destroyed in December and everything carried away out of it by British patrols. In the beginning of this month still, the house of Klein Frans van der Merve was similarly burnt by one of your patrols coming from the direction of Ramah. These cases are far from being the only ones.

With regard to our complaints that barbarians are encouraged by British officers to make attacks on Republican *burgher* forces, your Excellency quotes one of the instances, but, as it seems to us, without having been properly informed about the facts by your subordinates. The correctness of the allegation can be substantiated by good witnesses in spite of the denial of the probably guilty parties.

We beg to state, moreover, that we have in custody as prisoners of war two natives, both caught with arms in their hands fighting amongst the British troops against us. The one was made prisoner at Stormberg on 10th December. He went on firing at our *burghers* and wounded one of them, named Adriaan Greyling of Smithfield, after the white flag had been put up by the troops in token of surrender, as he could well see. The other *Kaffir* is one of many who are fighting against our *burghers* in the vicinity of Dordrecht.

\*\*\*\*\*\*

Note:—It is stated that in their attack on Derdepoort, Nov. 25, 1899, the Bakathia captured seventeen women and children, and two women were murdered, *viz.* Mrs. Pieters, an American wife of the storekeeper, and Anna M. M. Fourie. See *Boer Fight for Freedom,* by M. Davitt.

\*\*\*\*\*\*

Not only at the attack at Derdepoort, on the boundary of Rustenburg, did natives, led by British officers, fight against our *burghers* and commit terrible crimes against our non-combatant women and children, whereby two women were murdered and houses were destroyed and burnt in the South African Republic, but in many other instances also, as at Tuli, Selukwe, and Mafeking, natives were egged on and used by British officers to fight against our *burghers* or to take up arms, as will, amongst others, appear from the following official communication. *The Mafeking Mail* of 10th November states:

> The following official despatch was issued on the 4th November. The Colonial contingent under Captain Goodyear has done splendid service today in occupying a position at the brick-fields. The contingent, though opposed to a withering fire, maintained its position, and was supported in a capital manner by the Fingo contingent under Mr. David Webster.

It also appears most clearly from official telegrams found in the English camp at Dundee that strong endeavours have been made by the British Government to enlist Basutos, against payment of five shillings per day, for military purposes: endeavours which have been successful in many instances.

With regard to your Excellency's counter accusations against our *burgher* forces, it may be permitted us to point out that they are so undefined and vague that we are thereby precluded from either being enabled to investigate the same or replying thereto and giving explanations, possibly, of the instances to which reference is made. We unhesitatingly accept your Excellency's assurance as to your instructions issued to the British troops regarding the subject under discussion, and we cherish the hope that thereby the desired results may be attained for the future. We also wish to assure you that the like instructions have long ago already been issued on our side, and that if such should prove necessary will be stringently enforced.

With regard to the sending away of certain of Her Majesty's subjects from their dwellings to beyond the lines of those parts of the country occupied by our *burgher* forces, we can affirm to your Excellency that the instances where such—and that only quite recently—has occurred, it was necessary in the interest of our military operations, as in all instances there was at least strong presumption existing that they did not behave themselves quietly and occupy themselves solely with their daily avocations, but either themselves acted as spies or assisted spies to make our movements and positions known to the enemy.

We regret the inconvenience and loss suffered by them, but we feel convinced that they themselves were the cause of it by their conduct. If any case be brought to our notice where a peaceable inhabitant of the parts occupied by us has been hardly or unjustly dealt by, we shall at once see to it that the sufferer shall have justice done him, as happened in a case brought to our notice of a certain Mr. Diebel, whose flock of sheep was confiscated on suspicion of being intended for use of our enemy's troops in Kimberley, and to whom, on reasonably acceptable explanation being forthcoming, rebutting the suspicion, full compensation was made.

The foregoing communication was ready for transmission when we received your Excellency's supplementary telegram of the 12th inst. We have caused an investigation to be instituted on the allegations therein made, and will send further communication as soon as we shall have received report.

To this despatch, Lord Roberts sent a short reply on the 24th of February—

Paardbburg Camp, 3.45 p.m. Feb, 24, 1900
(Received Pretoria 8.39 a.m. Feb, 28.)
I beg to acknowledge receipt of your Honours' telegram of the 19th February, in which you complain of certain acts alleged

to have been committed by the British troops, and in reply to acquaint you that it is impossible to inquire into these cases in the field after the lapse of so long a time since they are said to have occurred.

I, however, am fully convinced that no wilful destruction of property by Her Majesty's forces has taken place except such as was absolutely necessary for military purposes. In some cases, where the Republican forces have threatened or violated native territory under British protection it has been found necessary to arm the natives to defend themselves, but I feel sure in no case have armed natives been employed in military operations with the Imperial forces. I am of opinion that such complaints as these would be much more satisfactorily inquired into if made by the military commander on the spot to the military commander opposite to him.

The destruction of property by the Boers in Natal, and especially of the contents of the farm "Longwood," to which Lord Roberts called attention, was not apparently inquired into as promised by the Boer officials, no doubt owing to the rapid advance of the English forces which immediately followed. That case, and others of a similar nature, though not so widely advertised, were, however, carefully investigated by Mr. Robertson during his visit to Natal, and clearly shown by him to have been mainly the work of natives, though begun by Boers and completed by British troops. (See *Wrecking the Empire*, by J. M. Robertson.)

The official return of estimated damage done by the Boers in eleven Natal districts amounts to £32,138, 13s. This is the joint claim of 285 Europeans. (Cd. 979, 1902.) It does not appear that any farm was burnt by the commandoes during the first invasion of Natal.

From these despatches, we learn that before February eighteen farms in the Jacobsdal district alone, besides two near Rustenburg, had been burnt. An equal number of families were therefore homeless, and others, frightened at the thought of a similar fate, piled their waggons with goods and fled to the fastnesses of the hills. Here they formed small *laagers*, protected by old men and boys. During the months of February and March, after Lord Roberts had joined the army, there seems to have been a lull, and a more settled feeling ensued, consequent on his influence and on the effects of the First Proclamation.

The day after the occupation of Bloemfontein, a proclamation was issued to the rank and file of the fighting *burghers*. (Proc. iii., Bloem-fontein, March 15, 1900.)

All *burghers* who have not taken a prominent part in the policy which has led to the war between Her Majesty and the Orange Free State, or commanded any forces of the Republic, or commandeered or used violence to any British subjects, and who are willing to lay down their arms at once, and to bind themselves to an oath to abstain from further participation in the war, will be given passes to allow them to return to their homes, and will not be made prisoners of war, nor will their property be taken from them.

It is a matter of common knowledge that this system of giving and taking an oath failed in its accomplishment and the results of its failure fell hard on the women and children. (For form of oath see Cd. 426, 1900.) The English forces could not effectively occupy the country, and returning commandoes exercised their legal rights to compel *burghers* to join their ranks or be considered traitors. The next step, on the reappearance of the English troops, was the eviction of the family and the burning of the house as that of a man who had broken his oath.

Moreover, the oath, nominally one of neutrality, was not always so considered in practice, and here was wide opening for misunderstanding. The people interpreted the word literally as meaning giving no help to either side; but constantly they found themselves punished because they did not report to one side the presence of the other upon their farms. Such a case in one of its many ramifications is that of Mr. Gideon De Wet, who has in consequence been undergoing two years' hard labour as a convict while his wife and family pined in Bloemfontein Camp. On this account, many homes were destroyed and many families rendered destitute.

Very little was heard in England of the farm-burning till May, by which time the accounts of war correspondents and private soldiers began to fill the papers, showing how general it had become. A few examples are given. The first, a letter from Private Stanton, must have been written in the early spring, being reprinted from the *Sydney Telegraph*,

Within 800 yards of the farm we halted, and the infantry blazed a volley into the house. Then we marched up to it, and on arrival found it locked up and not a soul to be seen, so we broke open the place and went in. It was beautifully furnished, and the officers got several things they could make use of, such as bedding, etc. There was a lovely library—books of all descriptions printed in Dutch and English. I secured a Bible, also a Mauser rifle. . . . After getting all we wanted out of it, our men put a charge under the house and blew it up. It seemed such a pity. It was a lovely house with a nice garden round it.—*Reynolds' Newspaper,* May 27, 1900. Letter from Private Stanton, N.S.W. Contingent.

The *Times* correspondent, writing from Bloemfontein April the 27th, says—

This column (General Carew's) had started with definite instructions from Lord Roberts 'to render untenable' the farms of such men who, having surrendered, were found to be still in league with the enemy, or were but making use of British magnanimity as a means to save their property, while they still actively favoured the enemy.—*Times,* May 21, 1900.

And that these orders were liberally interpreted seems clear from the account of Mr. E. W. Smith, correspondent of the *Morning Leader,* dated April 29—

General French and General Pole-Carew, at the head of the Guards and 18th Brigade, are marching in, burning practically everything on the road. The brigade is followed by about 3500 head of loot, cattle and sheep. Hundreds of tons of corn and forage have been destroyed. The troops engaged in the work are Roberts' Horse, the Canadians and Australians. I hear today that General Rundle burnt his way up to Dewetsdorp. At one farm, only women were left. Still rifles were found under the mattress. Orders were inexorable. The woman threw her arms round the officer's neck, and begged that the homestead might be spared. When the flames burst from the doomed place, the poor woman threw herself on her knees, tore open her bodice, and bared her breasts, screaming, 'Shoot me, shoot me! I've nothing more to live for, now that my husband is gone, and our farm is burnt, and our cattle taken!'

Mr. Filson Young, author of the *Relief of Mafeking,* published by Leonaur, describes an afternoon's work of this nature, and questions the wisdom of such methods—

Dry Harts Siding, May 8.

The burning of houses that has gone on this afternoon has been a most unpleasant business. We have been marching through a part of the country where some mischievous person has been collecting and encouraging insurgents, and this afternoon, in the course of about ten miles, we have burned no fewer than six farmhouses. Care seems to have been taken that there was proper evidence against the absent owner, and in no case, were people actually burned out of their homes; but in one most melancholy case the wife of an insurgent, who was lying sick at a friend's farm, watched from her sick husband's bedside the burning of her home a hundred yards away. I cannot think that punishment need take this wild form; it seems as though a kind of domestic murder were being committed while one watches the roof and the furniture of a house blazing.

I stood till late last night before the red blaze, and saw the flames lick round each piece of the poor furniture—the chairs and tables, the baby's cradle, the chest of drawers containing a world of treasure; and when I saw the poor housewife's face pressed against the window of the neighbouring house, my own heart burned with a sense of outrage. The effect on those of the Colonial troops, who in carrying out these orders of destruction are gratifying their feelings of hatred and revenge, is very bad. Their discipline is far below that of the Imperial troops, and they soon get out of hand. They swarm into the house, looting and destroying and filling the air with high-sounding cries of vengeance, and yesterday they were complaining bitterly that a suspected house, against the owner of which there was not sufficient evidence, was not delivered into their hands.

Further, if these farms are to be confiscated, as the more vindictive loyalists desire, and given over to settlers, why burn the houses? The new occupant will only have to build another homestead, and building is a serious matter where wood and the means of dressing stone are so very scarce as here. The ends achieved are so small—simply an exhibition of power and punishment, which, if it be really necessary, could be otherwise inflicted; and the evils, as one sees them on the spot, are many.—
See *Manchester Guardian*.

Reuter's telegrams during the month of May are full of the destruction of farms for one reason or another. In many cases abuse of the white flag was the reason assigned. On this point, there seems to have been continual misunderstanding on both sides. No doubt there were occasional instances of its abuse, but more often a shot coming from no one knew where, and fired by no one knew who, was enough, without investigation, to condemn the nearest farm where women and children were living under the protection of the white flag. Such a case appears to have been that of Christian Richter's house referred to in subsequent despatches, and described by Mr. E. W. Smith of the *Morning Leader*, who was with General Pole-Carew and General French.

> Two white flags were displayed over the house of Christian Richter; a shot was fired at random.
> The first sight which met my gaze was that of a score of men, some with their feet on the necks of turkeys, ducks, and fowls. Quicker than it takes me to tell the story, the women and children had been discovered in an outhouse; several troopers were occupied pouring paraffin about the flooring and walls of the house. Within five minutes the dwelling was ablaze. Still the womenfolk rushed in and out, trying to save what they could.

That hundreds of families were rendered homeless thus early in the war is certain, and the fact is implied in the pregnant sentence written at this time by the special correspondent of the *Daily Chronicle*:

> From end to end the Orange River Colony now lies ruined and starving. (Dated May 28.)

There were, however, some districts which did not suffer till later.

The Government Return on farm-burning only begins, it will be remembered, with the month of June, and does not include any of the destruction described above by so many pens. It was, however, sufficiently apparent to the enemy, for in the middle of May General De Wet addressed one of his brief despatches to Lord Roberts. (Cd. 582.)

> 19th May. Your Excellency's telegram C. 1575. Justice to his Honour the State President of the Orange Free State. I have the honour to reply to your Excellency's proclamation of 26th March. I have noted contents. I trust that the troops under your Excellency's command who have acted or will act in opposition to said Proclamation will be heavily punished. For your Excellency's information, I have been permitted to bring to your no-

tice the following farms and others, which have been destroyed by troops under your Excellency's command, *i.e.*, Perzikfontein, belonging to Commandant P. Fourii; Paardi Kraal, farm of P. Fourii, junior; and Leeuw Kop, farm of Christian Richter, all in the District of Bloemfontein. *Re* the other farms your Excellency will know about

Lord Roberts' reply gives reasons for the burning in these instances, though from Mr. Smith's description of the destruction of Richter's farm, which he witnessed, no time to investigate the charge of treachery seems to have been allowed.

C. 1737, 20th May. Your Honour's telegram of 19th instant I have taken ample measures to ensure the protection of public and private property by the troops under my command. At Perzikfontein stores of forage were destroyed to prevent them falling into the hands of marauding bands which infested the district, but the house was not damaged.

Paardi Kraal and Leeuw Kop farms were destroyed under my orders, because, while a white flag was flying from the houses, my troops were fired upon from the farmsteads. I have had two farms near Kroonstad destroyed for similar reasons, and shall continue to punish all such cases of treachery by the destruction of the farms where they occur.

The Annexation of the Orange River Colony was formally announced on the 24th of May, and on the 31st it was placed under Martial Law:

As a temporary measure and until further notice . . . as such law is understood and administered in British territory and by British officers. (Cd. 426.)

The following day it was announced that fighting *burghers* would be dealt with as rebels.

I hereby warn all inhabitants thereof, who after fourteen days from the date of this Proclamation may be found in arms against Her Majesty within the said colony, that they will be liable to be dealt with as rebels and to suffer in person and property accordingly.—Proclamation, Cd. 426, xv. Johannesburg, June 1, 1900.

Almost immediately followed the order of punishment when public property was damaged, such as railways and telegraph wires.

Pretoria, June 16. I . . . warn the said inhabitants and principal civil residents that, whenever public property is destroyed or injured in the manner specified above, they will be held responsible for aiding and abetting the offenders. The houses in the vicinity of the place where the damage is done will be burnt and the principal civil residents will be made prisoners of war.

Within three days, as we read in the *Times*, (of June 25), De Wet's Farm near Rhenoster was burnt, and his family evicted, in pursuance of this order issued by Lord Roberts to burn the nearest farm wherever the railway or telegraph were damaged. (Pretoria, June 19.) It became difficult to see how any farm could escape destruction or any family homelessness. If a house did not fall within the scope of any of the foregoing proclamations, it probably fell under the ban of fighting generals or local commandants. Reuter telegraphed from Maseru that:

> The Boers who are fighting in the Ficksburg district have been informed by General Rundle that unless they surrender by the 15th their farms and all their possessions will be confiscated.— *Times*, June 15, 1900.

Forgetting the principle laid down in Lord Roberts' despatch of February 5:

> It is barbarous to attempt to force men to take sides against their own sovereign and their country by threats of spoliation and expulsion.

General Rundle issued a notice under date June 30, calling upon all farmers to discontinue harbouring fighting *burghers* at night, and to give information of their whereabouts under penalty of the confiscation of their farms, the cancelling of payments due, and a heavy fine on their property. (*Trommel*, July 1. *Times*, July 3, 1900.)

A proclamation of sentences passed upon individuals was now issued at Bloemfontein.

## NOTICE.

(*South African News*, Sept 5. Proclamation printed by *Argus* Company, No. 602, Bloemfontein.)

Whereas by Proclamation dated the 16th day of June 1900 of Lord Roberts, Field-Marshal, Commanding in Chief Her Majesty's Forces in South Africa, it was notified to, and the inhabitants and principal civil residents of the Orange River Colony and the South African Republic were warned, that whatever wanton damage to public property, such as railways, bridges, culverts, telegraph wires, etc., took place, the houses of persons living in the neighbourhood would be burned, inasmuch as such destruction could not take place without their knowledge and connivance.

Now, therefore, it is hereby notified for general information that the following sentences have been passed in connection with the destruction of property, railways, etc., in the Orange River Colony, and have been approved and confirmed by Field-Marshal Lord Roberts.

SENTENCE.

The following persons to have their farms burned:—

A list of nearly forty persons is given whose farms are to be burnt, while many of the same are also fined. (See Appendix.) Not one of these appears in the Government Farm-burning Return which covers that period—unless indeed the Return is so carelessly prepared that initials and names of farms bear no significance.

Captain Ritchie's notice, published July 9 and modified on the 16th, is already well known.

V.R.

PUBLIC NOTICE.

It is hereby notified for information, that unless the men at present on commando belonging to families in the town and district of Krugersdorp surrender themselves and hand in their arms to the Imperial authorities by 20th July, the whole of their property will be confiscated and their families turned out destitute and homeless.

By order,

G. H. M. Ritchie,
Capt. K. Horse, Dist. Supt. Police.

Krugersdorp, 9th July 1900.

V.R.

PUBLIC NOTICE.

Notice is hereby given, that unless those persons of the town

and district of Krugersdorp who are now on commando surrender themselves and their arms and ammunition and take the
oath of neutrality, and further declare stock and supplies in their
possession, before the 20th July 1900, the whole of their stock
and supplies is liable to be confiscated.
The previous notice in this matter is cancelled.

By order,

G. H. M. Ritchie,<br>
Capt. K. Horse, Dist. Supt. Police.

Krugersdorp, 16th July 1900.

As a result of these two notices, a nucleus was formed which developed later into the Krugersdorp Camp. A telegram in the *Times*
indicates this.

Krugersdorp, Aug, 24.

A patrol under Sir R. Colleton of the Welsh Fusiliers came into
touch with the enemy's scouts today. There was no fighting.
*A farmhouse was burnt, the owner being away on commando.* The
women and children were brought in here for shelter and food.
They are being well looked after.—*Times*, Aug. 27.

Another local order shows that burning and consequent eviction
might be the penalty for a case of sniping on farms which were often wide in extent as an English parish, (See *South African News*, Oct.
31.)—

Bloemfontein, Oct. 24.<br>
O.C. Section.

The General Officer Commanding orders the following to be
made known to all farmers in the vicinity of your section:—

In consequence of a case of sniping which occurred last night,
he looks to them to co-operate with us in preventing these
outrages; they can themselves or through their servants (white
or black) scour the neighbourhood of their farms any evening.
It will be his unpleasant duty in the event of a recurrence of
this sniping to take very strong measures. In no case will the
nearest farmer be let off without a fine up to £200. The G.O.C.
will decide the amount; if the fine has no effect in inducing the
farmers, *he will burn the farm nearest the place of sniping.*
The G.O.C. looks on the failure of the farmer to help as a justification of the measures to be taken to prevent this sniping.

This should be widely made known.
By order,

A. H. Maundin,
Lieut. S.O. to O.C. Troops.

Official notes in various places put great pressure on the people, and under it a certain proportion succumbed. How hard it was for them to withstand must not be forgotten in the future by those of their neighbours who took the opposite view. Here is an instance of a note given to a quiet woman alone on her farm in the Transvaal with three children, her husband a hundred miles distant on commando, and sick.

From the Commandant, Paardekop, to Field-Cornet Franz-Badenhorst
I wish to point out to you the strong advisability of surrendering without delay. If you surrender voluntarily now you will be treated with leniency, and probably will not be transported, and at the end of the war you will be allowed to return to your wife and farm. I warn you that if you do not surrender your farm will be burnt and your cattle taken within a fortnight
(Signature)                    V., Lieut. Camp-Adjutant
Place, Paardekop, 2/10/1900.

A similar note was left with the sister of this woman and another neighbour—their cattle were taken before the order expired. Twelve days after the receipt of the order the place was burnt. Several women from Heidelberg have said they had a notice in Dutch put on their houses, and a notice in English given them, as follows:—

The contents of this house—all the livestock and eatables of ——, who is on commando, is confiscated.
J. M.V., District Commander.
Heidelberg, Oct, 31, 1900.

One of the latest of these notices was that of General Bruce Hamilton of November 1.

## NOTICE.

The town of Ventersburg has been cleared of supplies and partly burnt, and the farms in the vicinity destroyed, on account of the frequent attacks on the railway line in the neighbourhood. The Boer women and children who are left behind should apply to the Boer commandants for food, who will supply them unless they wish to see them starve. No supplies will be sent from the railway to the town.

(Signed)                    Bruce Hamilton, Major-General.
Nov. 1, 1900.

Only a few extracts can be given here from the writings of soldiers, war correspondents, and others, who draw a picture of the state of things brought about under these various proclamations and notices. Riding from Bloemfontein to Kimberley, the correspondent of the *Manchester Guardian* thus describes the country in July—

> The way is a line of desolation; the farmhouses have not merely been sacked, they have been savagely destroyed. The mirrors have been smashed, the pianos wrecked, children's toys and books wantonly destroyed. Even the buildings themselves have been burned and seriously damaged.

The *Cape Argus*, (June 21), says:

> Between Bloemfontein and Boshof, some thirty or forty homesteads have been burnt down—utterly destroyed. That is only one route. Many others have been burnt down also. Their homes destroyed, women and children have been turned out on to the *veld* in the bitter South African winter.

We read in the Sept.1900, *Natal Witness:*

> Yesterday (September 21), your correspondent went on a house-burning expedition (in O.R.C.) under Colonel H. B. Gumming of the Kaffrarians. During the day sixteen houses were destroyed. Many of the homesteads were occupied, and it was pitiful to see the women and children removing the furniture from the house before it was fired. The system of house-burning will probably have a good effect on the rebellious Boers; but I regret to say that the system is not carried out in a consistent manner.

The *Cape Times* correspondent at Winburg says—

> Along the line of march General Campbell has practically denuded the country of livestock and grain stores, whilst the sight of burning farmhouses and farm property is of daily occurrence. A number of old men, many sickly, who until recently

held good-conduct passes, have been made prisoners, and accompany the column. There are cases where women and children, the families of prisoners of war either at Green Point or Ceylon, have been reduced to utter destitution, and are subsisting upon the charity of their neighbours, who, however, are but little better off than themselves.

That the task assigned them was in most cases uncongenial, seems evident from the feeling often expressed in the rough descriptions of the soldiers. It would be tedious to insert here more than one or two samples of letters which dated from all parts of the two Republics, and reiterated the story of burning and pillage.

Bethlehem, July 8, 1900.
Since we are with Clements we have had plenty of work burning farms. It is very hard sometimes. Last Sunday six of us went out with an Imperial officer to a fine farmhouse, giving the occupants five minutes to clear out all their goods as well as themselves. There were an old grandmother, three married daughters, and several children, crying and asking for mercy, but no, when the time was up we burned it to the ground.—Trooper Morris, Brabant's Horse, *Morning Leader.*

Bethlehem, Sept, 22.
For the past month, we have had some, although exciting, very unpleasant work—namely, that of burning farms of those still fighting—I assure you in some instances very heart-rending. In one case twenty of our fellows rode up to a farm and told a woman and two daughters to take a few things and quit in ten minutes. We then cleared out everything and set the whole place on fire. The mother and two daughters dropped on their knees and prayed and sang, weeping bitterly all the time. One of the girls went to an organ and commenced singing some hymns. They sang 'Rock of Ages,' and then commenced to laugh loud and long hysterically, muttering all the time. A doctor who saw her before we came away tried to soothe her, but the poor woman had then gone raving mad.—Yours, etc.,
Arthur.
(Received by Mr. C. A. Harrison, King's Arms Hotel, Wood Green. Published in *Tottenham Herald* and *South African News* of Dec. 12.)

Today we marched into Senekal, and the Boers retired towards Bethlehem. For the last four or five days, we have been burning the farms of the men who are absent from home and who are suspected of being away fighting for the Boers. If the farmer was away, down the house had to come. No matter whatever the wife said to excuse her husband, the farm was destroyed. The farms burned well, there's no mistake. But we gave the wives time to get everything out of the houses they wanted before setting fire to them. I must say that I felt very sorry for the poor little children who were turned out of their home. They had, I suppose, to sleep in the open. The women did not seem to care a bit; but it must have been all right to stand by and see their homes set on fire.—*Barnet Press,* Private H. Philpott, 2nd Bedfordshire Regiment. *Morning Leader,* Nov. 1, 1900.

Mr. Hervey de Montmorency, writing later in the *Daily News,* June 22, 1901, gives his recollection of the period with which we are now dealing in these words—

When we retreated from Rustenburg in August of last year, after the evacuation of that town, every building in the neighbourhood of the northern-most road to Commando Nek was burned to the ground without discrimination. No single act of treachery on the part of the Boers occurred on the road. It would be interesting to know what was the motive for the malignant destruction of these farms. I speak of things I know, '*quaeque ipse miserrima vidi.*'

Captain March Phillipps' fuller story coincides with the above—

Hospital, Kroonstad, Sept, 6.

. . . . The various columns that are now marching about the country are carrying on the work of destruction pretty indiscriminately, and we have burnt and destroyed by now many scores of farms. Ruin, with great hardships and want, which may ultimately border on starvation, must be the result to many families. . . . I had to go myself the other day, at the general's bidding, to burn a farm near the line of march. We got to the place, and I gave the inmates, three women and some children, ten minutes to clear their clothes and things out of the house, and my man then fetched bundles of straw and we proceeded to burn it down. The old grandmother was very angry. She told me though I was making a fine blaze now it was nothing compared to the flames that I myself should be consumed in hereafter. (*With Rimington,* Letter xxiii., by L. March Phillipps.) Most of them, however, were too miserable to curse. The women cried, and the children stood by holding on to them and looking with large frightened eyes at the burning house. They won't forget that sight, I'll bet a sovereign, not even when they grow up. We rode away and left them, a forlorn little group, standing among their household goods—beds, furniture, and gimcracks strewn about the *veld*; the crackling of the fire in their ears, and smoke and flame streaming overhead. The worst moment is when you first come to the house. The people thought we had called for refreshments, and one of the women went to get milk. Then we had to tell them that we had come to burn the place down. I simply didn't know which way to look. One of the women's husbands had been killed at Magersfontein. There were others, men and boys, away fighting; whether dead or alive they did not know.

I give you this as a sample of what is going on pretty generally. Our troops are everywhere at work burning and laying waste, and enormous reserves of famine and misery are being laid up for these countries in the future.

Finally, we have the account of General John Smuts given in his Report to Mr. Steyn, and published by the *New Age*, part of which refers to the months now before us—

I feel altogether incapable of giving a description, even a mere sketch, of the devastation brought about by the enemy; of the pains and troubles caused to us, which have touched the hearts of our women and children as if they had been pierced by steel. Let me take as an example that part of the Krugersdorp district situated between the Magalies and Witwaters mountains; one of the most beautiful, most fertile, and best cultivated parts of South Africa, the so-called 'fillet.' When I came to these parts in July 1900, the land was green with an uninterrupted series of cultivated fields, gardens, and charming houses and farmsteads, a delight to the eye, and a proof of what our people had been able to do with respect to agriculture in half a score of years. And now? It is now a withered, barren waste; all the fields have been destroyed, the trees of the gardens cut down or pulled up by the roots; the homesteads burnt down, the houses in many cases not only destroyed by fire but blown up by dynamite, so that not a stone was left unturned; a refuge only for the night-owl and the carrion-birds. Where, till lately, everything was life, prosperity, and cheerfulness, death now reigns. No living animal, no woman, no child, not even a *Kaffir* woman, is seen but with the traces of anxiety, misery, nay, even with starvation, distinctly visible in their faces.

Oh! one needs the pen of Isaiah or Jeremiah to be able to describe these horrors of destruction. . . . But I want to give another example of the manner in which our dear country is being destroyed.

In the afternoon, I went on a scouting tour along the Doorn-rivier (a tributary of the Elands River), which part had been visited by the army of General Douglas the day before. I was well acquainted with this neighbourhood, as our forces had encamped here when the camp of Colonel Hore on the Elands River had been besieged. It was night, but the moon was out, when I arrived there. My companion and myself came to the first farm, and found that everything had been destroyed and burnt down here. I came to the second farm, which had not been burned down, but plundered, and not a living soul was left in it; that same night I passed by some twelve or fourteen farms successively, which had all been burnt down or looted, and not a living being left behind in them.

Truly, it rather resembled a haunted place than that magnificent thriving neighbourhood which I had left in all its glory about a month before. Late that night I lay down to sleep in the yard of one of these deserted places. Everything in that beautiful property (Doornkom) had been plundered and destroyed. The owner, Mr. Mostert, is a prisoner of war in St Helena, his wife has died, and some little orphans were left behind alone, with some relations. But even their innocence and youth, and the exile of their father, could not satisfy the vindictiveness of the enemy.

That night I reflected upon the fate of the many families of that district, and in the morning I found to my great surprise that they all appeared from the neighbouring hills like badgers from the ground. The women had fled with their children to those parts, thinking that they were safer with the wild beasts in the field than under the protection of the colours and armies of Her Majesty. . . . That afternoon I rode from Boksloot to Coster River, where I met with the same devastation and misery. No fewer than seven families, consisting of women and little children, were living under the trees in the open air, in spite of the heavy rains. Even the tents had been burnt.

The document goes on to mention the generals responsible for this devastation.

The condition of families in July was so serious as to evoke another protest from the *Commandant* General of the Boer forces—

To my regret I must again approach your Excellency with reference to the wanton destruction or damaging of private properties, and also the inhuman treatment and even assaults on helpless women and children by Her Britannic Majesty's troops in the South African Republic.—General Botha to Lord Roberts, July 4, 1900.

Complaints are repeatedly reaching me that private dwellings are plundered, and in some cases totally destroyed, and all provisions taken from women and children, so that they are compelled to wander about without food or covering. To quote several instances:—It has just been brought to my notice by way of sworn affidavit that the house of Field-Cornet S. Buys, on the farm Leeuwspruit, district Middelburg, was set on fire and destroyed on the 20th June last. (This is not included in the Government Return, Cd. 524.) His wife, who was at home, was given five minutes' time to remove her bedding and clothing, and even what she took out was again taken from her. Her food, sugar, etc., was all taken, so that for herself and her children she had neither covering nor food for the following night. She was asked for the key of the safe, and after it was given up by her she was threatened with a sword, and money was demanded. All the money that was in the house was taken away, all the papers in the safe were torn up, and everything at the homestead that could not be taken away was destroyed. The house of Field-Cornet Buys' son was also destroyed, the doors and windows broken, etc.

It has also been reported to me that my own buildings on the farm Varkenspruit, district Standerton, as well as the house of

Field-Cornet Badenhorst, on the adjoining farm, have been totally destroyed, and such of the stock as was not removed was shot dead on the farm. (These are not mentioned in the Government Return.)

Further, there is the sworn declaration of Mrs. Hendrik Badenhorst, which speaks for itself—

I cannot believe that such godless barbarities take place with your Excellency's consent, and thus I deem it my solemn duty to protest most strongly against such destruction and vindictiveness as being entirely contrary to civilised warfare.

I trust that your Excellency will take all the necessary measures to punish the doers of such deeds, and in the interest of humanity I call on your Excellency to use all your power and authority to put an end to the devastation wrought by the troops under your Excellency's command.

A few days later General De Wet makes similar complaint in relation to the Free State, though he makes no mention of the destruction of his own farm or consequent eviction of his own family—

Field near Bethlehem, July 10.

Your Excellency,—It is with a feeling of great indignation that I have from day to day noticed the reckless devastation of property in this State by the troops under your Excellency's command. Houses and other property are under all manner of excuses destroyed and burnt, and defenceless women and children are treated with scorn, and driven on foot out of the houses to seek accommodation under the bare heavens. Through such action great unnecessary suffering is caused. Amongst many others, this has happened to the following, *viz*:—

Near Lindley: the farms of Hermanns Pieterse, Jacobus Pieterse, Christian Hattuigh, Roelof Fourie, Adriaan Cilliers, Daniel Momberg, and Gert Rautenbach. (None of these seem identical with any named in the Government Return.)

Near Heilbron: of Hendrik Meyer, Mathys Lourens, and Jan Vosloo.

Everything belonging to these persons has been burnt and destroyed.

The wife of General Roux, at Senekal, has been driven out of the manse, while the wife of Mr. J. G. Luyt, at Heilbron, was treated very scornfully, and the wife of Commandant P. H. de

Villiers has been driven from two houses at Ficksburg. There are many other cases which have been brought to my notice, but for my purpose it is not necessary to send your Excellency a complete list.

I trust that, in the name of our common civilisation and humanity, your Excellency will have the culprits punished, and prevent the perpetration of such acts in the future.

However, should the troops under your Excellency's command continue to unnecessarily devastate the country in a manner contrary to the principles of civilised warfare, I shall feel obliged, however much against my own feelings, to take such reprisals on the houses and goods of British subjects in the Orange Free State, as well as of British subjects in the Cape Colony and in Natal, as I may think proper, in order to put a stop to these atrocities.

Imbued with the desire to carry on this unfortunate struggle in terms of the dictates of humanity, I have felt obliged to write your Excellency this letter, trusting that your Excellency will receive and consider same in the same spirit in which it is written.

The following replies to the two Boer leaders were sent by Lord Roberts. He gives General Botha a detailed answer refuting the charge in the case of Mrs. Badenhorst, and goes on to say—

July 28

I have not yet received replies from General Officer Commanding Standerton, as to the alleged destruction of buildings on your Honour's and the adjoining farm. I hope the reports may prove unfounded, as I have given most stringent orders that except in certain cases where railway or telegraph line has been cut, or our troops fired upon from farms, homesteads are not to be destroyed. As far as I know, up to the 4th July, the date of your letter, none of our troops were in the Middelburg district. (Cd. 582.)

The despatch to General De Wet contains no detailed answer to the instances enumerated by him—

Pretoria, Aug. 3.

I have today received through General Sir A. Hunter your letter dated 10th July 1900.

As your Honour is well aware, the utmost consideration has invariably been shown to every class of inhabitant of the Orange River Colony since the British troops under my command entered the country.

Latterly, many of my soldiers have been shot from farmhouses over which the white flag has been flying, the railway and telegraph lines have been cut, and trains wrecked. I have therefore found it necessary, after warning your Honour, to take such steps as are sanctioned by the customs of war to put an end to these and similar acts, and have burned down the farmhouses at or near which such deeds have been perpetrated. This I shall continue to do whenever I consider the occasion demands it Women and children have thus been rendered homeless through the misdeeds of the *burghers* under your Honour's command, but your Honour has been misinformed as to these poor people having been badly treated, as everything possible has invariably been done to lessen the discomforts inseparable from such evictions.

The remedy lies in your Honour's own hands. The destruction of property is most distasteful to me, and I shall be greatly pleased when your Honour's co-operation in the matter renders it no longer necessary.

Not satisfied with the answer received from the Commander-in-Chief, General Botha wrote again—

Aug. 15.

On inquiry, I have discovered that it is a fact, which I can have supported by affidavits, that well-disposed families living on farms are driven from their houses, and all their property taken away or destroyed. In every case the private conveyances are taken away, so that there are instances where women with their children who, deprived of their property in this manner, were obliged to walk for miles in order to seek for food, shelter, and protection from our *burghers*. I cannot here refrain from remarking that, in such cases, the action of the troops under your Excellency's command very much exceeds the teachings of civilised warfare.

I bring these facts to your Excellency's notice because I cannot believe that they are your Excellency's instructions, and as it is done by the troops under your Excellency's supreme command, I expect that your Excellency will make an end to these atrocious deeds and barbarous actions.

In this connection I wish to remark that everywhere small bodies of troops axe captured far from their main force, and who allege that they are scouts, but who in point of fact go about to rob, and that it cannot be expected that such robbers, when captured, be in future treated as prisoners of war.

The case of the house of Acting-Commandant Buys mentioned by me in my letter of the 4th July last was in the district of Heidelberg and not in the district of Middelburg, as your Excellency appears to think. This arbitrary destruction of houses still continues, and I must again most strongly protest against same. I also wish to bring to your Excellency's notice that in many cases houses in which are only women and children are now bombarded.

This despatch evoked a short stern reply from Lord Roberts—

Pretoria, Aug. 23, 1900

Your Honour represents that well-disposed families living on their farms have been driven from their houses, and that their property has been taken away or destroyed. This no doubt is true, but not in the sense which your letter would imply. *Burghers* who are well-disposed towards the British Government, and anxious to submit to my authority, have had their property seized by the Boer commandoes, and have been threatened with death if they refused to take up arms against the British forces. Your Honour's contention that a solemn oath of neutrality which the *burghers* have voluntarily taken in order to remain in unmolested occupation of their farms is null and void because you have not consented to it is hardly open to discussion. I shall punish those who violate their oath and confiscate their property, no *burgher* having been forced to take the oath against his will.

The misunderstanding which was evident finds some explanation in this passage written from South Africa by Mr. J. M. Robertson—

Cape Town, Aug. 13, 1900

I have already told how, according to trustworthy reports received up-country, there occurred in the Free State acts of blundering provocation of the sort that have abounded under martial law in the Colony. I now learn, on very high authority, that in addition to these there occurred wholesale provocation by some provosts-marshal, and acts of so-called vengeance which were really gross miscarriages of justice. Much has been said of Boers firing on British soldiers from farms which flew the white flag. What actually happened again and again was that women and non-combatants flew the white flag on a homestead, and that armed Boers carried on hostile operations on other parts of such farms without any regard to the doings of those in the farmhouse, which might be miles off—a Boer farm being often as large as an English parish.

But when farm-burning was once begun, it was not restricted to cases where the white flag could be pretended to have been misused. Many where burned on the sole ground that the owner was absent, presumably on commando. Even at this stage, different generals proceeded on different principles, just as has happened under martial law in the Colony. Some burned, and some spared. A concrete case, reported in a telegram, will serve to show how things are going in the Transvaal—

*Johannesburg, Aug. 17.*—On Tuesday evening. Private Richards, of the Railway Pioneers, was mysteriously shot near Witpoorje, four miles from Krugersdorp. He was doing patrol duty, and when picked up yesterday he had five bullet wounds, including one through the head. As he was sniped by some resident in the vicinity, the people were called upon to produce the murderer. As they did not, some *four houses* were demolished, and the occupants sent to Johannesburg."—*Morning Leader*, Sept. 1900.

The confusion in the minds of the *burghers* was not lessened when on August 14 another proclamation was issued repealing either the whole or important parts of previous promises. Under Section 6 of this, a man who had given and was keeping his oath of neutrality became guilty if he failed to "acquaint Her Majesty's Forces with the presence of the enemy." (No. 12 of 1900.) In a word, he must no longer be neutral. Commenting on this and other passages in this proclamation, under which concentration becomes almost inevitable, the *St. Jame's Gazette* says—

We pointed out that it would be more business-like on our part to adopt the policy of General Weyler's 'reconcentration order' in Cuba. After delays. Lord Roberts has come round to our way of thinking. We observe, not without some amusement, that this adaptation of the methods of General Weyler has met with general approval, and is only mildly condemned in quarters where it once would have caused able editors to fill the heavens with eloquence. There are reasons not unconnected with the sale of papers for the change of tone. Where the women and children give active help—then all are combatants. In any case, we have undertaken to conquer the Transvaal, and if nothing will make that sure except the entire removal of the Dutch inhabitants, they must be removed—men, women, and children. They (the Dutch) would be justified in shooting every Englishman, in refusing to give quarter, and in killing the wounded."—*St. Jame's Gazette*, Aug. 20, 1900.

Their correspondent in South Africa appeared to take a different view of the working of the same proclamation, for, writing from Ficksburg, he says—

... On the night of September 6 General Campbell reached Generals Nek.... Generals Nek is three hours, or about twenty miles, from here. Colonel Oakes wished to send despatches to him, and I volunteered to ride there. On my arrival at Generals Nek I talked for some time with General Campbell, as, in addition to the despatches, there was much information to be given by word of mouth. On discovering that I knew the district and the inhabitants, through having worked for some two months under the district commissioner, Major White, he requested, or rather ordered, me to remain in camp that night and to march with him the following day.

The general told me that he had received orders to "sweep" the country, and a view of his following soon made it obvious that he had not failed to carry out his orders. All farms on the line of march were cleared of horses, cattle, sheep, waggons, carts, etc., the forage being burnt, and the owners bidden to join the ranks of the prisoners, of whom there were already a goodly number. In several cases I ventured humbly to point out that many of these men, in fact most of them, had been paroled, and allowed to return to their farms, and had received a protection certificate for their property from the District Commissioner. Some of them were Britishers, who rather than take up arms against their country had sacrificed all and taken refuge in Basutoland.

My pleas were of no avail. All who had once been on commando, in spite of having been paroled, were retaken prisoners. Britishers were allowed to remain at liberty, but their livestock was taken and their stacks burnt I knew that in many cases our leniency had not been appreciated, and that such punishment was thoroughly deserved. But it was with mingled feelings of dismay and regret that I beheld the work of settlement on which we had been employed for more than two months all upset in a couple of days.

I was afterwards given a copy of a proclamation issued by Lord Roberts on August 14, on which General Campbell based the justification of his action. The meeting between General Campbell and Captain Ward, Assistant Commissioner for the Lady Brand and Ficksburg Districts of the Orange River Colony, was anything but a pleasant one. Each had been carrying out a policy antagonistic to the other, and for a very simple reason. We had never received any notification of the proclamation of August 14, and we had consequently been working in accordance with those of earlier dates. Why we have never received any copy of the proclamation from the authorities at Bloemfontein is inexplicable. I observed that the proclamation was issued 'to the inhabitants of the South African Republic' I am still wondering whether it is intended to be applied to the inhabitants of the Orange River Colony. General Campbell assured us that it was so intended.—Ficksburg, Sept. 14. *St. James's Gazette*, Oct. 17, 1900.

Comparatively few people have read the correspondence which took place at this date between Lord Roberts and General Botha on the subject of the expulsion of the women. It was first published in the *Handelsblad*, subsequently in the *Manchester Guardian*—

Lord Roberts to General Botha.

Sept. 2, 1900.

Sir,—I beg to address your Honour in regard to the actions of the comparatively small bands of armed Boers who conceal themselves in the neighbourhood of our lines of communication, and who constantly endeavour to destroy the railroad, thereby endangering the lives of passengers, both combatants and non-combatants, travelling by the trains.

2. I address your Honour on this subject because, with the ex-

ception of the districts occupied by the army under your Honour's personal command, there are now no properly organised Boer armies in the Transvaal and the Orange River Colony, and the war degenerates into the actions of irregular and irresponsible guerillas. This would be detrimental to the country, and so regrettable from every point of view that I feel compelled to do all in my power to prevent it.

3. In order to put these views into practice, I have issued instructions that the Boer farmhouses near the spot where an effort has been made to destroy the railroad or to wreck the trains shall be burnt, and that from all farmhouses for a distance of ten miles around such a spot all provisions, cattle, etc. shall be removed.

4. In connection with the forgoing, the time has also arrived when I must again refer to my despatch C. in C. 670 of August 5, 1900, which your Honour answered on August 15. I feel that when the war has once entered upon the stage of irregular or guerilla fighting, I should be neglecting my duty towards the national interests if I continued to allow the families of those who still fight against us to live in towns which are guarded by our forces. This is no longer a matter of commissariat, but rather of policy, and in order to protect ourselves against the transmission of news to our enemies.

I would therefore consider it a favour if your Honour would warn all *burghers* on commando whose families are living in districts occupied by our troops, to make timely preparation for receiving and sheltering their families. The expulsion of these families will commence within a few days, a start being made with those now in Pretoria. They will travel by rail to the British outposts, to be then transferred to the person whom your Honour might appoint for their reception.

I will keep your Honour informed of the number that may be expected from day to day, and I take this opportunity of informing your Honour that since nearly all the carriages of the Netherlands South African Railway Company have been removed eastwards, the families, to my regret, will mostly have to travel in open trucks. I will endeavour to provide Mrs. Kruger, Mrs. Botha, and as many of the other ladies as possible with closed carriages, but as I am not certain of succeeding in finding one, I desire to suggest to your Honour that you should forward suitable carriages for them.

I need not tell you how repugnant these measures are to me, but I am obliged to resort to the same by the evidently firm resolve on the part of yourself and your *burghers* to continue the war, although any doubt as to the ultimate result thereof has now ceased to exist.—I have the honour to be your obedient servant.

The answer to this letter was prompt—

General Botha to Lord Roberts.

Sept. 6, 1900.

Inasmuch as our entire armed force is only a small one in comparison with that of your Excellency, it cannot, of course, be expected that strong commandoes should be in the field everywhere, and it naturally follows that now, as during the war, what is incumbent upon us must be done by small forces. Moreover, we have been compelled to still further scatter our commandoes in order to be able to check the looting patrols, under your Excellency's chief command, who scour the country to carry off cattle and provisions from the different farms.

2. As regards your contention that, with the exception of the *burgher* forces under my command, no other Boer forces should be in existence, I most strongly deny this, since our armed forces are still disposed and directed in the same manner as in the beginning of the war, and in accordance with the country's laws.

3. In paragraph 3 of your letter, with which I am now dealing, it is already known to me that barbarous actions of this kind are committed by your troops, under your command, not only alongside or near the railway, but also in places far removed from railways. Wherever your troops move, not only are houses homed down or blown up with dynamite, but defenceless women and children are ejected, robbed of all food and cover, and all this without any just cause existing for such proceedings.

4. With regard to paragraph 4 of your Excellency's letter, I extremely regret to learn that my *burghers'* and my own determination to persevere in the struggle for our independence is to be visited on our wives and children, and this is the first instance

of this kind known to me in the history of civilised warfare. I can only protest against your proposed measures as being in opposition to all principles of civilised warfare and excessively cruel toward the women and children, cruel especially towards elderly women, and above all towards the wife of His Honour the President of this State, who, as you must be well aware, is not able to travel without risk to her life, so that it would be simply murder to compel her to undertake such a journey.

The pretext alleged by you, *viz.*, that by so doing your Excellency desires to protect yourself against transmission of information to us, clearly lacks all substance, since such proceedings were not considered necessary at a time when our troops were encamped in the immediate neighbourhood of Pretoria. It is needless to state that we have never, by means of women and children, received information regarding operations of war.

5. If your Excellency still intends to persevere in carrying out your Excellency's plan, which I hope will not be the case, I request your Excellency to give me timely notice of the period and particulars of the expulsion, as I wish to arrange for the direct transport of the families to Europe. With regard to your Excellency's remark about proper accommodation, I am prepared to send proper carriages to a place to be indicated, and also, if required, a cog-wheel engine for the track between Waterval Boven and Waterval Onder, provided that your Excellency guarantees the safe return of such carriages and engine.

6. In conclusion, I desire to give you the assurance that nothing you may do to our women and children will deter us in continuing the struggle for our independence.

On September 7 Lord Roberts again urges his reasons for the rigorous methods which appear to have increased throughout September and October—

Lord Roberts to General Botha.

Sept, 7, 1900

I beg again to direct your Honour's attention to paragraphs 2 and 3 of my letter dated 2nd September, in which I pointed out that, except in the districts occupied by the army under your Honour's personal command, the war is degenerating, and has degenerated, into operations carried on in an irregular and irresponsible manner by small and, in very many cases, insignificant bodies of men. Your Honour's own statement that your commandoes are being more and more split up, bears this out, and I am convinced that, except within a district which is daily becoming more restricted, your Honour can exercise little or no control over these guerilla bodies.

I should be failing in my duty to Her Majesty's Government and to Her Majesty's Army in South Africa, if I neglected to use every means in my power to bring such irregular warfare to a conclusion. The measures which I am compelled to adopt are those which the customs of war prescribe as being applicable to such cases; they are ruinous to the country, entail endless suffering on your Honour's fellow-countrymen, and must, I regret to inform your Honour, necessarily become more and more rigorous.

General Botha replied from Warmbaths, Oct. 17—

I regret to note that the barbarous actions of your Excellency's troops, such as the blowing up and destruction of private dwellings and the removal of all food from the families of the fighting *burghers*, against which I have already been obliged to protest, have not only met with your Excellency's approval, but are done on your Excellency's special instructions. This spirit of revenge against *burghers* who are merely doing their duty according to law, may be regarded as civilised warfare by your Excellency, but certainly not by me. I feel obliged to bring to your Excellency's notice the fact that I have resolved to carry on the war in the same humane manner as hitherto, but should I be compelled by your Excellency's action to take reprisals, then the responsibility thereof will rest with your Excellency.

So far as appeals from the Blue Books, the correspondence between the two generals ends with this announcement from Lord Roberts—

Pretoria, Oct. 23, 1900

With regard to the remark of your Honour, as to the state of organisation which exists among the *burgher* forces at the present moment, I am compelled to point out to your Honour that their tactics are not those usually associated with organised forces, but have degenerated into a guerilla warfare which I shall be compelled to repress by those exceptional methods which civilised nations have at all times found it obligatory to use under like circumstances.

It has been since recognised that the Boer warfare, though guerilla in some methods, was carried on throughout under an organised system, and at its remarkable close there was absolute order and discipline. Meantime the families rendered homeless by all these military operations were seeking refuge, some in neighbouring farms, or even Kaffir *kraals*, others in *laagers* formed by the Boers; others, again, in hiding-places among the hills. A few fled to friends in Cape Colony, while a considerable number flocked into the towns, where it soon became necessary to provide them with food. In Lord Roberts' report from Pretoria, July 2, he mentions that several families of men fighting against us were being fed, and some of them were in a state of destitution. (*Times*, July 4.) From the middle of July, it became evident that the women and children who were homeless had so swelled in number that it was becoming a serious problem how to deal with them.

Far away near Mafeking a camp was formed in this month where some of the wanderers in the north-western districts were received, but no other was yet established, only *laagers* formed by the Boers for their protection. It was midwinter, and the cold at night very intense. Charitable people in some of the towns tried to stem the tide of distress by taking out waggon-loads of supplies to country districts, but military rigour soon made this impracticable. It was resolved that the responsibility of feeding these families should be shifted on to the shoulders of the *burghers*. Telegrams at that period speak of a proclamation calling upon the wives of Boers still fighting to report themselves, (Pretoria, July 18. Reuter), with a view to being sent into the enemy's lines, and describe waggon-loads of women and children leaving the town for that purpose. (Reuter, July 19. See also *South African News*, Aug. 22.)

This eviction was carried out at Johannesburg, where, on the authority of the correspondent of the *Daily Telegraph,* we are told that "on August 10 and the following days trains left the town conveying 1550 children and 450 women." We have seen in Lord Roberts' letter to General Botha his proposal to carry out this plan at Pretoria on a large scale, including such ladies as Mrs. Kruger and Mrs. Louis Botha, who were not themselves amongst those receiving rations from the military authorities. In the end these ladies were not molested, and the eviction was, it is believed, confined to women of a class unable to support themselves.

Soon after the Proclamation of August 14 a new feature presented itself, in the voluntary arrival and submission of occasional refugees, who brought in their families and stock, hoping by this means to save themselves from the transportation or imprisonment threatened by Lord Roberts. With the exception of the Western District refugees already in July formed into the camp near Mafeking, the first intimation of these *bonâ fide* refugees seems to be in Lord Roberts' report of September 3, where he speaks of an officer at Eerste Fabricken reporting that ten men, with several women and children, had come into camp, bringing with them their cattle, waggons, and carts. (*Times*, Sept. 3.)

In various localities, a few of these men appeared and sought protection for themselves and their goods. It became an instant duty to provide for them, and on 22nd September General Maxwell issued the order which established the system of Refugee Camps.

Camps for *burghers* who voluntarily surrender are being formed in Pretoria and at Bloemfontein.

J. G. Maxwell, Major-General,
Military Governor.

Pretoria, Sept, 22, 1900.
(Government Notice No. iii. of 1900, Sec. 4.)

This is the first official notice of the formation of camps. They really were Refugee Camps in that they were established for that class of person. Had they been true to their name, and kept for refugees only, they would have remained small in size and few in number. Till about this period the people of the land had been as one body. But now a rift was formed which widened and deepened as the months rolled on. The individuals who feared transportation, imprisonment, or material loss, (see Proclamation No. 12 of 1900. Cd. 426), surrendered and came in as refugees, and a distinction was formed between them and the great mass of the people who remained patriots and were known as "undesirables."

From General Botha's point of view, it became necessary to nullify the terrorising effect of a proclamation which was weaning some of the people from alliance to their country, and he issued a circular reminding the people of their duties and threatening punishment for those who laid down their arms. It was clear that from one side or the other suffering must come.

This Circular of the Boer generals, dated Roos, Senekal, October 6, 1900, is the subject of an extraordinary error in the Blue Books.

Lord Kitchener in his despatch of December 6, 1901 (Cd. 903), quotes General Botha as saying in this Circular:

> Do everything in your power to prevent the *burghers* laying down their arms. I will be compelled, if they do not listen to this, to confiscate everything movable or immovable, and also to burn their houses.

But the Circular referred to contained no such sentence. The words quoted are taken, as appears from the White Paper (Cd. 665, p. 5) published six months earlier, from a letter from General Botha to the Landdrost of Bethal, in which the Circular was enclosed. The Circular itself is given at length in Mr. M. Davitt's book. (*Boer Fight for Freedom.*) After informing the *burghers* that the Executive Council had given leave of absence to the State President to assist their deputation in Europe, and that the government continued under Mr. Schalk Burger as Acting President, General Botha exhorts them to be true to their cause and their leaders, and in the final clause issues this warning—

> The *burghers* are also warned against fine words used by the enemy to deceive them so as to make them put down their arms, because, according to the proclamation of Lord Roberts, they will all be transported to St. Helena or Ceylon as prisoners of war, and they put their property, as it were, between two dangers, for in future I will deal severely with all property of those who put down their arms.

Two months later, in another Circular, dated Ermelo, December 3, 1900, General Botha defines more carefully how this property of surrendered *burghers* is to be dealt with. Nothing is said of the burning of houses or of immovable property, because General Botha had no legal right to touch these things, but by a decision of the *Kriegsraad* the movable property of traitors was confiscate, and he was bound to seize it in obedience to that rule, under certain limitations.

> The movable property of these persons must be taken and a proper inventory made by the field-cornet concerned, in conjunction with his *commandant* and his general of division for commando purposes. Care must be taken in all cases that sufficient means of livelihood are left for the support of the wife and family.—Cd. 663. Enclosure 1. in No. 5.

From these documents, it is clear that the suggestion that the Boer generals adopted the avowed policy of punishing desertion by burning farms is without foundation. By a strange oversight, Lord Kitchener has confused what is at most, if correctly translated, General Botha's personal expression of opinion in a letter to an individual as to the mode of punishment which he *may* be driven to adopt, with an official announcement of a settled scheme of reprisals. The plea that concentration was rendered necessary by the burning of farms by the Boers themselves thus falls to the ground.

Lord Kitchener says that many surrendered *burghers* made complaints to him of ill-treatment received after they had laid down their arms, but no instances are given by him, nor is mention made of any farm being burnt. The only instance of eviction and devastation hitherto made public for the year 1900 is that of Mrs. Viviers, who published in the *Bloemfontein Post* an account of her ill-treatment. This happened shortly after the issue of Botha's Circular. She does not say her farm was burnt—

After explaining that she is an Afrikander of Dutch-French extraction, whose son had gone out on commando and been wounded at Magersfontein, Mrs. M. E. O. Viviers states that after the British occupation of Bloemfontein and the submission of the *burghers* in her neighbourhood, peace and order were restored until the autumn of 1900, when Badenhorst's commando arrived. 'On November 30 he sent twenty-one armed men to search my house and to loot it I closed the doors and refused to open them. Lieutenant Jan Lubbe, of Aarpan, district of Boshoff, broke open the door, and shouted, "We will fire," and I flew with my daughter and "*bijwoonster*" and her children through the other door. Lubbe gave a man the order to see that we did not run away, and that man stood guard over us while the others were looting my house.

'When Lubbe (he had also taken the oath, although later on he became one of the greatest rebels) entered the door, he said, "*Burghers*, take what you want" They went through every room, and turned over everything; they even turned over the beds. They also took all saddles, halters, etc., which I had packed in my son's room. They took all the watches, my daughter's watch, and many more articles. The green fruit was taken from the trees, the young vegetables were destroyed, as well as my beehives. . . . After Badenhorst had taken the best of everything on my farm, he sent his brother Christoffel Badenhorst . . . to let me know that I had to go into the enemy's lines. On that day I was laid up. . . . My daughters asked Krause to give us time till I felt better. He replied, "When I heard that your mother was sick I sent a message to Badenhorst. His reply was, 'Give them an hour and a half.' I must fulfil my orders, and if you refuse to go I will be obliged to use force." I had to go in my spring waggon, inspanned with six oxen, some bedclothes and clothing, leaving behind all I had—the work of many years—to live a poor life amongst strangers.

'Under this escort of Piet Krause and Casper Willemse, of Aranslaagte, district Hoopstad, who had also taken the oath, we had to pass the night on the *veld*. They had not given us time to prepare any food at home, and they fed us, once a day, on a piece of sandy meat, pumpkin boiled in water, and a cup of corn coffee. When we arrived at Hagenstad we were handed over to Field-Cornet Jan van Wijk and twelve armed men, to bring us on farther. They led us across the Modder River, and there gave our native the order to bring us into Bloemfontein. They then went back. I am now temporarily in Bloemfontein, and my son, from whom I was separated for six months, was three months in the Refugee Camp at Norval's Pont. He states that he had nothing to complain of there.'—See *Times*, Feb. 17, 1902, quoted from *Bloemfontein Post* of Jan. 24, 1902.

A return of farms burnt or damage done by the Boers has been published, but refers only to destruction in British territory, and gives the few forms which were burnt in Cape Colony as reprisals. (Cd. 979.) The cases enumerated by Mr. Tobias Smuts are mentioned in a later chapter. (See Part 2 chap. 1.) It may be that more will come to light as time goes on, but this is doubtful, as it was not the Boer policy, and was against their principles.

On the other hand, homeless "undesirables," or patriots, were so largely on the increase, that in the uncertain state of the line they could not all be sent away to Natal or the Coast, and it was probably thought that their influence over the men in the field was too powerful to make it prudent to continue sending them to the commandoes, at any rate as regarded the women of the higher classes.

Humanity forbade, at this stage, a continuance of the practice of their being left outside their ruined houses, and so it came to pass that they were brought in by convoys and placed in the small camps which had been formed for refugees. Those small handfuls of people were soon swamped by the inundation of new-comers, and large camps sprang into existence in 1900 at Bloemfontein, Johannesburg, Irene, Potchefstroom, Norval's Pont, Kroonstad, Vereeniging, Heidelberg, and Winburg, besides Port Elizabeth and Pietermaritzburg, which last were wholly for "undesirables." The severance of the people, which might have been avoided by a wise and equable treatment, was, on the contrary, aggravated by the primary administration of the camps, and became complete.

Certain distinctions of food and various facilities were made in favour of the surrendered families, and these were often given paid employments and placed in positions over the patriots, acting in some cases as spies who carried trivial words and tales to those in authority. The patriots, on the other hand, felt and expressed contempt, often undeserved, for these neighbours, and nicknamed them "hands up-pers." The deportation of women and children had now become an event of daily occurrence, and it was a common sight to see whole train-loads of families packed into trucks passing the stations or shunted on to sidings. The following are samples of the telegrams which announced the same thing from many parts in the country:—

Oct. 19.

. . . At Heidelberg, the General Commanding has taken a wise step in bringing families known to have been harbouring the Boers into the town. The depleting of the farms round Vlakfontein of all food-stuffs continues.—Reuter, *Times*, Oct. 22.

Ventersburg, Oct. 31.

Numbers of families with their goods and chattels have been sent by the railway.
The enemy plead they cannot trust the proclamations.
Numbers have taken their wives and families to a *laager*.—Reuter, *South African News*.

Durban, Saturday,

The work of deporting 'undesirables' from the Eastern districts of the Orange River Colony is proceeding with some vigour. Two hundred and fifty women and children from Harrismith and vicinity have been sent to Ladysmith, and one hundred and ninety men to Durban.

Bloemfontein.

Some more women from Jagersfontein have reached Bloemfontein, and are encamped with the first batch a few miles outside the town. It is rumoured at Bloemfontein that strong punitive measures have been taken at Bothaville, and that the Dutch Church is the only building left standing there.

Bloemfontein, Nov, 22.

Seven waggons with refugee Boer families arrived from Thaba 'Nchu this morning."—*South African News*, Nov. 28.

Standerton, Nov, 17.

... One hundred Boer women and children have been sent to Natal.—*Times*, Nov. 19.

Capetown, Tuesday

The Rev. Colin Fraser, of the Dutch Church, Miss Fraser, and a number of other Dutch partisans, have been removed from Philippolis by the military authorities. Mr. Fraser has been sent to Bloemfontein.—Reuter, Oct. 31.

Mr. Fraser, here mentioned as having suffered deportation, is a venerable clergyman of Scotch parentage, and the father of Mrs. Steyn, the President's wife. His brother, Mr. John George Eraser, obtained his release and he returned to Philippolis. Some months later he was with his wife deported to the camp at Norval's Pont, and thence sent down to East London. Miss Emmeline Fraser, his daughter, a girl of twenty-one, has herself told me how she was sent up in a coal-truck from her home, and then had to trudge from the station at Bloemfontein, some three miles, out to the camp, carrying her own things, beneath a burning sun and with armed soldiers behind her. The thoughtful act of a soldier who helped to carry her bundles alone redeemed the bitter humiliation of that day.

Many telegrams spoke of the exile of a large number of families from Jagersfontein and Fauresmith to Port Elizabeth.

When a batch of these unfortunates arrived in the south of Cape Colony, the sight aroused a storm of indignation; it brought to Cape Colonists the first realisation of how the brunt of the war was falling upon helpless women and children.

Reuter's message runs—

Port Elizabeth.

Yesterday I visited the Racecourse Encampment, where the

Dutch women and children, who were sent down from Jagersfontein and Fauresmith are quartered They are practically prisoners, as a military guard has been placed over them; but everything has been done that is possible to make their incarceration within the enclosure as comfortable as circumstances permit. Many of the women and children have lived in affluent positions, and are now housed in tin cabins of circumscribed space. The wives of the Mayor of Fauresmith and the Dutch Reformed Minister, and the sister of the Resident Magistrate, are among them.—*South African News*, Oct. 31, 1900.

The supply of families for deportation, which seemed unending, was kept up by the devastation which increased rapidly in the latter months of the year. From October to December a series of telegrams from various districts echoed the news in sad refrain. Here are a few contributed by Reuter:—

Vryburg, Oct, 1.
General Settle's Column, after relieving Schweizereineke, proceeded southward to Christiana, pacifying the country as they went along; . . . some farms were burnt, including that of Pretorius, formerly member of the Second Raad."—Reuter. See *Times*, Oct. 5, 1900.

Kroonstad, Oct. 26.
The column arrived at noon, destroying farms on its way.(*South African News*, Nov. 7.)
Not a single Boer house in the country between Dundee and Vryheid has been left standing. All have been burned by the British troops as a punishment for the treacherous acts of the resident Boers.
The British patrol sheds are affording shelter to the Boer women and children, and the British are also supporting them with the necessaries of life.—*Central News* Telegram.

Bloemfontein, Nov. 5, 1900.
It is stated that the village of Ventersburg has met with a fate similar to that of Bothaville, having been destroyed on account of its having been used as a Boer depot.—*Times*, Nov. 7.

Belfast, Nov, 6.
. . . General Dorien Smith . . . determined to destroy every farm that had given cover or shelter to the Boers. . . . Farms

were burnt or blown up as the force proceeded.—*Times*, Dec 6, 1900, from a correspondent.

Orange River, Nov. 23.
The farms belonging to Scholz, who destroyed the line near Belmont, have been destroyed.—*South African News*, Nov. 28. Reuter.

Pietermaritzburg, Dec. 24.
A force from Heidelberg has destroyed 37 farms, sweeping off the livestock.—*Daily Mail*, Dec. 25.

As earlier in the year, the letters of soldiers fill up the bare outline of Reuter's messages. Here are a few sentences from Lieutenant Morrison's well-known letter—

Belfast, Nov, 21.
There were a number of very fine farms nearby, and we saw the Boers leaving them and making off. The provost-marshal came up from the main body, removed the Boer women and children with their bedding, and proceeded to burn or blow up the houses. From that time, on during the rest of the trek, which lasted four days, our progress was like the old-time forages in the Highlands of Scotland two centuries ago. . . . We moved on from valley to valley, 'lifting' cattle and sheep, burning, looting, and turning out the women and children to sit and cry beside the ruins of their once beautiful farmsteads. . . . It was a terrible thing to see, and I don't know that I want to see another trip of the sort, but we could not help approving the policy, though it rather revolted most of us to be the instruments. . . . We burned a track about six miles wide through these fertile valleys, and completely destroyed the village of Wilpoort and the town of Dullstroom.

In similar language Captain March Phillipps continues the story from other parts—

Nov. 23.
Kroonstad, (*With Rimington*, Letter xxiv.), Lindley, Heilbron, Frankfort, has been our round so far. We now turn westward along the south of the Vaal. Farm-burning goes merrily on, and our course through the country is marked, as in prehistoric ages, by pillars of smoke by day and fire by night. We usually burn from six to a dozen farms a day; these being about all that in this sparsely inhabited country we encounter. I do not gather

that any special reason or cause is alleged or proved against the farms burnt.

If Boers have used the farm; if the owner is on commando; if the line within a certain distance has been blown up; or even if there are Boers in the neighbourhood who persist in fighting—these are some of the reasons. Of course, the people living in the farms have no say in these matters, and are quite powerless to interfere with the plans of the fighting Boers. Anyway, we find that one reason or other generally covers pretty nearly every farm we come to, and so to save trouble we burn the lot without inquiry; unless, indeed, which sometimes happens, some names are given in before marching in the morning of farms to be spared.

The men belonging to the farm are always away, and only the women left. Of these there are often three or four generations; grandmother, mother, and family of girls. The boys over thirteen or fourteen are usually fighting with their papas. The people are disconcertingly like English, especially the girls and children—fair and big and healthy looking. These folk we invite out on to the *veld*, or into the little garden in front—where they huddle together in their cotton frocks and big cotton sunbonnets while our men set fire to the house. Sometimes they entreat that it may be spared, and once or twice in an agony of rage they have invoked curses on our heads. But this is quite the exception.

As a rule they make no sign, and simply look on and say nothing. One young woman in a farm yesterday, which I think she had not started life long in, went into a fit of hysterics when she saw the flames breaking out, and finally fainted away. . . . The fire bursts out of the windows and doors with a loud roaring, and black volumes of smoke roll overhead. Standing round are a dozen or two of men holding horses. The women, in a little group, cling together comforting each other, or hiding their faces in each other's laps. In the background a number of Tommies are seen chasing poultry, flinging stones, and throwing themselves prostrate on maimed chickens and ducks, whose melancholy squawks fill the air.

Farther off still, herds and flocks and horses are being collected and driven off, while on the top of the nearest high ground a party of men, rifles in hand, guard against a surprise from the enemy, a few of whom can generally be seen in the distance watching the destruction of their homes.

Of the vast number of farms burnt in the year 1900, only a limited number seem included in the Government Return. (Cd. 524). It covers the months from June 1900 to January 1901, and does not deal with the first five months of 1900, nor the last sixteen months of the war. Of the large number of farms destroyed in June and July, it gives for June only two and for July three. Tidings of this wide destruction of their property reaching the prisoners of war in their camp at Green Point, they drew up a protest, and on October 22nd forwarded it to Sir Alfred Milner. It seems as if only two of the farms they instance appear in the Government Return. (Protest of Boer Officers, Prisoners of War, to Sir A. Milner.)

Your Excellency,—May it be permitted to us, military officers of the *burgher* forces of the Free States and the South African Republics, at present prisoners of war at Green Point, to bring the following respectfully to the notice of your Excellency:—

To our great grief we daily receive information regarding the destruction of private property by Her Majesty's troops within the territories of both Republics. Not only is the property of *burghers* still on commando destroyed, but the same measures have in several cases been taken with reference to the farms and property of persons who are prisoners of war in the hands of Her Majesty's Government, and even of women and widows.

About the destruction of the property of *burghers* who are still fighting we shall at present say nothing, though we deeply regret it, and do not wish to be understood to acknowledge that such a measure is called for by military operations; but in the interest of humanity we feel constrained to make an appeal to your Excellency with reference to the burning of the homes of the wives of prisoners of war and of widows, and to protest respectfully against it. Women have never been combatants, while, as regards the property of a prisoner of war, it cannot be said that he allowed his farm to be used in such a way that the military leaders were obliged for military purposes to have the same destroyed. We could cite numerous instances in which property has been destroyed in this way, but it is sufficient to enumerate the following from one district, *viz.*, Winburg:—

1. B. Wessels, at present at Green Point, taken prisoner February

1900; his dwelling at Stydfontein was burned in the month of July.

2. J. de Bruyn, at present at Green Point, taken prisoner May 5; his farm, Beste Hoop, burnt on September 13.

3. Mrs. Jacobs (widow); farm, Gevelkrans (district of Winboig), onde Witte Bergen, burned about September 1900; no one living there, all her sons prisoners of war, deported to Ceylon. (Cases 2 and 3 are amongst those in the Government Return.)

4. Mrs. Ferreira (aged seventy-five); farm, Onegegund, burned down; all sons prisoners of war, except J. Ferreira, of Destadefontein, district of Ladybrand, who was killed at Oliphantsfontein.

5. Louis P. Venter; made prisoner May 10; farm, Doorndraai; district, Winburg; burnt down September 1900; only women and children on farm.

6. Jacobus Coetzee; taken prisoner May 10; died at Green Point, July 1900; farm, Schilder Kranz; district, Winburg; burnt September 1900.

7. Willem A. Venter; farm, Schilder Kranz; burnt in September 1900.

8. Mrs. Elizabeth Venter (widow); house at Doorndraai; district, Winburg; burnt September 1900.

9. Sarel van der Walt; house at Doorndraai; burnt September; said Van der Walt a blind man.

10. Jacobus du Plessis; farm, Zronhuwfontein; district, Winburg; taken prisoner February 27; farm burnt September 19.

In support of what we have the honour to bring to your notice, we are able to refer to the accounts of the burning of houses and removing of stock which so often appear in the newspapers.

Trusting that your Excellency, as the representative of a powerful and Christian nation, will take into favourable consideration this communication, and trusting that your Excellency will express your disapproval of such actions, and that by your friendly intervention a stop will be put to the same, we have the honour to be, your Excellency's obedient servants.

(Signed by all the Boer Officers.)

Oct. 22, 1900.

By November it was recognised that the burning of farms and villages had become indiscriminate, and the commander-in-chief issued an order defining its limitations—

> As there appears to be some misunderstanding with reference to burning of farms and breaking of dams, commander-in-chief wishes following to be lines on which general officers commanding are to act:—No farm is to be burnt except for act of treachery, or when troops have been fired on from premises, or as punishment for breaking of telegraph or railway line, or when they have been used as bases of operations for raids, and then only with direct consent of general officer commanding, *which is to be given in writing*; the mere fact of a *burgher* being absent on commando is *on no account* to be used as reason for burning the house. All cattle, waggons, and food-stuffs are to be removed from all farms; if that is found to be impossible, they are to be destroyed, whether owner be present or not—Order xl. Cd. 426, Nov. 18.

On November 30th, Lord Kitchener succeeded Lord Roberts as commander-in-chief.

A committee of surrendered *burghers* had been formed, and Lord Kitchener addressed these men at Pretoria, offering protection to their families. A proclamation was issued embodying this offer, under which a certain number of small farmers, mostly Transvaalers, came in to save their goods, and formed waggon *laagers* in some of the camps. Their families thus secured comparative ease and comfort

> Pretoria, Dec. 20
>
> It is hereby notified to all *burghers*, that if after this date they voluntarily surrender they will be allowed to live with their families in government *laagers* until such time as the guerilla warfare now being carried on will admit of their returning safely to their homes. All stock and property brought in at the time of the surrender of such *burghers* will be respected and paid for if requisitioned by the military authorities. (See *Morning Leader*, Dec 28. Reuter.)
>
> (Signed)                                 Kitchener.

CHAPTER 2

# Women in 1900

*The wife, whose babe first smiled that day,*
*The fair fond bride of yester eve,*
*And aged sire and matron grey,*
*Saw the loved warriors haste away.*
*And deemed it sin to grieve.*

William Cullen Bryant.

The preceding chapter will have made it clear that the year 1900 had seen almost the whole of the two Republics reduced to chaos. From January onwards helpless families had been wandering homeless, captured, exiled, deported hither and thither on foot, in trucks, trolleys, waggons, and trains. It may be long before they can fully speak or write the story of that twelve months. Some women here and there wrote cautiously to friends, intimating rather than dwelling upon their experiences. It is my object in this chapter to give a few of these letters, written as they were unconsciously, and with no view to publication, so that by this means the story may be told in their own words by themselves.

To these are added accounts from a few people who occupied no official position, but gave them help in their troubles. Space forbids including all the letters which came from one district after another in gloomy succession. In nearly every case I hold the originals of these letters, though some of them have already been published separately. The name of the writer where withheld is known to myself, but prudence in some cases forbids its publication for the present.

The spirit in which the bulk of the Boer women faced their troubles is well conveyed in this anecdote—

In the beginning of this year, when the cause of the Boers

began to look uncertain, their leaders appointed a council to consider the dangers of the situation. On that occasion. General Smuts, in the presence of his men, of whom many had their wives with them, addressed his own wife in these words:—

'The moment is come in which we must choose between surrender and war to the utmost, war without end. I have duties to you, wife, and to our children. I must fulfil these duties. I must not hesitate. I must surrender and sacrifice the independence of the people. But you, I, and our children, we have also duties towards the country. And if we are true to these duties, then we must sacrifice ourselves.'

The general's wife opened her mouth to speak, but her husband silenced her with a sign, and continued: 'First you must know all, and then answer. If we choose the country, the sacrifices we must make are immense. Listen to me well. I must expose my life day by day, hour by hour, as long as the aim is not yet reached. In other words, I must forget all those I love—and you, wife, you and your children, you must forget every claim that you have upon me. Let us say goodbye to each other as if we were already stepping into the valley of death, and then go away as far as possible, that no temptation come over us to see each other again and to falter in the face of the enemy. Choose now between ourselves and our country.'

The woman answered these three words: 'Go, John—farewell!' And all the women said even so.—"Wives of the Boers," *Upright Harlem Newspaper,* 1900.

For the first few months of the year little was heard of the privations of the women and children, though it was known that their troubles had begun. As early as May 4 the correspondent of the *Manchester Guardian*, describing his stay at Brandfort, dwells upon the sorrowing families there, and calls it "the town of miserable women."

An Englishwoman who lived at Potchefstroom wrote to me about the state of that town in June and the succeeding months. She says—

Last June, and through the ensuing months, there were several families whose relations were fighting and had done much harm turned out; their goods were confiscated and used by the English officers, and in many cases sold by auction on the open *veld*. Naturally on the English evacuating Potchefstroom the Boers endeavoured to give these families back their property, but much was either destroyed or stolen. On the English again coming they took the same measures as before. In September last the wife and family of Commandant Francis were treated shamefully; they were turned out of the house, some of the children being sick, and would have died had it not been for kind friends who fed and kept them from starvation. The mother herself was compelled to go with the English.

At this time, too, there were in the town many from Griqualand West, who had sought refuge and had been living on the kindness of us all. (I gave them an empty house, and my husband helped them with a few bits of furniture and food, as most of them had *nothing*, not even a bed.) These people, who had been living under the English flag, had been terrified by reports that the English would kill or treat them even worse, so that many of them tried to get away to Boer *laagers* for protection.

Those who were left in Potchefstroom were disgracefully handled by rude soldiers, *forced* to climb into waggons, some poor women on the eve of confinement, and were taken away. I heard as a fact that two poor women of this latter class died from the effects. . . . The English evacuated Potchefstroom August 9. The next date of their coming was September 10, when they arrested my husband, and sent *Kaffirs* into town all round to arrest Hollanders, Boers, and those who were not allowed to remain. They all left on the 16th. Captain Maxwell (the only officer who treated women in a kind manner) wrote to me very kindly the morning my husband was taken. . . . The English did not return till October 29.

One night some sniping commenced at 7, while we were at supper, myself and my little boys, and we ran into the front room, laid flat on the floor, and there had to remain till the small hours of the morning. This sniping occurring rather oftener than was pleasant, we took to sleeping in town, and on our return about a week after were ordered to remove. Some of my belongings, such as beds, books, etc., which stood in the outside room, were stolen, and when I asked for the bed, which I wanted to sell, I was told I could not have it. . . .

One more word about the women and children, who are now the chief sufferers in this sad war. I think there are between two and three hundred brought away from their homes round Potchefstroom, no proper provision whatever having previously been made for them, (Sept and Oct. 1900, birth of Potchef-stroom Camp), mostly all deposited on the *veld*, or given such asylum as can be got quite irrespective of numbers and *sex*; these poor souls, before being able to obtain food, had to stand hours *outside* an office door waiting each her turn for admission to ask permit to get her 'daily bread.'

When the permit is procured, she, with her fellow-sufferers, trudge off to another office, and there stand again and wait till her turn comes to receive perhaps one or more slips of paper permitting her to obtain a few meagre groceries and milk, for which each must send at a stated hour. I have heard myself the officer telling women to come at 7.30 a.m. to receive their food, and having come were told to come back again at ten.

I could fill many pages with the sufferings that well-to-do people are at present enduring. I will tell you anything you wish to know, as this subject lies very near my woman's heart.

Mrs. George Moll, the wife of a prisoner of war, tells her own story in writing to Mrs. Steytler of Cape Town. In this instance publication was asked for—

You will no doubt be surprised to get a letter from me, who am quite a stranger to you, but I feel as if I must make our case known to you noble women of the Cape, so that you can publish it in one of the Cape papers. What I intend telling you I declare before God is the solemn and honest truth.

My husband was taken prisoner at Elandslaagte thirteen months ago. I had to manage alone with my two children, which I (did very well until the British came to Vrede the 23rd August. We lived about an hour from the town. At the time when they came I was staying in town, as I had just had a baby which was a month old. The British went out to the farm and destroyed all my furniture and clothing.

From there they went to the *veld* and took all the cattle belonging to me. The herdsman told them that the owner of the cattle had been captured and that I was in town; but the answer was 'she ought to have been here on the farm,' and that they would take everything; so, I was left without anything. The second time the British occupied Vrede (a month later), they first went to my sister's house (Mrs. Cornelius Moll) and drove her and her children oat of the house without anything, so she fled to my house.

A little later they came and told us to keep ourselves in readiness to go to Standerton. We had only a few hours to get ready, when they sent a bullock waggon to load us up for the journey. We didn't go very far when the side of the waggon gave way. We almost fell between the wheels. They shifted us into another old waggon a very little better. So, we had to travel to Standerton. When we got there, we were locked up in a dirty old schoolroom. The door was guarded by armed men. They thought us food after we were almost starved, which consisted of six tins of bully-beef and some biscuits (*klinkers*) in a dirty grain-bag, which was thrown down in front of us; the poor children could not eat the biscuits as they were too hard.

Next morning early, we were marched to the station, and ten of us were packed into a third-class compartment and the door was locked. We had to sit up straight for two whole days and a night without being allowed to go out once. Our poor children wanted to get out but they could not. They were almost starved. They would not allow me to get food for my baby, who was then little more than two months old. She had to travel all the way, you may say, without anything. Miss Marie le Roux (who is now in Caledon) and I warmed some water over a candle (as I wasn't allowed to buy spirits or anything) to mix a little condensed milk for the child.

Along the road they told the *Kaffirs* to drive us nicely as they were going to marry us when we got to Natal. When we got here we had to stand for ever so long with our tired, hungry children, not knowing where to go. After a lot of bother we were marched off to a private boarding-house, and we were kept there for a week, when we got notice that we would have to pay our own expenses in the future. We had no money. We only left with a few pounds in our pockets. You can never imagine what we had to go through. We managed to hire a cottage, so we took in a few of our people who are on parole here—Mr. Enslin, our Dutch minister from Vrede, and a few others, so we have to manage along. We can hardly make ends meet.

We heard from some of the inhabitants of Durban that the military say we asked them for protection, which is a falsehood—we never did anything of the kind. That's why they say we were sent down here. We have to report ourselves every day like the men. My sister was very ill just before we left Vrede. She was taken away sick and has been sick ever since. She asked the doctor here for a certificate to show the military that the heat was too much for her.

Mrs. Roman has just come from Harrismith. She says a few days before she left the British brought in a lot of families from different farms. One poor lady was sick and had to rush into the first house she could get, and a few minutes after that she was confined.

It is most heart-breaking if you hear all these things, knowing how we had and have to suffer.

Mrs. Van Vuuren, deported from her home in the Free State, wrote to Mrs. Koopmans de Wet in gratitude for help given when destitute—

Cape Town, Sept. 18, 1900.

How shall I thank you for helping me in my great need—and one who is a perfect stranger to you? Was it not good of our Heavenly Father to have given it in the heart of the lady in England to send you the money?

I started cutting out at once, and now we have finished several undergarments. My costume is also finished. Thank you so very much for the great gifts.

If anyone had said to me a year ago that I would before the end of 1900 be homeless and penniless in a strange country, I would have said, 'It can never be.' Ah, how many of my dear country-women are in the same condition; and, alas, many are worse off than myself . . .

You know so little about my sad experience, as I was here only two days when your loving heart found its way to a poor and lonely stranger, that I must tell you how I came here.

My dear husband and three sons left me last October 1899. My eldest boy, twenty-one years, was killed in January. How I felt the hand of the cruel war—yet not once have I regretted that he went out to fight for his dear country. Yes, for his own country, bought with the blood of forefathers, which the cruel money-seekers want to take from us.

The next blow was that my husband and two sons were sent to Ceylon.

How terrible the news was to us to hear that our dear ones

must go so far away. Here in Cape Town we knew were many Christian hearts who did for our people what they could to sweeten the bitter cup. It is so hard to know that we are separated from our dear ones by a vast expanse of water. I was then left alone with my only little girl of nine years, and my darling boy of thirteen years.

All that last week of August last the report was that 'General De Wet was in the vicinity of Wepener.' Our hearts rejoiced to think that once more would we poor women be protected. We were always in fear and trembling while the soldiers were about They would open our doors, march in, search every room, and take whatever they fancied. Not once, but time after time.

Each Dutch woman had to sleep in her own house, and we were never allowed to get another friend in to sleep with us, whether alone with a *Kaffir* boy or otherwise. I have heart disease very badly, and have often tried to have some friend with me for the night, but could not get permission.

On Friday, August 31, another dark cloud was near. My little boy was busy giving the horses water, when two policemen took him away. I ran out and asked what was wrong, one turned round and said—'We have orders from the major to put him across the border (that is Basutoland) for some days.' I asked for permission to bid him goodbye, but was not allowed. I felt my heart would break.

My heart got a fearful shock. I was quite sick. We sent for the doctor. I thought my cup of sorrow was filled to the brim, and that if anything else came I would be crushed. But my cup was not yet full, for on the Sunday evening, when I was already in my room for the night, there came a loud and harsh knock. I at once felt it could bring no good news. My little girl at once said—'Oh, mother, it is surely a soldier. What shall we do? Don't open the door, mother.' I knew I had to open the door or else they would burst it. I called out to wait for a moment. While putting on my bodice it was one long question: 'Oh, what can it be? Is my cup not yet full?' I opened the door.

There were two policemen and a cart. 'You have five minutes to get ready. You must go away by this cart for a few days. On Wednesday, you will be back again.' I asked if they would ask my neighbour to come over so that I might leave directions re my property. Of course, that was refused. I asked why they were sending us away—they did not know, were only carrying out orders. I was told that I may not take a single thing with me. I asked if I might take a rug since it was a cold night That the hearts of stone did not refuse. We travelled all that night to Bloemfontein—my little girl and I in a post-cart, and only one rug to cover us with.

The next morning, we were put on the train. A ticket was given us but nothing said. A few minutes later the train steamed out of the station. I was so taken aback, and everything came upon me so unexpectedly, that I had no time before for reflection. My last thought was Cape Town. But so it was, as the ticket said so. Imagine how I felt on seeing that no money, no food or rugs. Neither did the kind, civilised major think of seeing to the needs of a poor, barbarous Boer woman. If only he had told me to provide for a long journey. But our God, who has so wonderfully helped us in this unrighteous war, was with me even on the train. The wife of a Dutch minister travelled part of the way with me, and she helped us.

Never shall I forget the awful feeling of loneliness which got hold of me on arriving in this great and strange city. Where should I go? Who is there to help me? Alone and without money. May the major's wife never have a similar experience. At last someone took me to the Refugee Relief Committee. On hearing that I was a Boer woman, was told—'No, we cannot help you, your people are fighting against our people. Go to the Dutch ministers to help you.' They gave me the address of the Rev. Van Heerden. He then brought me to this Home, where I was most kindly received. I at once felt easier. I was then amongst my own people. I immediately wrote to Colonel Heyman at the castle, saying the military sent me down here and they were to provide for me. His reply was—'We know nothing about you and can have nothing to do with you.'

If only I could go back to my home. Then I would be nearer my darling little boy. It is so terribly hard to be torn away from kith and kin like this. And what is so hard is that mine is not an isolated case, but there are hundreds of such cases. Never can you people down here know what we, women and young innocent girls, have to suffer. Do you wonder that we cannot bow down to English rule? Not if you knew everything. We are willing to suffer more, and for another year, if only we get our independence back. That is all we want No gold or silver. Will our faithful God then not hear us?

I must write no more, as I feel it is exciting me.

May our dear Heavenly Father crown you and the dear unknown English lady with His richest blessing, and spare you both to be a bright and cheerful ray of light to many a sorrowing heart. Once more thanking you very much,—I remain, yours gratefully,

Gertruida Van Vuuren.

This was written in those far-off days when as yet it was not held credible that women should be turned penniless from their homes, and deported at the will of the military. A lady in Cape Town thinking, therefore, that there must be some mistake, wired to the officer commanding Wepener—

Cannot Mrs. Van Vuuren return to her home? At whose expense is she here?

The reply received was as follows:—

I cannot have Mrs. Van Vuuren here. She is on her own expense so far as I am concerned. She may live where she likes except in the districts of Moroka and Wepener.

Major Wright, Officer
Commanding Wepener.

The next letter is from Miss Ellie Cronje to Miss Hauptfleisch.

Wellington, Cape Colony, Nov, 6, 1900

No doubt you will be very surprised to hear from me, and wonder why we are at Wellington.

My mother, a lady friend, and I were sent here by the military authority.

Knowing what an interest you take in our people, I would like to give you an account of my experience during this war. I hope you will understand, after having read my story, how much the homeless women really do suffer in the Free State. My story is quite true. Our farm lies three hours from Winburg. My father, General Cronje, who served in Natal, and later on in the Free State, and four brothers, joined the commandoes in the beginning of October, the fifth brother left for the front on the 8th of January. One of the four who went first, being ill, came home, but for a short time only. Two of my brothers were taken prisoners, one with General Cronje in February, and one after being wounded at Koedoo's Rand was taken prisoner at Bloemfontein. On the 10th of May, we had our last visit from my father, since then we have not seen him.

My mother, a lady teacher from a neighbouring village, and myself, with our servants, were alone on the farm after May 10th. A week after that date General Macdonald camped for the night on the farm. Next day we received our passes from two policemen sent out to the farm by order of the provost-marshal. General Colville with his force passed a few days later, they also camped on the farm for the night; the general sending up a night watch to guard the house, only a few of the soldiers called at the house to buy food.

On July 6, General Brabant camped about half an hour's distance from the house, remaining for a few days. Lieutenant Morris came to the house, with his men and other soldiers; they bought food, some paying for what they got and others not. They poured into every room in the house except my mother's bedroom; they took many things from the sitting, dining, and bedrooms. The house was a fairly large one, containing drawing-room, dining-room, six bedrooms, kitchen, and pantries, a verandah and *stoep* run round three sides.

There was a poster on the door of the waggon-house, given by order of the provost-marshal, saying that nothing was to be removed without his orders; of this they took no notice, and took our bullock-waggon, horse-waggon, mealies, harness, and vegetables, also a load of forage, 12 oxen, poultry, and other things. We asked Lieutenant Morris for a receipt, he said we should get one from his men, but they said they had no right to give receipts, so we got nothing for all these things. Our oxen were sent to Ficksburg by one of our native servants, who on his return showed us—gave us—his pass, which stated that he was not to be interfered with as he had been sent in charge of '*Captured Stock*'; this pass we kept for future use, but after a little while the 'boy' demanded it, and for fear of annoyance we gave it to him.

After this troops passed several times, but gave us no trouble. A force again passed in September; we asked a captain who the general was, and he told us General Colville; this was not so, for we soon found that it was someone else. A few officers with their soldiers (Highlanders) called at the house to buy eggs, butter, and ham, which they paid for. They were very nice. Then some other officers and men came, who were very uncivil. They took the cart, etc., and cleared the waggon-house, leaving us no means of getting about. They took dried fruit and blankets, and from the loft even servants' clothing was taken.

An officer marched into the kitchen, and asked all sorts of silly questions—did we do any work? who killed our pigs and sheep for us? He went into the pantry and said, 'I'd better take all the things (canned fruit, etc.) or else you will give and make nice things for the Boers when they come again.' In the dining-room he told me he was going to burn the house, and asked what reasons could I give that he should not do so. I said, 'In the first place it is cruel to treat families as you are treating them, and in the second place what is to become of my poor mother?' He said, 'Oh, you must not think of your old mother now, when the house is burnt you must go and live with the *Kaffirs*; you will like that, won't you?' To my mother, he said, 'Go and fetch your old man by his beard and fasten him to the table and tell him to plough his lands.' He also said we would not get an inch of ground even if my father did come back, and, further, that we were the most cunning, slyest, cleverest people he had ever had to do with. 'You send the Boers nice things, have news of your father, and when we come and ask where the Boers are you pretend to be quite innocent, and say "We have not seen them for months." He left, and sent two waggons for forage, etc. On September 16, a small fight took place close to the farm. On the 17th six English came to the house to ask where the Boers were. On the morning of the 18th two men came to the house and asked who the owner of the farm was, whether he was still fighting, who my mother was, and whether any of my brothers were still fighting. I answered these questions. They then asked if the Boers called at the house when passing, and whether any of them actually entered the house, and who these were. We told them the Boers did call when they passed; how could we prevent them, our own people, when we could not keep the soldiers out? Mother said she never asked their names, and added, 'I do not ask you what your name is; you go away and I never know to whom I have been speaking.'

Then they tried to find out about the Boers from the *Kaffir* boys. Just before riding away they called the boy aside, and told him to tell mother to carry out her furniture because they were coming back with Colonel White's men to burn the house. We had about an hour to carry out furniture from the drawing and bedrooms, our piano and sideboard. While we were busy the troops came. They poured something over the floors to make them burn, and soon the dwelling-house and outside buildings were in flames, and soon our comfortable home was gone.

My mother, our lady friend, and I remained outside amongst the furniture we had removed and watched the burning. One of the men asked where we intended sleeping that night I said, 'If I had burned the house I would have known where to have gone and what to have done.' Others said, 'You have to thank Presidents Steyn and Kruger for this. Why do they not come and give in, why do they go about like robbers?' So, we said, 'They will never, never give in; they are fighting for their country, and you are fighting women because you know they will not shoot back.'

We also asked would they give in if we were fighting them and started burning their houses and sending women into the open *veld* without a morsel of food because their husbands and fathers and brothers would not give in? While we were still carrying out things the cutlery was taken from the sideboard drawers, along with a lot of things from the kitchen.

A soldier helped himself from our butter-barrel with his hands, and when we asked him to leave that alone he replied we might be thankful we had saved something, by rights everything should have gone. That night we kept out among the furniture standing on the '*werf*,' the wind carrying sparks over our heads. Twice during the night, the stables caught fire, and we got up to put it out so that we might have some shelter for the next night. Next day we had the stables cleaned and our goods carried in there, and there we slept the second night. They now took our remaining horses, cattle, and other things, and were going to send to gather the sheep. I asked for one cow to be left The reply was, 'Not one—not one.' Thirteen waggons were sent to take all the homeless women to the town.

On that day seventeen other families had been made homeless. Most of these are very poor and have a lot of little children.

We did not want to go to the town, and asked to be left on the farm, hoping to be allowed to remain in the stables; there was no help for it, we had to go. We have our own house in the town, and were promised we might go into that On this (Thursday) morning we were just going to have our breakfast in the ruined kitchen when a major came in and hurried us out of it to get our bags of clothes, etc., on the waggon. While we were doing this a soldier told me this major was eating our breakfast; I went in and asked was he not ashamed of himself seeing this was all the food we had? he appeared to be, and then tried to get us something.

At ten we were put in an open bullock-waggon and were sent in to town, which we reached at half-past seven that night, after having been exposed to the hot sun all day. The major calmly said, 'You are only common working people and used to such a rough life.' When we got to town they refused to give us our house and sent us to the hotel—paying for us. This was on September 20. On the 23rd the *commandant* came to see us, and said we were to go either to Bloemfontein or to the Colony; should we refuse we should be sent later on with the other women in open trucks to Bloemfontein and placed in tents there—these were his orders. He farther promised that if we went to Cape Town we would see our prisoner brothers at Green Point every afternoon. An officer standing by said, 'No, my dear girl, you will never see them; you might see them through the bars but won't be allowed to speak to them.'

At Winburg there were a number of families less fortunate than ourselves, who were obliged to crowd together; they received food from the military, but were without any comforts for the little children, the sick, and the old women. These people had been able to bring nothing with them. One of these women, in my presence, told the military that when she tried to save some of her children's clothing the soldiers threw these back into the flames. Another woman had with her twins of five months old, children of her daughter, who had died soon after their birth— when sent in she had asked for milk for these children, but it was not given her.

These are only a few instances out of many cases of equal suffering. These unfortunate women were told by the *commandant* that on no account would they be allowed to remain where they were, they would be sent to a women's camp at Bloemfontein. Can anyone imagine, without indignation, the misery of such a place—no privacy, the herding together of young and old, and barely the necessaries of life?

I did not think my story would be so long, but I only hope this will give you some idea of what the poor homeless families must suffer in the Free State. My statements are all true.—

Yours sincerely,

Ellie Cronje.

The above is that letter from Miss Cronje which was published by Mr. John Morley in the *Times* of November 17, 1900, and which caused such a wave of feeling throughout the country. The farm is amongst those mentioned in the Government Return, Cd. 524, (Welgelegen, Dist. Winburg) as having been burnt on September i8, 1900, and the reason given is an "order to lay waste the Doornberg district." The Return gives seventeen farms as having been destroyed that same day, which agrees with Miss Cronje's statement that seventeen families had been made homeless.

When I saw Miss Ellie Cronje she was living in exile with her mother in Cape Colony. She received me very civilly, and seemed relieved to tell me her story. There was not a trace of self-pity in the way she dwelt upon her sufferings—on the contrary, she gloried in them; it was a source of strength and comfort to the girl to feel that she too had suffered for her country—but she is anxious the world should know how they have suffered and what hard things they have endured. She was delicately careful not to hurt my feelings, and there was not a shade of bitterness expressed either by the girl or her mother towards the English people or the Queen.

Mrs. Cronje, who spoke only Dutch, is a quiet, dignified woman. Her first remark was to express sorrow for the many English soldiers who had fallen. "Both sides have suffered much," she said, "and neither English nor Boer is to blame; it is the fault of the millionaires." She made no allusion to her own losses. Miss Cronje said five farms in their family had been burnt; their own, those of her two married sisters and of her two married brothers. In her sister's case the soldiers came when it was early and she was but partially dressed, with her hair all down her back. In this state the poor thing had to watch her house burnt, while Kaffirs tore the rings off her fingers. Then, as all vehicles had been taken, she and her five children had to trudge into the town, a two hours' walk.

Miss Cronje spoke with gratitude of General Colville's conduct towards them. "We all loved him," she said. At one time, he sent up a guard to protect their house at night On the other hand, the women shrank from some of the officers. One of them said to her, in answer to her question why the houses should be burnt, "We burn them because your men won't give in, and if that won't do we'll burn the women next"

"Then why not begin with me?" she replied; "I am here, and quite ready to suffer for my country."

"But there are bad Boers too," wound up Miss Cronje, "and there are good English. I was very grateful to an Imperial Yeoman who, seeing our condition, most considerately offered me money or any assistance, and said he felt ashamed of the things done and said."

The next letter describes the eviction of Mrs. John Murray, wife of the missionary in the district of Waterberg, Transvaal. The mission station, which appears to have been burnt in September or October, is not mentioned in the Government Return—

Mrs. John Murray to a Relative.

(Received Dec 17, 1900.)

At last I am able to write you a few lines. I took ill the very day I arrived here, and have been three weeks in bed. I only got up for the first time this morning.... During the past year of war I tried in various ways to write letter after letter to you, but after some months all our letters were returned to us again. You can imagine how disappointed we were. We received some of your letters, but not all. We had always food in the house, although we had sometimes to pay tremendous prices for it.

But last month our provisions were getting so low, and there was no way of getting anything, so on the 17th J. left me by cart for Delagoa Bay to telegraph to Mr. R. for his salary that he might buy provisions. The day after J. left, W. H. drove out to our mission station to fetch me to spend a few days with them. J. had asked him to take care of me.

I had only left a few days when the British came. We were then on the fighting line, and our people with General Grobelaar were about a mile from the house we were in, on the mountains, and the tremendous English camp about ten minutes from us.

We had cannon and rifle firing over the house for more than two weeks; we never hardly put our heads out of our doors during the day; and it was dreadful to see the dead and wounded being carried forth. The English took all the food we had, leaving us hardly enough for a fortnight It was terribly hard when we had no more bread for the little children. Then I applied to the British for food, but they said they could do nothing. Then they gave us two hours' notice to leave for Pretoria; Mr. and Mrs. A. and their children, Mr. and Mrs. H. and child, and myself and three children. We were all put into cattle-trucks. I was not even allowed to send home to fetch some clothes for the journey.

We were all sent away because the officer said every homestead was to be burned down, so you can imagine with what grief and sadness we left our houses. I told the officer that our mission station was Colonial Church property, but he said it made no difference! It is hard to think we have perhaps lost everything. I expected J. the week before we left, but the officer said he would not be allowed to get through, so I cannot think what has become of him. The officer said if J. had been in the station he would have been taken prisoner and sent to Ceylon, adding that ministers, missionaries, and Boers are all treated alike! I feel very anxious about J., but I know the dear Lord will take care of him. Oh! you cannot think what poverty and misery there is in the Transvaal, not so much in towns as in farms. It is dreadful to see the homes burned down, and not a living thing about

Mrs. Murray gives further particulars upon another occasion. The officers said to her, "You women are the cause of this war, if you were to give in your husbands would give in too. You must go and tell your uncle Louis Botha to surrender."

"Louis Botha will care nothing what I say," she replied.

Mrs. Murray asked an officer why the British were burning all the farms, and he replied, "Oh, because when you are all poor we can buy your farms for pretty well nothing, and then your husbands will be our servants and you women will serve our wives."

When the troops came, they were ordered to give up all their supplies—the meal, the rice, eta, which, with the milk of the cow, Mrs. Murray and the children had managed to live on up to then. "But what is to become of us?" she asked. "If anyone is to suffer you must be the ones to suffer, not we," they said, and gave her two bags of hard mealies. "But the baby cannot live on these," she exclaimed in horror.

"It is all you will get," they replied. If she had not previously secreted a little meal under a mattress the baby must have died, as she was not nursing him herself.

When the order came to burn down the house, Mrs. Murray protested, on the score of the house not being her own but Church property, but they turned a deaf ear to all she said. She hurriedly put together a few parcels of clothes, and placed them on the *stoep* for putting on the waggon, but the soldiers tossed them all away. She was obliged to come away in the old dress she was wearing about the house, and all she carried was a small hand-parcel of a few necessaries for the baby. They were placed on the waggon and driven through the British camp towards Warmbaths.

Soldiers guarded the waggon with fixed bayonets both in front and behind. At Warmbaths they were put into a dirty cattle-truck which had carried cattle the day before and not been cleaned out, and sat there exposed to the cold without wraps from 10 a.m. to 10 p.m., when they arrived at Pretoria. She asked to be allowed to go to her aunt, Mrs. Louis Botha, but this was refused. Mrs. Murray argued that her children would perish of cold if they sat all night long in the cattle-truck Upon this they were allowed to go into the ladies' waiting-room, and locked in. Every scrap of furniture had been removed from this room, even to the carpet, and there was nothing on which to sit or lie but the bare floor.

It was lighted above by a skylight, which was out of order and would not shut, and the night was bitterly cold. She lay down on the floor with her maid and the children, and the wind streamed down from the skylight and they could not sleep. She took off her own skirt and wrapped one child in that, and the other was wrapped in the maid's skirt. The baby screamed all night from cold and hunnger. In the morning Mrs. Murray called out to the soldiers from the window, "If you do not let us out this child will die."

At first, they said she must stay where she was, for she was to be taken down to the Women's Camp at Port Elizabeth, but finally they allowed her to go and see her aunt Mrs. Botha took her at once to Governor Maxwell, and through her influence Mrs. Murray was allowed to proceed to her parents in Natal. Her health, however, was severely, and it is to be feared permanently, injured by all she had undergone. In Natal, she was three weeks in bed, and on coming to Cape

Colony to live with relations she was four months in bed, and had to undergo a bad operation. The doctor said had she gone to a camp she must have died.

At Green Point, prisoners were beginning to learn from letters and also from newcomers of the capture of their wives and children.

To a Prisoner of War from his Wife.

Natal, Sept, 1900

Dear ——, I received your letter; I had just written to Ceylon and St. Helena to hear if you were there when your letter came; you cannot think how thankful I was. *We cannot find out why we are taken prisoners.* We left Vrede in two buck-waggons, and had only two hours to get all ready. From Standerton, we went in third-class carriages, *ten of us in one compartment.* For two days and one night *we were locked up in these carriages* almost without food. Baby takes a bottle, but I was not allowed to make food for her; I had a little spirit stove, but they would not let me buy spirits for it At first, they paid our expenses, but now we must manage for ourselves or go to the Refugee Camp, where we should get 7½d. a day. We thanked them, and preferred to pay our own expenses.

We have hired a nice house, food is cheap, so we are comfortable. We must report ourselves daily at the office. Our home is totally ruined, everything smashed in it and all our cattle taken except a few goats. Myrtle is grown a great deal, so has Eric; baby (born while the father was in prison) is very like him. What shall I call her? She is not yet christened. Willem is prisoner here on a ship. Yours, etc.

To A Prisoner of War from his Wife.

Durban, Sept. 12.

Much Beloved,—You will be surprised to hear that I and our children have all been taken prisoners and are here in Durban. The little one (only four months old) is such a strong, healthy, and pretty child.

To A Prisoner of War from his Mother, giving earliest personal account of Bloemfontein Camp.

Bloemfontein, Oct, 17.

We were taken out of our house and the house was burnt It is today a week since we arrived here (Bloemfontein). We were

15 days at Winburg and had a comfortable house belonging to Mr. ——, who was willing to do everything for us, but to punish us we were sent to this place. We were not allowed to take anything with us but our clothes; we get rations (chilled meat and baker's bread). It is very hard to be beggars, but I hope everything will come right We are half an hour from Bloemfontein, in a camp; they call it the Refugee Camp.

There are 13 families in the camp. We are placed 12 in one tent, and your mother is cook, for we were forbidden to bring servants. You can imagine what it is to wash clothes, etc., in a small bath. They cart the water here in two vats for the use of all the people. You can fancy what things look like; and we must gather for ourselves and drop the green bushes to make a fire. There are no cattle here, and we have to use mule dung to light the fire with. Your loving mother.

To A Friend in Cape Town.

Translation.

Bloemfontein Female Prisoners' Camp, Nov. 30.

Dear ——, Only a few lines to tell you that I was taken (caught) last Sunday and sent to Sanna's Post. I then asked that my children (aged 5 years, 3 years, and 18 months) might be sent for to be sent along with me, as I could not think of them alone on the farm. Now we are all here in a tent; old Aunt N. and my sister also. The latter they brought here with her three little sons. They would not even allow her to bring her baby.

Oh! unless God come to help us, I do not know what is going to become of us. I must perish in my misery with my children. I entreated them to let me go into a boarding-house, but it was positively refused me. I had to go to a camp. No mercy! I am hoping and trusting in God. He will hear us and send us deliverance. If I have to endure ever so much I shall remain an Afrikander.

Do, dear, pray much for us all. God alone knows what we have to suffer. I may not write or I would tell you all. Christie and John are both ill, as they sent us in an open cart six hours' distance in the glowing hot sun. And now here in the tent it is very hot. No animal can live in it Here are many people we know from different places. Uncle P. T. and his aged wife. Do write soon. I am longing to hear from you.

OCCUPANTS AND FURNITURE OF ONE CELL TENT SOON AFTER ARRIVAL FROM THE FARM, APRIL 1900.

The oats that I got sown are now standing beautiful on the field. When I went away I sent C. (the *Kaffir* servant) to reap it, but I do not believe they will allow it.

Loving greetings from myself and the children.

Mrs. J. R. Green who, as is well known, visited the prisoners of war in St Helena, has kindly supplied from her notes a few anecdotes which show clearly the anxiety felt by the men for the safety of their families in the unsettled state of the country—

Wednesday, Oct, 10, 1900.

. . . Among the new prisoners there are, I am told, about sixty farmers taken up *on their farms* and sent off without any reason given. . . . One told me his wife and three children were now left alone on the farm—the eldest girl 13, the eldest boy 11—three miles from the nearest neighbour. There were others in the same distress. The country unsettled, prowlers, and men stealing what they could get, and the like. The father of the three children, when his arms were taken some time ago, had begged to keep one Mauser, given him by Joubert, to protect his farm.

When the English came to his farm first they took the black boy and asked him where he had buried his arms. The boy did not know. They beat him badly. Still he did not know. 'You must know,' they said; 'you were the boy who drove and went everywhere with him.' 'That was my brother,' said the boy, 'and he went away many weeks ago.' The *Kaffirs* were frightened at all this, and left the farm, all but three.

I asked if he was charged with concealing ammunition. 'No, there was no charge,' he said. 'I was a Progressive member of the Raad' (he was a very educated and superior man), 'and for ten years I have been struggling to avert this war.' 'Your sorrow must be great?' I said. 'Oh, Mrs. Green, I cannot tell it. I am like a son mourning for his mother; and what I fear is that now there will begin a set of horrible murders, such as history has never told of before. I used to hear that if you burned a man's house you turned him into a soldier. Now I have seen it all round me, and I know that if you burn a man's house down you turn a coward into a hero. When a man has seen his wife and children turned out of doors with nothing but what they have on, and the house blown up, that man does not care from that time what he does.' The men out now are desperate men.

Mrs. Green continues—

Then I was fetched to Roos's tent ... A very young-looking boy was brought, Du Toit I thought him about 17. He was 21. . . . He was taken on September 10 at Potchefstroom. . . . On the 15th his mother was taken as 'prisoner of war' and put in prison. At eight in the evening he was sent out with a guard to fetch the baby to her. There were five other children, the eldest girl 16, the youngest 3—and these were left alone. He does not know where they are. His mother and the baby were sent to prison in Johannesburg.

No reason was given for the arrest. He has no idea why she was taken. (Waldeck said he heard the mother had been out on the farm some little time before to drive in the horses, and found a wounded Boer lying in the field, and had carried him not to her own house, but to some other shelter. He thinks that may have been the charge.) Of the ten mothers, he thinks eight were sent to Naauwpoort: thirty-one women and children taken in all. The whole house was sacked; everything taken out of it but the mattresses, and the farm wasted, and every beast or fowl on it cleared off, and then these five children were left ...

. . . . They cannot tell why women are seized. Some say to keep the Boers from firing on the troops with prisoners. Some think it is to force the husbands to come and give themselves up and set the wives free. Zinn, in the hospital, had been also on the journey with the women prisoners. He said it was a pitiable sight. The number of children, many in arms, not a year old, wailing and crying. His anger is very, very hot

Oct. 12, 1900. Friday.—Commandant Wolmarans . . . asked me to lunch in tent, Commandant Viljoen with him. . . . Talked of the women and children turned out 'God knows, no one else knows, how they can live.' Old white-haired Viljoen never spoke. . . . Wolmarans asked me to stay, and poured out his story with vehement animation. His wife died seven years ago. His house was shut up, he being away. One son of 14 was living near with a married sister. The soldiers came (these new prisoners report), tore the roof off the house, wrecked it, and took everything away. They drove off his cattle, every single thing on the farm.

The boy of 14 ran after the cattle to try and drive them back. They took him prisoner of war to Johannesburg with another boy, and kept them in gaol some days. Then had them out, gave them ten strokes with a stick, and turned them out. One boy shrieked and cried. Wolmarans' son said not a word nor dropped a tear. When it was over he said, 'Now I will shoot the English.' Wolmarans tells that these blows, which must have been given by an official's order, are worse to him than the destruction of all his property. To all of them it was a horrible insult.

This story and others have given all the camp a new fear as to what may have happened to their families. They had expected under Roberts' proclamation that the farms of surrendered men would be protected from the English soldiers. They still think they ought to be.

Mrs. P J. Botha to a Sister in Cape Town.

Bloemfontein Camp, Dec. 20.

This is just to let you know our whereabouts. I and my family were sent here eight days ago, with thirty other families from Philippolis. You can well imagine how longing we are to hear from our dear ones—it was in September we had the last letters. Communication has been cut off since then, and now we are here. I need not tell what camp life is like, being placed with all classes and all conditions in one place; it is too rough to describe to any one, I never knew tent life was so hard. I have a bell-tent, with all my children (5); in dry weather it is very hot, but don't speak of wet weather, when the water runs in under one and wets all one's bedding, and water leaking from above. You would be amused and sad to see your poor old sister trotting after the water-cart to get a water supply, then up the *kopjes* to gather wood; we have to find it all ourselves. We get government rations, meat, bread, sugar, coffee, *no luxuries*. Still we are satisfied, it might have been worse. We are not allowed to go into town or else I could go and see A—— (brother), and they are not allowed to come to camp or send any eatables, but he sent me a mattress and chairs and waterproof to make our tent a bit comfortable.... I tried to get a permit to go to Cape Town, but was refused.

Mind, Hessie dear, in a way I feel proud to suffer with my people, for one can never really sympathise before being placed in the same circumstances, and now I assure you I can in full sympathise with all. . . . I have very much to be thankful for, it might have been worse.

I hear our dear boy has been sent to Ceylon—from my husband I have not heard for months. . . . I will never be dissatisfied with anything again, for I have had it too hard; all my things I have lost. When I was driven out of my house and home and went into Susan's house, I stored all my things in a room of a Mr. Gertenbach, and that has all been destroyed, so we have nothing to lose more. Naked we came into the world and naked we will have to leave it I have much to write, but for the present we must be satisfied. I find it very difficult to write as we have no table to write on.

From a Free State Lady, describing the Early Camp at Bloemfontein.

Oct, 29.

Oh! it is so wearying, and one looks forward fearfully. Boers are brought in daily, some as prisoners and others who have laid down their arms. The wives and children of many of our well-to-do farmers, whose farms have been burnt out and everything taken, are dumped down in tents in the direction of Spitz Kop on the dusty veld. The bread supplied them by the military authorities is so bitter they cannot eat it, and there is much sickness.

From the same Lady.

Bloemfontein, Nov. 14.

Only yesterday more women and children were brought from the camp to be sent to Norval's Pont, scarcity of water being the reason given; and along the street some insolent natives chaffed the native drivers, shouting, 'Where did you pick up that lot?' Poor weeping women and children, and the guard not manly enough to protect them from insult! I could fill pages. Misery and suffering are everywhere, and poverty gaunt. Yesterday was a terrific day—a fierce wind raged, and about two o'clock the clouds gathered and we hoped rain was really coming, but dust storm upon storm raged all the afternoon, and at sunset it blew madly and the whole western sky was vermilion. I thought of those poor women in camp with the little babes. The weather is truly awful, and natives say, 'It can never rain again, there is too much blood in the land!' What is before us? God only knows.

The poverty is overwhelming—no ploughing, no sowing, people depressed beyond telling—depressed but dogged.

A British subject who resided in Bethlehem wrote me a description of her deportation to Natal. She gives an account, which is the earliest we have, of the camp at Pietermaritzburg, where food and necessaries were always comparatively abundant It would be a mistake to suppose that the large tents and furniture she describes were provided in all camps, or indeed in any after the very first weeks. The people were brought to bell-tents *really* bare.

Cape Colony.

In October 1900 (26th) we were taken away from Bethlehem. We were stopped by a fight with the Boers on Mr. Van der Merwe's farm, Mooihoek, about two hours from Bethlehem. The Boers were on the *rand* and *kopje* at the back of the house; there were none in the house or garden.

The English bombarded the house, where the women and children were, at intervals from about nine in the morning until five in the afternoon. One bomb fell on the schoolroom where the women and children were sitting; they escaped only just in time. Owing to the bombs falling on the house they had at last to take refuge behind the garden wall; the bombs and bullets were falling thickly around them all the time.

When the general came to the house he told Mrs. Van der Merwe and Mrs. Pretorius to take out what they wanted quickly as the house was to be burnt; as quickly as they brought them out some of the soldiers carried back the things, so that in the end they had very little besides what they had on. They were brought into camp late that night, having had to walk quite a long distance to reach it.

In speaking about the matter to Captain Webber, I told him that Mrs. Van der Merwe had told me that there were no Boers in the house or garden, and that she had not even known that they were on the farm. He said that Mrs. Van der Merwe was telling a lie. I know Mrs. Van der Merwe to be thoroughly truthful.

Our waggons were just at the back of the cannon, and we saw the Boers on the rand but none in the garden. There were three generals with their forces at this place, but I believe that it was General Rundle who took Mrs. Van der Merwe and Mrs. Pretorius away. The husbands of these two ladies had both been taken prisoners in August. There were about 150 women and children in our company. Each family had a waggon, with a small tent at the one end; at night, each family was provided with a small bell-tent; the tents and waggons then formed the sides of a small square in which the women and children could walk about when encamped.

The corporal and his men who had charge of the women did all they could for their comfort. The party arrived at Harrismith on the 30th, and remained there for a week; then half of them were sent by train to Maritzburg; the first part of the way they were put into second-class carriages, at Ladysmith they were put into third-class.

On arrival at Maritzburg they found tents ready for them, but nothing else; before evening, however, blankets and food were supplied. The tents were the large oblong tents with double canvas, one for each family. The furniture consisted of iron stretchers with straw mattresses, five blankets to each person, a table and two benches, a tin basin, a bucket, and a campkettle. The food was prepared by the women themselves; a fair amount was given.

The women did their own washing; a shed with good water had been put up for the purpose. The great drawback was the intense heat, and there was no shade for the children to play outside. The women were allowed to go out visiting their friends in the town or to go shopping.

After spending a fortnight in the camp, I was allowed to go home to my friends in Cape Colony.

From a Clergyman's Wife to a Friend at Stellenbosch.

Pietermaritzburg, Nov. 1900.

My dear Mrs. Louw,—You will no doubt be surprised to receive a letter from me from this place. I am now also experiencing camp life, and do not find it very convenient. Last Sunday I was still at Heidelberg, getting ready to come away. Mrs. O. and I were sent off together. When I last saw her she was still in a hotel and not on parole yet I was at once put on parole, and stayed in an hotel one night, but could not stay longer as the room I had was engaged for the next day. I tried to find another place, but that was unprocurable, as it is holiday time, and between that and the exiles every vacant place was already occupied, so I had no alternative but to come to the camp on the understanding that as soon as I could get a moderate boarding-place that I would be allowed to go out.

I am here with the two youngest children; my boy had to remain behind as witness in his cousin's case, which had to come off last week, but I was so undesirable that it was impossible to leave me a few days longer. My daughter and the boys will come on later. A certain colonel is to go into my house; he means to get his wife out I doubt if I shall ever see any of my things again. This is a very large camp. I hear some 500 families are here. I daily find people I know. Life would not be so hard if one could get a marquee tent for a family, but now there are so many in one small tent. (See previous account a month earlier; over-crowding had now begun.) Part of the camp will be removed to Howick sometime next week.

The women really behave splendidly, making the best of all the hard jobs, chopping wood, carrying water, cooking outside, etc. I should like to see a lot of Englishwomen placed in these circumstances, you would not be safe to come near for all the quarrelling there would be. Last night we witnessed a sad sight, about 130 persons, women and children, were marched out to this place from the railway station (three miles off). Just as they arrived a heavy shower of hail and rain came on, and before everyone had a tent they were soaking wet; to see wee little children drenched to the skin was so sad, and the tents were as wet as they themselves.

All the luggage was still behind, and they had to turn in for the night as they were. We fortunately had heard in the afternoon that some eatables were sent for the camp from some good people at Greytown, I believe, so Miss B. and I went to find out the committee and asked for some bread for the new arrivals (as they had hardly had any food all the way down here), which they willingly gave us, so although the poor little things were wet they could be fed.

Some of the women who arrived were very ill and wanted medical attendance at once, especially one woman who had sickened on the road for her confinement. I have not yet heard what became of her. The tents are so alike that it is hard to find a person here. Two other women arrived, one with a baby five days old, the other is seven days old; imagine them arriving in a thunder and hailstorm. One of these women was taken away by ambulance-waggon this morning, so I make out that she has been taken worse, as they only take away those that are seriously ill. ... New arrivals tell us they had tidings of our people as still in excellent health and spirits; they wish us all to be of good cheer and as confident as they are.

From Rev. N. P. Rousseau to the Committee in Cape Town.

Pietermaritzburg, Dec. 10.

There are more than 1000 men, women, and children together in the camp. They have pretty large comfortable tents, but complain bitterly of not getting enough of meat and bread and of being without any clothing whatever. I am not sure of this being the case with the women from Heidelberg, but of most of the others I know that after a moment's notice, in many instances, their houses, with all in them, were burnt down before their eyes, while they were not allowed even to take an extra bit of clothing with them. Some are in a terrible plight ... I have been to the *commandant* about their food supplies. ... We are doing what we can.

We have a Ladies' Committee which cares for the clothing and shoes for the most needy. The military authorities have offered help in this respect also; but there is so much of red-tapeism about it, and they want each one to sign for what he or she gets so as to pay back after the war, that they do not wish to avail themselves of this help. (It is well to note this proposed repayment for clothes supplied) .... Of course every penny is welcome. ... There is a talk of some of them being removed. ...

A Clergyman to Helpers at Stellenbosch.

Pietermaritzburg, Dec. 29.

I have received your note re the Boer women and children in the so-called Refugee Camp here. ... With regard to the hundreds of our poor women and children here, I am sorry to say that the most of them are sadly in want of clothing; our Ladies' Committee here has received a list from the Committee in the camp, from which it appears that there are hundreds who need help, and the account will certainly amount to more than £100 sterling. Many of the women and children are almost naked. Some have no underclothing whatever. They say they were driven out of their homes just with the old things they had on at the time, and that they were not allowed to take anything with them however much they begged to do so, while their houses were burning even before they had fully left.

Others just had time to take a single box of clothing with them and some bedding. Others, again, did save some of their furniture even, but had to leave all behind, as they were driven away by the soldiers. Some have money with them, but the majority of them have not a penny. I cannot describe to you the misery these poor people are in. Here some of them arrived while it was pouring with rain, and were just put into those small round bell-tents, sometimes ten in one of these tents, where they are almost burned to death in these hot summer days when the sun shines.

I was in several of these tents yesterday but could not endure the heat in them for a few moments, and yet in these very tents there are sick women and children of a few days old. In one tent, I found a mother who was confined on the way to this— she lay there with her baby of a few days old in the burning heat. She was taken out of her comfortable home, where she was already ill in bed, and carried out, while her house was set fire to. The only crime of these women seems to have been that their husbands are away with the Boer commandoes.

The food these people receive is so little that they cannot exist from it I have complained to the *commandant* about all this, but as yet we have had no redress.

I gave some money to the most needy families so as to buy some more food for themselves. I got some money from the Committee in Cape Town, and today £40 has been wired me again.

The Greytown and Maritzburg people are doing what they can to relieve this distress, but many are in great want. I visit them regularly and preach for them at stated times. We need help, but as the camp is to be shifted to Howick, or at least a part of the camp, I have not yet decided what steps to take for securing the help of a brother minister. There are those who have plenty of money amongst them, and others, alas, who cause us a deal of sorrow by their conduct ... But we certainly do need help and much of help. We dare not write, and I am afraid even what I have written now might do harm.

Turning to the Transvaal, we find a lady occupied in mission work writes at this time—

Near Johannesburg, Nov, 1900.

If we look around us at the needs of others, we feel that we dare not open our mouths, our privileges have been great. We are hard up, but we can manage with the little our Church gives to procure food and clothing. We had a very terrible experience about a fortnight ago. Four men entered our house at ten o'clock in the evening and would not be persuaded to go out. We did not know what to do; but as always the way to the throne of grace was open, we knelt down and cried to God.

Even then they hardened their hearts and took not the slightest notice of what we were doing. They stood talking to us as if nothing was happening; I just felt I could not let the Lord go before He heard us and answered, and when they saw we were determined not to give them their way they stepped out and closed the door behind them. You will hear more about this later on. M. and S.'s nerves were so shattered that they were obliged to be sent away for a fortnight's rest.

A friend writes, (*South African News*, January 9, 1901):

Johannesburg, Dec. 8, 1900.

Words cannot express the extent of misery which is meted out to our womenfolk here in this country. Today about fifty families were brought in from the Potchefstroom District, all past my door, and they were all dumped down on the Robinson Deep men's quarters. I then went down to see, but my heart wept within me when I saw the misery. Children were crying with hunger, and mothers the same, and had nothing to give them to eat. They had not had anything to eat since yesterday. They have been removed from their farms. I took as much milk and bread as we had and divided it among them.

I sent Johannes with money into the town to try and buy bread, but he could not get a single loaf, so they will have to hold out until they get something from the relief. You can never form an idea of what it is, and we can't realise what the end will be. Food is so scarce that even money can't buy it; . . . but there are, you may say, thousands whom starvation is staring in the face. I hear all, or most, of the women in the two Republics are to be brought here. Ophirton is as full as it can be, so is the Racecourse, and now I hear they are to be put in the compounds.

The letter continues—

Dec, 18.

I have written about the treatment of the women here, but the worst I have not told you.

A certain train arrived from Potchefstroom full of females all loaded in open trucks, and three women confined in the open trucks in the midst of children. On arrival at Braamfontein Station it was found that one had died under confinement, together with the baby. Others on alighting at the station fainted from sheer exhaustion. We have arranged with the authorities and got permission to send refreshments to the station when the trains arrive, as the poor people are without anything to eat for days.

Rev. Mr. Meiring of Johannesburg wrote also to friends in Cape Colony describing the early want in Johannesburg Camp—

Johannesburg, Dec. 1900.

There is much sickness amongst the people, ascribable very largely to want of sufficient and proper food, the promised improvement in the rations not coming up to our expectation. The whole matter both of feeding and clothing our poor people is causing us much anxiety. We are resolved, if we can get no satisfaction with the local authorities, to appeal to the commander-in-chief, and if need be to higher officials. The people have, very many of them, no change of raiment, and without soap, as a result cannot cleanse themselves.

We cannot of course supply all this from our own wardrobes, although some seven waggon-loads of old clothes have been sent out there by us from time to time. We cannot clothe 2000 or 3000 women and children. These poor sisters were in many cases brought away from their homes with nothing but what they had on, or what they could gather in the few minutes allowed them; and while they have till now been accustomed to food and respectable living, they are at present as the offscouring of the country.

We have asked for another interview with the governor to discuss this matter and to ask for immediate improvement. It is heartrending to move among these sisters and witness their silent sufferings.

Very important, with its detailed information, is this letter published first in the Algemeen *Handelsblad* of February 21, 1901, and in the *Daily News* of March 1, 1901—

Johannesburg, Dec, 2, 1900.
During my stay in Johannesburg I had the opportunity of attending the public meetings which were held in December by a Committee charged with the distribution of the 'Dutch Church funds for the relief of prisoners of war and captured women and children at Johannesburg,' and, being a prisoner on parole myself, I naturally took a great interest in all that was being done for these poor people. I state nothing but that of which I have immediate personal knowledge. On December 2, a deputation from the above-named Committee had a meeting with the military governor of Johannesburg with a view of seeing what could be done to provide for the lodging and feeding of the captured women and children who were to be sent there. The deputation, as the result of this meeting, was referred to the architect Mr. Nicholson, and to Major Cavaye, the officer charged with the distribution of the Imperial Relief Fund. The architect exhibited the plans for the buildings which were to be erected for the reception of the prisoners.

Three sheds were to be erected, each 200 ft. long by 25 ft. wide. In each of these sheds 400 adults were to be lodged; wooden cribs would be supplied, but the prisoners must supply their own bedding. Major Cavaye informed the deputation that, in accordance with a new ration scale which he had received from Lord Kitchener in Pretoria, only 7 lbs. of maize meal, 4 oz. of coffee, 4 oz. of salt, and 8 oz. of sugar would be provided weekly for each adult. The children would receive the same quantity of sugar, and half rations of the other articles.

The major admitted that this diet was not sufficient to keep body and soul together, and stated that he had on his own authority allowed 2 lbs. of flour and 5 lbs. of maize meal to be given instead of 7 lbs. of the latter. In face of these facts, it is needless to say that the lot of the prisoners of war in St Helena and Ceylon is infinitely better than that of their wives and children left behind. On the 19th December the chief medical officer addressed the following letter to the military Governor of Johannesburg:—

> Sir,—In my capacity as Chief Medical Officer of the Boer camp, I have to report that I consider the rations served out to the refugees to be insufficient to keep them in health. The great majority of these people are women and children who are not in a condition of health to withstand the sudden change in their diet, for, as is well known, most of them have been accustomed to a diet consisting largely of meat. The consequence of this sudden change is that much sickness has broken out amongst them.
>
> Most of the women, and almost all the children, are suffering from a more or less acute form of diarrhoea. In this state of things, the supply of drugs and medical comforts forms a very large item in the expenses of the camp. I would suggest that in addition to the present ration of maize meal, flour, coffee, sugar and salt, meat and fresh vegetables should be supplied at least three times a week to those who are not in a position to purchase them for themselves.
>
> (Signed)                                    R. P. Mackenzie,
> District Medical Officer.

On December 9 also the Secretary of the Committee wrote to Major Cavaye, pointing out that the 282 women and old men, and the 547 children, confined on the grounds of the Robinson Deep, Mainreef, and Ferreira Mines, were obliged to procure their rations at the Racecourse, three-quarters of an hour's walk away. As they had no means of transport, they were obliged to walk there and back in the burning sun, a terrible hardship in the case of people nearly all of whom were suffering and ill. The Committee prayed, therefore, that a depot might be established at the Robinson Deep Mine to lessen in some measure the hardships for the women, old men, and children. The lot of these unfortunate people here is thus, it may be seen, a terrible one, but the treatment they undergo on their way from their homes to Johannesburg was no less cruel. A letter addressed by the Committee to the Military Governor on December 27 throws some light on the matter.

In this letter the Committee speak of an interview they had

had with the governor, in which he had consented to their supplying the women and children who were arriving at Johannesburg by trainsful with coffee and biscuits on their arrival; for the poor creatures were given no food or drink on the journey, and arrived in an almost starving condition. They go on to state that the military shops refused to sell them the coffee and biscuits for this purpose, and pray that he will give orders that the goods shall be sold. I will now show how for, up to the 15th of January, the requests of the Committee had been acceded to, and the promises of the authorities fulfilled.

The promised buildings on the racecourse have not been erected, and the women and children have to sleep 16 together in rooms 12 by 14 feet 626 of them are lodged in the workmen's quarters of the Robinson and village Mainreef Mines, and the remaining 2300 are packed in tents under the blazing sun. The suggestion that meat and vegetables shall be supplied three times a week has not been carried out, but a portion of meat is supplied once a week. No depot has been erected on the Robinson Deep Mine, so that the prisoners still have to take their trying walk for their scanty rations. Nothing has been done for the women and children arriving by train; only on one occasion have we been able to supply them with a little maize gruel and coffee.

One must have seen one of these trains arrive in order to form any conception of what the poor unfortunates have to undergo. The crying of the starving children, the moaning of the suffering women, are enough to melt a heart of stone. On one occasion when I was present the soldiers themselves could stand it no longer, and divided their rations among the poor wretches. I heard one of them say, 'I am a father of a family myself, and I know what it is when the children cry for bread.' I was often present at the arrival of the trains, and could not wonder at the feeling of bitter hatred with which the sight filled those present, making them more than ever determined to continue the struggle till death.

In conclusion, let me give a letter addressed by the Secretary of the Committee to Major-General French at Johannesburg. The letter is dated December 15—

> Sir,—with reference to a conversation held last Friday between a deputation from my Committee and a mem-

ber of your staff, I have now the honour to bring the following matters before you in writing:—

(*a*) ... (hardly relevant).

(*b*) Failure to inform the local authorities of the despatch of trains containing women and children to Johannesburg.

The deputation begs to inform you that on various occasions trains full of women and children have been despatched from or have arrived at Johannesburg without notice having been given to the local officials, with the result that the prisoners have had to wait for a very long time on arrival or before departure in the goods' sheds. They have even been kept from 24 to 30 hours in open trucks standing on the line, without any attention being paid to them, and exposed to much unnecessary inconvenience owing to the lack of lavatory accommodation on the train.

The deputation wish, therefore, respectfully to request that the stationmasters be instructed to notify the officials of the station at which a train is to arrive of its departure from their own stations—and that the railway officials shall give immediate notice to the officer in charge of the arrival of all trains containing captured women and children.

(*c*) The short notice these people receive of the intention of the military authorities to deport them, leaves the women and children frequently only a few minutes in which to prepare for their journey, so that they have no opportunity to get together the food, clothing, and bedding they require. Only in exceptional cases are they allowed to bring provisions with them, but articles such as flour are brought outside by the soldiers, the sacks cut open, and the contents strewn on the ground, quantities of fresh potatoes, newly harvested maize and other foodstuffs, destroyed and burnt, articles which in almost every case the women and children themselves have sown and reaped, working late into the night, as their cattle have been taken from them.

And these women and children who have worked so

hard to save themselves from want, are carried off into the towns and fed on starvation diet. The deputation would respectfully request that wherever possible these unfortunate people—in cases where their removal from their farms to prison camps be still considered necessary by the military authorities—be allowed to bring with them provisions, cattle, and clothing for their own use.

(Signed)                                          Van Os (Secretary).

To this letter General French vouchsafed no answer, and up to the middle of January no improvement had taken place in the lot of the unfortunate women and children.

From the neighbourhood of Kimberley came similar stories. The account given here by Mrs. Hurdus of the women brought from Potchefstroom coincides with that given in an earlier letter—

Kimberley, Oct, 1900.

I proceeded to Modder River with a few pounds given by kindly colonists, which, although it gave some relief, seemed like a drop in the ocean when distributed amongst the destitute families. I was sadly impressed with the desolate appearance of the once pretty spot, the only green spot to go to from Kimberley, the general picnicking place.

The second farmhouse I came to belonged to Mr. J. Fourie, and was one of the best houses on the river. To my surprise, I found a heap of sand where the house stood. Mrs. Fourie and children were in an outside building, put up by her husband shortly before his death. The husband was arrested on suspicion—no evidence against him. After being kept in gaol for months, without trial, he was released, to return to a heap of ruins.

We have several such cases. Another sad thing is the condition of two old people, about 80 years of age, whose earnings have been stolen. They are old, destitute, and helpless, and there is no workhouse in South Africa to send them to.

The suffering and wrongs endured by women and children in the martial law districts would move the hardest to tears. A lady named Cotzee, at Modder River, gave birth to a baby just after the arrival of the British troops. The poor creature was turned out of her bed and made to walk a great distance. The baby died a few minutes after, through neglect and exposure.

One old woman said to me, 'If our queen, who is a mother herself, who has also lost husband and children, could know how her Dutch subjects are treated, and what terrible suffering is caused by this war, she would never allow the war to continue.' This simple soul did not understand that our queen does not govern, and that the real state of things never reach her. I, too, believe that if the queen was able to hear and see the facts, and could be made acquainted with the truth of this war, she would see that justice is done, even though at the loss of fame and worldly honour.

About two weeks ago, six mothers, with 20 children from one month to 16 years, from Potchefstroom, were brought into Kimberley by the military. These women were taken from their homes, and mounted *Kaffirs* conducted them through the streets to the gaol. They were kept there a night and day without food and bedding, with their children. The next day these women refused to go into the railway trucks, not knowing where they were to be sent to, and refusing to leave behind children, as two of these unhappy mothers had a child sick in bed. These mothers do not know what has become of their children. They were then taken by force and put into trucks for Johannesburg. They showed me their clothing, torn by soldiers who took them out of the cell. When I visited these poor women in their tents, they were sitting down in the bare sand, and one woman was very ill. They were treated with kindness and respect by the officer that took charge of them from Johannesburg, and also received all attention from the officer in command at Kimberley, who gave all assistance possible to provide for them, and is not able to say why these women were sent here at all. By the aid of friends we succeeded in making them as comfortable as possible under the circumstances.

Mr. Truter deserves all praise for his self-sacrificing deeds. He gave a house free of rent, as did Mr. Lingefield. As house rents are high, and those gentlemen both suffered heavy losses during the war, they deserve all praise for their charitable and unselfish conduct.

The names of the women are as follows:—Mrs. Van Wyk and family, Mrs. Myburgh and baby, Mrs. Marais and child, Mrs. Grobbelaar and children, Mrs. Benade and family, Mrs. Kruger and family. I give these names as somebody may hear of a lost wife, mother, sister, or friend, and by giving these names I may afford some trace of a lost one. These women are originally from Griqualand West Their husbands were commandeered by the Boers at the commencement of the Kimberley siege, and some taken prisoners. The wives followed, but lost all trace of their husbands.

State-Attorney Smuts in his Report to President Steyn, issued in the beginning of the year 1902, describes the lamentable state of homeless women in the Western Districts of the Transvaal—

During the month of July 1900 I was ordered by my government on a mission to the Western Districts, which had been cut off from communication, and from Balmoral Station set out for these districts, but on arriving at Elandsrivier I was recalled by the government on pressing business, and returned by way of Bronkhorstspruit Station. I arrived here late in the afternoon, and on that high table-land and in the middle of winter it was so fearfully cold that I could hardly bear it, and (according to official reports) many English soldiers had succumbed there with starvation.

Hardly had I arrived there when I saw in a cart two women and some little children. One of the two women was an old widow, Mrs. Neethling of Tierpoort, the mother of the magistrate (*landdrost*) of Klerksdorp, and a relation of the much-respected clergyman of Stellenbosch; the other woman was her daughter, Mrs. Du Toit, and her children. Their condition in that bitterly cold climate was most heartrending, without any food, without any covering, with nothing else about them than the clothes on their backs. That old mother, over 70 years old, told me the following things. Tierpoort some weeks before had been lying in the field of battle during the skirmishes which preceded and followed upon the great Battle of Donkerhoek, and from the fields behind her dwelling our men had repeatedly fired at the patrols of the enemy.

At one time some Boers had ventured as far as the house, and she had given them a loaf of bread; when one evening, a short time afterwards, an English officer came to the house with a strong patrol, and gave her notice to leave her house that same night, as the place was to be burnt down next day. She called his attention to the fact that this would be impossible, as all the cattle and the carts had been taken away by the English, and that she was too old to walk so far to the Boer lines.

He remained inexorable, and was so impudent that the grown-up daughter of Mrs. Du Toit, who was her interpreter, told him that he ought to feel ashamed of persecuting defenceless women and children in this way, instead of fighting the Boers; upon which he in so far forgot who he was that he gave her a slap in her face. As he would not give in, a messenger was sent to the Boer forces that same evening to fetch an ox-cart When the cart had arrived, this knightly officer (an Australian Colonist) refused to allow that some food, clothes, or bedclothes were put in the cart, and in this wretched condition these poor people had to be sent out into the wide, wide world.

Her youngest son, Johannes Neethling, was with me at the time, to her immense joy, and whatever I could spare I gave her to take along with her on her journey to the Boschveld. Having only in the world her daughter and grand-daughter, she was however full of courage and strong in faith, and even succeeded in cheering us up. I do not mention this as a rare case, but as a typical example of what happened in hundreds of other places."

Mr. Smuts passes on to speak of the formation of Boer *laagers* for the women as a protection from the natives, and of the sickness and misery there endured. No statistics as to the death-rate in these laagers are yet forthcoming.

I shall therefore speak of another subject, namely, how the enemy avails himself of the help of *Kaffirs* to make our women and children suffer greater pains. I do not intend to speak about the old story, how natives were enlisted and imported by the English officers along the Western and Northern borders of the land, which, as your Honour knows, has been proved by documents now in possession of the government. The massacres at Derdepoort and at other places on the Western border have been surpassed by what has happened since May last. The *Kaffir* chiefs having joined the enemy, crossed the Western border and committed murders and cruelties from which even English soldiers shrank back. The consequences were that the greater part of the Western and Northern Districts had to be abandoned by us, because the women and children were constantly exposed to being murdered.

Camps for the women were then made in the central parts of the Western Districts, and the women provided with carts, tents, food, and placed under the protection of old men who were less fit for military service. It was expected that the enemy from a sense of pity, which is even found with animals, would have left these camps for women alone. But not at all! he repeatedly marched upon them, burnt the carts, tents, and the food, seized the aged guards who had not been able to fly, and caused so much misery as cannot be described. And when he did not appear himself, the enemy sent the *Kaffirs*, or rather the hordes of *Kaffirs* always formed a wing of the British forces, and completed the work of destruction which had been undertaken by the English troops.

Many a time it was my task to visit these women–camps, and I cannot help saying that I had never expected to be a witness of such scenes of misery. The women and children, suffering almost every one of them from malaria, fever, and other diseases, in consequence of privations and bad food, without physicians, without medicine, without any consolation in this world, almost without any clothes, and, after hostile raids, without any food at all And all these women did not belong to the poorer and lower classes, but some of them belonged to the richest families of our country. But privation could not curb the spirit of these noble martyrs, and by one consent they advised me and the *burghers* to persevere to the bitter end.

At Port Elizabeth Camp the number of persons affected was comparatively small, hundreds in place of the thousands in the north. Undoubtedly their preliminary sufferings were great, but with no martial law in the town public opinion could and did make itself felt. Many friends came forward with help, and as a consequence the conditions of life were soon made healthy and tolerable. Many accounts exist of this one little camp, numbering only about 380 people, for the horrors of war were first vividly depicted in these poor women when they arrived carrying their bundles and their babies; there is, however, little space here for letters which filled the Cape papers at the close of the year 1900. Soon after the arrival of the exiled women, a lady at Port Elizabeth wrote to her friends in Cape Town as follows:—

Port Elizabeth, Nov, 12.

.. . . I have been with them twice, but now the authorities have become more severe. Yes, it is quite true that nearly all the farms are burnt I do not think Piet Visser's is, though Groenkloof, the

Rabie's, is burnt, Vlakfontein and Huctelspoort Poor old Mrs. Coetzee of Vlakfontein is also here. Old Mrs. Hertzog's house was blown up a quarter of an hour after she quitted it. It is too pitiful to see all the misery and suffering. Poor old Mrs. Hertzog said to me, '*Ach, myn kind, stuur toch voor my een ketelje en een wenig goede koffe.*' ("Ah, my child, send me a little kettle and a little good coffee." The story of the Mrs. Hertzogs is appended to this chapter.) Fancy, they have no tables, chairs, or bedsteads, they are just on the floor—on mattresses—sometimes ten in a room, or rather hut.

It is so awful to see the soldiers with fixed bayonets guarding defenceless women and children. . . but one must not say many things.

In November the Cape Town Relief Committee took the sensible step of applying to the military authorities for the release of those in the camp, (letter to Military Authorities, Nov. 19, see *South African News* of Dec. 12), who had friends to receive them, or whose expenses could be paid for by subscription; and some Dutch ministers, Mr. Rabie and Mr. Pienaar, who were asked to visit and report on the camp, also advocated this course as the most sensible and best calculated to allay unnecessary feeling. (See Report of Dutch Ministers, *South African News*, Dec. 1900.) To this application, Colonel Trotter sent an answer in the negative.

To the appointment of Miss Hauptfleisch as matron was largely due the rapid improvement in the organisation of this little camp, and when the primary discomforts had abated Mrs. Leroux was able to report favourably of the progress made in a letter to the *South African News*. (Report of Mrs. Leroux—Railway Missioner, *South African News*, Dec. 19.)

Dec. 14.

Sir,—Requested by Miss Nellie Hauptfleisch to give a report of our visit to the exiled women, I will try to do so in a few words.

We spent two days (Saturday and Sunday) in the camp, and had two meetings for children in the camp. I am glad to be able to give a more favourable report now than last time. The women find a decided improvement in the cooking of the food. The quality of the food now sent out is better than before. Mr. Smith has promised not to give any more 'bully' beef. If the dinner is always (with a variety in the preparation of the meat) as it was on the 8th inst., there is not much room for complaint in that respect.

The way the meals are served out is, I daresay, the best under the circumstances. We cherish the hope when the unfortunate exiles are in their new quarters (which promise to be an improvement on the present) things may be arranged more to the taste of civilised people. I am happy to report that there are bedsteads now in all the tents and huts. In the medical line, too, there is an improvement. Dr. Casey pays more attention to his patients than did his predecessor.

The military have given Miss Hauptfleisch every opportunity to visit the camp and see what was wrong. They have taken most of her suggestions into kind consideration. Colonel Salmond is very kind to all the exiles, and is respected by all.

All the improvements do not alter the fact that the women are still in pole-tents and kept as prisoners. Why are they so jealously guarded if they must not be considered prisoners of war but exiles? Call a spade a spade. Your readers can form their own opinion. I give facts as I found them,—I am, etc.,

M. H. Leroux, Railway Missioner.

Thus, the year ended with some relief at the thought of the reform effected in the camp at Port Elizabeth, but at the same moment away in the north far greater sufferings and privations were being endured, and these were preparing the ground and sowing the seed of diseases which must inevitably yield a rich harvest for the Reaper Death.

MRS. HERTZOG.

*Women! who shall one day bear*
*Sons to breathe New England air,*
*If ye hear without a blush*
*Deeds to make the roused blood rush*
*Like red lava through your veins*
*For your sisters now in chains—*
*Answer! Are ye fit to be*
*Mothers of the brave and free?*—J. R. Lowell.

In Port Elizabeth Camp, there were three ladies of the name of Hertzog, the mother of the Commandant Judge Hertzog, his wife Mrs. Barry Hertzog, and his sister-in-law Mrs, James Hertzog. These two ladies were sisters, daughters of Mrs. Neethling of Evergreen,

Stellenbosch, and British subjects born. Mr. James Hertzog had been taken prisoner early in the war, and his wife being alone in her house at Jagersfontein, her sister Mrs. Barry Hertzog came from Bloemfontein to visit her. While there, measles broke out, and both the Mrs. Hertzogs' children were down with it when the military authorities seized the mothers with their sick children and sent them to Edenburg Station, exposed in open waggons for two days. (By post-cart this place is only five hours distant.) The Hertzogs' house was then laid waste, blown to dust with dynamite.

Arrived at Edenburg, the children were pronounced too ill to travel farther. Hearing this, their relatives at Stellenbosch at once applied for a permit for the two Mrs. Hertzogs to come on parole to their father's house, and after considerable trouble this permit was granted. But in the meanwhile, the families had been removed to Port Elizabeth, notwithstanding the condition of the children, and this though they prayed to be sent to Stellenbosch. When the authorities heard that they had been removed to Port Elizabeth, they withdrew the permit. No necessary comforts could be procured on the journey or on arrival in the camp, and the consequences were fatal. The first death notice from the camps appeared in the papers when Mrs. James Hertzog's boy died.

Hertzog.—On the 12th November 1900, Prisoner of War in the camp at Port Elizabeth, Charles Neethling Hertzog, in the 8th year of his age.—The sorrowing grandparents,

Charles M. Neethling.<br>W. Neethling.

Evergreen, Stellenbosch.

Sixteen thousand children have followed him to the grave.

After this sad event a lady wrote thus to Miss Neethling, urging her to come to the help of her married sisters. She shows how rough and unsuitable the arrangements were to which these ladies were at first subjected—

Port Elizabeth, Nov. 17.

Have you heard anything again from your two sisters at Port Elizabeth except that they are there as prisoners? It makes one's blood boil to think of the poor people there—it is a crying shame. Mrs. Jordaan, with whom I am here, returned from Port Elizabeth this morning; she saw both the Mrs. Hertzogs, so I'll be able to give you more particulars than they may write from the camp. Mrs. Jordaan and another lady from Cradock were sent to Port Elizabeth by their '*Dames Comite*' to go and see what they could do for the women prisoners there. She says she can never tell and make us understand how miserable and uncomfortable the state of things is at the camp. When she speaks of what she saw there the tears run down her face.

Mrs. Jordaan thinks it urgently necessary that some of you should come to Port Elizabeth and try and get the Mrs. Hertzogs out on parole. She thinks perhaps you might be successful; it seems impossible that anyone can survive in those miserable iron sheds and tents for many days longer. But if you could not get the mothers out you might at least take the children with you. The military officers say that they are awaiting further orders from headquarters, and they expect to have things improved in a few days' time. (Still it would be much better to get the children away.) Mrs. J. came to the camp just after Charles (Mrs. James Hertzog's son) was buried. She thinks Mrs. Hertzog wonderfully calm under the sad circumstances—probably through the many prayers sent up for her at Stellenbosch, Mrs. J. says.

There are no chairs, no beds! the bedclothes lie on the ground in the dust, and the people must either sit on the ground or stand about. The military had the decency to give Mrs. (Rev.) Malherbe a chair to sit on as she watches by the side of her child down with fever (that was the only chair to be seen). One of the officers said to Mrs. J.: 'You must understand that the less you speak about the state of things here, and the less fuss you make about it, the better it will be for the prisoners.' (The better it will be for them, the military, he meant to say.) They are afraid of having things brought to light. Mrs. J. told the Intelligence Officer that she will not promise to keep quiet; but the sooner they let the women out the better it would be for them, and that it would lessen the strain on the colonists.

Miss Neethling visited the camp as requested, but did not succeed in obtaining the release of her sisters. After many applications and much red-tapeism, however, she was successful in securing the release of Mrs. Barry Hertzog's baby boy, aged then about 17 months. The child was weak and pining, and she took it back to the home at

Stellenbosch without its mother. From that day to the end of the war repeated efforts were made to secure the release of the two sisters, but in vain. I give a copy of the refusal received by Mr. Neethling, who, on hearing of the concession made by Mr. Brodrick in June 1901, that all women separated from their children, or having friends ready to receive them, might be allowed to go, made instant application on behalf of his daughters.

B. 3795, 17A.

The Castle, Cape Town, Aug, 4, 1901.

Sir,—I am directed to inform you that your application to Lord Kitchener, dated July 12, with reference to Mrs. Hertzog and family, now at Port Elizabeth, has been noted; but that the G.O.C. regrets that in the present state of affairs in the Colony he cannot yet sanction their removal to Stellenbosch.—I am, Sir, yours faithfully,

L. Heyman,
Lieutenant-Colonel S.O. Prisoners of War.

Mr. C. M. Neethling, Evergreen, Stellenbosch, C.C.

After the formation of the camp at Merebank, specially set apart for women whose husbands failed to surrender on September 15, 1901, Mrs. Barry Hertzog was suddenly transferred thither, and this in spite of the fact that Port Elizabeth was a small and healthy camp, while Merebank was very crowded, and condemned as marshy and unhealthy. Thus, from December 1900 till June 1902 Mrs. Hertzog was separated from her only child, and no chivalrous voice was upraised in England strong enough to insist upon the release of this lady, or to condemn a system of warfare which included the wholesale imprisonment of women, and, in this case, necessitated separation from a young child, if that child's life was to be saved. Exposure and rough camp life have seriously affected Mrs. Hertzog's health.

SKETCH OF MY LIFE FROM THE OCCUPATION OF BLOEMFONTEIN.
BY MIJNIE HERTZOG.

On the evening of 11th March 1900, my husband left Bloemfontein. When the British came on the 13th several officers came to requisition my house. I protested, and eventually they desisted, resting satisfied with some bedding and furniture. On July 3 I left for Jagersfontein to visit my sister. On September 30 I requested permission from the military authorities to return to Bloemfontein, receiving from them the answer, that as my husband was Acting President it could not be granted before inquiring from Bloemfontein whether my return was desirable. It was found not, and I had to stay. On the day of my asking for the permit, Major Hall, sitting in an adjoining room, yelled out, "She shall not go," whereat another officer, a lieutenant, jeeringly asked me if I did not feel proud of the distinction conferred upon my husband.

At 4.30 a.m. on October 16, the *burghers* attacked and entered the town. After releasing the *burgher* prisoners from gaol, a party of them came up to my sister's house, where I was informed by them that my husband was in command. About 9 a.m. the *burghers* left the town, and at 10 a.m. there appeared at our door Lieutenant Rudledge with a party of soldiers in search of Boers. Finding none, he turned his men loose on our pantry, telling them to take all eatables they could get. At my instance, he seemed to relent, and stopped the soldiers from further depredations.

Before sunrise on the 19th of October we were roused by a sergeant, with orders that I and my sister with our sick children were to leave within 15 minutes for another house. Dressing hurriedly, we did as ordered, shifting our children, 3 in number and all ill of measles, as best we could, without any aid, and taking nothing with us but a few blankets and pillows. The house assigned us contained 5 rooms, and we were 13 families to occupy it. To myself, sister, and sister-in-law with 5 children was allotted half the parlour. Under strict guard we were kept here until Sunday with no food, except a little milk for our sick children, which after much trouble we obtained from a compassionate townsman.

On the morning of our arrival here, an officer coming up to us had declared in angry tone that we could starve here, a threat which they now seemed to be executing. On Sunday morning, the townsman referred to again came to our assistance, sending us a bag of bones. While still rejoicing over the prospects of having soup, orders came that we were immediately to start for Port Elizabeth. I was allowed to run over under guard to fetch some clothes. My house, however, had been plundered, and all my belongings gone.

Famished, I returned and had our children examined. Two doctors declared that they were unfit to travel. Orders came, however, that we had to go. About 11 a.m. Sunday morning the convoy started. We arrived at Edenburg Monday evening at 7, having had nothing to eat all the time barring a small crust begged at a farmhouse on Sunday, and again a few mouthfuls at another place on Monday. On my arrival at Edenburg, my child, whose temperature on the day of removal registered 102°, was now, through exposure and privation, a mere skeleton. Also, my sister's children had a relapse. In consequence of the illness of our children, we were the following day left behind, a tent being erected for our accommodation. No permission was granted to leave our premises, and having no food we were left unsupplied until the following Sunday. The stationmaster's wife having in the meanwhile learned of our distress, kindly provided us with necessaries. On Sunday, Dr. Johnson from Bloemfontein hearing that we were subsisting on charity, interceded for us. Thenceforth we were regularly supplied.

After 13 days' stay at Edenburg, our children then being convalescent, we were sent on to Port Elizabeth. Arriving there, we were placed in a small iron shanty about 7 x 10 ft., having to share this with 5 other persons. In order to find sleeping accommodation, we ten had to be packed like sardines. Thus, we lived about 2 months, my sister's little boy 8 years old dying 12 days after our arrival. About the same time, I was taken ill of fever, while my child was growing worse every day. Later on, I was removed from this dingy hole to the English Refugee Hospital, a favour granted me after much supplication.

After a fortnight I was obliged to leave the hospital because of the conduct of the matron, who seemed to grudge me even the little food I got. My sister, Miss Neethling, having come from Stellenbosch to inquire into our state, and finding how weak I was, took back with her my child, then a mere skeleton. I never saw him again until peace was declared, though I had frequently requested to be allowed to proceed to Stellenbosch where my parents were living, who were desirous to have me with them.

Our food, which was as bad as our accommodation, was prepared and distributed to us by a very inferior and insulting class of Johannesburg Refugees, who treated us alternately to boiled bully-beef and maggoty salt fish, which they did not scruple to ladle with their hands. Finding that we were starving for want of nutritive food, I complained, saying that if the food were not improved we should be forced to try and escape, a threat which probably gave colour to the absurd story published later that I had tried to run away.

We were later on shifted to a new camp, where both food and accommodation were substantially improved.

After a year at Port Elizabeth, in November 1901 I suddenly got notice to leave for Durban. At East London, the boat stopped for 3 days, but I was not allowed to go on land. After 8 days, I arrived in Durban. The following morning I was by my guard taken to Mere-bank Camp, a marshy hole, later on condemned by the Commission of Inspection from England. Separated from all my relatives and acquaintances, for reasons unknown to me, I arrived here a forlorn stranger with only a few pounds in my purse, for the money deposited by my husband in the bank for me I had never received.

The rations obtained from the authorities being both insufficient and unfit for my constitution, I found it necessary to obtain additional supplies. I therefore tried to earn a little money by giving lessons in music. My provisions1 had to fetch from the commissariat store, having at times to wait hours before obtaining them. My wood, in large blocks, I had likewise to fetch thence once a week, and chop up as best I could. Being insufficient, I had to supplement it from the fields, that is to say when the authorities could be induced to grant a permit More than once I was on my way back deprived of my little bundle, collected under the greatest difficulties. Cooking had to be done in the open air.

One day His Excellency the governor visited us for the object of hearing and inquiring into complaints. He heard them, but postponed the inquiry indefinitely. We asked for the erection of soup kitchens for the convalescent, better bread, more soap, and an increase of food in general, etc. Suffice it to say that, after treating some of us with scant courtesy, he dismissed all with an increase of, as far as I can remember, half an ounce of soap to our weekly supply.

On the 3rd of June 1902 I was set at liberty, and granted a free pass to Bloemfontein.

CHAPTER 3

# Feeling in Cape Colony

*Are we pledged to craven silence? O fling it to the wind!*
*The parchment wall that bars us from the least of human kind—*
*That makes us cringe and temporise, and dumbly stand at rest,*
*While Pity's burning flood of words is red-hot in the breast!*

James Russell Lowell.

Those to whom the social structure of South Africa is familiar, will at once understand the effect produced in Cape Colony by the events of 1900. Family and religious ties bound the people of the old colony to those of their race in the younger States. This was not only the case along the borders, where constantly members of the same family were found living on either side of the boundary, but throughout the Cape Colony there was hardly a family without blood relations who had settled in the north, and become full *burghers* of one or other of the two Republics. As family after family became destitute, anxiety deepened. It was the anxiety of those whose kith and kin were suffering.

News was hard to get, and the strain was intense. A stray letter, a traveller from the north, or a soldier's story—these brought bits and scraps of news, worse in their effects than a whole knowledge of the truth would have been. As the months rolled on, feeling could no longer be restrained, and the women of Cape Colony were driven to break through their usual domestic habits, to organise meetings, and speak their mind. From June to August sixteen meetings were held, and more followed. Letters which came from the Cape at that time indicate the depth of the feeling aroused.

One lady wrote, (Aug. 29, 1900):

In the balance, hangs—*not* whether the Republics will preserve their independence—in the balance hangs whether England

107

shall continue to be a great nation. Just as personal acts of dishonour and dishonesty shut out individuals from the society of the honourable, so with nations. England will pronounce her own doom by the behaviour she shows to the Republics. She is at a turning-point of her political existence. May the good and true and noble prevail, the preserving salt to save the nation from ruin. . . . And now you have us to think of in the Cape Colony. England kills our brothers, and now she is on the point of killing our respect for her. From Zoutpansberg to the Cape Town docks there will be a solid phalanx of men and women and children—the women the bitterest because we feel our loved ones have been treated needlessly hard. It is not thus that a Boer is subdued. At such acts, one's anger against England for the moment vanishes and one begins to pity her.

Do you not feel how almost impossible it becomes for colonists to keep calm? . . . We look to the good amongst you women whose influence is boundless, for if there is a force against which even the devil is in the long run powerless it is a good woman.

And in the same strain writes another, (Sept. 1900):—

I cannot tell you what a real drop of comfort it is to us who have been brought up to love and honour England, and who have had such a rude awakening, to feel that she still holds women who will work for justice and England's honour. I am a South African of Dutch and French Huguenot descent, and have never left this country, but my education and ideals were based on an almost entirely English foundation. Judge what it means to have all that swept away. Not only have our eyes been opened to England's present policy of injustice, but we feel compelled to lift the veil behind us as well, and we see there former acts of wrong. Ireland's years of oppression, the seizure of the Kimberley Diamond Fields, the Jameson Raid— Our blindness was the blindness of love; our children will not be blind.

The debate in the Cape Parliament gave an opportunity, embraced by several prominent members, for strong protest against the devastation proceeding in the north. But it was not until November 10, 1900, that the profound sorrow and disapprobation of the bulk of Cape Colony found expression if not relief in a remarkable gathering held at the Paarl. This was a Women's Congress, and upwards of 1500 women of Dutch and English race were present; while from far and wide letters and telegrams expressed the regret of those who could not attend. The condition and treatment of the women who were their kindred formed the subject of the Resolutions which were carried unanimously:—

1. This meeting of South African women desires to enter its solemn protest against the imprisonment and deportation of unprotected women and children without investigation, in defiance of all the laws and usages of modern warfare.

2. This meeting earnestly protests against the burning, plunder, and destruction of private property, whereby women and children are rendered destitute, and claims that this is in contravention of the resolutions of the Peace Conference at The Hague—resolutions which England supported, and to which she subscribed.

The Congress will be long remembered. It was held in the open air beneath the great oak trees of the Paarl. The speeches, delivered though they were by women wholly unversed in public speaking, had the unconscious eloquence which is born of deep feeling. It was a solemn protest, solemnly recorded.

The following month, (Dec. 6, 1900), a great People's Congress gathered at Worcester, and here beneath the mouths of English guns another protest was made against the treatment to which women and children were subjected, which would "leave a lasting heritage of bitterness and hatred, while seriously endangering the future relations between civilisation and barbarism in South Africa."

But the feelings of the Colonial women were not satisfied with empty words. Relief was active. The Prisoners of War Fund, started in the previous April, now extended its work to aid the wives and children homeless and alone. In November twenty-seven cases of clothing were despatched to Port Elizabeth, and in December twenty cases to Norval's Pont, and forty-one cases to Bloemfontein. Feeling it impossible to stem the tide of distress from the overtaxed resources of the Cape Colony, the Committee issued an appeal, (Oct. 12), to the women of the civilised world. European countries and the United States responded generously to this appeal. In various Colonial centres, small local societies were formed to collect funds. At Kimberley, where there were destitute families scattered on each side of the boundary, the difficulties of relief work were thus described in October. (Oct. 19, 1900. South African Mothers' Christian Union.) The Committee went out with waggon-loads of supplies wherever possible—

They wrote:—

It is the only way in which we can reach the people whose farmhouses have been burnt and everything taken from them by the British. . . . We must go to them personally, and this means traversing whole districts which have been simply devastated of everything. The farms are so scattered that people (colonists) cannot get to assistance. They simply watch their houses being burnt, and are then left on the *veld*. . . . We had a permit from the military authorities a month ago, to go over the border and traverse the districts, but the country round here is in such an unsettled state just at present, that the military authorities have given strict orders not to allow any person to go out of the town.

In England, the year was well advanced before relief work was begun. So little news relative to farm-burning was permitted in the Press, and so little sympathetic imagination was brought to bear upon what was known, that only the few who had followed the fortunes of the South Africans with appreciative intelligence had formed any conception of the straits to which women and children were reduced. Very quietly a few local collections were made and forwarded to the Holland or Cape Town Funds, but no public subscription list had been set on foot

In the late summer, I read of the hundreds of Boer women who, having been made homeless by our military operations, were deported from the towns we occupied, where they had collected for sustenance, and sent to the Boer lines. A picture of wretchedness lay beneath the bald telegraphic words! That these poor families, bandied from pillar to post, must need protection and organised relief, was certain, and from that moment I determined to go to South Africa in order to help them. Late in September I tried to start a fund on the broad grounds of pure and simple benevolence towards those made homeless by the war.

For some weeks, it was difficult to persuade even those most interested either that there was any real need, or if so, that any considerable sum could be collected, or if collected could be administered. Mr. Stephen Gladstone in a kind letter, (Oct. 11), was the first to give real encouragement—a name that ensured success. Lord Lansdowne was approached and asked whether, in the event of the formation of a fund, facilities for distribution could be given. The application was transferred to the Colonial Office as more properly belonging to that department. At that moment, the war was considered at an end, and the people we desired to help were our fellow subjects of two annexed colonies.

A small Provisional Committee met and agreed to adopt the following outline as a basis for their proposed fund, and this was forwarded to the Colonial Office. The South African Women and Children's Distress Fund, as it was named, was purely benevolent and non-political. Its objects were—

To feed, clothe, shelter and rescue women and children, Boer, British, or others, who had been rendered destitute and homeless by the destruction of property, deportation, or other incidents of the military operations.

Its distribution was to be placed in the hands of persons deputed by the Committee, and not to run counter to the requirements of the local, civil, and military authorities.

The reply from the Colonial Office informed us that Mr. Chamberlain "sympathised with the object in view," and a later letter communicated Sir Alfred Milner's message that such a fund might be useful, as though the people received military rations they were "in want of everything beyond the bare necessities of life."

A large number of influential people of all shades of thought, who it was hoped would unite in a work of mercy, were invited to be signatories or to join the Committee of such a fund. The replies received were most discouraging. Practically all refused to give their names or help the cause unless they happened to belong to the party who had been in opposition to the war throughout It was most unfortunate, for the movement was entirely outside of politics, had no political aims, and has maintained a purely philanthropic attitude from the beginning. The refusals were, however, characteristic of English sentiment at that date. One prominent clergyman thought that to keep Boer women and children alive might "prolong the war." Another eminent preacher was apprehensive lest such a charitable fund would reflect on the "honour of our soldiers," and had not Lord Roberts said they were all gentlemen? Such was the tenor of the replies received.

Privately, many people sent me sums for the assistance of the women and children whom I might reach, and as it was my wish to go to South Africa in a private capacity, and independent of any body of people, I did not wait for the complete formation of the Executive Committee, but left England in the first days of December.

The Society of Friends started their fund about this time, and work parties were also organised by a separate Committee which dealt only with clothing. Though the charitable help of England has fallen far short of that from other countries, yet from that time to this hardly a ship has left the docks which did not carry one or more bales of material and clothing for the victims of the war.

CHAPTER 1

# More Homes Destroyed

*Waste are those pleasant farms, and the farmers for ever departed!*
*Scattered like dust and leaves, when the mighty blasts of October*
*Seize them, and whirl them aloft, and sprinkle them far o'er the ocean.*

Longfellow.

A debate, upon the issues of which depended the lives and well-being of thousands of women and children, took place on the opening of the new Parliament, (Dec. 7, 1900). The Opposition then questioned the success of the severer policy of the last half of the year, but Mr. Chamberlain's and Mr. Brodrick's speeches were reassuring. (See *Times*, Dec. 8, 1901). The Colonial Secretary thought the destruction would, when statistics were forthcoming, be found to have been brought about by the Boers more than by the English troops. He said they had treated their countrymen barbarously.

Moreover, he thought the extent of the farm-burning had been greatly exaggerated, and from an economic standpoint would be found unimportant, as the houses were little better than labourers' cottages. (Mr. Chamberlain, it is believed, has not yet visited South Africa). He said this particular punishment, which both government and generals thought should "be used as sparingly as possible," would be still less employed in the future. The deportation of women, which "sounded like something serious," would be found, he was sure, to be done only for their protection both from marauding bands of Boers and from natives. Mr. Brodrick dwelt on the fresh orders recently issued by Lord Roberts, carefully defining the limits of farm-burning, and said that in the humane conduct of the war there was every reason to believe the new commander-in-chief was entirely at one with the government. (See also Part 1. chap. 1.)

The year 1901, however, opened with a renewal of the devastation so widely practised in 1900. Sweeping movements were carried out in many districts. Reuter telegraphed, Jan. 8, 1901:

The country round Kimberley is being cleared, and women and children are being brought in by waggon and train. (*South African News*, Jan. 16.)

The destructive work of January is also described by Private M'Cormick, who found leisure to write from the hospital at Potchefstroom—

I suppose you have read about Kitchener's proclamation telling the Boers to lay down their arms and go to their farms. Well, I have travelled through the Free State and the Transvaal, and I can say for a fact that there is not a farmhouse fit for habitation in the Free State or Transvaal. They are nearly all burnt, and those that are not burnt are deprived of all woodwork, such as window-frames, doors, and beams. Wood is very scarce here. As for pigs and fowls, there won't be one left in the two countries when the war is over. Everyone who has a fowl has to get wood to cook it, and they go to farmhouses and wreck them for wood. In *January*, we were a month burning houses. (Private M'Cormick to Mr. W. E. Jones, Branch Sec Nat. Union of Dock Labourers, 17th March, quoted in *Methods of Barbarism*.)

Some of the Warwickshire Yeomen who returned about April 1901 gave similar accounts of their experiences. One in particular spoke very freely during an interview with a journalist. (*Warwickshire Advertiser*, June 1901.) He had been attached to Paget's column, and since Christmas had been chiefly occupied with the burning of farms.

'What farms did you burn?' this Yeoman was asked. Not understanding the question, it had to be explained to him that the English at home had been told that only those farms on which concealed Boers or arms had been found had been subjected to this unpleasant treatment. He was surprised at these statements, and, as his reply shows, failed to acknowledge their accuracy. 'I don't know,' he says, 'about finding Boers or arms. All I know is this, that some days we would start off early in the morning and try, during the whole day, to burn as many farms as we could. I never saw one in some districts that was spared. We used to ride up—half a dozen of us—to the farm door, dismount, and rap loudly with our rifles on the wood. We didn't wait for an invitation. In we went with a rush, and said to the woman, "Come on, pack up, missus; there's a cart waiting for you." And we gave her ten minutes to get a few things together, and then, with the youngsters, she was packed into the open waggon and driven off to the nearest camp.'

'Did you ever find Boers or ammunition hidden away?' 'Never, during the whole time, except a few loose bullets lying about in different rooms.'

'Then why did you burn the farms?'

'By the general's orders. We used to have plenty of fun. All the rooms were ransacked. You can't imagine what beautiful things there were there—copper kettles, handsome chairs and couches, lovely chests of drawers, and all sorts of books. I've smashed dozens of pianos. Half a dozen of us would go up to as fine a grand piano as ever I've seen. Some would commence playing on the keys with the butts of their rifles. Others would smash off the legs and panels, and, finally, completely wreck it. Pictures would be turned into targets, and the piano panels would be taken outside and used as fuel to boil our tea or coffee. And then we could enjoy ourselves if it was cold; but,' he added ruefully, 'it was generally hot—boiling hot. After this we would set the building on fire, and as we left, riding together or detached over the sandy waste, we could see the flames rising up, and soon there would be nothing left but black smouldering embers. We would do the same with the next farm we came across.'

The speaker then went on to describe how news of their approach had often been carried to the inhabitants of the farm, and before the punitive party arrived the house had been deserted, and all the cattle and valuables carried off. On these occasions, they undertook the task of making a bonfire of the building with even greater relish than on ordinary occasions.

'How did the families take this farm burning?'

'Well,' he replied, the smile on his face abruptly dying away, 'to tell you the truth, we had to shut our eyes to a great many sights. The mothers would implore us with the little English they could muster to leave them in peace, and then, as we would not listen to them, they would dry their tears and curse and swear at us. We were the '*verdommte rooineks*' (red-necks), and often they would say, 'You kill my father or brother at the war,' and straightway fall to heaping all sorts of bad names upon us. It was not always pleasant. I have often seen a mother in this situation, with a two months' old baby at the breast, and little ones around her, with a number of *Kaffir* women howling in sympathy. But we had to do our duty.'

Mr. Cowley, whose letter is written April 17th, describes the events of his various treks in the previous weeks from Heilbron—

Perhaps you will be interested in a brief account of our doings. The first day out from here was quiet, but we burned all farms, native *kraals*, out-buildings, and other places that might afford shelter for the Boers in bad weather; we also killed all fowls, ducks, geese and pigs, turkeys, or any kind of poultry, and collected all horses, cattle, and sheep into herds, and drove them along with us, and I could not help thinking what a waste it was to kill good things for the sake of killing, after we had halted; but it was grand sport chasing young cockerels and chopping geese's heads off, hearing pianos play as they were rolled upside down on to a fire lit in the middle of a room, piling pictures and brackets, etc. on a deal table and then putting a straw mattress underneath to start the blaze.

Well, it was a go and no mistake, but all the fun is spoiled when you are tired out at the end of the day, and you have to go on outpost, instead of having a sleep, and particularly if the rain sets in. On the second day, we had over twenty fires on the go before nine in the morning, and had got about six or seven miles from our last halting-place when we got a check for a couple of hours. We destroyed the nicest residence I have seen in the country. I forget his name that used to live at it, but he was next in position to the President of the late Orange Free State Republic. It took us all the afternoon to get it all destroyed. The threshing machines made the best fire, but the most interesting part for me was to see the explosion of a traction engine that worked all the farm machinery. It was built in England, because it bore the makers' name-plate—Clayton and Suttleworth, Lincoln—and it was over an hour from the time the fire was lit before the boiler burst.

The work we get now has very little interest for a soldier, and the sooner the Colonial Office is prepared to start its work the sooner we can leave.—*Boston Guardian,* June 8, 1901. From Private G. Cowley, Reservist, Oxford light Infantry, to Mr. C. J. Phillips.

By mid-January the *burghers* were so incensed by the sufferings of their women and children, consequent upon the devastation, that President Steyn and General De Wet issued a letter to their commandoes announcing their resolve to invade the Cape Colony a second time, in order to make reprisals on the property of British subjects. Here was a prospect of more innocent people being made to feel the pressure of the war, though the women and children were to be excepted from molestation. These leaders said in their circular:

> But, the *burghers* would be less than men if they allowed the enemy to go unpunished after ill-treating their wives and destroying their houses from sheer lust of destruction. Therefore, a portion of our *burghers* have again been sent into Cape Colony, not only to wage war but to be in a position to make reprisals . . . but at the same time, to avoid being misunderstood, (*verklaren wy hier openlyk, dat wy nooit de vrouwen en kinderen lastig zullen vallen, wat ook de Engelsche troepen de onzen aangedaan mogen hebben,*) we hereby openly declare that the women and children, will always remain unmolested, despite anything done to ours by Her Majesty's troops.—Proclamation of Steyn and De Wet, Jan. 14, 1901. See also *Sequence of Events,* by F. Mackarness.

As a result of the clearing movements of January, families brought in from the country to the various centres were largely on the increase. From Johannesburg, we learn that a "large number of families of Boers still on commando are being fed and housed by the military authorities;" (Reuter's Service, Feb. 13), while from Standerton large numbers were reported as being sent to Ladysmith daily, where there were then fully 500 families of "surrendered" people already encamped. (Reuter, Feb. 15. *South African News,* Feb. 20.)

The intimations of continued devastation indicated by the telegrams at that period were sufficient to occasion further debate in the House of Commons. (Feb. 25. *Times,* Feb. 26). Mr. Bryn Roberts brought forward the notice already alluded to signed by General Bruce-Hamilton, by order of which the women and children of the burnt village of Ventersburg were to be abandoned to starvation, asking if it could be true, and what did happen to the families so threatened. (See Part 1, chap. 1.) Mr. Brodrick at once explained that the commander-in-chief had indeed directed the burning of the village, but had not approved the wording of the notice, which was withdrawn and the families given rations from the Army Stores.

Mr. Dillon persevered in an attempt to present the whole question of the dealing with non-combatants in its moral light, and deprecated the imprisonment of women and their guardianship by armed sentries. (*Times*, Feb. 26.) But the debate failed to have any good effects as far as releasing the imprisoned women was concerned, or preventing the capture and deportation of thousands more.

Just two days after this debate took place the memorable interview between Lord Kitchener and General Botha at Middelburg. (Feb. 28, 1901.) Lord Kitchener, who describes this meeting in the Blue Book, (Cd. 902), says he took occasion to bring before General Botha the numerous complaints made to him in the early part of the year by surrendered *burghers*, who had stated that after they laid down their arms their families were ill-treated and their stock and property confiscated by order of the Commandants-General of the Transvaal and Orange Free State. He thought the acts were in consequence of General Botha's circular, already commented on, of the preceding October, (Oct. 6, 1900. See Part 1, chap. 1.)

Lord Kitchener writes:

> I told him, that if he continued such acts I should be forced to bring in all women and children, and as much property as possible, to protect them from the acts of his *burghers*. I further inquired if he would agree to spare the farms and families of neutral or surrendered burghers, in which case I expressed my willingness to leave undisturbed the farms and families of *burghers* who were on commando, provided that they did not actively assist their relatives. The *commandant*-general emphatically refused even to consider such an arrangement. He said, 'I am entitled by law to force every man to join, and if they do not do so to confiscate their property and leave their families on the *veld*.'
>
> I asked him what course I could pursue to protect surrendered *burghers* and their families, and he then said: 'The only thing you can do is to send them out of the country, as if I catch them they must suffer.' After this there was nothing more to be said, and as military operations do not permit of the protection of individuals, I had practically no choice but to continue

my system of sweeping certain areas into the protection of our lines. My decision was conveyed to the *commandant*-general in my official letter dated Pretoria, April i6, 1901, from which the following is an extract:—

> As I informed your Honour at Middelburg, owing to the Irregular manner in which you have conducted and continue to conduct hostilities, by forcing unwilling and peaceful inhabitants to join your commandoes, a proceeding totally unauthorised by the recognised customs of war, I have no other course open to me, and am forced to take the very unpleasant and repugnant step of bringing in the women and children.
>
> I have the greatest sympathy with the sufferings of these poor people, which I have done my best to alleviate, and it is a matter of surprise to me and to the whole civilised world that your Honour considers yourself justified in still causing so much suffering to the people of the Transvaal, by carrying on a hopeless and useless struggle.

From this date, April 16, 1901, it became the avowed policy of the commander-in-chief to adopt the clearing process which had already been so widely practised. A bargain had. been proposed by which, if surrendered *burghers* were unmolested by Botha, the families of those on commando should also be left alone by British troops, provided they did not actively assist the enemy. Was this a tacit avowal that till then proof of active assistance of the enemy had not been required? The bargain failed; for General Botha argued that the law of the land justified his orders, and his punishment of those who disobeyed. This law, however, limited his control so far as goods were concerned, to *movable* property, which he was bound to confiscate. Immovable property he had no legal right to touch, and he therefore refrained from all destruction of homesteads, as did also the other Boer generals.

It is difficult at present to find instances of families who have suffered punishment from Boer hands. That of Mrs. Viviers has been given. (Part 1, chap. 1.) The letter of Mr. Tobias Smuts, published as a Parliamentary paper, mentions three farms which he affirms were burnt by General Chris. Botha. Mr. Smuts had himself burnt the village of Bremersdorp in Swaziland, and had been told by General Botha that this act was "against their principles." Unable to give reasons for his action satisfactory to the *commandant*-general, Mr. Smuts was suspended, and subsequently discharged from his command. In his letter, he protests against this dismissal, and urges that the "principle" of not burning houses had been already broken. (Sept. 2, 1901, from District Ermelo.) He says—

> Already, several months ago, General Chris. Botha burned houses in Sambaansland, which is not neutral territory. About the same time Bremersdorp was burned, the farm of Mr. Bernardus Johnstone, District Wakkerstroom, was burned, or partly burned, by General Chris. (Botha), and also the house of Franck Johnstone, and I have not heard yet that his Honour has been suspended or dismissed for it. When we were at Pietretief the house of Van Brandis was burned, and I was told that this happened by 'High Order.' It is, in my opinion, not the number of houses that breaks the 'principle.'
>
> Also in connection with the transport of women, we took up the same standpoint as a principle, but still I got the order from you to send the women away against their wish, and when I asked you what to do if the English refused to take the women, your answer was that in that case I had to load them off within the lines of the enemy.

✶✶✶✶✶✶

See Cd. 933. It must be remembered that this letter of Mr. Tobias Smuts (who must not be confused with General J. C. Smuts) was but one of a correspondence, all of which must be read to understand its due proportions. The women whom he was told to send away against their wish were a certain few who had been discovered giving regular information to the enemy.

✶✶✶✶✶✶

With regard to these burnings. General Meyer supplied the information that they were not burned by General Chris. Botha, who is son-in-law of the owner, Mr. Johnstone, but that Lieutenant Von Wichmann burnt the waggon-house only, which he found stored with forage for military use, Mr. Johnstone having surrendered. The house of Van Brandis was burned, but not by "High Order." It was the act of a *burgher* whose name is uncertain, and said to have been done privately as an act of revenge.

From the date of the Middelburg Conference the Boers washed their hands, as it were, more completely of the families of surrendered *burghers*, and, regarding them as English subjects, sent them into the English lines. One of these cases is alluded to by Mr. Conan Doyle.

(See *The War: Its Cause and Conduct,* by A, Conan Doyle, later Sir A. Conan Doyle). He mentions that Commandant Albert communicated to the English officer at Krugersdorp his desire to send several of those families *whose husbands had surrendered* to their rightful protectors. Mr. Conan Doyle adduces this as a proof that the Boer families had no objection to the Concentration Camps.

From the one side or the other it was clear that the Boer women with their little ones must suffer. They were between the devil and the deep sea.

On June the 10th, Mr. Ellis had asked in the House of Commons whether the policy and practice of burning farm buildings in South Africa for military reasons had been discontinued, and if so, at what date and on whose instructions.

Mr. Brodrick had replied—

I informed the House some time ago that, except in cases of treachery and certain recognised military offences, farmhouses would not be burned. Specific orders to this effect were given by Lord Kitchener on 7th December 1900, and I have every reason to think they have been observed.—Hansard, vol. xciv.

This statement indicated that the discussion of December 6 in Parliament had not been fruitless, but had resulted in fresh orders by Lord Kitchener for more careful discrimination in the work of burning, and it would have been eminently satisfactory had it but tallied with other accounts. In a letter to his friends, Trooper Victor Swift, 53rd Company, East Kent Imperial Yeomanry, describes his work in the first fortnight of July:

We burn every farm we come across, and are living like fighting-cocks. We think it a bad day if we haven't a couple of chickens and a suckling pig apiece. It's funny to see us with fixed bayonets chasing the pigs round the farmyard. I have an appetite like a wolf.

We went to Vrede next, and after a day's rest left that place in a shocking state. We killed thousands of sheep, and put them in every house. The stench in a week will be horrible. It is to prevent the Boers from returning.—*Daily News,* Aug. 17, 1901.

Soldiers' accounts are liable to exaggeration, but this one agrees with that contributed by the Rev. Samuel Thompson of Rivington, Bolton, Lancs., who writes—

It is popularly believed that the farm-burning in South Africa is now a thing of the past, but I send you an extract from a letter written by a soldier at the front which shows that it still goes cruelly on. The letter is dated July 5, 1901.

> 'It is very cold out here, especially at night-time: that is the reason that I want a woollen scarf, so be sure and send me one as quick as you can. . . . I have trekked hundreds of miles. I have been out with a column, and it is sickening work. We burn every farm we come to, and bring the women and children to the Refugee Camps. No matter where we go we burn the crop, leaving nothing but a waste of country behind us.'—*New Age*, Aug. 1901.

It mattered little, however, from the point of view here taken, that of the women and children, whether a farm was actually burnt or otherwise destroyed. The immediate effects for them were the same. Large numbers of houses, not burnt, were destroyed, all the woodwork taken, and the furniture broken up for firewood. From the scarcity of fuel, it is hard to see how otherwise the troops could have cooked their food. The results of the clearing movements were seen in the great increase of the size and number of the camps. Telegrams came from many quarters announcing the arrival of convoys with women and children.

Early in August (the 7th) was issued Lord Kitchener's proclamation calling on all *burghers* to surrender before September 15, under pain of banishment; and about the same date notices were sent out by the Boer leaders appointing two days for Thanksgiving and Humiliation.—*Morning Leader*, Sept. 10, 1901. They met for this purpose on the estate of Willem Pretorius, in the Heidelberg District The spirit shown by the women formed one of the subjects of thanksgiving. A force was sent to break up the meeting, but it was already over; there was no one left when the soldiers came but a number of women and children on the farm, who were carried off, and the building was burnt.

These were the subjects of thanksgiving and confession, (Proclamation: Thursday, Aug. 8, Thanksgiving Day; Friday, Aug. 9, Day of Humiliation):—

1. For the greater and smaller victories gained over the enemy, not only in the beginning of the war but even in recent times.

2. For the miraculous preservation and glorious deliverance from the hands of our enemy and his superior powers.

3. For God's paternal care to provide us with our daily wants as to food, clothing, and ammunition.

4. For the enemy's failing in his endeavours to rob our country altogether of cattle and grain, and thus to starve us.

5. For the glorious spirit of perseverance and courage, to be found especially with our women and children, who even do not lose courage in captivity and the misery attending it; in one word, for the maintenance of us as a nation during a violent struggle of nearly two years, which distinctly shows us that God takes no delight in our fall, but desires us to return to Him and to live.

DAY OF HUMILIATION, AUGUST 9.

We wish to confess before the Lord that though He repeatedly delivered us since we have existed as a nation, when we were in distress and called upon Him; we, however, turned from Him and served other gods; and then ask the Lord to deliver our people; and we wish not only to confess our sins so that is only mouth honour which is an abomination in the eyes of God, but beseech the Lord to teach us that we may rightly know what sins we have committed; and to make us willing, without considering to what rank or station in the nation we belong, to leave off sinning, and confess sins of various kinds, such as: sins for breaking the Lord's Sabbath, drunkenness, unbelief, lip-devotion, infidelity towards each other, laying down arms, cupidity, theft, slander, etc. etc. But the names of other sins we dare not mention, as their name is 'Legion.'

Let us, the government and the people, seriously beseech the Lord on the day of humiliation to give us strength to have ever and exclusively before our eyes in future, as well in our government as in our legislation, the honour and glorification of our Lord.

(Signed)                    Schalk Burger, M. T. Stevn,
                Christian De Wet, Louis Botha, J. A. Smuts.

Lord Kitchener's proclamation evoked replies from all the generals. Some took the form of counter-proclamations, and the following passage in that of General De la Rey deals with the fate of the women and children, and the cost of their maintenance:—

> Contrary to the laws and customs observed in waging civilised war. His Majesty has removed our wives and children like criminals, burned their homes, and now keeps them as prisoners of war; and to recover the cost of maintaining them there. Lord Kitchener now threatens to confiscate our landed property. One finds it nowhere stated in God's Word or in Civil Law that any person is guilty and punishable because he in self-defence protects his life and property.—Proclamation of De la Rey, Aug. 16, 1901.

Towards the end of September General Louis Botha's house on his farm at Vryheid was blown up with dynamite.

A list has been forwarded to me of 58 farms burnt or destroyed in September and early October. The families were brought in to Irene Camp, where the affidavits were taken. I am not at present allowed to make known the name of the person who collected and vouches for the reliability of this information. But it is a responsible person, known to several people of high authority. The list is given in Appendix C.

In Cape Colony, a Reuter message of August speaks of anxiety on the part of families in certain districts from the actions of the Boers, and lack of adequate protection from the British—

> Waterkloof, Cape Colony, Aug, 6.
> The families who are being removed from Waterkloof express eagerness to leave that place, as their position is intolerable. During the absence of the British columns the Boers constantly live on them, while at the same time they fall under suspicion of the authorities."

The account given by Mr. Cloete, Magistrate of Steytlerville, shows there was justification for their alarm. The threatened reprisals had begun. This gentleman, who was a prisoner with Scheepers' commando for fifteen days, and was then released, said that the commando consisted of about 300 men, most of whom were young rebels from Cape Colony, Scheepers having brought only 70 men with him from Orange River Colony. All were well clad, equipped, and fed. They were strongly mounted, and led remounts. They had no transport or pack-horses, and lived solely on the country through which they passed, keeping in touch with every farm, and looting freely whatever they required.

*Scheepers issued orders to destroy the homesteads of all men known to be serving with the District mounted force.* Mr. Cloete reports that many houses were accordingly burnt. The inmates were allowed to remove a few blankets and some bedding, and the premises were then fired. Mr. Cloete, during his captivity, travelled nearly 300 miles. He was kindly treated throughout. None of the commando are older than Scheepers himself, who was about twenty-four years of age.

Earlier in the year the Marquis de Kersauson tells of the burning of a farm in the Colony by Scheepers. In his diary, under date March 19, 1901, he writes, (French edition, published in the *Petit Bleu*):—

Our object was to reach the nearest little village, Jansenville, which we would gain by following the course of the Sunday River. On the way, at Uitkomst, we met Scheepers' commando. He had just been setting fire to a farm in the district. This farm, of which the proprietor and his son were English, had been turned into a regular military post, working against the Boers; and the farmer had recruited *and armed 12 Kaffirs*, and sent them in pursuit of us. In the interior of the house Scheepers had seized several Lee Metford rifles, and two belonging to the *Kaffirs* in question, whom he had shot, following the terms of the proclamation, interdicting the natives from taking up arms on pain of death. Then he made the farmers leave their house, and set it on fire.

In November, Mr. Schalk Burger and Mr. Reitz, representing the Transvaal Government, forwarded through Lord Kitchener a long letter to Lord Salisbury. (Nov. 21, 1901. Cd. 902.) This appears in the Blue Book, and bearing, as it does, almost entirely on the case of the women and children, is here given in full. The protest was no doubt prompted by the tidings which must have penetrated to the commandoes, of the appalling figure which the October mortality in the Concentration Camps had reached—346.72 per 1000 for the aggregate.

In the Field, Nov. 21, 1901.

Excellency,—The handling of affairs with reference to the removal of families of the *burghers* of the South African Republic by British troops was hitherto left entirely in the hands of his Honour the *Commandant*-General, who has from time to time directed protests to his Excellency Lord Kitchener, but as these protests have led to nothing, and the request of the *Com-*

*mandant*-General to appoint a Commission—among whom a medical man—to make a thorough investigation into the state of health in the women's camps, was refused by Lord Kitchener, as will appear from the correspondence carried on with him, this government feels herself called upon to bring the facts of this question direct to the notice of the Government of His Britannic Majesty. With indignation, the government and the people were surprised with the policy followed by the British military authorities in removing families of *burghers* from their dwellings.

This removal took place in the most uncivilised and barbarous manner, while such action is moreover in conflict with all up to the present acknowledged rules of civilised warfare. The families were put out of their houses under compulsion, and in many instances by means of force, the houses were destroyed and burnt with everything in them—such as bedding, clothes, furniture, and food; and these families, among whom were many aged ones, pregnant women, and children of very tender years, were removed in open trolleys exposed for weeks to rain, severe cold wind, and terrible heat—privations to which they were not accustomed—with the result that many of them became very ill, and some of them died shortly after their arrival in the women's camps.

Many of the conveyances were also very rickety, and loaded with more persons than they had accommodation for, so that accidents necessarily took place, whereby more than one was killed. Besides these dangers, they were also exposed to insults and ill-treatment by *Kaffirs* in the service of your troops as well as by soldiers.

As a variation to the above treatment, families have lately been compelled to go out of their houses; the houses, with everything in them, burnt and destroyed, and the women and children left under the open sky without food or covering, whereby some were obliged to accompany the enemy, in order not to succumb to hunger, and to being exposed to storm and wind, as their natural protectors, who would in some way have been able to provide for them, are either on commando, or have been taken prisoners, or killed.

And, be it further noticed, that when Lord Kitchener circulated his proclamation of the 7th August last, a number of women were granted passes to betake themselves to our lines for an unlimited period. It may be asked why these women have returned. The reply is simply because their children are kept in the camps as hostages—this is calculated to give the British Government and public the false impression that such families have *voluntarily* placed themselves under the protection of your troops.

Such cruelties are almost unbelievable, and might indeed be sought for in the histories of former centuries, but not in the enlightened twentieth century.

And they have gone still further. British mounted troops have not hesitated in driving on foot for miles before their horses, old women, little children, and mothers with sucklings to their breast

But still more pitiable was and is the lot of these families in the women's camps—several of which camps are situated in the coldest winter (*sic*) and most stormy places in our land, namely, at Belfast, Middelburg, Standerton, and Volksrust. The great majority of these families are property owners, and were in a well-to-do position until they were totally robbed and exposed, as has already been described. They were taken away from their comfortable homes, where they had every comfort, and were well provided for with good food for themselves and their children, and were able to get sufficient servants. From these places, they were transferred to packed and uncomfortable tents, and which moreover did not give sufficient shelter from storm and wind, while the majority of them have been deprived of the help of their servants.

On account of the stingy supply of fuel which is allowed, women of the most noble families of South Africa have been obliged to gather with their own hands fuel consisting of dry cow-dung in order to prepare food for themselves and their children. At the same time, they are obliged personally to wash their clothes and other linen besides, because, as has already been stated, they have been deprived of the help of their servants. Besides this, according to information given to this government, the food is not sufficient, nor sufficiently varied, and the class of food not nourishing enough, especially for children.

The abnormal and terrible number of deaths in these camps must be put down to what has been said above, and very likely is increased by insufficient medical help. One of the facts in connection with this case is that very young children, as soon as they become ill, are separated from their mothers, and all this on medical orders. The mothers are only now and then allowed to visit their children. That such treatment must injure the health of the child speaks for itself.

It was alleged as a reason for the removal of the families, that if they were left on their farms they would act as a commissariat for the commandoes. It therefore surprised us to see that later, in the English Parliament, it was alleged as a reason for such removal, that the families would succumb to hunger if not removed in this way. These two reasons are directly in conflict with each other, and neither of the two is the truth. That the wives of the *burghers* have not acted as a commissariat for the commandoes, is apparent from the fact that the *burghers* in the field have still been continually provided with the necessary food. From the above it must therefore be clear to everyone that the 'Refugee Camps' is an unjust and misleading representation.

This government therefore most strongly protests against all the aforementioned actions employed by the British military authorities in connection with the removal of the families, and insists on improvement (or amendment), also because of the houses from which these families have been forcibly removed, hardly a single house now stands on the whole area of the two Republics—not, as was lately alleged in the British Parliament, five hundred (500), but at least thirty thousand (30,000) dwellings having been burnt and destroyed by orders of your military authorities, and to say nothing of the villages that have been totally destroyed.

At the same time, this government repeats the request already made by his Honour the Commandant-General, that a Commission from our side, of whom at least one member will be a medical man, shall be allowed to visit the women's camps to render a report to her (the government).

We have the honour to be your Excellency's obedient servants,

S. W. Burger, Acting State President,

F. W. Reitz, State Secretary.

Lord Kitchener, in forwarding this despatch to the Home Government, enclosed also a copy of the reply he had made to the Boer leaders. The communication was brief—

Dec. 1, 1901.

I observe from your Honour's communication, which you have asked me to forward to Lord Salisbury, and which I have so forwarded, that you complain of the treatment of your women and children, and the camps which we have established for their reception.

Everything has been done which the conditions of a state of war allowed to provide for the well-being of the women and children, but as your Honour complains of that treatment, and must therefore be in a position to provide for them, I have the honour to inform you that all women and children at present in our camps who are willing to leave will be sent to the care of your Honour, and I shall be happy to be informed where you desire they shall be handed over to you.

Commenting on the foregoing correspondence, the commander-in-chief wrote explaining that in his opinion it was clear that the responsibility for the condition and sufferings endured by the women and children lay with Generals Botha and De Wet rather than with himself. However, that may be, it is probable that Mr. Schalk Burger's letter resulted in a change of policy, for an order was given in December to bring in no more families. The statistics of the camps show that on the whole this order was carried out. The populations remained stationary, or rather showed only a decrease consequent upon the high mortality.

The despatch of Lord Kitchener ran as follows, (Cd. 902. Dec 6. 1901):—

It will, I believe, be perfectly clear that the responsibility for the action complained of by Mr. Schalk Burger in his letter of 21st November 1901 rests rather with the *Commandants*-General of the Transvaal and Orange Free State than with the Commander-in-Chief in South Africa.

It is not the case that every area has been cleared of the families of *burghers*, although this might be inferred from the despatch under discussion. On the contrary, very large numbers of women and children are still out, either in Boer camps or on their own farms, and my column commanders have orders to leave them alone unless it is clear that they must starve if they are left on the *veld*.

★★★★★★

Accounts received since peace was declared speak of some 10,000 who were under the care of commandoes. See Part 3, chap. 1.

★★★★★★

In addition to the families of surrendered *burghers* who either came in of their own accord, or were brought in solely to save them from the reprisals of the enemy, there are three other classes represented in our Refugee Camps:—

(*a*) Families who were reported to be engaged in a regular system of passing information to the enemy.

(*b*) Families from farms which were constantly used by the enemy as places from which to snipe at our troops.

(*c*) Families from farms which were used as commissariat depots by the enemy.

(*a*) and (*b*) speak for themselves. Mr. Schalk Burger seems to consider that (*c*) is in conflict with the statement that such families would have succumbed to hunger if not removed. If, however, a Boer commissariat depot is found with perhaps regular messing arrangements for thirty men and thousands of pounds of flour and mealies, of course these supplies have to be withdrawn, leaving only a margin of a few weeks' food for the resident inmates of the farm. At the close of a few weeks the family runs in danger of starvation and has to be brought in, so that the want of logic complained of is merely an attempt on the part of Mr. Burger to make a clever point on paper.

The majority of the women and children in the Refugee Camps are those of surrendered *burghers*, (Lord Kitchener seems to have been totally misinformed on this point), but neither they nor the wives of prisoners of war, nor of men on commando, make any serious complaint, although they are constantly being invited by commissions, inspectors, etc., however little it may be, against the arrangements made for their comfort, recreation, and instruction.

Mr. Burger is anxious that a Boer Commission should be permitted to visit the women's camps and render a report upon them. Indeed, this is the one practical suggestion contained in his letter. It is strange, to say the least of it, that no mention is made by Mr. Burger of the fact that I have already told the

130

*commandant*-general I would permit a representative appointed by him to visit the Refugee Camps in order that an independent report might be furnished on the subject. Nor is there any reference to the inspection of these camps which was actually carried out by Captain Malan.

It will be remembered that I immediately acceded to General B.Viljoen's request that he might depute an officer for this purpose. He selected Captain Malan, who went around asking if there were any complaints, and who afterwards expressed his entire satisfaction with the arrangements which had been made on behalf of the Boer women and children. (He does not appear to have been allowed to visit more than *one* camp, *viz.* Middelburg.)

I take this opportunity of stating that I would make no objection to Commandant-General Botha himself, accompanied if he likes by General De la Rey and Mr. Steyn, visiting these camps, provided they undertake to speak no politics to the inmates, who as a rule appreciate the general situation much better than their husbands or brothers on commando.

Finally, I indignantly and entirely deny the accusations of rough and cruel treatment to women and children who were being brought in from their farms to the camps. Hardships may have been sometimes inseparable from the process, but the Boer women in our hands themselves bear the most eloquent testimony to the kindness and consideration shown to them by our soldiers on all such occasions.

I enclose copy of letters which I have just despatched on this subject to Mr. Burger, Mr. Steyn, and to General de Wet, offering to return to them any women who may be willing to join the Boer commandoes in the field.

No information has yet been received as to how this offer was met by the Boer officers, and we do not know if the permission was made known to the women in the camps.

Late in December 1901, General De la Rey sent his official report to Mr. Kruger and the Boer representatives in Europe. This, published in England and on the Continent, gives the following picture of the country as it appeared at the close of the year:—

Our land is one heap of ruins.

Nothing remains but the walls of buildings, except where even these were blown up with dynamite. Nothing has escaped this destruction. The properties of neutrals as well as of *burghers* killed in battle, and of those who are now prisoners of war, and of the widows and orphans—everything has been destroyed. Neither churches nor parsonages nor schools have been spared. In my division, the villages of Wolmaransstad, Bloemhof, Schweizer-Reineke, and Hartebeestfontein, which have not been occupied by the enemy, have been totally burnt.

It is exactly the same in the Eastern Districts of the South African Republic, where General Botha is at present.

The treatment of women and children, defenceless creatures, is really the darkest page among the many dark pages of this sad war. At first hundreds of our women who were living in the villages were taken prisoners and sent to the commandoes. We formed women's camps at several places, where our women and children were taken care of. But soon the enemy changed his conduct Our women who had been taken prisoners after the homesteads had been burned, were sometimes carried along with the columns on trolleys for weeks.

At night the women were placed around the *laagers* as a protection against a night attack from our side. When the women realised what was the object of the enemy, they tried to escape, but were pursued. They were even fired upon. Sometimes they were caught again, and then they were removed to greater distances, and placed in tents. But from the camps hundreds of sweet messages reach us, telling us not to worry about them, but to continue the struggle for our country.

Many women have already lost their lives either from wounds or from the misery they have endured My own wife was ordered by Lord Methuen to leave her home and everything she possessed. She has been wandering about the country for over twelve months with six small children. My mother, an old woman of eighty-three, who has been a widow for nine years, has been carried away as a prisoner. All her cattle have been taken away, and her house burnt She has been removed to Klerksdorp.

FAMOUS ANTI-BRITISH CARTOON OF THE PERIOD

BURNING A BOER FARM

BURNING A BOER HOUSE

A burning Boer farmhouse

Burning out a Boer family

FARMS BURNING ON THE VELDT

THE BURNING OF COMMANDANT TUBBETS' FORTIFIED FARM
BY GENERAL BABINGTON'S CAVALRY

# CHAPTER 2

# January to June—Visit to the Camps

*A naked people in Captivity,*
*A land where Desolation hath her throne.*

William Watson.

I reached Cape Town the 27th of December, in time to see the opening of the New Year and the New Century. It was my first visit to the country, but whatever my ignorance of South Africa, her language and her people, at least I knew that thousands of women, no matter what their usual condition, were at that moment undergoing great privation and sorrow, and I believe that suffering and the desire to relieve it know a common tongue, which cannot be misunderstood.

★★★★★★

*The War: Its Cause and Conduct,* chap. vii. by A. Conan Doyle. Mr. Conan Doyle has said that in consequence of complete ignorance in these particulars my "conclusions" concerning the camps are "untrustworthy." I notice Mr. Doyle has put forward conclusions on the camps without ever having visited them at all. But he and the critics of whom he is a sample forget that Concentration Camps are not the normal condition of life in South Africa, and it is only indirectly that the normal life of the people bore upon the conclusions formed in respect to life in those camps. I may remark that I had taken a course of lessons in Dutch, read books relative to the lives and customs of the Boers, and was intimate with many South Africans, who supplied me with detailed information.

★★★★★★

How to approach these sufferers, or exactly where all the existing camps were situated, I did not know when I landed. Port Elizabeth was the only camp known of in England when I left, but in Cape Town I heard at once of the large camps at Johannesburg, Bloemfontein,

Potchefstroom, Norval's Pont, Kroonstad, Irene, and other places. Unfortunately, a few days before I landed, martial law had been declared, (Dec. 20, 1900), over a number of fresh districts of Cape Colony, and now extended nearly to the coast Hence moving about with freedom was impossible even for purposes of relief.

Permission from the highest authorities was essential I therefore took my introduction to Sir Alfred Milner, and had at his invitation the opportunity of putting before him my objects, and of asking his help to reach the destitute women. From him I received every kindness and promise of assistance, subject only to Lord Kitchener's military decision. He was himself agreeable to my visiting every camp both in the Transvaal and the Orange River Colony, but Lord Kitchener's telegram when it arrived limited my permit to Bloemfontein. The High Commissioner also suggested I should be accompanied by a Dutch lady, but Lord Kitchener thought this unnecessary, and refused permission.

Sir Alfred Milner was aware of the uneasy feeling prevailing amongst the Cape Colonists with respect to the women in the north, and he felt it fitting that a representative of their Relief Committee should help in the work. Lord Kitchener, on the other hand, was right in supposing that I should find assistance wherever I went, but he failed to perceive what a great victory might have been won over the hearts of the Dutch by allowing their anxiety and wounded feeling this reasonable outlet Clearly also he did not understand the vastness of the need, the wide scope of a work in which such help would have been invaluable. I carried his permit, together with the High Commissioner's letter which follows, to all the camps I visited.

Letter of Authority from Sir A. Milner.

Government House, Cape Town, 21/1/1901.
Dear Miss Hobhouse,—I have written to General Pretyman, the Military Governor of the Orange River Colony, asking him to give you any assistance in his power.
'Personally I am quite willing that you should visit *any refugee camp in either T. V. or O.R.C.* if the military authorities will allow it. As you are aware, Lord Kitchener is not prepared at present to approve of your going farther than Bloemfontein. But as he has expressly approved of your going as far as that, I do not think that there can be any difficulty about your visiting the camps *either there or at any place on the railway south of it.* In any

case, you can show this letter as evidence that as far as I am concerned such visits are authorised and approved of.—Yours very truly,

A. Milner (High Commissioner).

I accepted gratefully Lord Kitchener's limited permission, trusting that the future would bring opportunity for getting forward to the more northern camps, such as Kroonstad, Winburg, and Johannesburg, of which at that time I heard very sad accounts. Sir Alfred Milner further helped me by providing a large truck, in which I was able to pack several hundred pounds' worth of groceries, clothes, and hospital necessaries. With this I left Cape Town January the 22nd, and reached Bloemfontein the afternoon of the 24th. My first duty was to call on General Pretyman at Government Buildings, who received me very kindly. He gave me a permanent pass to the camp, introduced me to the superintendent, with an intimation that any suggestions I should make should be considered, and asked me to let him know later what I thought of the camp, and from time to time I did so.

I could form no scheme of work till I had seen the camp and the people. Thus a few days were spent talking to the officials and to the women, learning the conditions of camp life in general and that one in particular. It was a time of war. There was pressure on the lines of communication, pressure on the supplies, pressure on the transports, on the exchequer—pressure everywhere, unless we except the time and brains of subordinate officials. Obviously, then, the lowest possible standard of comfort compatible with health and life itself must be the one adopted as the standard to attain to in the camps. And here I may remark that to this standard I sternly adhered during my sojourn in South Africa. So definitely did I draw the line, that I even regarded candles as luxuries except in cases of sickness. It was a hardship to sit in the dark, but it could be endured by those who could not buy, and I saw my funds must be spent on what would nourish, cleanse, or give warmth.

Soon from a crowd of minor details certain facts loomed large. I realised that the barest necessities of life were lacking or inadequately supplied. I had come to give little extras or comforts or garments, such as the authorities could not at the moment be expected to provide, and I found what really lacked were bare necessities.

The shelter was totally insufficient When the 8, 10, or 12 persons who occupied a bell-tent were all packed into it, either to escape from the fierceness of the sun or dust or rain storms, there was no room to move, and the atmosphere was indescribable, even with duly lifted flaps. There was *no soap* provided. The water supplied would not go round. No *kartels* or mattresses were to be had. Those, and they were the majority, who could not buy these things must go without. Fuel was scanty, and had at that time to be cut by the people from the green scrub on the *kopjes*. The earliest ration lists then in vogue ran thus:—

### SCALE OF RATIONS.

| *Refugees.* | *Undesirables.* |
|---|---|
| ½ lb. fresh meat. | ½ lb. fresh meat. |
| ½ lb. either meal, rice, samp, or potatoes. | ½ lb. either meal, rice, or samp. |
| 1½ oz. coffee. | ½ oz. coffee. |
| 3 oz. sugar. | 1 oz. sugar. |
| 1 oz. salt. | 1 oz. salt. |
| $\frac{1}{12}$ tin of condensed milk. | $\frac{1}{18}$ tin of condensed milk. |

### " ASSISTANT PROVOST-MARSHAL, O.R.C."

The above scale is undated, but was, I believe, the earliest, and superseded by this one, dated January 16, 1901 :—

### " LINE OF COMMUNICATION ORDERS BY LIEUTENANT-GENERAL SIR A. HUNTER, K.C.B., D.S.O., COMMANDING LINE OF COMMUNICATION FROM NORVAL'S PONT TO WOLVERHOEK.

#### " BLOEMFONTEIN, *Wednesday, Jan.* 16, 1901.

#### "SCALE OF RATIONS FOR REFUGEES.

| *Refugees.* | *Families who have members on Commando.* |
|---|---|

**Adults and Children over 6 years of age.**

| | | | |
|---|---|---|---|
| Flour or meal. | . 1 lb. daily. | Mealie meal | 3 lbs. daily. |
| Meat . . . | . ¾ lb. „ | Meat. . . | 1 lb. twice weekly. |
| Coffee . . . | . 1 oz. „ | Coffee . . | 1 oz. daily. |
| Sugar . . . | . 2 oz. „ | Sugar . . | 2 oz. „ |
| Salt . . . . | . ½ oz. „ | Salt . . . | ½ oz. „ |

**Children under 6 years of age.**

| | | | |
|---|---|---|---|
| Flour or meal | . ½ lb. daily. | Meal. . . | . ½ lb. daily. |
| Meat . . . | . ⅜ lb. „ | Meat. . . | . ⅜ lb. twice weekly. |
| Milk. . . . | . ¼ tin „ | Milk . . | . ¼ tin daily. |
| Sugar . . . | . 1 oz. „ | Sugar . . | 1 oz. „ |
| Salt . . . . | . ½ oz. „ | Salt . . . | . ½ oz. „ |

Either of these was sufficiently small, but when, as I constantly found, the actual amount given did not come up to the scale, it became a starvation rate. Yet, marvellously enough, there was little or no complaint on the score of food. This was due partly to the fact that many still had private means by which to augment the rations, and partly that probably the people themselves did not realise how impoverished the system would become on food at once so meagre and so monotonous. I certainly did not fully realise it, and said little on this head, except to suggest rice as an occasional alternative, and milk for the hospital and young children; and the good sense of the women was most striking, an ordinary remark being, "We know it is war-time, and we cannot expect much."

Periodically a consignment of coffee or sugar would be bad in quality, or the meat would be putrid and then the results were serious. Mr. Methuen has called attention to the doctor's analysis of the food given in Johannesburg Camp at one period, (*Peace or War in South Africa*, A. M. S. Methuen), and I have coffee and sugar in my possession which a London analyst has pronounced in the first case to be 66 per cent, adulteration, and in the second the sweepings of the warehouse.

As their money became exhausted, it was so hard to live, that many women were driven to borrow from friends or storekeepers or business men in town at high percentage.

In January, there were 1800 people in Bloemfontein Camp, and many other large camps awaited my visit. To provide the bare necessaries urgently wanted in this camp alone would have swallowed up the resources then at my command. It seemed clearly the duty of the government to provide the actual necessaries for the people whose own means they had destroyed, and who were prisoners of war, as well as for the few who had come for their protection. The sum committed to my care was intended to give the people small extras to alleviate their lot. But my hand was stayed, for while necessaries are lacking comforts cannot be considered. Acting therefore on General Pretyman's instructions, I laid before the superintendent these several needs.

Unfortunately for the camp, there was a continual change of authority at this period, which made consistent and organised work impossible. My request for soap was met with the reply, "Soap is a luxury," and the further argument that soldiers do not receive soap in their rations. I urged that that was a matter which lay between them and the War Office, but did not affect the question of its necessity for women and children. Finally, it was requisitioned for, also forage—more tents—boilers to boil the drinking water—water to be laid on from the town—and a matron for the camp. Candles, matches, and such like I did not aspire to.

It was about three weeks before the answer to the requisition came, and in the interim I gave away soap. Then we advanced a step. Soap was to be given, though so sparingly as to be almost useless—forage was too precious—brick boilers might be built—but to lay on a supply of water was negatived, as "the price was prohibitive." Later on, after I had visited other camps, and came back to find people being brought in by the hundred and the population rapidly doubling, I called repeated attention to the insufficient sanitary accommodation, and still more to the negligence of the camp authorities in attending to the latrines. I had seen in other camps that under proper administrative organisation all could be kept sweet and clean. But week after week went by, and daily unemptied pails stood till a late hour in the boiling sun, (see also Cd. 819, Dr. Becker's "Report on Bloemfontein in June 1901"), and the tent homes of the near section of the camp were rendered unbearable by the resulting effluvia.

With regard to the outlay of the fund with which I was entrusted, it was too responsible a matter to give other people's money at haphazard, and it would, I felt, be necessary to get some broad idea of how and where it was most needed. To obtain this, I determined to proceed by a methodical system of investigation. By getting answers to a certain simple set of questions, (see my report), I was able to learn quickly what had been the position of a given family, what was now its condition and what its prospects. Having obtained this simple information, the answers could be easily tabulated, and an idea arrived at as to the kind of help most widely needed—amongst whom—and what proportion of the funds should be kept to give on the return home of each family.

At that date, few thought either that the war would last so long or that the camp system would grow to such proportions. Sufficient advance was made with this plan to gain for myself a clear general view of the situation, when I found the people being brought in on all sides in such great numbers as to render the scheme quite impracticable. Had the camps remained stationary at the size I first found them, a good system of relief could soon have been organised. It was evident they were to attain far larger proportions, and with such a mass of impoverished people it took all the time and the money to find out and deal with instant cases of necessity.

Every day made it more evident that camp matrons were essential to do work which could not be done by a man, nor by those nurses whose time should be wholly occupied in hospital work, nor indeed spasmodically by any one, but only by a capable head with a large staff of regular workers. As far as Bloemfontein was concerned, and in other towns where such existed, the local committee of ladies were most anxious to help in every way, and had it not been for their efforts in providing clothing, sad indeed would have been the condition of the helpless people. But here as elsewhere they laboured under a disadvantage. It became clear to my astonished mind that both the censorship and system of espionage were not merely military in character, but political and almost personal, so that even to feel, much more to show, sympathy to the people was to render yourself a suspect. Hence many a charitable scheme in Bloemfontein and in other places was nipped in the bud by the chill of disapprobation.

Such schemes which had no aim but the bettering of hardships would have saved many a valued life if freer scope had been allowed to the workers. Life and work in the camps was made intolerable by the presence of spies who carried tales founded on nothing. Everyone knows what class of men accept the work which means spying upon neighbours, and can draw their own conclusions as to the value of such reports. The subject is alluded to simply to show the difficulties of voluntary helpers, whose unstinted work has been so unfairly criticised and condemned. One can neither initiate, organise, or work one's best when conscious that suspicion is in the very air one breathes. If ladies not only in Bloemfontein but elsewhere had not been baulked at every turn, and made timid by censorial methods, their womanly common-sense and ready help would have averted much of the tragedy we all deplore.

I made a tour to visit other camps, and found that though in some respects they were superior to Bloemfontein, yet broadly the same needs prevailed in each, varying according to local circumstances, such as are enumerated in my Report. I saw Norval's Pont, Aliwal North, Springfontein, Kimberley, Mafeking, and Orange River, in some cases paying repeated visits. On returning to Bloemfontein, I found Major Goold-Adams had just arrived to take up the position and work of Deputy Administrator. Hitherto the camps had been under military control, now they were to pass under civil administration. Undoubtedly in the long run this has proved for the best, but at the moment, with sickness rife in the camps, with a constant influx, with a crude organisation, the change from one authority to another caused great friction and enhanced the difficulties of the situation.

Moreover, civil superintendents rarely possessed such knowledge of organisation and discipline as pertain to military men. In some ways, however, the military still retained control and an endeavour to get anything done was met with continual shunting of the responsibility from one authority to the other. In addition, expense was a continual difficulty. This may seem strange to those who have formed their ideas of the camps on Mr. Conan Doyle's description. In the fairyland of his fertile imagination, "no money was spared," and "every child under six had a bottle of milk a day"; (See *War: Its Cause and Conduct*, by A. Conan Doyle), but we are dealing with facts.

Major Goold-Adams entered with interest into the condition of the camps. He discussed the question of mattresses, and I drew up and sent him a memorandum of the cost of covers and making to provide one for each tent. It seemed to me of paramount importance to lift the people off the ground at night I volunteered to manage the whole supply, and even to undertake the entire cost, if the government would provide forage of some kind for stuffing. The military refused this, as too precious, and no sufficient quantity of anything else could be procured. The *veld* was bare of grass, which might otherwise have afforded good material.

The only bright spot in the camp life at this period was the little schools; these the wisdom and energy of Mr. Sargant were gradually creating out of chaos. They were gladly welcomed, and recognised as an improvement upon the many little classes which had been inaugurated and carried on here and there in the camps by energetic Boer teachers under the most adverse circumstances. Good administration, too, where met with, brought more cheerful elements in its train.

This was the case in the very earliest days of Aliwal North under Major Apthorpe, and I have frequently in public meetings and elsewhere dwelt upon the superiority of the camp at Norval's Pont, which passed in March under the administration of Mr. Cole Bowen. This camp had been from the beginning fortunate in its commandants. The first to organise it was, if I am correctly informed. Lieutenant Wynne of the Imperial Yeomanry, whose conduct won for him the title of "Father of the Camp," and the affection of the people committed to his care. I do not know who he is, but I mention this thinking he may like to know that long after he had left the place his memory was treasured with love and respect.

After a spell of the firm military discipline of Major Du Plat Taylor, the camp passed into the hands of Mr. Cole Bowen. This gentleman showed marked administrative powers; his rule was firm, just, and kind, and he seemed possessed of unlimited resources. Such a management brought more alleviation than any outside help could do, to the privations which were the lot of all. As a consequence, the entire spirit of the camp was on a higher level.

It was my wish and suggestion that Mr. Cole Bowen should be asked to visit other camps, in order to inaugurate his superior methods, and so obviate needless suffering. The idea, however, was not adopted until in the last months of the year the Ladies' Commission made the same proposal, and Mr. Bowen became travelling inspector, with effects for which in Bethulie alone that ill-fated camp can never be too grateful

Some weeks elapsed during my second tour before I returned to Bloemfontein. In the interval, all through March and part of April, fresh sweeping movements had resulted in the advent of crowds of families into the camps. In all directions, I had witnessed this, and read of it as happening elsewhere. I had seen families swept close to the railway line near Warrenton and Fourteen Streams; I had seen a crowded train crawl the whole long day into Kimberley—the people, old and young, packed in open trucks beneath a cruel sun—kept at the station without food until late at night, brought up at midnight to bare tents, where, groping in the dark, they sought their bundles and lay down, finding no preparation, no food or drink.

I had seen them in crowds by railway sides in bitter cold, in streaming rain, hungry, sick, dying, and dead. I have seen these patient people packed in train-loads for Bethulie and elsewhere, and I never doubted but that every countrywoman of mine, had they seen and known, would have felt as I did, great sympathy with their forlorn condition and a desire to alleviate it I believe most of the soldiers round me shared my thoughts.

My first visit to the camp at Bloemfontein after the lapse of a few weeks was a great shock. The population had doubled, and had swamped the effect of improvements which could not keep pace with the numbers to be accommodated. Sickness was increasing, and the aspect of the people was forlorn in the extreme. Disease and death were stamped upon their faces. Many whom I had left hale and hearty, full in figure and face, had undergone such a change that I could not recognise them. I realised how camp life under these imperfect conditions was telling upon them, and no impartial observer could have failed to see what must ensue, unless nurses, doctors, workers, and above all extra food, clothing, and bedding, could be poured out in abundance and without delay.

I sought the deputy administrator, and represented to him the death-rate already worked out in the adjoining camp at 20 *per cent*, and asked if nothing could be done to stop the influx of people. He replied that he believed that all the people in the entire country, with the exception of towns on the line, were to be brought in. His kindness and courtesy often encouraged me to put before him not only the bodily needs of the women, but other troubles or punishments which weighed upon them, which seemed unnecessarily severe, and appeared to be creating sores which even time would not have power to heal. His policy was no doubt dictated from higher sources, his humanity too evidently crippled by lack of means. My fund was but a drop in the ocean of such a need.

There were two courses open to me. To stay among the people, doling out small gifts of clothes, which could only touch the surface of the need, or to return home with the hope of inducing both the government and the public to give so promptly and abundantly that the lives of the people, or at least the children, might be saved. It seemed certain that in South Africa itself adequate expenditure would never be authorised.

But I first determined to make the effort to visit and take relief to Kroonstad, where I had been repeatedly invited by the superintendent of that camp.

******

It is worth remarking that the incessant getting of permits and passes increased very materially the difficulties and fatigues of the work. It swallowed up hours, and even days, involving not only waste of time, but also severe that both of physical strength and of patience.

******

As Lord Kitchener reiterated his refusal to allow me a permit north of Bloemfontein, I referred the matter to the High Commissioner, who telegraphed his regret that it was impossible. I next laid the facts before Major Goold-Adams, asking if his aid was sufficient to help me at least to Kroonstad. His reply was in the negative, and at the same time he dwelt a little upon what were evidently the real reasons of the refusal given me to go farther on. It was said that I was showing "personal sympathy" to the people. I replied with astonishment that that was just what I came to do, to give personal sympathy and help in personal troubles. He believed that gifts could be dealt out in a machine-like routine. I said I could not work like that, I must treat the people like fellow-creatures, and share their troubles. He believed this unnecessary.

It had also been brought to his notice from Pretoria that letters from me had been read at a meeting in London which he understood to be a political meeting. As I had that day had similar news by post, I was able to tell him that it was a *private* meeting of subscribers to the fund, which had met in my uncle's house, and was not a political meeting. Naturally people desired some account of what was being done with their money.

By this conversation, the situation was made clear to me.

It was no question of political sympathy. On that score I always maintained a negative attitude. *Personal* sympathy was to be discouraged. This wholly unexpected policy accounted for much of what had struck me as peculiarly painful in the camps in the general attitude and tone adopted by many of the officials towards the women in their care, whatever their social standing might be. This sympathy, so needed by a sick and bereaved womanhood, was to be denied them, not only when offered by people of their own race, as the local committees, but even when offered them by an Englishwoman, who believed that whatever might be the issue of the war every friend so made would be a link with England.

I had come amongst them as a woman to women, and talked to them on no other ground. After all, one individual whose methods were thus unconsciously in antagonism to the professed attitude of the authorities, could do next to nothing, faced also by the enormous populations of the camps. Disease and death were already let loose in their midst, and if adequate help was to come in money, kind, and working staff, if an immense death-roll was to be averted, it could only be done by a strong warning to the government of the serious state of affairs, and a mandate from England to lift the entire system on to a higher level.

The arrival of occasional English newspapers confirmed me in the fear that the facts as they existed were wholly misunderstood at home. It was true that efforts made in the House of Commons had brought about a discontinuance of the half-ration system, though treatment of the "undesirables "in other ways still remained different from that of refugees; but I read with dismay Lord Kitchener's message, communicated by Mr. Brodrick, that the people had "a sufficient allowance, and were all comfortable and happy." (*Times*, Mar. 2, 1901.) I saw, too, that the Secretary for War, relying no doubt on the scanty information contained in telegrams, told the House that the people came to the camps for protection (true only of a minority), and that those who came might go. (Feb. 25, 1901. Hansard, vol. lxxxix). I knew they were miserable and under-fed, sick and dying. It was clear that there was a misunderstanding, and the country as a whole was ignorant of the true position of affairs. Yet this was what the Boer women so often asked me: "Do the English people know what we suffer?"

"Let us not," said the colonel commanding one of the towns to whom I went for help in my work, "let us not call it the Refugee Camp. These people are *not* refugees." I willingly agreed, feeling with him it is always best to face facts as they are.

Shocked at the misery I had seen, and conscious that equal suffering prevailed in some thirty other camps, certain that with right administration much of it could be removed, and strong in the faith that English humanity if made aware would not tolerate such conditions, I formed my determination to return home, and I left South Africa with poignant regret but with no delay.

It was clear that reform to be effectual and life-saving must come from England, must be on a large scale, and at all cost must be instant.

BOER IN A CONCENTRATION CAMP

BOER WAR CONCENTRATION CAMP, 1901

BOER CONCENTRATION CAMP

WOMEN BEING TAKEN INTO BOER CONCENTRATION CAMP

WOMEN AND CHILDREN IN BOER CONCENTRATION CAMP

FRENCH POLITICAL CARTOONS

# CHAPTER 3

# June to December

## SECTION A

*Milton! thou should'st be living at this hour:*
*England hath need of thee; she is a fen*
*Of stagnant waters: altar, sword, and pen,*
*Fireside, the heroic wealth of hall and bower,*
*Have forfeited their ancient English dower*
*Of inward happiness. We are selfish men:*
*Oh! raise us up, return to us again.*—Wordsworth.

In the last chapter, a sketch has been given of the predominant impressions regarding the camps, so far as the country had any impression at all; and with but few exceptions no more was known. As illustration of the general vagueness about this great movement, I may mention that the editor of a prominent London paper was under the impression that there was only one women's camp, and that one somewhere in the vicinity of Cape Town. My advisers in England were anxious to facilitate the collection of funds for the relief of the camps by the publication of a few extracts from my letters, descriptions written on the spot to my family and friends.

Before deciding to appeal to a wider circle by means of these letters, I desired as my first step to lay my information before the Secretary of State for War. A recent speech, (*Times*, May 25, 1901), he had made in the House increased this desire, for he had then spoken of the "women coming for food and protection against the *Kaffirs*"—of "20,000, 30,000, or 40,000 women who had placed themselves in our charge "—of "no occasion in which in these camps food ran short," and of "immense improvement," etc.

I wrote, therefore, to Mr. Brodrick, asking if an interview would be agreeable to him, (May 31), and I mentioned that though my first duty was towards the Committee whose funds I had been administering, yet I wished to lay all information before the government before any publicity was given to my statements, in the event of that course being decided upon.

In reply, I was invited to see Mr. Brodrick; (June 4), and so for as could be done in a short hour, I explained the condition of the camps—the insufficient supplies—attempted improvements swamped by increased numbers—the great sickness and heavy mortality—that the great majority were there by compulsion, and were prisoners not allowed to leave, though health and life itself were endangered.

I was listened to with kindness and attention, and requested to send my suggestions in writing. This was done the same day, and they were subsequently embodied in the Report. which the Committee of the Distress Fund issued a fortnight afterwards. This Report drew general attention to the Concentration Camps. Meagre as it was, it aroused considerable sympathy, creating, as Lord Spencer put it, "a profound feeling of compassion throughout the country." Previous to its issue there had been a debate on the Concentration Camps in the House of Commons on Mr. Lloyd George's motion of adjournment. (June 18.) He first graphically described the situation, and, supported by Mr. Ellis, appealed to the humanity and Christianity of the House to take immediate steps to alleviate the sufferings of the women and children.

Mr. Brodrick adopted the apologetic attitude, (*Times*, June 19), and asserted that the fault of these women being in camps at all lay with their own men, who did not "recognise their own responsibilities in the matter." It was even, he said, "owing to the action of their own friends." He urged the difficulty, which has always been obvious, that in war-time it is hard to keep 63,000 people (the numbers at that date) sheltered and fed in addition to a great army.

So obvious is this fact, that most people would have thought that some preparation would have been made for it before entering upon so vast a military movement. Mr. Brodrick assured the House that those who had been out there to distribute gifts, and had since returned and spoken to him, had told him "that things, so far from going from bad to worse, have been steadily ameliorating." My own effort had been to impress Mr. Brodrick with the view that such improvements as had been effected, and they were few, were nullified by the increasing number of families brought in.

Very clearly in my remembrance of that debate stands out Mr. Herbert Lewis's attempt to fix the attention of the House on the humanitarian side of the question. The House was unsympathetic, and neither knew nor cared to hear. Humanity was appealed to in vain, and Mr. Lewis was literally howled down by continual noise and wearied shout of "Divide" from the crowded Ministerial benches. The picture thus exhibited of callousness and impatience, not willing even to listen to sufferings innocently endured, contrasted badly with scenes fresh in my mind in South Africa. In common with the Boer women, I had felt sure that English humanity would not fail to respond instantly if the facts were clearly understood. I was wrong; no barbarisms in South Africa could equal the cold cruelty of that indifferent House.

The first part of Mr. Brodrick's speech on this occasion was answered by President Steyn in his despatch to Lord Kitchener, and may be interesting in this connection—

> To say that they are in camps of their own free will is altogether opposed to facts, and to assert that these women were brought to the camps because the Boers refused to provide for their families (as the Minister of War is said to have done recently in Parliament), is a slander which wounds us less than the slanderer, and which I feel sure will never bear away your Excellency's approval. M. T. Steyn.—From Reply of Mr. Steyn to Lord Kitchener's Proclamation, dated Aug. 15, 1901.

A few days after the issue of my Report, the Secretary for War sent me the following answer to the Recommendations which had been forwarded by me at his request:—

War Office, June 27, 1901.

Dear Miss Hobhouse,—The Recommendations contained in your letter of June 4 on the subject of the Concentration Camps have been most carefully considered, and I am now in a position to give you the opinions which have been formed on them by the government, and which, I think you will agree, generally speaking meet with your wishes. As regards—

Questions and Answers.

1. You ask that all women who still can, should be allowed to leave—

(*a*) Those who, themselves penniless, yet have friends and relatives in Cape Colony;

(*b*) Those who have means and could support themselves in Cape Colony or in towns on the line;

(*c*) Those who have houses in town to which they could go;

(*d*) Those divided from their children who wish to find and rejoin them.

*Answer.* We have communicated to Lord Kitchener our view that any women coming under these four headings should be allowed to go, unless there is some military objection. The question of refugees going to Cape Colony in large numbers is open to grave objections, and is one on which in any case the wishes of the Cape Government would have to be consulted.

**2**. Free passes into all towns nearby for all wishing to find work there.

*Answer.* We understand this to be already the practice in most camps.

**3**. In view of the size of the camps, the sickness and mortality, a resident minister in each camp, or free access to any minister living close by.

*Answer.* Lord Kitchener has telegraphed that ministers are resident in or near all Refugee Camps, and regular services are held.

**4**. That, considering the countless difficulties ahead and the already overcrowded state of the camps, no further women or children be brought in.

*Answer.* We believe that every care is being taken to check overcrowding. We cannot undertake to limit the numbers who, for military reasons, may be brought into Concentration Camps.

**5**. That, considering the mass of the people are women and children, and seeing the successful organisation of the matron at Port Elizabeth, a matron conversant with both languages be appointed in every camp. Many women would undertake this voluntarily.

*Answer.* Every camp now has a trained matron, with a lady assistant, and also a qualified medical officer and superintendent, with efficient staff. The nurses include women selected from the refugees, who receive payment for their services. The whole staff is chosen with a special view to their knowledge of the Dutch language.

**6.** That, considering the congested state of the line and the ever-increasing lack of fuel, any new camp formed should be in a healthy spot in Cape Colony, nearer supplies and charitable aid.

*Answer.* Careful attention will be paid to these points in selecting the site of any fresh camps.

**7.** That because all the above, and much more not mentioned, including the economical distribution of clothing, demands much careful organisation, detailed work, and devoted attention, *free access* should be given to a band of at least six accredited representatives of English philanthropic societies, who should be provided with permanent passes, have the authority of the High Commissioner for their work, and be responsible to the government as well as to those they represent Their mother-wit and womanly resource would set right many of the existing evils.

*Answer.* We think it more desirable to work through local committees and persons sent out by the government to act with them, and shall shortly send out certain persons to aid the committees in distributing charitable funds.

**8.** That the doctors' report on the condition of the children in Bloemfontein be called for and acted upon.

*Answer.* This report has been called for.

**9.** That the women whose applications are appended be at once allowed to leave the camp. They are good women, and their health and strength are failing under the long strain.

*Answer.* Copies of these applications have been sent to Lord Kitchener.

All the above Recommendations have been forwarded to Lord Kitchener, who will no doubt act upon them, except in any case where military necessity may preclude him from doing so, though I do not foresee any difficulty of that kind. Meanwhile, the government has accepted with pleasure a suggestion that funds should be raised to provide comforts in the camps beyond the actual necessaries which the government can properly supply, and is willing—through the local committees or persons sent out from England by the government, to act in co-operation with the local committees—to be responsible for the distribution of any such funds, whether intended for the Concentration Camps or for loyal subjects of the Crown who have suffered through the war.

You will doubtless have seen a letter by me to Mrs. Alfred Lyttelton on this subject which appears in the press today. I have every hope that within the necessary limitations imposed by camp life all reasonable provision will be found to have been already made in the Concentration Camps, for adequate food and the necessaries of life, with proper medical treatment, schools of instruction, religious ministration, various forms of labour, and amusements for the inmates. No doubt the assistance received from the funds referred to above will help to make the lot of those who are suffering from the effects of the war as comfortable as the circumstances of war and the difficulties of the country will permit.—Yours faithfully,

St. John Brodrick.

Anyone familiar with the Recommendations as sent to the War Office will observe in this reply the omission of the word "equally," from No 2 and the entire omission of the original No. 3. These ran:—

**2.** Free passes into towns for all *equally* wishing to find work there.

**3.** Equality of treatment, whether the men of the family are fighting, imprisoned, dead, or surrendered.

My reply will show that I feared that the first important concession would prove a dead letter unless friends were at hand to make it known and smooth away the difficulties, and indeed events have proved it to be no more than a paper concession. Had it been acted upon, the lives of many would have been spared. I wrote:—

Dear Mr. Brodrick,—I feel greatly indebted to you for your letter to me containing the opinions of the government on my Recommendations concerning the Concentration Camps. Everyone will share a feeling of relief and thankfulness at hearing that all women coming under the four headings *a, b, c, d* will be allowed' to go. The clause 'unless there is some military objection' appears to me, who have seen the complexities in the working of martial law, to give ground for some apprehension lest the above permission be rendered nugatory. I will hereafter venture to make a suggestion on this point I may be allowed to express my entire concurrence with your suggestion that the Cape Government should be consulted with regard to the question of large numbers going south to form new camps, and I trust that their opinion may be sought without delay.

The initial difficulty of removal would be considerable, but it would surely prove of advantage in the end, especially if, as I gather from your reply to No. 4, there is every probability that the numbers in the camps will be augmented, and I know from experience that it is already impossible to prevent overcrowding in the existing camps, owing to the impossibility of obtaining enough tents so far from the coast. The supplies would be easier and cheaper, the line proportionately relieved for military use, and I cannot doubt that the effect universally desired, of arresting the abnormal mortality, would be in large measure obtained. (If the co-operation of the Cape Government can be obtained, I have the permission of my Committee to place my services at your disposal for the personal supervision of such a removal; whilst the funds of the Committee could be usefully employed in supplementing the government supplies with things necessary to women and children in such circumstances.) With regard to Recommendation 2, I am fully aware that it is, as you have understood, already to some extent the practice in most camps to grant passes, but I desired to point out, by the use of the word 'equally' in my first letter to you, that the passes are at present granted or withheld for reasons not easily understood and often apparently capricious, and I would urge that the rule should be laid down that passes should be freely granted unless there were some clear and unmistakable reasons for denying them in a special case.

No. 3. With regard to ministers, what is urgently needed is not so much the holding of regular services as ministrations to the sick and dying and the burial of the dead. These functions can clearly not be performed for large bodies of people by clergy resident in neighbouring towns in addition to their own parochial duty. Could not Dr. Andrew Murray's suggestion, that ministers from Cape Colony already British subjects should be invited to take up their residence in the camps, be more widely acted upon? This has been already successfully arranged at Norval's Pont

No. 5. I fear that I cannot have made plain that my suggestion with regard to matrons had reference to the necessity of matrons for the camps as well as for the hospitals. The hospital matron, often the only trained nurse, is fully occupied in her own sphere. What is needed is a lady in each camp, holding the position occupied by Miss Hauptfleisch at Port Elizabeth, who has enjoyed the entire confidence of the military, and whose womanly tact and power of organisation has had a success attested by all who have seen the camp under her control I believe that a sufficient number of competent ladies, both English and Colonial, are at this moment forthcoming who would undertake the work without remuneration, so that if it were thought necessary to retain the present superintendents at high salaries, little if any extra expense would be incurred.

I will further venture to make here the suggestion alluded to earlier, that the camp matrons should be authorised to act as intermediaries in cases in which women were applying to quit the camp, and should be allowed to investigate and represent the circumstances of the applicants, especially when any objection was felt in the first instance by the military authorities. In such cases that came under my notice I have felt sure that the military objections must have rested on a misunderstanding or the incompleteness of the evidence presented, and this might have been removed by the kind of assistance which might be rendered by a responsible person on the spot

In respect to the distribution of charitable funds through the medium of the local committees (some of which I myself helped to set on foot, and of whose work I had considerable experience), I feel sure that the work will be done most satisfactorily if some of the persons whom you propose shall be sent by the government to act with them, were persons nominated by the committees of the several funds raised in England and submitted to the government for approval. I am not in a position to speak for the other funds, but with regard to the South African Distress Fund I am authorised to state that such a mode of distribution would meet the approval of the Committee. For obvious reasons, they would not feel justified in delegating to others the entire responsibility of distribution.

In conclusion, bearing in mind the great extent of country, the masses of people, the gigantic responsibilities of the whole undertaking, the pressure of work resting on all local officials, it will at once be apparent to anyone who has worked at this subject on the spot, that the successful carrying out of the instructions of the government, as well as the desires of the English charitable public, will practically depend upon full facilities being accorded to a sufficient number of voluntary but accredited workers.—I am, etc,

Emily Hobhouse.

Early in July, Lord Ripen, as acting Chairman of the Distress Fund, had approached the War Office with a suggestion that ladies should at once be sent out to the camps, and had given my name as one prepared to go on this mission.

On the 9th of July, the reply came—

. . . I am directed to assure you that His Majesty's Government view with satisfaction the readiness of various philanthropic associations to supply funds and give service for the amelioration of the condition of those suffering by the war; though they would regret that such efforts should be confined to (the Distress Fund gave irrespective of nationality), one part only of those who have been rendered homeless or penniless by the course of hostilities. But these proposals, by their number alone, make it impossible for the government to accede to them. The Secretary of State for War has three such proposals before him at this moment, and it is obvious that it would be impossible to introduce a variety of authorities into camps organised and regulated by the government.

Thus, there were three proposals to send helpers, and nearly 40 great camps to divide them amongst, and all would have been willing to work under the government; none proposed "to introduce a variety of authorities." The help so sorely needed was offered and refused. Months later it *had* to be sent.

The letter proceeded—

The Secretary of State has every reason to believe that, allowing for the obvious difficulty of temporarily accommodating so large a population as is now congregated in the camps, all proper arrangements have been made for the food, clothing, medical attendance, and spiritual supervision of those in the camps. Schools have been established, and a properly qualified matron, (it was many months before this was done), has been appointed in each camp. Beyond this the government will shortly send out certain ladies to visit the camps and co-operate with the local committees in the distribution of comforts or gifts of money which may be entrusted to them.

From this rosy description of the camps it was evident to me that I had failed to present the matter in its most urgent and serious light to Mr. Brodrick. The long delay before sending workers and the rise in the death-rate combined to make me seek and obtain a further interview with the Secretary of State. (July 18.)

The conversation was confidential in character, but the refusal of the government to let me return to the camps was reiterated, and as it was confidently expected by the public in many parts of England that I should so return, I asked for and was promised a letter containing the government's reasons for this refusal Not having received this letter by the 26th July, I wrote as follows, and received an immediate reply:—

July 26, 1901.

Dear Mr. Brodrick,—When we parted on the 18th you promised to send me a letter giving the reasons why you could not allow me to return to my work in South Africa. Such a letter has not reached me, and I hope you will forgive me if I rather urgently press that it should be immediately sent. I am continually asked on all sides when I am going out again. It is generally expected I shall soon start, which is, indeed, my own desire. Since you have adopted, in principle, almost all my recommendations, I can scarcely think any ground of objection can be regarded as tenable against a proposal to resume work the results of which have been accepted by yourself.

It has occurred to me that you might say that any help on my part was unnecessary, because you have yourself selected certain ladies to visit and report upon the Concentration Camps. In relation to this, may I be permitted to urge that the number you have sent is really quite insufficient for the work entrusted to them, considering the largely increased number of refugees now found in the camps, unless they have supplementary assistance; that they must spend much time and labour before they will have acquired the preliminary knowledge necessary for useful action; and, if I may speak of myself, that my experience in the camps, my acquaintance with the people, and to some extent with their language, ought to enable me, and I trust would enable me, to be a useful auxiliary to them in the discharge of their duties?

I would fain hope that the delay in sending your letter may mean a disposition to reconsider my appeal for leave to revisit the camps in South Africa. In spite of improvements that have been made, there is much suffering and misery still wanting alleviation, and I do most earnestly press you to grant me permission to return at the earliest possible moment to the work in which I have become so deeply interested.—I have, etc.

War Office, July 27, 1901.

Dear Miss Hobhouse,—I am sorry if there has been any delay in writing you a letter on the subject which, with others, you mentioned when I saw you on the 18th, but as I was forced to refer to the matter publicly in reply to questions in the House of Commons, I hoped I had done what was necessary to explain the action of the government. The only considerations which have guided the government in their selection of ladies to visit the Concentration Camps, beyond their special capacity for such work, was that they should be, so far as is possible, removed from the suspicion of partiality to the system adopted or the reverse.

I pointed out to you that for this reason the government had been forced to decline the services of ladies representing various philanthropic agencies, whose presence in an unofficial capacity would be a difficulty in camps controlled by government organisation. It would have been impossible for the government to accept your services in this capacity while declining others, the more so as your reports and speeches have been made the subject of so much controversy; and I regret, therefore, we cannot alter the decision which I conveyed to you on the 18th instant.—Yours, etc.,

St. John Brodrick.

Thus the principle laid down as a guide in the choice of the ladies for this Commission was that "they should be removed from the suspicion of partiality to the system or the reverse." This good rule was unfortunately not followed, because two of the women selected had already expressed themselves with some warmth in the public Press. Mrs. Fawcett, who was made principal of the Commission, had written a criticism of my Report, which was in substance a defence of the concentration system. (*Westminster Gazette,* July 4, 1901.) In one phrase, she had spoken of the formation of the Concentration Camps as "part of the fortune of war." One wonders in what war Mrs. Fawcett had read of such a system, unless it was the Spanish action in Cuba, which was condemned by every civilised nation. Or did she refer to the wars of Shalmaneser and Nebuchadnezzar to find precedents for the wholesale uprooting, capturing, deporting, imprisoning, or exiling of the whole non-combatant portion of a country. In that case, more wisdom was displayed, as we are expressly told that the husbandmen and poorest of the land were left to till the soil.

Dr. Jane Waterston, on her part, was inspired by the tidings of English efforts to improve the camps, to write at some length in the Cape papers. (*Cape Times,* July 22, 1901.) Here are a few of her sentences, written before she herself became engaged in ameliorating the camps—

> Judging by some of the hysterical whining going on in England at the present time, it would seem as if we might neglect or half starve our faithful soldiers, and keep our civilian population eating their hearts out here as long as we fed and pampered people who have not even the grace to say thank you for the care bestowed on them.
>
> At present, there is the danger that the Boers will waken up to have a care for their womenfolk, and will go on fighting for some time, so as to keep them in comfortable winter quarters at our expense, and thus our women and children will lose a few more of their husbands and fathers.

After reading this, one wonders how Dr. Waterston could be so cruel to our soldiers as to accept a post on the Commission, and it is to her credit that, as we learn, she at first declined to serve.

It was tragic to feel that instead of a great number of good nurses, and, above all, voluntary workers as camp matrons, being at once despatched in early June, only six ladies started in a leisurely way towards the end of July, not themselves to work, but to make more inquiry.

★★★★★★

The Commission sailed without either Mrs. Fawcett or her companions making any effort to see me with a view to obtaining information, which might save time, when time was all-important. Mrs. Fawcett was invited to meet me, but declined on domestic grounds, and did not delate a colleague to do so. She recently stated in a London meeting (*Times*, March 24, 1902) that she could get no help whatever from our Committee, and in a subsequent letter to the *Times* excused herself by saying that she had asked me through a relative for information in writing. It was a pity that she did not choose the far simpler method of approaching me direct, instead of employing a medium. I never saw the letter to which she alludes, but the impression made by it at the time and conveyed to me, was that she evidently did not desire any help I might be able to give her.

★★★★★★

The death-rate rose, and after the August mortality list had been published, (see Appendix), I made one more appeal to Mr. Brodrick, entreating immediate action. A few weeks after, the control of the camps passed into the hands of Mr. Chamberlain.

Open Letter.

Sept. 29, 1901.

Dear Mr. Brodrick,—Three months have passed since I approached you on the subject of the Concentration Camps in South Africa, three terrible months in the history of those camps. Can the appalling figures just shown in the government returns for August and the preceding month pass unnoticed by the government and by the great mass of the English people? Will you bear with me for a moment if I approach you again on this sad topic, and with these latest figures before us make one more appeal to your clemency, and through you to the humanity of the country?

If we leave for the present the coloured camps and speak only of the white people, the returns show that the population of the camps has increased gradually during June, July, and August from 85,000 to 105,000 souls. In the past month of August 1,878 deaths occurred among the whites, of which 1,545 were children. The total number of deaths for the three months for which we have returns is 4,067, of which 3,245 were children. We have no account of the hundreds who passed away in the first six months of this year and part of last year. What is there to indicate the probability of any abatement in this fearful mortality? The cold winter nights are happily passing away, but rains are falling in many parts, and the increasing heat will bring sicknesses of other kinds. Scurvy has appeared. Daily the children are dying, and unless the rate be checked a few months will suffice to see the extermination of the majority.

Will nothing be done? Will no prompt measures be taken to deal with this terrible evil? Three months ago, I tried to place the matter strongly before you, and begged permission to organise immediate alleviatory measures, based on the experience I had acquired, in order thus to avert a mortality I had plainly seen was increasing. My request was refused, and thus experience which I could not pass on to others rendered useless. The repulse to myself would have mattered nothing, had only a large band of kindly workers been instantly despatched with full powers to deal with each individual camp as its needs required. The necessity was instant if innocent human lives were to be saved Instead, we had to wait a month while six ladies were chosen.

During that month 576 children died. The preparation and journey of these ladies occupied yet another month, and in that interval 1,124 more children succumbed. In place of at once proceeding to the great centres of high mortality, the bulk of yet a third month seems to have been spent in their long journey to Mafeking, and in passing a few days at some of the healthier camps. Meanwhile, 1,545 more children died.

This was not immediate action; it was very deliberate inquiry, and that, too, at a time when death, which is unanswerable, was at work; nay, when the demands of death, instead of diminishing, were increasing. Will you not now, with the thought before you of those 3,245 children who have closed their eyes for ever since last I saw you, on their behalf, will you not now take instant action, and endeavour thus to avert the evil results of facts patent to all, and suspend further inquiry into the truth of what the whole world knows?

In the name of the little children whom I have watched suffer and die, and whom I cannot for a moment forget, I make bold to plead with you once more. In the name of our common humanity I urge that immediate steps may be taken by those qualified and empowered to act, lest one day we are bowed down by the humiliating and grievous thought that we have sat still and watched calmly the extermination of a race brave and strong enough to have kept the British Empire at bay for two long years. I need not recapitulate the proposals which I made to you, some of which you seemed to adopt, though, alas, even your adoption has appeared to be powerless to secure the effectual employment of the most important. I ask at least for effectual amelioration.

Yet is it not conceivable that we might go further? The men cannot end the war. The women will not end the war. Cannot the children help to bring about that peace which both sides so earnestly desire? Thousands have given their innocent lives. Thousands more are sick and like to die. Is it not enough? What the children need of proper food, clothing, and shelter cannot be brought to them; transport is too difficult, supplies too scarce. They must die, die where we have placed them, in their hundreds and their thousands, unless the war ends and sets them free. 'The cry of the children' comes to us now not from our own mines and factories, but from across the seas.

Will it be heard and answered? Will not your own and every parent's heart in England respond to their cry, and beat in sympathy with those mothers who have bravely borne the loss of homes and possessions, but stand aghast and enduringly resentful as they witness their children swept away? There are cases where women have entered camps with eight and ten children, and death has claimed them all. Do we want 'unconditional surrender' at the cost of so much child-life? Is it worth the price? For the men of either side I say nothing. They have chosen their part and must abide by it.

For the women also I do not now plead; they are always strong to endure. But I do ask, in the name of the innocent and helpless children, that England's humanity may triumph over her policy, so that the sacrifice of the children may be stayed. Is there a nation that will not honour her the more? In the earnest hope that you will listen to my appeal,—I have the honour to be, yours faithfully,

Emily Hobhouse.

Appeals for relief for the camps had been periodically made throughout the spring by the Committee of the Distress Fund, and in April had appeared a letter from Lady Maxwell, wife of the Military Governor of Pretoria, who appealed to the American public through the *New York Herald,* April 16, 1901. She is herself an American, and gave as her reason for turning to American charity, that England was too exhausted by other claims to give in this direction. We have never heard it hinted before that England has not money enough and to spare for destitute women and children, taken either willingly or unwillingly under her protection. Such a letter as Lady Maxwell's, coming straight from Pretoria, and from the wife of an officer, would, if it had been addressed to the English public, have reaped a harvest of ready subscriptions.

At any rate, we who are English feel it was our duty as well as our privilege to provide for the health and comfort of these victims of the war, likely also to become our fellow-subjects. She wrote:

> It is in the name of the little children, who are living in open tents without fires, and possessing only the scantiest of clothes, that I ask for help.

Lord Hobhouse's eloquent appeal had been issued simultaneously in England. It was addressed, he said:

> . . . . to all English people who have hearts to feel for the sufferings of fellow men and women, and to all who are thinking what course of action at the present moment is most likely to bring honour and permanent rest to our country.—*Speaker*, April 20, 1901.

He went on to describe something of the conditions of camp life, and touched on the mental suffering, which was at all times the deepest—

> Numbers crowded into small tents: some sick, some dying, occasionally a dead one among them; scanty rations dealt out raw; lack of fuel to cook them; lack of water for drinking, for cooking, for washing; lack of soap, brushes, and other instruments of personal cleanliness; lack of bedding or of beds to keep the body off the bare earth; lack of clothing for warmth, and in many cases even for decency; no needles or thread to mend tatters; shelter only in tents of single canvas, now scorched by a very hot sun, and now drenched by rain, and very slender appliances to meet the maladies consequent on such exposure. We do not dwell on wounded feelings, the anguish of separation, the despair of watching the children, unable to help while they waste away. These are griefs which money can alleviate but little. But every kind of physical affliction seems to be ac-

cumulated in these camps, or at least in some of them, containing thousands of people: hunger, thirst, nakedness, weariness, dirt, disease; and money judiciously applied may alleviate these things.

We add that our proposal is to give help wherever sufferings and a chance of alleviating them are found; all without reference to the national character of the recipients.

About the end of June another group of people became at last aware of the want which had been so long distressing the women and children in South African camps, and a new fund was formed under the auspices of the Victoria League. (*Times*, June 25, 1901.) This fund, like the South African Women and Children's Distress Fund which had been so long at work, was non-political in intention, though not sufficiently withdrawn from partisanship to work in concert with the existing Committee. Some of those instrumental in forming this fresh fund had been asked but had refused to join the Committee which had pioneered the work of relief. They also received the approbation of the government, and their collection was administered by the Commission, the members composing which were some weeks after announced by Mr. Brodrick.

The Committee of the Distress Fund, anxious to add to their resources by a wider dissemination of facts, arranged to hold a meeting for that purpose in the Queen's Hall, Langham Place, where I could plead the cause of the sufferers in the camps. The Bishop of Hereford promised to preside. During the voyage home I had had some conversation with Lord Milner with regard to permission either for myself or for other women to go to the camps, and he had promised me a speedy decision. As this had not reached me, I wrote, (June 7), with the sanction of the Committee, to tell him of the proposed meeting, adding that it would give great satisfaction if he could enable me to announce to the audience that we had his permission to bear their gifts to the destitute people.

A fortnight later, (June 24), the day of the proposed meeting, the reply came, saying that the matter having now passed into the hands of the government, it would be better to learn from them direct what decision had been arrived at. Feeling the delay serious, I wrote again to Lord Milner, begging no more time might be lost if the dying children were to be saved. The arrangements for the projected meeting in the Queen's Hall had continued, the hall was hired and the meeting advertised. Suddenly, three days before the appointed time, the lessee of the hall, Mr. Robert Newman, withdrew his consent, breaking the contract. The excuse offered was that a political meeting had been held by other people in his hall during the previous week, and some roughs, outsiders not connected with the meeting, had made a disturbance; therefore Mr. Newman suddenly resolved to refuse the hall for a philanthropic meeting with a bishop in the chair.

The secretary of the Committee had been making final arrangements with the lessee on the Saturday morning, and in the afternoon received word of this change of mind. The expenses incurred in advertising the meeting on the strength of Mr. Newman's agreement were never made good. The minister of Westminster Chapel, hearing of this incident, offered the use of his large church, and plans were in train for holding the meeting there. But the timidity which possessed the metropolitan police and Mr. Newman infected four out of the six deacons of this chapel, and neither would they allow a cause to be publicly pleaded, funds for which had the open sanction of the government. The meeting was perforce abandoned, and the Bishop of Hereford sent the following letter to the *Times*:—

June 24.

Sir,—As the meeting on behalf of the South African Women and Children's Distress Fund, at which I had promised to preside tonight, has been unavoidably postponed, I desire to appeal to your readers for subscriptions to the fund.

Every humane person who reads Miss Hobhouse's report must feel a desire to alleviate the misery described, and would be sorry if what has occurred should stop the supplies which Miss Hobhouse and her friends have been using so well and so kindly.

While making this appeal, and to avoid misunderstanding, I desire to add that the proposed meeting was not intended to be in any sense a political or party meeting.

The object of its promoters was purely philanthropic and charitable. Their work is a work of mercy. Lord Roberts might take the chair at such a meeting, and it would accord with his well-known kindness to do so. Lord Milner could do no better service in the cause of peace and goodwill between Dutch and English in South Africa than to preside at one of Miss Hobhouse's meetings.

It is a comparatively new phenomenon in English life for such meetings to be rendered dangerous or impossible by a portion of the Press and the lawless and brutal element in the community. Let us hope, for our national credit's sake, that it may soon disappear.

The natural instinct of the English people is to give very generously in relief of such a pitiable lot as that of those poor women and children, and I hope the fountain of charity may flow freely on this occasion; for those who give to this good work will not only be joining in a work of mercy and Christian benevolence, but will also be helping to sow in the hearts of the sufferers seeds of pity and loving-kindness which can hardly fail sooner or later to bear good fruit and to come back to us in grateful memories and consequent goodwill.—*Times*, June 25, 1901.

Unable for the moment to help the cause in any other way than by the collection of money, I proceeded to accept invitations to address meetings of a non-party character for that purpose. Owing to the interest awakened by the issue of my Report, these invitations were numerous; but evil communications corrupt good manners, and the example set in London by Mr. Newman and the four deacons spread to the provinces, and several halls already engaged shut their doors at my approach. These meetings, at which I appealed only to the sympathy and humanity of my audience, aroused in a certain section of the Press and the people a most intolerant resistance.

Various facts which came to my knowledge combined to show that the opposition to my lectures was not spontaneous, but organised by people who did not appear. In several places the police allowed themselves to be made the instruments of this opposition, affecting fear that they would not be able to keep order. The spectacle of the Press and police force of the country affecting alarm at the quiet gatherings in which I described suffering women and sick children would have been ludicrous, had it not been the outward sign of an inward intolerance, inhumanity and pseudo-patriotism, lamentable to all who hold their country's true honour and dignity at heart? The Society of Friends, whose ears are always open to the cry of the distressed, came to my assistance, and offered the use of their meeting-houses.

Having no intention of abandoning my projected tour because of this foolish agitation, I publicly stated that the more I was opposed the more determinately I should continue to carry out my plans, and it would be for the benefit of the agitators to desist from further interference. This, combined with the fact that those from whom it is probable the opposition emanated began to see that the agitation was ridiculous, and merely served as an advertisement, had its effect, and I proceeded quietly with my work.

I spoke at forty public meetings in the course of the summer, and with three exceptions every one was peaceful and orderly. Cheltenham excepted, a deep interest was evinced in each place, and marked enthusiasm in some towns. The three disturbed meetings were Bristol, New Southgate, and Darlington. At Darlington, the audience itself was large and orderly, the disturbance being entirely due to some ten roughs who sat together under a leader, evidently engaged to obstruct by singing songs the whole evening. The meeting reassembled in a private house next day. Bristol and New Southgate were attended by a good many rowdies, who made quiet presentation of the subject impossible, and were unamenable to reason. They deemed it patriotic to end their proceedings by throwing sticks and stones, with more injury to themselves than to me.

Efforts to nullify the effect of my story, lest public sentiment should be aroused, took two forms, *viz.* criticism of myself and justification of the camps. I was labelled "political agitator," a "disseminator of inaccurate and blood-curdling stories." (*Times*, June 19, 1901.) A discredited South African wrote insinuating that my mission had been a political propaganda. (*Hansard*, vol. xc.; *Daily News*, June 27; *Times*, June 25.) My Report was described as a "weapon" (*Times*, Aug. 27), used "wherever the name of England was hated." I was "deficient as an investigator," and had not the competence to compile "charges against us." (*Ibid.*) This last remark brings to mind a similar fault found with Mr. Burdett-Coutts. During a debate on the Hospitals Commission, he said—

> I consider it an attack upon my motives to convert the statement of facts I made into an attack upon Lord Roberts. (Opposition cheers.)
>
> *Mr. Balfour:* You did criticise somebody, and who that person can be if not the responsible officer we have been unable to discover.
>
> *Mr. Burdett-Coutts:* I criticised nobody; I criticised a state of things. (Opposition cheers.)
>
> *Mr. Balfour:* There is no such thing as criticising a state of things.

(Loud cries of 'Oh! oh!') You may describe a state of things, but not criticise it (Cries of 'Oh!' and Opposition laughter.)

*Mr. Burdett-Coutts:* I am extremely sorry to interrupt again, but I ask the right honourable gentleman in what words, where, and when I criticised any person and who that person was. (Opposition cheers.)

Mr. Balfour replied that the honourable gentleman's criticisms were of a vague and obscure character. (Opposition laughter, and cries of: "Then why appoint a Commission?")—*Western Morning News,* July 6.

Finally I was "hysterical" and put "implicit belief" in all that was told me. (*Times,* June 20.) Mr. Conan Doyle has gone still further on this point, distinctly saying, in misquotation of words used at Derby by my friend and cousin Mr. Charles Hobhouse, that "some of my statements would not bear examination." (See *The War: Its Cause and Conduct,* by A. Conan Doyle.) Mr. Doyle's attention was repeatedly called to this error, which had gone out into the world in a quarter of a million copies, but he let months elapse before making any public withdrawal of his words, and then did so in such scant fashion that I am obliged to make the correction myself. Drawing my cousin's attention to the misrepresentation of his words at Derby, I received the following reply, which he gave me leave to publish. I do so with my answer—

Letter from Mr. Charles Hobhouse, M.P.

I had already seen the reference in Dr. Conan Doyle's book to which you allude. I wrote to him pointing out that I was in no position to admit that some of your statements would not bear examination, that I had never stated anything of the kind, and that as to the accuracy or inaccuracy of your Report I could say nothing because I did not *know.*

The meaning of my words at Derby was dear to myself if not to others. Your Report purports to be a careful review not only of the state of the Concentration Camps, but also of the conditions under which persons were brought into those camps. The extracts which you give from statements made to you impugn not only the want of foresight by the authorities, but the individual humanity of officers and soldiers ordered to carry out what was, I believe, an uncongenial task. If such accusations are to be made at all, and are, moreover, to carry conviction to those who can only judge of events at second-hand, I am strongly of opinion that they should only be made upon the evidence of persons whose names are given in full, and whose assertions are verified and corroborated by others, and not upon the *ex-parte* statements of people whose identity is veiled behind initials and blanks.

From this it is plain that Mr. Hobhouse did not say "my statements would not bear examination," (*vide* Dr. Doyle, now Sir A. Conan Doyle), but that he wished other people's statements made to me could have been examined. This I also wish and hope it will one day be done. I replied to him as follows:—

My Dear Cousin,—I am much obliged for your letter. I now understand that by an unverified statement you mean one taken down from the lips of one or more eye-witnesses, and published precisely as taken. If you had made this clear in your speech (at Derby), I think you would have avoided some misunderstanding. On p. 36 of my Report I particularly mention that the individual name of the person making the statement is in each case known to me and the Committee. I have withheld the names of these witnesses for reasons which will be apparent to all who have lived under martial law.

You will have noticed that the name of the farm is given in each case. It was an essential part of my work with a view to relief to clear up the question whether the women came into the camps voluntarily or otherwise. This could only be determined by their own narratives, and if the narratives were to be given at all, they had to be given word for word as received. I may remark that for your private information I am willing to give you any name you may desire, but without the consent of the women concerned I cannot at present make them public.

In investigation work, when a number of people from wholly different places and quite independently of each other make statements which are found to be in agreement on certain main points, such statements are, I believe, looked upon as in a sense corroborative evidence. . . . Perhaps a stronger testimony is offered by letters and books written by soldiers, and accounts given me in South Africa by soldiers themselves were the strongest of all. Naturally, amongst so many men, characters and manners varied infinitely. I quite agree that cousinly considerations should not interfere with one's public work, but Dr. Doyle's grave misrepresentation of your words, which I had previously determined to ignore, has made it necessary to defend myself in the interests of my cause.

The existence of the camps was justified by sundry reasons self-contradictory in nature, (see note following)—*e.g.* "The camps are an absolute military necessity"; (*Times*, Aug. 30), again, "We have voluntarily and out of humanity gone out of our way to undertake certain obligations in regard to the families of our foes." Later, it was asserted that they were formed as reprisals. The mortality was explained as due to the habits of the Boer women, and their inferiority as careful mothers. (*Times*, June 20 and July 20.)

★★★★★★

Note:—Since peace was proclaimed, reasons for the camps have been more fully dwelt upon by the *Times* special correspondent (*Times*, July 12, 1902):—

Lord Kitchener's first intention undoubtedly was definitely to clear the country of stock and inhabitants by mobile columns operating from the railway. The impression generally prevailed in South Africa, that the Boers, on account of their proverbial domesticity, could not long endure separation from their wives and families.

Also for military reasons it was necessary to remove the occupants from their farms. . . . We had promised protection to such *burghers* as surrendered and returned to their estates—a promise which ought never to have been made, and which, in but few instances, could be fulfilled. . . . Partly to meet the apparent breach of faith to the surrendered *burghers*, consequent upon the withdrawal from the occupation of outlying townships, and in the main to further the 'clearance' scheme, the Concentration Camps organisation was conceived.

It is possible that the conception of the Concentration Camps and the inordinate haste in which Lord Kitchener pushed hurriedly-recruited mounted troops into the field, are the only two serious blots upon the handling of a campaign fraught with difficulties. . . . The formation of the Concentration Camps did not bring about the desired results. In fact, it rather increased the difficulties of the situation. The undesired interference of inquisitive and notoriety-seeking persons brought the Concentration Camps into public notice, so that they became a lever in the Pro-Boer campaign at home and on the Continent, which has been the most nauseating circumstance of the whole war. But that was a lesser evil in comparison with the effect which the camps had upon the military situation. The scheme, *which as designed to bring pressure upon the Boers in the fields instead of goading them into sur-*

*render*, was welcomed by them as a means by which to rid themselves of impedimenta.

(I have shown earlier that the Boers sent no families into the British lines except those of surrendered *burghers.*—E. H. )

✶✶✶✶✶✶

Attempt was also made to minimise it by proof that the normal death-rate in South Africa was high and the population consequently slow in increasing.

Mr. Letherby of Plymouth contributed a letter, (*Times*, Sept. 16), on the death-rate in the Cape Colony village of Middelburg, (which has no connection with the camp of that name). Others writing in the same strain induced a leading article from the *Times*, (Oct. 19, 1901), full of unverified and ill-digested facts—

> The death-rates in the camps look enormous to people ac-customed to the rates obtaining in English towns. But heavy as they are, they are not enormous judged by South African peace standards, for our correspondent mentions that the rate in Middelburg, Cape Colony, before the war was 150 per 1,000. He also observes that the increase in the population of the Or-ange Free State between 1896 and 1900 was only 11 per 1,000 *per annum*, and this among a proverbially prolific race. Obvi-ously, the normal death-rate must have been appalling, judged by English standards.

Mr. Brailsford's answer, (*Times*, Oct. 25, and *Morning Leader*, Oct. 24, 1901), to this muddle of figures and facts was complete—

> You suggest that a death-rate which seems high, if judged by English standards, would not appear so by 'South African peace standards.'
>
> I find that the death-rate among the European population of Cape Colony has varied during the period 1896-98 from a fraction over 15 to a fraction over 16 per 1,000. As the English rate is a fraction over 19, it seems clear that there is no such contrast between English and South African standards as you imply.
>
> You further cite the increase of the Free State population be-tween 1896 and 1900. The reference in your correspondent's letter is to 1886 and 1890, and the figures in the leading article appear there, no doubt, by an oversight How your correspond-ent obtained his figures I do not know, as the census in the Free

State is taken decennially. The white population in 1880 was 61,022, in 1890 it was 77,716. There was, therefore, an annual increase per 1,000 of 27.4, which is, I think, more than three times the rate in the United Kingdom. How your correspondent reached his figure 11, I am at a loss to guess.

Mr. Brailsford goes on to show that the mortality of Middelburg in 1899 brought forward by Mr. Letherby was so exceptional that a special report on it was presented to Parliament. The population there, which consists largely of English consumptives and natives officially described as dirty, filthy, and lazy, was 1,666 persons, and there were 125 deaths in the year, giving a death-rate of about 75, not 150. The normal death-rate in South Africa (something over 15) appears to be lower than that of the United Kingdom.

In relation to this, a doctor who has long practised in the Free State, told me recently that he thought it would be quite easy to get a return of the deaths in that country when the war is over. Deaths were not formally registered, but each little town had its one undertaker— the town of Bloemfontein possessing two. They did all the necessary business, and their books and those of the practising doctors would give all deaths and the information needed to compile returns.

During the summer, white papers were issued which showed the rapid increase of the mortality. Yet in the midst of this a telegram from Lord Kitchener was published, which said—

> Goold-Adams has made tour of inspection Refugee Camps, Orange River Colony, and reports people well looked after and completely satisfied with all we are doing for them.—Lord Kitchener to Secretary of War, Aug. 3. See *Morning Leader*, Aug. 6, 1901.

It was constantly affirmed that the people were thus "completely satisfied," and this was relied upon by men who do not seem to have made any effort to understand their attitude. Mr. Chamberlain dwelt upon it in his speech of August 14. (*Times*, Aug. 15.) He said, too, that the women could all escape if they wished to do so, and the fact that they did not do so (with perhaps half a dozen young children) was proof, in his opinion, that they had no complaint. Evidently Mr. Chamberlain has never known what it is to be shut up, as many of these people were, in an enclosure of barbed wire 8 feet high— curiously enlaced, nor to find himself ringed by armed sentries and military camps.

In spite of these preventions, women in some camps did escape with the help and connivance of soft-hearted English soldiers, who often objected to being the armed guardians of women and children. On the same occasion Mr. Chamberlain alluded to the suggestion of the Natal ministers, of charging the maintenance of the Boer families to the fighting *burghers*. (Part 1, chap. 2.). As was revealed in an earlier chapter, subordinate officials had already made this idea familiar to the women of Pietermaritzburg in the matter of clothing. Mr. Chamberlain limited the proposal to a charge only upon those to whom the families belonged.

In September, public opinion on the camps was further consoled by an account of an inspection of Middelburg by the *burgher* Lieutenant Malan, (*Times*, Sept. 13), a young unmarried officer in the artillery. This was permitted by General Blood, and Malan was said to be "agreeably surprised," "satisfied," "finding the people content" In his despatch Lord Kitchener alluded to this visit in the plural, as if Malan had visited several camps. It was, however, only Middelburg. Judgment must be reserved until we have seen Malan's own signed account of this visit. From the manner in which the *Times* has transformed my own opinions, I should hesitate to accept as accurate anyone else's presented in its pages.

Supposing, however, Malan's opinion is correctly given, what does it prove? It was said this fighting Boer's verdict would be worth more than any report drafted by a commission sent from England. ((*Times*, Sept. 13.) We ought then to tear up the report of the Ladies' Commission on that camp, and condemn them for dismissing its superintendent. In the face of the death-roll of those weeks at Middelburg Camp—of the various accounts of it in the Blue Books—of many a woman's letter received from there—Lieutenant Malan's reported opinion is of little worth.

He may be a good soldier, but is evidently a bad investigator. Possibly he judged from the superficial aspect of the camp, as many, Dutch and English, have done before him, notably the *Times* special correspondent and sundry members of the Women's Loyal Guild; but that the women did not, as asserted, complain to him is no criterion that they had nothing to complain of. I do not know the Boer woman who would by complaints of her own sufferings weaken the arm of her countrymen in the field, while I do know that women of all nations can, if they choose, easily deceive a man about what they personally undergo.

★★★★★★

Since writing the above, I have heard that the medical inspection asked for by the Boers was distinctly refused by Lord Kitchener, and that Malan's visit was not authoritative. Happening to come in with despatches, he was conducted by General Blood through the camp.

★★★★★★

The arrival of my Report in South Africa, and the news of the appointment of a Commission of Inquiry, occasioned an outburst of the most "loyal" Colonial opinion. Owing to martial law, opinion could only be expressed by one party, with one or two valiant exceptions. Dr. Jane Waterston's long letter of indignation has been alluded to. Mr. Victor Sampson, M.L. A., and Colonel Harris describe how they walked up to Kimberley Camp one afternoon, (*Times*, July 28), and found everything satisfactory, all the children plump and well fed. (*Times*, Aug. 27, 1901.) Yet in July, 59 died out of 3,624, (Cd. 819), persons, and in August 163 out of 3,701, (*Ibid*), in that camp.

Canon Orford writes from Bloemfontein that "the families of those fighting us are being better fed and cared for than our own people." A batch of letters were published by Mrs. K. H. R. Stuart, chiefly from members of the Guild of women she represents. (*Times*, Aug. 20.) Most of the writers had not seen a camp, and the others had only paid a passing visit if one happened to be near at hand. The upshot of their remarks is, that if the women in the camps are not very comfortable they ought to be. They show also a tendency to rush into comparison of the camp prisoners with those loyalist refugees who came south early in the war.

If the Committees who distributed relief to this set of war victims allowed them to want they are surely to blame, but that is no reason why another class of war victims should also be neglected. It was a surprise to me to learn that any of these loyalist refugees were still in want, when so large a sum as £240,000 had been expended on their behalf. I had therefore determined on my second visit to South Africa to investigate their needs in the coast towns side by side with those of destitute exiles deported from the north. The result will be remembered.

I was prevented from even landing at Cape Town, and forced to make the return voyage when physically unfit, in a way greatly to the discredit of those official servants of the country who conceived the plan and carried it into practice. Mrs. Stuart published more letters as "protests" against my "misleading Report." (*Times*, Sept. 7, 1901.) Does she consider the whole group of Blue Books also misleading, and will she continue to protest? The Cape year ended with the self-congratulations of the *Cape Times*, (Dec. 25, 1901), based on some Christmas amusements wisely prepared for the children in the camps—

> It is a consoling thought at this festival of the Christian year, that no war that was ever waged has been so tempered and civilised by the influence of Christian sentiment, as this in South Africa. The British people is supporting at this moment, in all the comfort that can possibly be extended to them, 120,000 of the helpless dependents of our enemies. We are glad to know that Christmas time is not to be allowed to pass in the Concentration Camps without some effort at a suitable celebration. The superintendents of all these camps are authorised to incur some expense for this object. Sports, Christmas trees, and treats of all kinds are being arranged, and everybody will wish these people as merry a Christmas as is possible under the circumstances. Next Christmas, let us hope, they will all be restored to their homes, with memories not altogether unpleasant of their prolonged Feast of Tabernacles.

## SECTION B

Turning from the comfortable assurances of the *Times* and the anger of Cape Colonists, we find expression freely given to many weightier views on the camps both on one side and the other, only a few of which can be cited.

Lord Hugh Cecil's letter to the Times, (June 24, 1901), which that organ eulogised as "vigorous and entertaining," is a plea for the justness and rightness of their existence, and seems to be called out by Sir Henry Campbell Bannerman's well-known phrase "*methods of barbarism.*" Lord Hugh argues:—

> Since the generals think so, we must take it that these measures are military necessities. This raises the issue, however necessary, can they be justified? Are they not morally intolerable for whatsoever purpose they are taken? If anyone has his misgivings on this point, let me ask him to consider a single argument. Would not all the suffering involved in devastating and concentrating be considered quite allowable if inflicted not on dwellers in the open, but on the inhabitants of a besieged town? . . . Morality cannot depend upon fortifications. . . . But the example of a siege plainly shows that all that has been done and very much

more—is justifiable if it be necessary to achieve the object of the campaign. And that it is necessary we must accept on the authority of the best military advice at our disposal.

Lord Crewe at once replied to this, (*Times*, June 26), "as far as Lord Hugh Cecil argues it seriously."

Lord Hugh's propositions are two—first, that responsibility rests in the main not on the government, but on the military commanders; and, secondly, that suffering undergone in one of these camps may properly be compared with the hardships endured in a besieged fortress.

He regards the conditions as strictly analogous if not identical . . . Lord Hugh seems to ignore the essential fact that the difference is not between fortifications and no fortifications, but between the results involved by active resistance on the one hand and passive submission on the other. A scheme of defence applied to a particular place . . . will involve certain consequences, familiar since war has existed, upon non-combatants who remain there.

Similarly, if a farmhouse on the *veld* is held by armed Boers, women and children who are there must take their chance of being shot, or of having nothing to eat so long as resistance lasts. . . . In the one case, it is impossible to distinguish parts played by individuals in maintaining the resistance, except by showing respect to the Geneva Flag; in the other case there is no resistance, and the 'devastation and concentration' are the acts of a Stronger Power alone. These people are in fact . . . 'prisoners in Refugee Camps,' and they have a claim to be treated with the consideration due to prisoners at any rate. In fact, Lord Hugh's fallacy, like so many of its kind, breaks down by proving too much. He would be the last to suggest that these women and children ought to undergo the privations of most sieges.

The other argument which fixes responsibility on the generals is an old friend. . . . It is not courageous . . . but a pusillanimous plea may be technically sound. This plea, however, is not even thus sound. Those who abhor the method entirely will condemn the government only; but let it be granted that devastation and concentration' may in extreme cases be admissible military acts. I say "in extreme cases," because the method is new, risky, and open to grave abuse; but I am willing to admit the possibility. Now there are three stages in the business—devastation, deportation, and detention. In the case of each cleared district these three may be humanely carried out, so far as humanity is possible; or there may be shortcomings, with a ghastly result, in any or all of them.

Can it be conceived that a commander-in-chief, holding the tangled skein of enormous operations, can supervise in person the triple process in each case? Of course not Public opinion will not so burden Lord Kitchener, but it certainly will lay heavy responsibility on the government for any proved failure to meet the plain needs of the case. The whole question, indeed, is one of degree. A proved military exigency—its results foreseen, its processes carried through with every possible precaution—such is the case the government has to make for itself. It may be right to suspend judgment until all the facts are known; personally, I think it is.

The real mischief, however, of such a contention as Lord Hugh's is the unintended encouragement it gives to a certain sinister sentiment, which can be traced between the lines of not a few articles, public letters, and speeches nowadays. The war is terribly costly and tedious, it is whispered; let us finish it as best we can, and not ask too many questions about the means. Even the mortality in Concentration Camps may (under Providence) have its use, by convincing the Boers of the futility of further resistance. To Lord Hugh himself such pernicious views would, of course, be absolutely abhorrent. They would be equally odious to Lord Milner and to Lord Kitchener, in whose humanity the country at large has complete confidence. It is all the more to be regretted that Lord Hugh Cecil's unfortunate letter should be open to a misinterpretation which nobody would deplore more entirely than he himself.

Speaking at Southampton early in July, Sir Henry Campbell Bannerman put the subject strongly before the country on the grounds of humanity, morality, and policy. He reiterated boldly the phrase "methods of barbarism." He said—

I wish to say a few words on some of the methods pursued in the conduct of the war. I take strong exception to those measures. I do so not merely on the grounds of humanity and morality, but on the ground of policy, because our objects being what I have described them to be, namely, to bring the war to an early close, and establish good relations and kindly feelings after the war, these practices seem to me to be specially designed to defeat both these objects. I have called them methods of barbarism. So they are. . . . Between 60,000 and 70,000 women and tender children are imprisoned in camps, huddled together in tents under blazing sun and icy winter winds. Everything has been done by the *commandants* of these camps that was in their power to modify the hardship of existence, but such has been the want of proper food and other necessaries, and such the dangers, that the average death-rate over all the camps has been 116 in the thousand. I do not know what the death-rate in Southampton is, say 13 or 14, and in these camps, it is 116. The death-rate is an unerring test which knows nothing of prejudice or sentiment.—*Times*, July 3.

Sir Henry was supported not only by Liberal politicians, but by many of the ablest thinkers of the country, some of whom wrote or spoke from time to time. Mr. Frederic Harrison lectured and wrote indefatigably, Mr. William Watson and Mr. Herbert Spencer were not silent

Mr. Goldwin Smith wrote:—

Things are being done which may bring a lasting stain upon the honour of the country. . . . The Boers were regular belligerents. What right have we now to veer round and treat them as rebels, deport them to Ceylon, burn their farms, and turn their women and children out to starve?—*Manchester Guardian,*

No opinions carried so much weight, and none were more striking, than those of the veteran soldier, Field-Marshal Sir Neville Chamberlain. Mr. Herbert Spencer has told in his book, (*Facts and Comments*), the difficulty which Sir Neville Chamberlain had in getting his opinions made public, how the *Daily Chronicle* delayed and demurred; and he has himself complained to me how, after his letter was published by the *Manchester Guardian*, the rest of the Press boycotted all allusion to it. Yet few opinions on the military side could have more value. He wrote, *Manchester Guardian*, Aug. 5, 1901:—

The necessity, has never been made clear to the nation to justify a departure from the recognised laws of international warfare. I mean the frequent injudicious if not reckless burning or sacking of farmsteads or homes of the Boers, the removal or destruction of the food stored in their houses for the maintenance of their families, the sweeping away of all cattle and sheep, the destruction of mills and implements of agriculture, as also the forcible removal into camps of all the women and children, and there being kept in bondage. I do not wish to imply that extreme measures are never justified during war, but I do assert that the daily reports which have appeared in the Press during the past seven or eight months indicate that a great wave of destruction has been spread over the Orange and Vaal States, such as has never before been enacted by our armies. . . .

In times past British generals have earned an honourable repute for moderation and humanity in their dealings with the people of the country in which they had to operate, and the history of our nation tells us that war can be carried on with safety to the troops and with brilliant success without resorting to methods of oppression, and the more especially against the families of the combatants and non-combatants. . . . The conditions and the suffering of which Miss Hobhouse assures us she was a witness ought to be enough to make it impossible for them ever to be repeated.

It surely can never become a recognised episode in war for wives to be forcibly torn from their homes and to know not what had become of their children; for women about to become mothers to be forced into railway trucks and to have to travel tedious journeys and then remain in camp devoid of the comforts needed for maternity; for women and children to be sent to live in bare tents, and often exposed to sleeping on the bare ground or to be drenched under leaky tents; or for mothers to see their little ones dwindle and die for the want of suitable nourishment. . . .

What would be the indignation in the United Kingdom if anything approaching to such miseries were enacted by an invading army in our own country, where even the nests of the birds are under the protection of the law? Admitted that measures have lately been taken to remedy many of the evils that formerly beset the Concentration Camps, still the suffering and the indignity have had to be endured and cannot now be whitewashed. . . . Finally, let me add that when the war is ended, the nation will, I believe, be made to realise the truth of the saying of Sir

Philip Sidney—'*Cruelty in war buyeth conquest at the dearest price.*'

A few weeks later, Sir Neville Chamberlain was again constrained to express his view.

The Swiss Branch of the Evangelical Alliance had issued an appeal on the subject of the war to the Christians of Great Britain. It appeared to them that unnecessary suffering was being meted out to innocent people. To this appeal the Bishop of Liverpool replied on behalf of the Evangelical Church. Dr. Chavasse spoke through the medium of the *Record*, and expressed "distress" and "dismay" at the charges they had formulated, but acknowledged that if they were true, Great Britain would deserve the condemnation of the civilised world. (Aug. 19, 1901. See *Manchester Guardian*, Aug. 22, 1901.)

> That our government have made mistakes we admit, but that we have been inhuman, oppressive, and unrighteous, we emphatically and indignantly deny.... Terrible as the farm burning has been, it was only ordered when absolutely necessary by a British general whose character for humanity and godliness is beyond dispute."
>
> The Boer women and children, were crowded into camps because they could not be kept alive in any other way. Their own friends could not help them, and starvation stared them in the face. No doubt they have suffered hardships, but so have our own soldiers and civilians. No doubt the death-rate in the Concentration Camps has been lamentably high, especially among children, but so has it been in our own camps amongst strong, seasoned men. . . . The best answer to your unhappy charge of cruelty to women and children is that the Boers themselves sent their families for protection to British territory, and that Mr. Kruger left his wife behind in Pretoria under British rule.
>
> ******
>
> Note:—Dr. Chavasse omits to state that this was only done by "surrendered" Boers, whose families had special facilities. Mrs. Kruger remained in her own house, not in a camp. These had not then been thought of.
>
> ******
>
> The great mass of Evangelical Christians I am sure would support the Government policy, because it involves the complete civilisation of South Africa and the evangelisation of the native races. (The bishop may be unaware of the Dutch activity in

missions to the coloured races.)

Dr. Chavasse concluded by saying he felt sure the Swiss Alliance had acted on "seriously defective information."

It was to this letter of the Bishop of Liverpool that Sir Neville Chamberlain, with his wide knowledge of military affairs, replied in words which perhaps few people in the country have yet had an opportunity of reading. (*Manchester Guardian*, Aug. 29. Letter from Field-Marshal Sir N. Chamberlain to the Bishop of Liverpool. —

He (a commander) is held responsible to his own nation for conforming to the dictates of humanity, and further, any departure therefrom deserves, in the words of Dr. Chavasse, the condemnation of the civilised world. The right reverend prelate emphatically and indignantly denies that any measures taken during the war have been 'inhuman, oppressive, and unrighteous.' I am unable to concur in that conclusion. . . . We have the assurance of Dr. Chavasse that he read the appeal of the Swiss Alliance with 'distress and dismay.' What then must have been the distress and dismay of the simple Swiss Protestant ministers to discover that a prelate of the Church of England could view as unavoidable the horrors that had already devastated and are still devastating the two Boer States?

Never before has anything approaching to such wholesale destruction or abduction of families been enacted by a British Army. . . . The existence of Concentration Camps is justified by the reverend prelate on the plea that starvation stared the women and children in the face. It was so because their homes were burnt over their heads and the food they contained carried away or destroyed. Further, where is any analogy to be found, as referred to by the bishop, between helpless females and infants suffering rigorous treatment, and the condition of the troops, who are only discharging their duties as soldiers employed on active service?

So ignorant of facts, or so blunted have become the minds of our people on the subject of the women and children, that they have come to believe that the Press is justified in extolling the great kindness and liberality which have been shown to these poor prisoners.

Perhaps the best way of giving some idea of the loss of life that has taken place among the women and children in the

Concentration Camps during the past month of July, is to give the following figures, (subsequently much increased), which are taken from the Governments return:—

| Women in camp. | 31,225 | Died | 187 |
| Children in camp. | 44,594 | Died | 1117 |
| Total. | 75,819 | | 1304 |

These figures, reduced to a few simple words, imply that about ten women and children have died in the Concentration Camps in July, as compared to one who would have died in London. Who is guilty for the excess of the nine?

My letter may be ended by calling to mind the humanising words of the Scotch peasant poet Burns—

*These movin' things ca'd wives and weans*
*Wad move the very heart of stanes.*

Twice during the autumn Dr. Haldane wrote, (*Westminster Gazette*, Sept. 29 and Dec. 4), drawing attention to the death-rates of the camps, and also to the scale of rations as affecting it.

The months following those upon which his calculations were based were, of course, still more disastrous to life. He says—

I venture to think that the apparent apathy with which these returns are received depends largely on the fact that to most persons the significance of a high death-rate is not easy to grasp. The following analysis of the figures for the last three months may therefore be of service, as showing roughly the deaths among Boer women and children which may be put down to insanitary surroundings, as compared with deaths which might be expected under normal conditions:—

| | Actual deaths. | Deaths under normal conditions. | Deaths due to insanitary surroundings. |
| --- | --- | --- | --- |
| Women | 606 | 96 | 510 |
| Children | 3245 | 272 | 2973 |

The deaths under normal conditions are calculated from the last decennial return for England and Wales, children being taken as under fifteen years, and women as averaging about forty years old.

The actual normal death-rates are not, of course, available; but the figures given are more likely to be too high than too low.— Letter to *Westminster Gazette*, by Mr. T. S. Haldane, M.D.F.R.S.

Dr. Haldane's second letter is of importance, showing as it also does the insufficient food allowed the soldiers, on the basis of which ration the women's allowance appears to have been drawn up.

In addition, it must be remembered that not infrequently the supply ran short of the allowed weights, and the quality was inferior. He writes—

Dec, 3.

On November 28, I addressed to the editor of the *Times* a letter (which has not yet appeared) on the Concentration Camp statistics, and at the end I referred to the inadequacy of the rations specified in the recent Blue Book. As the question of diet in these camps is one of immediate importance, I venture to write to you more fully on the same subject.

In any diet the most elementary condition which requires to be fulfilled is that the food should contain a sufficient amount of available potential energy to support the activities which are indissolubly bound up with life. The actual requirements of the body, as regards potential energy, have for long been clearly established by numerous experiments; and it is generally admitted that for an adult the energy required is equivalent to about 3,000 calories (units of heat).

For children, the amount is, of course, a good deal less; but in proportion to its weight a child requires far more food than an adult If the food is insufficient, the body supplies the deficient material at the expense of its own tissues. When the insufficiency is only a slight one, the balance is gradually re-established at a lower level of nutrition.

If the insufficiency is great, death occurs—usually from intercurrent disease—after a period which varies from a few weeks in the case of absolute starvation, to many months, or even years, in partial starvation. In children, this period is shorter.

On looking over the diets specified in the Blue Book, I have been able to come to no other conclusion than that grave mistakes have been made as regards their sufficiency. Nor can I find any evidence that these mistakes have been clearly recognised or more than partially rectified.

The supposition that any British officer would deliberately un-
derfeed women and children under his care is out of the question.

The mistakes have undoubtedly been made in complete ignorance, for which it will probably be found that the combatant
officers are in no way responsible.

After discussing the subject with others who are more familiar
with military matters, I feel little doubt that the miscalculations
have had their origin in official ideals as to the amount of food
required by a soldier.

The diets of the Concentration Camps seem to have been
calculated by comparison with the food allowance which still
constitutes the so-called 'daily ration' of a British soldier on a
peace footing.

In the case of the inmates of the Concentration Camps, a certain addition has even been made to this 'daily rations,' in order,
apparently, to leave no doubt as to the sufficiency of the allowance.

The normal energy requirements of the body at the respective
ages referred to being taken as equal to 100, the actual energy
supplied in the British soldier's 'daily ration' and the Concentration Camp rations are stated approximately in the following
table.

The references are to pages in the Blue Book.

In the case of children's rations the probable mean age of the
children is stated:—

|  |  | Percentage supplied of what is required. |
|---|---|---|
| British soldier's "daily ration" . . . . . | | 48 |
| Class 2 (p. 21). Families of prisoners and men on commando, December, 1900—March, 1901, Transvaal. | Adults . . . . | 57 |
| | Children, mean age 6½ . | 65 |
| Class 1 (p. 21). And all "refugees" after March 1, 1901. | Adults . . . . | 63 |
| | Children, mean age 6½ . | 75 |
| "Amended" ration (pp. 37, 101). O. R. Colony. | Adults . . . | 50 |
| | Children, mean age 8 (?) . | 97 |
| "Amended" ration (pp. 194, 225). Transvaal. | Adults . . . | 61 |
| | Children, mean age 9. . | 107 |
| | Children, mean age 3½ . | 81 |
| Kaffir ration (p. 37). O. R. Colony. | Adults . . . | 85 |
| | Children, mean age, 6·5 . | 122 |

188

Note:—The British soldier's figure is, in my own opinion, an over-estimate of what is supplied as compared with what a young soldier absolutely requires if he is to become really efficient.

The table speaks for itself. Nothing but seething discontent, an enormous death-rate, and very great expenditure in hospitals, doctors, nurses, 'medical comforts,' etc., can be expected in Concentration Camps with a dietary calculated on the same scale as the miserable official allowance to the British soldier. A soldier can supplement his ration out of his scanty pay, but a 'refugee' in a Concentration Camp, and without money, is in a very different position.

An article in the *British Medical Journal*, quoted in the *Times*, Nov. 8, 1901, thus summarised the probable causes of mortality and suggested remedies:—

The camps appeared to be a military necessity, and it was doubtless regarded as more humane thus to mass the women and children than to leave them on their half-ruined homesteads. The results have been calamitous. . . . The conditions of life in these camps are doubtless responsible for the greater part of the evil. Dysentery and diarrhoea, enteric fever, and pneumonia, as well as measles, probably prevail in them. The habits of the Boers probably make matters worse.

But this is simply a further reason for not permitting the continuance of the concentration of persons under such unsatisfactory conditions. . . . But the whole matter is really one of sanitary administration, and we should like to have an assurance that the direction of these camps has been placed in the hands of experienced sanitary administrators, with authority and power to carry out the changes necessitated by the proved facts as to the unhealthy condition of the people detained in the camps.

The important point for the moment is what can be done immediately? The one essential thing is to split up the camps into a number of much smaller camps on new and unpolluted soils. Large numbers of cases of measles cannot be safely treated together, unless under the most favourable hygienic conditions. Failing these conditions, the aggregation of patients must be stopped.

What are the causes which are likely to have been productive of the present excessive mortality in the Concentration Camps?

1. Almost certainly measles and complicating pneumonia are not entirely the cause. When the story is completely told, it will most probably be found that diarrhoea and enteric fever have also been prevalent.

2. Some importance must be attached to the fact that a large proportion of the Boer children have probably never been previously exposed to measles, and have now been exposed under conditions which ensure concentration of the poison of this disease. The conditions are analogous to those of a workhouse into the babies' ward of which measles is accidentally introduced. Those who have experienced how fatal measles is under such circumstances will have little difficulty in partially realising the state of matters in the Boer camps.

3. The Boers are stated to be dirty in their personal habits, and difficult to control in regard to the elementary rules of sanitation necessary to maintain a large camp in a wholesome condition. Probably this is true. It is one of the strongest reasons for not permitting dense aggregations of people possessed of habits which are only safe in detached and lonely houses.

4. Possibly unsuitable food and deficient clothing, although every effort has doubtless been made to remedy these defects, greatly aided in producing the result.

5. In view of the excessive mortality from enteric fever among our own troops, to which we have repeatedly drawn attention, we are bound to suspect that the same unreadiness to make provision for probable contingencies has characterised the action of the responsible army authorities in this as in other health matters. The sanitary control of the large camps, whether for soldiers or for Boers, has been most unsatisfactory.

One of the most important recommendations of the recent South African Hospitals Commission was as to the necessity for appointing special sanitary officers, whose duty it would be to organise and control the sanitary arrangements of all large camps. The sanitary, as distinguished from the medical, organisation of the South African Army has been attended by calamities for which the War Office must be held responsible.

What remedies are practicable?

1. The immediate organisation of sanitary control of the camps on a scale sufficient to meet all requirements.

2. Splitting up of the camps into a much larger number of units, each having a separate organisation, visits from camp to camp being strictly prohibited. . . . Uncomplicated measles needs to be treated in a separate building from measles associated with broncho-pneumonia; and if disinfection is not required for measles, it is desirable for its complications. Such methods may not be practicable under the conditions of camp life. The alternative is that no considerable number of susceptible children must be grouped together.

The camps must be split up and to some extent scattered. This point is clearly brought out by Sir Walter Foster in a letter to the *Times*, and he also lays stress on the importance of placing the camps on nonpolluted soils."

Imperceptibly, by the force of facts, opinion was changing in England, and a desire to have the camps reorganised was forming. Warning notes of the serious position began also to filter through from South Africa. One of the first of these to write was Mr. Dewdney Drew.

There are just two points, on which I feel impelled to write to you, and they both relate to an essential mistake which we are making about the Boer people. They are not a people to be cowed, nor are they a people to forget This bears, for one thing, very relevantly on our conduct of the war. Every piece of terrorism, every 'severe measure,' has so far recoiled on ourselves. This burning and pillaging committed by our troops, and to which I can testify (having ridden hundreds of miles in their track), has merely put the very devil into the Boers. I have heard from their own lips and from the lips of their women how it has affected them.

To give names, I was dining one day last month with the mother and two sisters of the Commandant Kritzinger, now invading the Colony, and with the Miss Olivier (daughter of the *commandant* of that name) whom he is engaged to marry. These ladies are refugees in Basutoland, where I met them. They were unanimous in ascribing the continued resistance of their relatives and countrymen to the above-mentioned cause.

At Thaba 'Nchu, where my brother-in-law's farm is situated, there lives a Mrs. Adams, whom I have known for years. She is an English lady and ministers to the sick in hospital, showing them charity regardless of their nationality. She told me, too, as I travelled homewards from Basutoland, that the wounded Boers were giving the same explanation. From what I have personally seen of the ravages inflicted by our troops on the Free State by fire and pilfering, there are revelations yet to be made to the British public which will fulfil Mr. Kruger's forecast and indeed 'stagger humanity.'

I know nothing personally about 'Concentration Camps,' having never visited one. However, I have, when riding on the *veld*, met convoys of women and children, and have also seen them huddled by scores in open trucks which stood by the hour at Springfontein railway station until the line could be cleared for forwarding them to the Bethulie Camp. The last-mentioned contingent had come in the same day from Fauresmith owing to 'clearing' operations in that district There were, of course, inevitable discomforts, let such removals be planned as wisely as possible, but I do not think the Boer women would make much of these. What will never die from the memory of the survivors is the horrors which we have allowed to fall upon them, not, of course, intentionally, but through sheer muddlement.

The government returns as to the mortality in these camps furnish only too convincing proof, and I venture to predict that Miss Hobhouse's findings will be virtually endorsed by the Ladies' Commission which has now sailed. It is the same kind of neglect which caused the hospital scandals, and which I have with my own eyes witnessed going on in the fighting districts and in the near presence of the enemy.

A general sets out to 'clear' a given stretch of country. He is going to scoop human lives wholesale into his net, but has no notion of what he will do with them when caught. The capture effected, he dumps the unfortunates down on the nearest camp, whose officer is at his wits' end to provide for them. Then the troubles begin: children die for lack of milk, women are un-tended in child-birth, and the g

overnment have to compile a set of 'returns' which make an Englishman's ears tingle as he reads.—Letter from Rev. Dewdney Drew to Secretary of Colonial Mission, dated Cape Town,

July 24, See *Daily News,* Aug. 1901.

This tingling of the ears does not appear to have communicated itself to the *Daily Mail,* (Dec. 27.) Its correspondent wrote optimistically and reported that "the Commission was well satisfied with the condition of the camps generally." The more observant agent of the Central News Service spoke in strong terms, distinctly asserting that the death-rate had become so formidable as to become quite the most important question of the day. (Central News Special Service, Pretoria, Dec. 6. See *Manchester Guardian,* Dec. 30, 1901.)

A change of some kind, he argued, must be made at once, as "we are not warring against women and children." He considered "the extraordinary increase of disease due to the heavy rainfall which has converted the tent cities into veritable death-traps. The most feasible plan would be to allow them to choose some village not occupied by us, to allow them doctors, nurses, food, and liberty"; or, as an alternative, distribution in Cape Colony.

On the Continent and in America, where interest in and information about the camps had all along been more general than at home, philanthropic feeling was deeply moved, and on several occasions found public expression. At midsummer, Madame Waszkléwicz, President of the Women's League for the Promotion of International Disarmament, had addressed a letter to Mr. Brodrick pleading for the Boer women in the name of the women of Europe and America. (The Hague, June 23. See *Algemen Handelsblad.*) She offered to relieve the military authorities of all burden by forming an International Committee, on which Englishwomen should be represented, to deal with the care of the Boer families, and she suggested that the example of Sir George White at Ladysmith should be followed on a large scale, and all the women handed over to a piece of neutral ground. Her offer was refused.

The appeal of the Swiss Evangelical Alliance has already been alluded to; at Christmas, the women of Switzerland published an open letter to the women of England, and the women of Germany made a strong appeal in the same month. Numerous meetings were held and resolutions passed in America and elsewhere.

The mortality of September had been so high, (see Appendix B, also Cd. 819), that details were anxiously expected, and these were given for the Transvaal Camps in the first Blue Book issued in November. With the exception of Bloemfontein for one month only, no monthly reports have been provided for the Orange River Colony Camps.

It was realised that the country was getting roused; numerous letters were written to the papers, and the city of Manchester sent up a largely signed petition to the government, headed by the Lord Mayor and the Bishop. The issue of the second Blue Book, (Cd. 853, Dec. 1901), showed that the Colonial Office had already assumed control, and that Mr. Chamberlain was applying his energy and business faculties to the remodelling of the camps. Some of the suggestions urged by the Ladies' Commission were also being carried out.

The telegraphic correspondence reveals some impatience on the part of Lord Milner and others in South Africa at the importance attached to this work, and the attention required for its details, but Mr. Chamberlain rightly insisted; the order was at last given that no expense was to be spared, (Cd. 853), and Lord Onslow, speaking at Crewe in December, assured the country that "the civil authority under the Colonial Office had now taken over all the Concentration Camps from the military authorities. No pains and no money would be spared to put the camps in the most efficient and healthy condition possible."

Thus, the gloom of the year 1901 was lightened at its close with the hope that substantial reforms were really inaugurated and would work speedy and effective amelioration.

Camp huts, 1901

# CHAPTER 4

# Women in 1901, as Described by Others (Unofficial)

*Life may change, but it may fly not;*
*Hope may vanish, but can die not;*
*Truth be veiled, but still it burneth;*
*Love repulsed, but it returneth.*
*Yet were life a charnel where*
*Hope lay coffined with despair;*
*Yet were truth a sacred lie;*
*Love were lust—if Liberty*
*Lent not life its soul of light,*
*Hope its iris of delight.*
*Truth its prophet's robe to wear,*
*Love its power to give and bear.*—Shelley.

Early in the year (Feb. 7, 1901), Mr. Rowntree thus describes the more highly blessed camps of Cape Colony and Natal. In a former chapter, it has been shown how Port Elizabeth Camp was brought under excellent conditions in the end of 1900. Mrs. Fawcett has spoken of this camp as a "show camp." Mr. Rowntree writes—

> I was given a pass by Mr. Hess, who remarked he wished us to see the camp so that we could assure people in England how well its occupants were treated. He put a note in the margin of the letter he gave me to the captain at the head of the military organisation of the town, to the effect that it would have its use in England. There was barbed-wire fencing to a considerable height all round, and sentries with their rifles on at least three sides of the square. A sensible Afrikander woman came to greet

us. She took us into a hut. The iron walls were bare, and the room resounded with the voices of the infants in the adjoining shelters. Chairs are scarce, but neighbours lend willingly, and boxes are gracefully tendered also.

******

Note—The conduct of the inmates is excellent; they have a great regard for the matron. Miss Hauptfleisch, of whom I cannot speak too highly. She has managed the camp and the inmates with a wonderful tact and skill, and the present efficient state of the camp is entirely due to her exertions and sacrifice of her time and health to her sisters in distress.

There is a good deal of crowding in some of the rooms, as many as ten, eleven, and fourteen persons living in one room together.

Charles P. Piers, Captain.

March 27, 1901.—Cd. 819.

******

There are 330 souls within the wire fence, 80 of them are mothers, 10 of them are persons of culture and means, the rest being absolutely destitute. The needs for the body are fairly met They have clothing for the present, but the problem is, and will be, to keep the mind healthy and occupied and free from self-brooding in this life of enforced idleness. In the hospital today there were only two mothers and two newly-arrived infants. Any news we could give was drunk in most eagerly. One person with whom we conversed had heard nothing of her husband for many months, and evidently yearned for tidings.

We came later, to Pietermaritzburg (February 14), and learnt that of the 1,800 persons in the camp here at Christmas, some 500 persons have been taken to Howick. This camp became unmanageably large. I fancy several children died, and that changes were needed. The colonel is evidently a humane man, desirous to act for the best on the limited means allowed him. The food, said to have been insufficient, is now said to be improved, but is not apparently always up to the mark, and barely sufficient

We have spent the afternoon at the camp. The thermometer was 95° in the shade. It is a vast space, almost like a deer park, on a slope, with much long coarse grass. The Rev. Mr. Rousseau, who is able to go into and come from the camp as he pleases, drove us right in without challenge. We saw many boys about, and feared we should miss the school, but soon came on a biggish tent, bursting with boys and girls. The head teacher is a young man, a British subject who did not fight, but it was thought best for the Empire that he should live in a gaol, and so he did for eight months. He still thinks, poor man, that he should have been charged with some offence and tried, but this is a vain thought, and he is perhaps hardly sufficiently thankful that he is now moved to a camp.

We visited several tents. One old man had got a protection order for his farm, but some dynamite was found on the line about six miles away. He knew nothing whatever about it, but he and his wife were called out, and the house fired. They were very quietly sad. Many of the women had had their furniture, indeed practically all their goods except a little clothing, confiscated, without any receipt or attempt at remuneration, because their husbands or sons were on commando. In some cases, this has been done to women whose husbands or sons are in Ceylon.

One of them burst into tears when she said they took a lamp which her son had made for her, though she pleaded for it. Speaking generally, such statements were never proffered, only given in answer to questions, and often with remarkable absence of colouring. One lady said she would gladly shake hands with English soldiers, they often shared their rations with the hungry, but she would not with the officers, who sent them away hungry and cold on long journeys. One had come, with thirty-six others, in an open truck, in cold weather, for a day and a night.

To one tent the news was brought us that more prisoners were coming. Their quick eyes caught them detraining when I could not distinguish them at all. In an hour, the new prisoners came. A few soldiers first, who looked good-natured, and as if not particularly relishing their work, then a long straggling procession, broken often into clumps. Mostly mother and children, many babies in arms, many toddling alongside, clutching gown or hand, most of them weary, sad, grave, a look of destitution imprinted on faces and clothing alike. One little lad of seven or eight was so tired that he lay down twice on the grass, and was made to go on. All, down to the infants, had some little thing, presumably the most precious or necessary, in one hand, a water-bottle, a kettle, a small bundle of clothing; here and there

THE LAST OF SEVEN, WENE, 1901.

a bag with a few provisions; one lone woman was cherishing a cat.

One old woman, with a little child by her side, came in a *rickshaw*, the rest were all on foot and with no umbrellas against the sun. The general effect was very sombre and infinitely sad. I saw two or three in tears, and one had to move away by one's self for a time. My wife followed them to see if anything could be done in the way of food, but a cordon of soldiers was formed, and all others were kept away. We could not well object, but out of their penury the older prisoners were evidently very anxious to supply the newcomers with coffee, and share what they had.

February 27,

What is to be the future? The past is mainly very sad—the 200 persons we saw ten days ago, had been slowly collected. One woman, with a good face, told me today that she and her children had been driven for two days to Standerton, where they stopped nine days. Then they were a day and a night in open trucks, coming here, with no rations, and only the bare tent when they got here at sundown; no bedstead, no bedding. They are many of them fine people, very much like Lowland Scotch. Their hearts unlock quickly, even to kind looks. Your head may soon swim with quietly told experiences, and now and then you may get tired of one or two interposing too often, but as a whole they have the true strength and dignity of self-restraint.

Mr. Rowntree continues—

March 1

Large numbers of homeless women and children are being drafted down continually. There are about 3000 bereft of almost everything but a bundle of bedding and a box of some sort. The authorities begrudge rations to those who have any means. Mrs. showed me a formal notice she had received from the camp *commandant* stating he was ordered to discontinue rations to her, understanding that she had means of her own. . . . The British Government has confiscated most of these people's effects. Is it intended that they should become pauperised? As it is they have to beg of a Dutch Reformed minister for a postage stamp or a needle.

There was something indescribably sad, as Mr. Rowntree shows, in watching the passing group of exiled women.

A lady of Thaba 'Nchu, writing to her sister on the 29th of May cries:—

Oh! how *weary* I am of it all! The never-ending stream of poor women and children still continues to flow through here on the way to that awful camp in Bloemfontein, where they are dying off like sick sheep. About a month ago all the women from just round about Prynnaberg—about 230—were brought here and 'plumped' down. They were crowded into the Dutch Reformed Church, schoolroom and hall, and left here in the greatest discomfort for three weeks; many got ill, one woman and one child died here—the woman was Mrs. Van Wijk, Aunt Maria Sephton's mother. She was 77 years old, weak and ill, and not fit to be carted over the country in all sorts of weather in an old jolty buck-waggon.

The Van Niekerks and Boschmans and all the women you knew round here were of the lot. I used to go and see them and 'hold their hands' for them, there is so very little one can do for these poor women. If you see what they have to put up with, it just makes one 'boil.' . . . How I do boil, and one has to keep it all bottled in and 'keep smiling.'

Well, these poor women show one how to take things bravely; they laugh, and seem to get as much fun out of their misfortunes as they can; I do admire them. But there is the other picture too; lots of them just used to come and sit and weep out their miseries to me in my room, because I was your sister. Well, last week they were all packed into more buck-waggons to be taken to the 'camp'; when they got to the waterworks, the order came for no oxen to cross the river on account of the rinderpest having broken out here. So, these poor women are stranded on the flats with hardly any food and next to no shelter. They had been there for days when I heard from them, and I can't say if they have been taken on to Bloemfontein yet Some of them said they would let me know what became of them eventually if they survive it all, poor souls. The sick (about six families) are still here."

Mrs. P. Maritz Botha writes—

On presenting my ticket for admittance (to the camp at Johannesburg), the guard informed me that there were two or three thousand women there, also that he had just come from Potchefstroom District, where he had spent five or six months, being one of a column employed in destroying homesteads and farms in that district, and bringing in the women and children into the camp there. He condemned the practice, saying that retribution was sure to follow on the English.

In the camp, I found a lot of sick lying about in the iron sheds— ill principally with measles—though other diseases were rife. These people were of the superior class of Boers. In the small space allotted to each family were to be seen sick, dying, and dead.

I found one poor woman with her face turned to the wall, weeping bitterly. On my questioning her as to the cause of her grief, she turned round and said that she had just lost her sixth and last child, all having died in camp.

★★★★★★

Note:—Housing.—This leaves much to be desired. There is no provision for privacy . . . nothing less suitable for families could well be conceived. I leave out of the question such objections as the want of privacy. . . . There are to my mind more serious objections.

The buildings are very draughty, and in winter will be very cold. The earth between the floors will soon become very foul, etc.

Dr. Turner.

Cd. 819.

Month ending 31st May, population . . . 3379
During May, deaths      . . . .79
The health of the Burgher Camp, Johannesburg, during the month of May has generally been exceedingly good.(!)

Dr. Crook (Medical Officer).

Cd. 819.

Dr. Croizier Durham entirely failed to cope with the situation, and I returned him to the coast, appointing Dr. Crook in his stead. Already an improvement is noticeable in the general health and appearance of the women and children, owing mainly to his efforts and the assistance rendered by a committee of the members of the local Dutch Reformed Church, who have provided nurses and some medical comforts for the invalids.

Report of G. W. Goodwin,
General Superintendent.

Cd. 819.

★★★★★★

A great and righteous complaint amongst the women was, that for all the divers diseases and illnesses rife in camp, from enteric and measles to a broken leg, only two kinds of medicines were used, and these were served from two separate vessels. This treatment naturally caused suspicion, and the result was that the women took to what are called home remedies.

As far as rations are concerned, thanks to Governor Mackenzie, just at this time there were no complaints about the food, which a little while back had been practically unfit for consumption. Also at this time the D.R.C ministers were allowed to supply small sums of money, which helped to build small ovens.

The method of taking these women from their homes was truly conspicuous for its barbarity. They were literally robbed of everything they had before being sent away; and I know women, once well off, who were carted about the country for months without once being able to change their dress. Some were made to give up their rings, others even their precious heirloom Bibles.

One woman told me that, having hidden £35 in her breast for safety and to feed her children with, she was approached by an officer, who snatched open her dress and took the money from her.

I personally, on visiting some of the poor families at night who were brought into Pretoria, have seen a father, mother, and eight children huddled together in two tiny zinc rooms, with nothing either above or below them for warmth and protection; and I have given bedding from my son's bed just to aid these people who were left in this neglected state for weeks at a time.

Mr. H. A. Cornelissen and Mr. F. Smits Verburg, now in Europe, were both in the Concentration Camp at Irene as prisoners, and had therefore good opportunities for describing the life of the camp. Mr. Cornelissen was a war correspondent with the Boer forces, and, after being six months in the two camps of Irene and Pietersburg, was allowed to leave for Europe in October 1901. He attributes the high mortality to various causes. First, the exhausted condition of the women and children on their arrival at the camps; secondly, the fact of the inmates being housed in tents—no Boer would ever think of living in a tent with his family in winter on the South African *veld*;

thirdly, the inadequate medical aid.

★★★★★★

The sheep supplied have undoubtedly been in very poor condition. . . . . On the whole, the ration satisfies the people, especially since children were allowed 1 lb. of flour a day, instead of ½ lb. as formerly. The flour supplied has been of very good quality on the whole.

N. J. Schotz, Supt., Irene.

Cd. 814.

★★★★★★

His most serious complaint is about the bad quality and insufficiency of the food supplied. The meat generally had to be thrown away. He says that but for private charity the women and children would have perished with the cold. His story is endorsed by Mr. Smits Verburg (see *De Telegraaf*, Amsterdam)—

On the 2ist of April last I arrived at the Concentration Camp at Irene. It was a Sunday afternoon. There was to be no distribution of rations before Monday morning at eight. We had to live meanwhile as best we could manage. On Monday morning, we received 7 lbs. of Australian flour, 4 English oz. of coffee (roasted maize), 7 English oz. of sugar (black and tart), and half an oz. of rough salt. Every Wednesday and Saturday was served out, besides the above, an English pound of mutton, the sheep being so lean that they much resembled greyhounds.

What they got too little in meat was made up for by the living things which the flour contained—black corn-weevils and beetles. And hundreds of women I saw sifting such flour, without complaining, to free it from living animals and mouldy clots. I myself took it back for Mrs. Aart van Wijk, Renosterpoort, Zoutpansberg, and after a deal of talking and flattery managed to get for her as much other flour as the mouldy clots and weevils weighed which she had sifted from her flour.

One round tent was assigned to every twelve persons to live in, without considering whether they belonged to the same family, so that they lay very close together, almost the one on the other; which, however, had one advantage, that the want of a sufficient quantity of bedclothes was not so severely felt during the bitterly cold nights of that time, as otherwise would have been the case.

★★★★★★

Note:—The weather has been extremely cold at night, and on some days the wind extremely cold. I have done all in my power to assist the people and minimise their hardships, by issuing to them blankets, sheepskins, and canvas coverings. On the whole they are fairly comfortable. Complaints are inevitable in a camp with 4500 people. . . . The scarcity of wood has been the cause of considerable anxiety, and is one of the greatest hardships of the people. . . . There is more than enough work for another medical officer to do in the camp, as it is quite impossible for a man to visit more than fifty patients and give them proper attention in one day.

Dr. Green's Report.

Cd. 819.

★★★★★★

When I arrived, there was one doctor to look after the patients, afterwards there were two, but this number cannot be considered sufficient for a camp of 4000 souls. The number of funerals was every day ominously great.

Mrs. Bodde, an English lady whom I have the pleasure of knowing, wrote thus about Irene Camp. Parts of her letter were published last summer—

May 23, 1901.

When I left Pretoria there were 5000 men and children in the camp at Irene, and 1000 were reported to be sick. The camp itself is on the site of a camp previously occupied by the British soldiers when they were prisoners in Pretoria. The ground is high and sloping. The camp is surrounded by a fence of barbed wire, and guarded by sentries, who refuse to permit any entrance or egress excepting under military pass. There is no truth in the statement, which to my surprise I find repeated in London, that the women and children went to the camps by their own consent, or are willing to remain there.

In almost every case, these women, with their little ones, have been taken by force from their homes at a moment's notice. They have not even been allowed to take with them a morsel of food, or to be removed in their own carts. They were taken by the soldiers, and put into open cattle trucks and waggons, while their own beautiful waggons, carts, and vehicles were burnt before their eyes.

The work of the destruction of the goods of these unfortunate people was not by any means confined to food-stuffs or to houses that might shelter the enemy. Thousands of bales of valuable wool, in the Standerton and Ermelo districts, were destroyed by first saturating them with paraffin oil, and then setting them on fire. Bales of wool cannot be used for food.

The impression seems to prevail in this country that the work of farm-burning has ceased. Nothing could be further from the truth. When a sweeping operation takes place, and a column goes out for the purpose of denuding the country of supplies, the farmhouses are uniformly first gutted and usually set on fire. When Mrs. Botha received permission from Lord Kitchener to visit her husband, she crossed the country in a Cape cart, and stayed each night at a farmhouse *en route*.

After staying five days with her husband, she set out to return to Pretoria. She could not come back the way she went, because all the houses which had given her shelter had been burnt to the ground in that brief interval. The work of destruction is usually done in a desperate hurry, for the soldiers are afraid that they may be usually set a house on fire, or blow up the walls with dynamite if it is strongly built. The crops are destroyed, hundreds of bags of grain are ripped open and trampled underfoot, fruit trees are cut down, and all this has to be done in a few hours.

In most of these houses which have been destroyed are stored excellent tents, used by the young people of the Boers when they go out into the *veld* to pasture their cattle. If they had been permitted to remove them they would at least have had shelter over their heads, but no woman was allowed to bring with her a tent to protect her from the sun by day or the cold by night. The tents were burnt with all the other furniture of the household; and, thus beggared and homeless, they were carted off across the *veld*, and consigned to the camps, in which they remain prisoners to this day.

When I left Pretoria it was already very cold, even inside my own home. What it must have been outside in the tents on the bleak hillside I shudder to think. Yet that was only the beginning of winter. The number of deaths occurring among the children is appalling. Unless the death-rate is checked there will be no children left in the camp when the winter is over. The women and children sleep on straw mattresses, on the bare ground. The tents are without lining, and they afford hardly any protection against wind, nor have the women adequate clothing.

We are orphans and fatherless, our mothers are as widows.

Some were allowed to snatch a blanket from the bonfire which was made of all their goods and possessions, but if they had only been allowed to bring their bedding they would at least have been saved some of the intense misery to which they are at present doomed. As a rule, they were allowed to bring nothing with them but the clothes which were on their backs. There is also hardly any fuel in the camps, it being exceedingly scarce.

While the shelter is miserably inadequate, the rations are very bad. The military authorities have entered into an arrangement with a contractor, by which he supplies the camp with food for adults. No special food is supplied for children. The rations supplied by the contractor, which are by no means the regular army rations, consist of flour that is often bitter and unfit to be eaten. Even if it were good, the women are not accustomed to white flour, and do not like it. They have always used either whole ground meal or Boer meal, but white flour many of them touched for the first time when their day's ration was handed to them.

The coffee is hardly deserving of the name, and appears to be made largely of roasted acorns. The sugar is the result of the skimmings of the sugar boiler. The food is quite inadequate for adults, and the poor children simply starve and die. The mortality among children is really terrible. From one farm alone ten children have died, and there are cases in which every child in the family has perished. How can it be otherwise? Children under seven years of age require to have some kind of milk diet. Of course, I am well aware that milk fresh from the cow is impossible. Every milch cow is commandeered for the use of the sick in the military hospital, but that is no reason why children should not be supplied with condensed milk and Mellin's food. The statement that it is impossible to supply condensed milk to the prison camps may be made here, but I never heard of any such excuse in Pretoria. I know of my own certain knowledge that there is any amount of condensed milk in Pretoria. I brought my own baby up on it for the last two years, and never had any difficulty in procuring as much as was wanted, with the exception of the first four months after the occupation of Pretoria.

Not only is there any amount of condensed milk in Pretoria, but a Hollander Charitable Committee, which was formed for the purpose of relieving the distressed women and children, actually kept many children in the camp alive by distributing condensed milk and other foods to the little ones; but for some reason or other—I think it was about the month of April—the military authorities withdrew the licence by virtue of which the Hollander Committee had been able to distribute these necessaries of life to the children, with the result that the children are dying like flies. Why they should be deprived of condensed milk and other food necessary to keep them alive I do not know.

But you can hardly be surprised if it is misinterpreted by the Dutch. They are aware that the authorities did, as a matter of policy, order that the women and families of the men still fighting should only receive half rations and no meat whatever. (See Appendix A.) Since I came to this country I hear that the rescinding of this inhuman order was attributed to pressure brought to bear on Ministers in the House of Commons. We knew nothing about that in Pretoria. All that we knew was that the foreign Consuls protested against the refusal of full rations to the women and children whose husbands were still on commando, and the distinction was blocked in deference—so we always understood—to the representations of the Consuls.

A few nurses are allowed in the camp, but the doctors do not understand the language of many of their patients, and obstacles have been placed in the way of the granting of a licence to the Hollander Society, which undertook to supply medical relief to the sufferers.

It is merely human nature that the Dutch should take a rather sinister view of these proceedings.

The desire to improve the conditions of the unfortunate inmates of this camp took the form of an appeal to the foreign Consuls for their intercession with the military authorities—

Translation,

To his Excellency D. Cinatti, Consul-General of Portugal, and the other Representatives of Foreign Powers.

Pretoria, May 25, 1901.

Excellencies,—The condition of the women and children of our *burghers*, especially of those whose men are still fighting, is of such a nature that we, the undersigned women, consider it highly necessary to call in the aid of the Consuls. These poor helpless beings suffer indescribably; they have been so weakened by bad and insufficient food that they cannot possibly withstand the ravages of disease and cold. Already the cold is intense at Irene, considered to be a warm climate. We dread to think what it must be on the high *veld*, at Middelburg, Standerton, and Vereeniging, etc.

Only very few families were allowed to bring clothing with them, the others having nothing but what they were clad in when forced to leave their homes, and those are worn and soiled. A few were also allowed to take bedding, but the majority have insufficient or none, and are compelled to lie on the cold earth, only sheltered from the bitterly cold weather by canvas. Their food is mostly unfit for consumption.

We know of a case where the mother saw three children carried away within sixteen days. They died from diarrhoea, caused by bad meat, flour, coffee, and sugar; no other food is dealt out to the imprisoned women and children. Another daughter, 13 years of age, is still lying dangerously ill. Neither soap nor candles have been given to them; these are called 'articles of luxury.' Our African nation cannot exist on flour, even when of the best quality; the poorest are used to plenty of milk, and plain, but nutritious, food.

We are convinced that (this) pitiful state of affairs is aggravated by rough and heartless men such as Superintendent Scholtz at Irene. The women prefer to starve and suffer with their children, even when twenty are herded together in one tent, almost without bedding, rather than expose themselves to insults when they approach with their needs.

Is it considered such a crime in these present days to fight for home and independence, that it is wreaked on defenceless women and helpless children, in order to compel the brave little handful of lion-hearted men to surrender? We earnestly beseech you to take steps without delay to relieve the sufferings of these unfortunate beings. Our little nation is being exterminated. Already many prisoners at Ceylon and elsewhere, and *burghers* still in the field, are, without knowing it, wifeless and childless.

With the approaching winter in view there is no time to be lost Help us, in God's name and in the name of humanity. He will bless you, and you will have our eternal gratitude.

We have the honour to be. Excellencies, your obedient and sorrowing,

(Nine Signatures.)

The appeal of May 25, after due deliberation by the consuls, was handed to Lord Kitchener, who, however, did not acknowledge it After waiting nearly five weeks, the same signatories sent in the following petition—

Translation,

To his Excellency D. Cinatti, Consul-General of Portugal, and the other Representatives of Foreign Powers.

Pretoria, July 1, 1901.

Excellencies,—The undersigned Committee of Boer ladies, in name of the Boer ladies in South Africa, having taken into consideration the serious condition of the various camps of the imprisoned women and children, of the appalling death-rates in consequence of disease brought on by cold and starvation, seeing the danger our brave little nation is running—unless speedily relieved—of being totally exterminated, are turning to you once again as our only earthly help in our great and bitter need. We earnestly beseech you without loss of time to request your governments, for the sake of humanity, to use their friendly good offices before the Government of Great Britain in favour of helpless women and tender children.

For our men we ask nothing—they are men, and well able to bear all that it has pleased Providence to lay upon them—but for their imprisoned families we demand, in common justice, from mighty and wealthy England, sufficient and better food, warm clothing and bedding; also that no obstacles be laid in our way to visit the different camps for the purpose of aiding as far as we possibly can.

They have been dragged by force from their homes, their food and clothing destroyed by fire, and are now dying by hundreds weekly for want of these necessities. To compel our brave men to surrender, their families are tortured and on the way of being rooted out Although not much is known about the many other camps scattered all over the land, you are sufficiently aware of what is taking place at Irene Camp, considered to be the best, and thus enabled to give an account thereupon to your government.

We pray to God that your endeavours may meet with success, so that relief may speedily come to these unfortunate victims of a cruel and unjust war.

We have the honour to be. Excellencies, gratefully, etc.,

(Signatures.)

Substantially the same as Mrs. Bodde's account is this one sent to England by a leading Transvaal lady—

Pretoria, May 1901.

In almost every case they (the women) have been taken from their comfortable homes at a moment's notice, and not even allowed to take a morsel of food with them. They were, and still are, thrust into open cattle trucks and waggons, while their own beautiful waggons, carts, and vehicles are being burnt before their eyes, their homes set on fire, or blown up if too strongly built. . . .

The crops must be destroyed, hundreds of bags of grain ripped open and trampled underfoot, trees cut down, in many instances *below* the grafts, all this being done in a few hours. I could mention hundreds of people I know by name and personally. In the sheep-farming districts, Standerton, Ermelo, etc., thousands of bales of wool were destroyed by first saturating them with paraffin. It is said no foodstuffs must be left on the farms to prevent the *burghers* on commando from taking them. But bales of wool cannot be used as *food*. Then they say only the farms in the neighbourhood of railway lines are destroyed. This is an untruth.

Two-thirds of the Republics, with the exception of the towns and farms of those who have surrendered, have been destroyed. The blacks of the Cape, bastards especially, take an active part in the destruction and looting of properties before the eyes of the helpless women, insulting and sometimes outraging them. We have been told—and I hope it is true—that the Australian volunteers have refused to fight because 'they did not come to fight against women and children, but men.' The condition of the women and children prisoners is terrible, too awful for words. . . .

I am only speaking of Irene—we know nothing of what happens in the other places, but it is admitted that some of the camps are very bad. Irene Camp is on a hill, very hot during the day and intensely cold at night Already the deaths daily are appalling. . . .

One of my relatives, a widow with five children, had the misfortune to stay a few days at Irene; they tell me the tents are without lining, the women and children sleep on the bare ground on straw mattresses with little covering; she had plenty of her own, but even then the cold was unbearable. They are wet with dew in summer, and now with a piercing wind blowing they might just as well be on the open *veld*; when the beds are lifted in the morning the ground is perfectly wet underneath. If these poor helpless ones had only been allowed to bring their own bedding and their own tents they would have been comfortable.

Every Boer has an excellent tent; they are used to the life, at least the younger ones pass months in tents pasturing their cattle in winter, but they stand in the bush, well sheltered with trees, with plenty of fuel and every other comfort. But here they are half-starved, brought away by force from their homes with only the clothes they stood in; one woman told me—widow of one of our first Volksraad members (who was killed at Derdepoort by the harpies, *viz. Kaffirs*, commanded by English officers)— that she was made to take off her shoes, also her daughter and little children, and to walk with bare feet to the nearest camp.

The flour portioned out to these prisoners, women and children of every age, is rotten very often, unfit for dogs; coffee, some poisonous stuff mixed with acorns; sugar, the scum of sugar boilers. I have seen samples of all these, and was assured that they prefer to starve rather than to eat or drink such stuff. We are being rooted out as a nation.

I know of several cases where the husbands are either prisoners or fighting, the wife dead with her three children, or a mother lost all six children. One woman told me her husband was at St Helena, some sons fighting, her daughter's husband killed, and that since she was brought into Pretoria, from her farm alone ten children had died.

Believe, as God is my judge, I am not exaggerating. No one can make things out worse than they are. Our land is desolate, but we can build it up again. What we cannot do is to give back to our poor prisoners when they return someday their wives and children, their relatives and friends. . . .

They say we are worse than the men, but what have the little innocent children done to starve them and in consequence to kill them with disease and cold?

This is only May, and the night is bitter cold in Pretoria; what it is on the high *veld* and cold districts, and what it will be in July, no one who knows can bear to think. I belong to the unfortunates who cannot put their thoughts on paper. It would require the pen of an Olive Schreiner (God bless her ) to describe the sufferings of our women and children. . . .

Very interesting is Miss Malherbe's short review of the work done by the volunteer nurses from Pretoria. These ladies, who had borne the burden and heat of the day for five long months, were dismissed by the Ladies' Commission.

I went out on 7th April 1901, together with Mrs. Armstrong, Mrs. Stiemens, Mrs. Vlok, Mrs. Enslin, Miss Findlay, Miss Van Warmelo, Miss Celliers, and the Misses Dürr. We all went out voluntarily, and at the request of the women in the camp; and of course, in receipt of no salary, in fact we paid the majority of railway fares from and to Pretoria. As far as our mess was concerned we drew officers' rations, also the Hollander Relief Fund gave £3 per month towards our mess.

We worked in Irene Camp for six months, being dismissed on the 10th October; there was no reason whatever given for this dismissal.

We were more than sorry to leave the camp, and the women also showed their regret by drawing up a petition praying for us to be allowed to remain. Even General Maxwell expressed to one of us his regret that we should be removed from the useful work we were doing. It did seem as if we were far more suited to attend our women, knowing them and understanding them as we did, than English nurses, who could not understand a word of their language; and seeing that we even had to interpret for the doctor himself.

The routine of the day began at 8 a.m. and consisted of visiting the two hundred or one hundred and fifty tents allotted to each of us, and there making notes of the sick, taking temperatures, and giving medical comforts (these were obtained by the patients presenting a card given by us to the doctor in charge), as

JOHANNA VAN WARMELO
One of the devoted band of Pretoria volunteer nurses.

well as applying what medical remedies were necessary.

All the tents under the charge of each person had to be visited by one o'clock p.m. each day, so naturally the quantity of work debarred us from doing as much as ought to have been done to each patient, seeing that in the case of epidemic we had as many as 500 patients. The visits of the doctors to the tents under our respective charges were divided between the morning and afternoon, half the sick being visited at a time.

In the afternoon we again visited the sick-tents to see if patients had what they required for the night; before leaving them late in the afternoon, their temperatures were again taken, this being the last attendance of the day.

★★★★★★

Notes:—

Six ladies from Pretoria, who are voluntary workers, visit in the camp and live in tents. Each lady takes a ward, and visits every tent in the morning, and then reports to the medical officer the serious cases, and does what nursing for the sick that she can. These ladies do their work well, and it would be difficult and impossible for the present medical staff to do their work without them.

Dr. Green's Report.

Cd. 819.

Six (Pretoria ladies) are permanently resident in camp. They draw rations, have a large marquee for their mess-room, and four bell-tents. They do not encourage the people to send their sick to hospital; Mr. Esselen does, but the sick remain in their tents in much larger number than is wise or right. They gave us to understand that they drew the same ration as the camp, but we found they really drew staff rations— a double quantity of meat. They said the meat was so thin that the whole of their joint ration (8 lbs.) only yielded 1 lb. of meat when separated from the bone."—Cd. 893. Report of Ladies' Commission.

It is the opinion of the Commission that the ladies from Pretoria are a dangerous element in camp. They represent an antagonism to the authority of the (Mr. Esselsen), and act as carriers and 'go-betweens' between the camp and the town.—Cd. 893.

The six ladies from Pretoria who belong to the Red Cross .. stay here for one month at a time, when they are relieved by others from Pretoria. They are of great assistance to the medical officer, and are untiring in their visits and rounds in the camps amongst the sick.

G. F Esselen, Supt.

Cd. 819.

On the whole, their tone was to weep and bewail, but take no active steps to help the people to help themselves, or make the best of things.

We called on them about 3.30 in the afternoon, and found them in their marquee doing knitting and crochet.

******

I have seen it mentioned in a Blue Book that the Committee of ladies (sent out to inspect the camps) stated that they found us crocheting; this may be so, if it was it could only have been between the hours of one and three o'clock p.m.—these being given us for our dinner and rest; and anybody knowing anything about South African life is aware that it is impossible for women to work outside between these hours; also all the crocheting done by us was for the use of the women and children in the tents.

In the Blue Book, also is stated a deliberate falsehood, *i.e.* that we neither tried nor did start either a soup kitchen or a tannery; Mrs. Armstrong made repeated requests to the superintendent for facilities to start either, but evasive answers were always given her, and certainly no facilities to start them. In one other camp visited, V. D. Hovens', near Pretoria, a soup kitchen was started by some Boer ladies, and was put a stop to by the military authorities.

Another thing, home medicines were *not encouraged* by us, but when home remedies were used they were first obtained from the store set up by military authority for the use of the camp; the selling of these home remedies was afterwards stopped, but this is how they were obtained and used in the camp. As to the people being poisoned by these home remedies, the idea is ridiculous. They consist of the simplest ingredients of the chemist art, and have been used since Boers became Boers; why they should die of these remedies the first time they were used under the English flag is inexplicable. In my five months of work in the camp neither did I attend or did I hear of any patient dying of poison from home remedies.

The hospital consists of one brick building with two large wards, and seven marquees. There are about sixty beds in all. There are three doctors, one dispenser with two assistants, two trained nurses, three untrained nurses, and several camp assistants. As far as I could judge, the hospital was in excellent order. So far as complaints are concerned I might fill a book, but to

217

shorten them as far as possible. They were as follows:—There was in vogue an extraordinary way of punishing the women and children; they were for most petty offences—such as washing clothes in a wrong place—sent off to a wire enclosure, where they had to remain for hours at a time under a small tent. Again, the supply of fuel was so badly arranged, that I have known at times that for days together the people had no fuel at all, and practically never had they enough to burn for their wants.

★★★★★★

Notes, Cd. 893:—

Some of the ladies have been in camp five months. We asked them if they thought a soup kitchen would be useful; they replied in the affirmative, but they had done nothing to start one.

The sale of Dutch medicines is prohibited, but the 'Pretoria ladies' bring them out.

There is a wired-in enclosure for unruly women.

There is no definite fuel ration in this camp. In the week previous to that of our visit the want had been specially acute.

There were many complaints in camp from lack of fuel, and Mr. Esselen seemed to experience great difficulty in supplying it Irene is as well placed geographically for the supply of wood as Johannesburg or Krugersdorp, yet, owing to lack of method, the camp is far worse off than either of the two latter camps.

★★★★★★

As far as the schools were concerned they were very much appreciated, but, as usual, with that persistent annoyance which was always put upon the people of the camps, the Dutch-speaking teachers were in a short time removed; this, as may be imagined, could only be a source of great discontent to the people and a slackening of interest in school work.

Now for the rations of the people in the camp. Before we arrived, I believe, from the tales I heard from the women in the camp, things were considerably worse, but the quantity and quality of the food they received while we were there will speak for itself. I may mention in passing that the chief food of our countrymen consists of meat, as is natural from the herds of cattle and sheep they possess; in fact, they are used to have meat once a day at least, and the richer two and three times, as well as an unlimited supply of milk and eggs. Now for such people suddenly to be put on 2½ lbs. of meat a week for grown people, and ½ lb. for children, and this meat to consist of thin, hardly-driven sheep or tinned bully-beef, the result may well be imagined, the terrible mortality in the camps.

Again, and again have I heard the people complain of the insufficiency of food, as this bad meat was only augmented by 1 lb. of meal a day for grown and ½ lb. for children, and a little coffee and sugar a day for each; rice was given once a week.

The question of beds is another sore point; there are only beds in the proportion of one to four, so that the large majority of women and children sleep on the ground; in fact, an interesting parallel might be drawn between the present lives of these unhappy people and the *Kaffirs* of the country.

Another great grievance was the treatment of the women in the camps whose husbands were still fighting at the front. In several instances I personally know of, such women were subjected to every kind of annoyance; requests which were granted to others were refused to them; in fact, they were made to feel that their husbands were considered criminals.

Another of the Pretoria lady nurses, Miss Van Warmelo, gives a description of Irene Camp and her work there—

Irene, July 20, 1901.
During the first week of my stay at Irene, (May 12-19), the total number of deaths was 12. This increased steadily, and in the middle of June it was 27; then the following week, to our horror, it was 47, and since then it has been over 45 every week. There was an epidemic of measles raging through the camp at the time, and the children died in hundreds of the complications which followed—bronchitis, pleurisy, and bronchial pneumonia. For the month of June we had no less than 137 deaths, an appalling death-rate for a population of not quite 5,000 people, and of these quite 100 were of children under 5 years of age. Now that pneumonia has set in, I am afraid the death-rate will increase.

The following is an extract from the doctor's report for the month of June 1901—

For the month, there has been a high death-rate, due—

1. To the very severe epidemic of measles.

2. To the great difference between temperatures in the tents during day and night This is especially detrimental to the chances of measles cases.

3. To the superstition and aversion many have to fresh air and water.

4. Camp life, to which the people are unaccustomed.

5. Diet is spare and fresh milk absent, the meat very often being unfit for consumption.

6. No fresh vegetables obtainable.

7. Orders for drugs and medical comforts take a long time in being executed, and then are not fully executed according to order—this resulting in our running short of necessary foods and important medicines.

Sanitary arrangements are well carried out on the whole. The water supplied from one source to six tanks in the camp, and is fairly good after analysis.

There is one thing they forgot to mention, a very important item, the over-crowding of the tents. During the whole of May I had 20 people in one of my tents—3 families: Bronkhorst, Prinsloo, and Venter, 3 married women with 17 children, and though I reported it frequently, I could not get another tent for them. Afterwards, when measles broke out amongst them, there were 11 people down at the same time, 2 women and 9 children packed in rows like herrings, with hardly standing room for anyone else between them. They all recovered from the measles, but 2 of the children have died from complications that followed afterwards. In another tent I had 19 people, 5 women and 14 children; and in *dozens* of others I had from 12 to 15.

★★★★★★

Notes Cd 819:—

I think it would be much better to get more ladies or nurses to work in the hospital, and thus relieve the trained nurses of a great deal of worry and overstrain.

Dr. Green.

The condition of the inmates . . . in the ward under Miss Van Warmelo . . . was much worse than any other portion of the camp. In some of the tents there is distinct over-crowding. In one tent, for instance, there are two women—Mrs. Bronkhurst and Mrs. Prinsloo—and nine children. Some of the children are insufficiently clad; all poorly. In another tent there are three families (Venters, Prinsloo, and Dorfling), parents and children number fourteen. All had measles. Two children died last week. One is still very ill and not likely to recover.

Report of Dr. Kendal Franks.

\*\*\*\*\*\*

Some of my tents were the oblong ones, lined, but the majority were bell-shaped and unlined, bitterly cold at night and intensely warm during the day. Even in the winter the heat during the day is almost unbearable in those bell-tents, what will it be like in our tropical summer? I slept in one of them myself two nights, and know what it means. I made many complaints about the overcrowding, and earned for myself the name of 'Agitator.' Once I appealed directly to the governor, General Maxwell, but he said there was nothing to be done, and that the empty tents would be required for new arrivals. The general has always been most courteous and kind, and I believe has done all he could to improve matters, but his power is limited apparently, and I find that in most cases it is quite useless to appeal to him.

In the Johannesburg Camp not more than 4 are allowed to sleep in a tent, and there they have large public ovens where the women can bake, and boilers always full of boiling water, and public baths where the women can bathe. Why then should there be made so much difference at Irene? We have none of those comforts, and when I spoke to the Superintendent Scholtz about it, he said that the Irene people were of the worst sort, a class utterly unused to any of the comforts of life; that they were far better off in the camp than they could ever have been in their own homes.

*It is not true.* Some of them are undoubtedly quite without education, but the majority of them are the families of rich farmers, accustomed to every comfort and even luxury of civilisation, to food of the most wholesome and nourishing description, to fine homes and warm clothing. The reason why so many of them reached the camp in a state of utter destitution is because they were torn from their homes in great haste, with nothing but the clothes they had on.

A few were allowed to take some bedding and a few bits of furniture, but these are exceptional cases. Many of these people were poverty-stricken through having been cut off from all communication with the world nearly a year, since the occupation of Pretoria. They were out of clothing, but never knew what it meant to be hungry, for they have always had more than enough to eat and drink.

The absence of their men on commando made no difference to them, sowing and ploughing and reaping went on as usual, under the superintendence of the women, who were better off for native servants during the war than in times of peace, because the *Kaffirs* were afraid of the Boers, and eager to remain on friendly terms with them, and there was no difficulty whatever in procuring as much labour as was required.

Throughout the whole war the attitude of the natives has been most favourable, and it is only in the districts occupied by British troops that they became insolent and aggressive.

The censorship is very severe, and we know next to nothing of what takes place in the outside world, but now and then some paper comes in—no one knows how—and in this way I have found out that the general opinion in England is that these families have *voluntarily* placed themselves under British protection, and left their homes for fear of the natives. Nothing can be more untrue. There were only a few families in lonely districts who had anything to fear from the *Kaffirs*, and they may have fled to the towns for safety; but not one woman that I know of—and I have had to do with *hundreds*—asked to be placed in a camp in a tent without proper food and clothing.

I see also that there is a great cry that these people should be sent back to their farms without delay. That is quite impossible. Their homes have been burnt down to the ground, their crops ruined, their trees cut down; all is desolation and blackness throughout the land.

No; England must go through what she has undertaken, and what we demand now is proper and sufficient food. Our people were well able to support themselves, they asked for *nothing*, but now that they have been ruined and deprived of all their worldly possessions, the least they can have a right to expect is that their life in camp is made bearable.

It is terrible to think of the poverty in store for them after the war. Many women told me that they saw the natives carrying away their furniture, wantonly destroying what they could not remove, ripping up eiderdowns, bolsters, and feather mattresses, and scattering their contents to the winds, slaughtering pigs and fowls, and generally carrying on the work of destruction begun by the troops.... Albums were cut up, pianos, stoves, etc., hammered to a thousand pieces under their very eyes; all the treasured relics of a lifetime were trampled in the dust

But more than all, the women and children suffered in their journey to the camps. Exposed, in some cases, for twenty days to all the inclemencies of the weather, often for days without food or water, insulted and bullied . . . objects of scorn and derision to every chance passer-by, is it any wonder that they are broken-spirited, broken in constitution, crushed and dull with the apathy of despair and of helpless misery? And yet, in my dealings with them, I was continually impressed by their patience and fortitude, their willingness to suffer and die with their children, rather than say one word to induce their husbands to surrender.

So much has been said about the rations they receive, that I doubt whether I can give you any information on the subject. I know that a few improvements have been made at Irene lately, but still things are very bad. No child can thrive on a diet consisting of ½ lb. flour and one bottle of watery milk daily, and that is what all children under five get; and then no salt, no fat is provided, flour baked with water and *nothing* else. Their elders get 1 lb. flour daily and 2 lbs. meat weekly, as well as a little coffee and sugar.

Lately the meat has always been unfit for use, and is getting worse every day. They cannot even make soup of it, even if they had something to put into the soup. We were always allowed to write orders for rice, sago, barley, maizena, soap and candles, as 'medical comforts' in case of sickness, but when the dispensary was generally out of everything it was no use whatever writing orders. And we were for three weeks without a grain of rice or barley. Sometimes for a week or ten days there was not a drop of castor or cod-liver oil to be had, and the people had to go without

That clause in the doctors' report about want of cleanliness is absurd. I can believe that enteric and malaria are caused by dirt and neglect, but certainly not pneumonia, pleurisy, and bronchitis—and that is what they are dying of. In all the time that I was at Irene I did not have a single death from typhoid, but I am afraid that when summer comes and no alterations have been made, there will be an epidemic of fever. Most of my tents are very clean, as clean as can be expected where the people live in pulverised dust, when all they possess is on the ground, and they have no soap to wash with.

★★★★★★

Note:—In all these tents, poverty, dirt, and ignorance reign supreme. . . .To see the skin (of the sick children) it would be necessary to scrape the dirt off. Under these conditions the wonder is not that so many die, but that any recover. . . . The high death-rate . . . is in no way due to want of care or dereliction of duty on the part of those responsible for this camp. It is in my opinion due to the people themselves, to their dirty habits . . . to their rooted objection to soap and water, etc. etc.

Dr. Kendal Franks.
(After a seven hours' inspection.)

Cd. 819.

★★★★★★

When the dispensary is out of candles the sick have to lie in the dark. I know of a woman in my ward, Mrs. Pretorius, who had five children down with dysentery, and she was up all night with them without light, and she had not a bit of soap with which she could cleanse their soiled linen, until I was able to help her out of a private store sent to us by kind friends in Pretoria. Our appeal for help met with so much success, that we were obliged afterwards to get a separate tent for our stores, with which we were enabled to relieve a great deal of the misery, but it would require a million of money to make life in camp endurable for women and children.

The hospital, which is situated on a site a little way from the camp, is under the charge of English nurses and an English doctor, and is consequently in very little favour with the Boers. We seldom succeeded in persuading the women to allow their children to be sent there, which was a great pity, because the hospital patients have every care and comfort. When there are quite 500 *serious* cases in camp, there are from 15 to 20 in hospital, never more, and many of these are brought in by force or after much persuasion.

We six volunteers had nothing whatever to do with the hospital—our work lay in the camp, and was unique in its way, for it

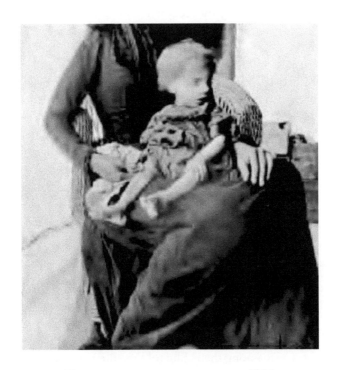

FEELING THE BRUNT OF THE WAR. 1901

brought us into daily contact with the people in their *home-life*. Every morning I went from tent to tent in my ward, one row up and another row down, issuing orders for milk, medicine, and food where necessary, making notes of the serious cases, to which I had to bring the doctor in the afternoon, encouraging, comforting, advising—no wonder the people regarded our daily visit as the one bright spot in their dreary existence.

I had at least 150 tents in my ward, over 700 people; and in one week I had 107 measles cases to report. It seems impossible for one person to undertake such a task, but of course the patients are much neglected and the nurses terribly over-worked, and yet we cannot get permission for more than six volunteers at a time. We relieve one another as frequently as possible. I hear on reliable authority that scurvy has broken out at some of the camps, and I dread to think what the condition of the people will be after another month or two of this life.

Miss Antoinette Van Brockhuizen relates an incident, one of many, which shows how unwillingly the women were brought in. The letter is dated Pretoria, September 14, 1901—

Yesterday I visited the women's camp close to Pretoria, to bring some necessaries. While there some women from Zwartruggies were brought in. Mrs. Vorster, a young woman of twenty-three years, with two children, the wife of one of our Volksraad members, was among them. She told me they had fled for three days trying to escape from being captured. At last the English surrounded them and opened fire on them. She got a bullet through her arm. She had lost an enormous lot of blood, and when she told me this she was as pale as a corpse.

After the expulsion of the volunteer nurses by the Ladies' Commission, it became increasingly difficult to obtain leave to see Irene Camp or to take relief to the people. Disquieted by rumours of the great sickness of October, Mrs. Joubert, widow of the general, made various efforts, and after obtaining a permit wrote thus—

Nov. 17.

'Till now not a soul has been allowed to visit the camps; but yesterday, after much trouble and innumerable applications, I at last obtained admission to the Irene Camp. I was desirous to see and hear for myself, after the frightful reports we were continually getting from there. And, indeed, it is awful, this distress in every degree and kind. Infinitely more terrible than it had been painted, and more awful than the wildest imaginings can picture! The people are dying like flies, of starvation, exposure, and disease. It is impossible to realise the condition and the sufferings of the women and children. Typhus is raging everywhere.

We are having an exceptionally wet summer, and heavy rains fall frequently in the evening, and again at midnight. All who know the Transvaal know these fierce storms. As the camps are generally situated on sloping ground, the water beats with the force of a torrent against the sides of the tents, flooding the whole place. Standing in deep water, the unfortunate creatures have to clutch their poor belongings, bedclothes, etc., to prevent their being carried away in the storm. Afterwards, they have to lie down to rest in several inches of mud.

If the war lasts another year, not a woman or child will be left The world knows this, and yet the mighty ones of the earth look on at these cruel murders, this barbarous slaughter. . . . The conditions in the Transvaal camps are worse than anywhere else; for everything we are at the mercy of these barbarians. No one is allowed to tend the sick except the willing tools of the officials. The men are fighting a heroic fight, and will never give in; the only result of all they hear about the awful mortality among their families is to strengthen them in endurance, determination, and courage. The burning of farms still continues. Armed *Kaffirs* in thousands are fighting in the English ranks.

On this same occasion, and with Mrs. Joubert, went the Australian lady, Mrs. Dickenson, whose account follows, reprinted from the *South Australian Advertiser:*—

The day before yesterday I visited the *burgher* camp at Irene, about half an hour by train from Pretoria, having first obtained a permit from the governor-general. Previously I had been introduced to a Mrs. Honey, whose niece was formerly one of the voluntary nurses in the camp, and she promised to act as my interpreter. She told me that old Mrs. Joubert, the widow of the General, was also going down. Irene had been described to me as one of the worst camps so far as the mortality of the children was concerned, but as I had found that Miss Hobhouse's suggestion as to allowing them tinned milk had been adopted at

Merebank, Maritzburg, and Howick, I was astonished to find that at Irene the rations were on a much lower scale. No condensed milk is allowed here as a regulation ration for a child unless it is ill; and then, instead of giving the mother a tin and allowing her to mix it, it is served out diluted, and of course quickly becomes sour.

I saw some terrible instances of emaciation among children which could only be matched by the famine-stricken people of India. One photograph I took of a child of five years, the skin hardly covers the bones. It was not in hospital and had no disease; it was simply wasting from improper food. After taking this child's photograph, I was told another mother would like to have her child photographed, as she thought it could not live long, but on reaching the tent I found the poor little thing had died.

The rations for a woman and three children for a week (I saw them) are two small tins of bully-beef, 1 lb. of unroasted coffee, 7 lbs. of flour, and 3½ lbs. of mealies (Indian corn). At Irene coals instead of wood (two buckets a week) are supplied, and the women have built clay ovens for baking their bread. No soap, candles, or matches are allowed as rations. Those families who have any money buy them, but the destitute go without Mrs. Joubert, who allowed me to take a photograph of her in the camp, is very kind to the poor families at Irene, but with 4000 people it would take a larger income than hers to supply them with what they require.

The Dutch Government have sent out a Relief Committee. (I was introduced to the secretary yesterday.) He told me the young Queen of Holland was personally much interested in it. The stipulation made is that they are to give no relief in camp unless to individual cases. Clothes, etc., are not to be handed over to the superintendent. This has debarred them from several camps where distribution to families except through the superintendent is forbidden.

Colonel Pickwood, commanding the military camp adjoining Irene *burgher* camp, told me that a couple of nights before, under cover of a dark stormy night, a party of fighting Boers broke into the *burgher* camp, but some of the Boer police, who have been organised to watch, gave him notice, and the troops were sent to clear them out. The soldiers fired on them, but apparently without effect. This incident shows how daring they are, and what constant supervision is needed. So far as their moral conduct is concerned. Colonel Pickwood gives a very good account of the Boer women. He says they behave in a quiet, dignified manner, and he has no difficulty in regard to the soldiers.

A friend has forwarded to me an extract from the letter of a young officer's wife, the latest unofficial description of that camp—

Pretoria, Dec 1901.

No one can realise till they have seen a camp what a wonderful work this is of ours. The letters of protest that appear in the English papers seem so wholly irrelevant. 'Tis such a huge and magnificent undertaking, this housing and feeding of all our new subjects, that the petty holes that are picked in the system seem nothing. As to the mortality, it is proved over and over again that if only the Boers would consent to be doctored by the first-rate doctors provided for them, instead of waiting till they are at death's door for their own remedies, and then coming to the doctors and giving them the blame, it would be a very different thing.

Quite early in the year the mortality at Johannesburg had aroused attention. A lady who signs her name was moved to write thus to the superintendent, suggesting the reason for the state of affairs. Camps differed widely, but in many there lacked the *sympathetic* service she questions as existing in Johannesburg—

Letter to Mr. W. K. Tucker, General Superintendent. (From the *Daily News*)

Johannesburg, June 6, 1901.

The information, sent by you from time to time to the local *Gazette*, about the cases of death which happen in the camp is of a sad and heart-rending nature, so sad, indeed, that one feels shocked and is overwhelmed with profound sadness, which makes it altogether impossible to look on quietly and passively when things are in such a horrible condition.

Anyone looking over these lists carefully, and considering the causes of death, can draw no other conclusion from them than that there is something quite wrong here.

Is it owing to the sanitary condition? No, it is not. The active, energetic superintendent did what was possible in this case.

Is it want of proper food? No, it is not. I repeat that the super-intendent, according to his duty and conscience, tried to make an improvement in the miserable food, such as it was, before he took upon himself the government of the place.

Is it owing to bad housing or insufficient clothing? On this head much can be said for the superintendent, who did his best to arrange everything. In this respect he met with many difficulties, owing to the state of affairs as it was under a former system.

There is, however, another and more serious question yet to answer—

Is it owing to a want of qualified medical assistance, or a want of sympathetic service of doctors and nurses?

It is rather difficult to answer this question, considering there is but one doctor to look after the whole camp, consisting of be-tween 3,000 and 3,500 persons, the greater part of them being children; considering that this doctor declares that he cannot treat all the cases of illness; that the greater number of cases is of such a nature that they need not end in death, or of a nature that, reasonably, patients can and may be expected to recover; that one knows that this doctor had only a small number of patients where he practised last, and employed his time in dia-mond washing; that this doctor is not only unsympathetic, but also rude to the wretches under his supervision; that one fur-ther learns that patients are beaten in the hospital, that the treat-ment of these people is hostile, and that there is no compassion or pity shown them; that the medical assistance to be given to old people, weak ones, and convalescents is restricted; that he scoffs at the religion of the *burghers* and their public worship; that he does not isolate serious cases of contagious diseases, as he should do, and as was to be expected that he should do, after the warning he lately got by experience.

If, moreover, we consider that the greater number of deaths were owing to trifling indispositions, not dangerous in them-selves, which people consider at home so trifling that they will cure themselves, then certainly the time has come that a change be brought about in the camp.

Under these circumstances, dear Sir, I appeal to your feelings of humanity and justice, and beg you to take into serious consideration the condition of the women and children, who have been dragged from their homes without any reason but that they greatly love their native country; who are now obliged to live together under such circumstances, while at least a kind and sympathetic treatment by doctors and nurses might be expected. I kindly request you at the same time to carefully examine into this affair, as a death-rate of 170 persons a week, in the 3,500 people, is a condition which certainly should not exist.—I am, your obedient servant,

Jessie Brandon.

One of the most diligent workers from the beginning of troubles for the relief of the women was the minister at Johannesburg, the Rev. G. P. Meiring, who, writing to the Committee in Holland, says—

July 25.

To answer your question about the condition of the camp is rather difficult if I do not want this letter to be kept back. I can, however, say this much, that, owing to the ardent zeal and liberal assistance received from hospitable Holland in the first place, and no less so from Germany and Switzerland, and even from England, the sufferings of our people have been much relieved, but the camps, considering they are ever on the increase, are *like a grave*, ever crying: Give! Give!

There is much want, nay, crying want, in some camps. The money is spent in providing for real want. An influential English lady (the wife of Professor Rendel Harris, Cambridge), in whose company I visited several camps in the land, was repeatedly much affected by the critical condition of some camps, especially when Death swept away his prey in such large numbers. It is such an agreeable task to be able to do something for these poor sufferers.

Nurse Geijer and Nurse Broers, two of the ladies who went from Holland to nurse in the camps, wrote home to their Committee at The Hague from Kimberley and Norval's Pont.

Nurse Geijer writes—

Kimberley, May 1901.

The way in which the measles are raging here is terrible, whereas almost all the children suffer from lung disease on account of cold, bad food and bedding. Warm clothing is much needed here.

The cold is intense here; every evening I suffer much from cold, and then think what these poor little fellows, with hardly any stockings on their feet or clothes on their backs, must suffer.

I live on rations, and receive a cupful of ground coffee and a cupful of sugar once a week; it is understood that I get some meat every day, but they often forget to give it me. The major one day asked me how I had got here, and I told him that I had been sent by a Committee. He asked me whether I received any salary from the Committee. I said, 'No.'

He said, 'Shall we give you some salary?'

I said, 'No; our work is done disinterestedly.'

Some three or four days afterwards he came back, and says, 'Sister, I have received orders to pay you 5s. a day for food, as the rations are not sufficient for you.'

I shall be very glad to learn from the Committee whether they have any objection to my accepting this money, for the rations are not sufficient at all.

The disease is spreading here day by day, and I should like to have another nurse with me. Today a girl was sent to help me. How much I should like to see God put an end to all this misery, for it is as bad as bad can be to have neither hearth nor house.

There is an excellent German doctor here who feels very much for his patients.

A few weeks later she continues—

July 19.

The condition of the camps here is sad in the highest degree; the number of people is now about 4,000. Want is greatly felt, and increases daily. In my first letter I requested that another skilful nurse should be sent, as more help is really wanted here. Last week we had nineteen deaths, so that you will understand that I am sorely tasked. Some toys sent for recovering children would be received with great gratitude. This morning at four o'clock a large tent was burned down, into which a number of women and children had moved at midnight

A little boy of five years was burned, and the shoulders and cheeks of the mother were injured by the fire. Two boys got seriously wounded. One of these two is not likely to recover.

Whatever they had been able to carry off from the farm, as beds, blankets, and some money, was also lost So one sad event here succeeds another. Not to be affected by what is suffered here one's heart must be of stone.

After improvements had been inaugurated, Miss Monkhouse, acting for the South African Distress Fund in Kimberley, writes (October 31)—

As far as I can judge, no effort is spared by the authorities here to ameliorate the condition of the inmates of this camp.

From the time we arrived up till now, things have been steadily improving. We did not set these improvements going, we came to find them begun—and they have been continued ever since, so that the condition of this camp has been steadily improving during the last three months. The terrible epidemic which was raging when we came is over. Soup kitchens have been started to give soup, with vegetables in, to the children who are at all weakly, and I believe about ninety children are now receiving soup.

A tennis and cricket set are the latest additions to the camp from government We have a minister resident here whose sole duty is to attend to the spiritual needs of the camp.

We have fenced in a small piece of ground just round our tents for a garden, but it is only small, and can in no way meet the needs of the camp. Still it may be of a little use, and possibly can help to supply a need for the sick people.

The hospital accommodation here is, I consider, good under the circumstances, and will probably be even more extended . . .

The sand-storms are the worst We had a terrible one yesterday, the worst yet.

Nurse Broers had the more comfortable conditions of Norval's Pont to describe—

June 8, 1901.

On Saturday last, in the midst of a terrible storm and shower of sand, five hundred newcomers arrived in the camp, among whom an old lady. The lower part of her body is lame, so that she has missed the use of her legs for the last thirteen years. She had brought with her her *Kaffir* girl, who, however, had stolen all the things and money the old lady had with her, and had then turned her back upon her mistress.

The commander did not know what to do with her, and sent for me. It was a terrible thing to see her when I entered the bare, empty tent in which they had set her down. With hardly any clothes on, she had been fastened upon an old cart I took her with me to the hospital tents, but one can hardly believe what the old lady, once so rich, has had to suffer.

We rise in the morning at six, and the first thing I do is to note down the temperature of my patients; then I help them to wash themselves, etc., and do whatever else there is to be done for patients suffering from typhus, measles, and lung-disease. At eight o'clock they get their breakfasts, which, in the case of most patients, consist of warm milk with an egg. Those who may have more food I give first a plateful of gruel, and then some bread, coffee, and an egg, which is quite a sufficient meal for these. At eleven they get a tumbler of milk, and at one, soup, rice, meat, and pudding; at three o'clock, once more a glass of milk; and at six, the same as at breakfast.

You'll understand that the patients get sufficient food, though the way in which the other people in the camp (there are 2,900 of them now) are treated is quite different

The number of deaths is large, principally among the children. If I were allowed to write down everything, I would have a strange story to tell. The want of warm clothing, stockings, and shoes grows daily upon us, and among the persons of this camp there are those who have been prisoners here for about six months, and were not allowed to take any clothing with them but what they were wearing at the time when they were picked up.

When the camp increased in size it was not so comfortable. Miss Broers continues—

It is a hard life we lead here at present The necessary food is hardly for sale here, and whatever you can get is difficult to digest. Of late my hospital has been quite full, and as the camp now numbers over 3,000 persons, five large tents with thirty beds will presently be added to the others. What you hear here is complaints; what you see, misery. Much of the money I received has been spent on poor sufferers, who are ill and have hardly clothes upon their backs; everything, however, is as bad as it is expensive.

Letter from Minister of Aliwal North Camp.

Sept. 1901.

When I arrived here I found a large outstretched camp, containing about 5,000 souls, and still ox-waggons bringing in more were constantly arriving.

The awakening desire to hear God's Word is great. Scarcely is early prayer on Sundays concluded ere the people begin to carry their stools, and so make sure of places at the 10 o'clock service. The church is quite too small for the congregation. Two hours before the time the stream churchward begins; an hour before service an elder announces that every seat is already occupied; half an hour later there is no chance of even getting near the door, and the churchwarden comes to say, 'You may safely begin, sir; there is no room for even a mouse!'

I regret to say that during this month my health has been far from good, and has sorely hindered me in my work. Thank God, the sore sickness that raged amongst the children during July and August has almost entirely ceased. . . . There is still much sickness, and the minister is in continual request at sickbeds and deathbeds. Here is a girl of about eleven years old, who wants 'so sorely to see the minister.' But the minister himself is ill, and forbidden to leave his tent. Presently he sees a sick person on a stretcher who is being carried to the hospital. He finds out it is the same little girl who so greatly desired to see him. The bearers bring her first to the tent of the Dominie; he says a few words to her, and she is carried away content to the hospital.

Then there is a father suffering from a deadly complaint from whom it can no longer be hidden that his end is approaching. He must be taught and helped and comforted. In the next tent lies a little sick child; the mother relates with streaming eyes how she has already lost two children, and now a third is hovering between life and death. Her husband—her stay—is away in far Ceylon. Under such circumstances the minister can with difficulty restrain his tears. Here it is almost literally true 'there was not a house where there was not one dead.' Most people are clad in black—the hearse passes constantly.

A few lines from Bloemfontein show the improvements in that camp effected in June and July. It is a letter to myself from Miss Fleck, of the local committee at Bloemfontein. In company with Mrs. Blignaut and others, this lady's self-denying work will be long remembered by women of that camp. Like the Pretoria ladies, this committee's work and visits were prohibited.

Bloemfontein, Aug. 22.

The camp has been divided into two now; the one part is situated over the *kopje* behind the *commandant's* tent, and the other over the *donga* to the right of the tent, a very nice, clear sweep of ground.

The camp is a gem to what it was when you were here.

The present superintendent and his assistant take great interest in the welfare of the people.

The death-rate has been high in this camp, and as it is thought that most die from measles, the lower hut has been knocked into one, and six large stoves set in to heat it I believe it is now quite full with patients; the women are as willing to send their children to this hospital as they were unwilling to send them to the other. The material for the wash-house has arrived, and the men have started it.

I go to the camp about once a week.

Water supply was always a prime difficulty in this camp, but one of the ministers writes:

Now, pipes have been laid on to the camp. Just now, however, it is brought in watercarts from the station 2½ miles away, and about half is spilt in the bringing. Yesterday a terrific hailstorm passed over the camp—one hailstone weighed 2½ lbs. Some tents were blown down, and others were blown away by a tremendous gust of wind. This sad fate also befell my tent, and my books were much damaged.

Another vivid sketch of his work and his people is supplied by the Dominie of a more northern camp.

Vredefort Road, Sept, 1901.

I find the work overwhelmingly great. Happily the Lord has put it into the hearts of some of the brothers to stand by me, both to assist me in the services and in visiting the sick and bedridden. As you can imagine, in a camp of 2,000 souls one finds a great variety of character. The majority show a spirit of patient endurance, but some have grown careless and indifferent, and are hardened under the chastisement of the Lord It greatly distresses me to find that while four or five corpses are being committed to the earth, at a short distance from the burial-place a crowd of people will have gathered for sports.

But while there is much to sadden there is much also to gladden. I have stood beside many a deathbed where in almost every case the language of the dying was the triumph-cry of the Apostle Paul, '*Death, where is thy sting?*' Thus, I have seen the promise fulfilled that for the dying death has indeed lost its sting. The Sunday services are very well attended, and there is great need of a roomy church. There are also very few seats, and the effect is strange and primitive to see each person stepping along with Bible and Psalm-book in hand, and in many cases a queer little stool on the back.

At the conclusion of the service each departs with his little load, doubtless fearing some mischievous lad may carry off the rare and much prized article. . . . The camp is neat and clean under the wise care of the superintendent, who does all in his power to soften and improve the lot of the people. The streets are regularly laid out, and the camp is under the charge of corporals—they being our own people. The health of the camp might be better than it is, and there are deaths daily. Yesterday soup kitchens for the sick and weak were started, and this will doubtless do much to improve the health of the people, for there is great need of softer and more suitable food for the sick. There is a sufficiency of bread and meat, but vegetables are sorely needed, and it will be easily understood that there is much sickness owing to the monotony of the food.

Ladies sent out by the Society of Friends thus write of their religious work at Volksrust. I quote from *The Friend* of August 30, 1901—

This morning (Sunday) we all went to the Concentration Camp at 10.30, and found a crowd of about 3,000 persons assembled for the service. There were quite too many for the building to contain, which does duty as a church and school, so they assembled in the open air. Mr. —— began by giving out a hymn, which was most heartily joined in by the great crowd, and he then read some portions of Scripture which had been selected by Mrs. H. It was most impressive to hear them sing in their slow, measured way the old Dutch Psalms.

Then in a few words he introduced her to the assembly, and told them also about us and our being members of the Society of Friends, 'sometimes called Quakers,' and that we had come amongst them in the love of God to tell them how much we felt for them, and to bring them what comfort and help we could in their time of great sorrow.

Then Mrs. H. spoke to them most beautifully and tenderly of that great love which broke down all divisions, in which, as the Apostle said, there was neither Jew nor Greek, and she might say to them there was neither British nor Boer, we were all one in Christ. And down those rugged cheeks the tears simply poured as she spoke to them of the great love of Christ which had constrained Him to leave His throne in heaven and suffer cold and hunger and anguish as no human being had ever suffered, and die that we might live, and being acquainted with human sorrow and grief He could comfort as no one else could do, and then she pleaded with them to come in all their sorrow and their trials to Him, the God of all comfort.

It was one of the most touching scenes I have ever witnessed. Miss T. spoke for a short time when Mrs. H. had finished, then there was another hymn. A service was announced for children at 2.30, to which older children might come if they wished, the benediction was pronounced, and then that vast crowd came up and shook hands with each of us, murmuring 'God bless you,' 'Thank you.' Some were completely broken down. One woman said to me, 'I have been living for myself, now I will live for God.' I never witnessed anything to compare with this, and feel quite unable to describe it. Mr. ——— told me afterwards that a man had said to him, 'I never thought there was any one in England cared for us as these ladies do.'

. . . At 2.30 Miss T. went back to the camp. A still greater crowd had gathered. The children were all in the front and centre, such a mass of them, and the older people all round. I have never seen such good children, or any who stood and sat so quietly as these. . . .

The nights are extremely cold. We sleep in our thick sleeping-bags, with warm wraps over the bed as well, and yet it is cold. Oh, what must the poor people in the tents suffer! . . .

Mrs. Dickenson relates an incident at Volksrust, which, she says, rather surprised her—

> A smart young woman in a Panama hat, but a nurse's cape, began to talk to one of the passengers in my carriage while the train was waiting, and told him she was a nurse at the Concentration Camp there. She remarked in a loud tone, 'I don't know one little bit about nursing—never did it in my life.'
> 'How did you get in?' said her friend.
> 'Oh, I just spoke nicely to the doctors, so they engaged me, and I haven't killed anybody yet' This, combined with an account I read today in a paper here of the trial of a dispenser in a camp near Bloemfontein for killing three children by giving them an overdose of strychnine, accounts for some of the mortality among the people in these camps.

There was, no doubt, often carelessness as well as great ignorance amongst the staff of a camp, but in the instance referred to by Mrs. Dickenson it should be mentioned that the accused was discharged.

> The trial has just been concluded by the Criminal Court at Bloemfontein of the chief dispenser to the Bloemfontein Refugee Camp, who was accused of improperly dispensing a preparation of strychnine so as to cause the death of three children of refugees. After a most minute inquiry, lasting a week, the accused was discharged. The most stringent regulations are in force in reference to medicines, doctors, and nurses, to prevent any mistake.—Through Laffan's Agency. (*Manchester Guardian*, Dec. 14, 1901.)

Of many far-off camps there is no unofficial description— only sometimes a few lines like this from Mr. Theunissen, the clergyman who distributed relief for the Holland Committee:—

Extracts from Letters to Committee in Holland.

Standerton, Oct, 18.

As I informed you by letter, I have already received from you £175. A considerable part of the money I spent on medicine. Death has ravaged the camps fearfully. During the last six months people died here at the rate of thirty-two per hundred a year. We hope and trust that some improvement will set in, though the minimum of deaths during the last fortnight was ten persons a day, whereas the number of inhabitants of the camp is now only 2,850.

The camp at Pietersburg was opened about May of this year. Only little by little the number of persons sent there reached the number of 4,000. And from May till the latter part of October already about 500 persons had died there.

One of the saddest of all the camps has been Bethulie, of which a lady, who visited a sick relation there, tells the following incidents, forwarded to me by the Committee at Cape Town, (compare Cd. 902. "Dec. 10 I have dismissed the superintendent for apathy."—Deputy Administrator):—

A man who had been rich before the war sent for the doctor, told him of how he had been weakened by privations and exposure, and begged for a little brandy; he was sure that that would make him all right. The doctor gave the certificate for the brandy, which the man took to the office, and was curtly ordered to be gone. Next day, when the doctor visited him, he was surprised that the man had not received the brandy, and went with him to the office, where both were ordered to leave at once.

'But,' pleaded the doctor, 'the man will die if he does not get a little brandy.'

'Oh, let him die, he is only a Boer!'

And he died.

When the people came begging for a candle in order to have a light with their sick ones, they were ordered off, even when there were boxes of candles which had been sent by the Committee from Cape Town, and when the Ladies' Local Committee begged for a few to distribute, they were refused as often as not, or given a little bit, or made to pay. (Of course nothing was allowed from Bethulie town to the camp.)

When the people had to make coffins for their dead, no arrangements were made for an adequate supply of. wood. As often as not, there was nothing to be had; many a wealthy man or woman had a coffin knocked together from bits of candle and soap boxes bought at exorbitant prices, but 'most of our beloved dead,' a lady told me, 'had to be consigned to the earth wrapped in khaki blankets, (see also Ladies' Report on Vredefort Road and private letter from Middelburg), oh, it hurt us terribly'! . . . . The two clerks, a De Villiers and a Percival, were inhuman, and made fun of the sufferings. *They are both dead.*

Of course the head-superintendent was horrified over all this, and since his visit things have, thank God, been better. But picture yourself standing with me and a few others as we stood in the graveyard there.

Mr. Otto said, 'Look! here I laid my son in August; from then, this whole place has been filled—1,300 *in six months out of a population of 5,000!!'* Tears would not come; it was just an 'O Lord, how long?' . . . Then to hear of how people, who had a little money with them, died because those in authority would not or could not give them a little food.

A lady told me of how she visited a wealthy woman who had had every comfort and convenience before the war, but now in a wretched bell-tent, just kept calling, 'Hungry, hungry! When I am dead, publish in the papers that I and my two daughters have all died of hunger.' It was just the same in tent after tent, day after day, that this same cry went on: 'Hungry, hungry! I am dying of hunger.' Lying on the floors, on the bare earth with only a blanket—those who had been accustomed to every luxury—died.

★★★★★★

Note—The quotations following are all from the Report of the Ladies' Commission. Cd.893:—

The village was out of bounds for the camp, and there was said to be no going backwards and forwards without passes.

The supply of coffins at one time had been short, and the dead had been buried in blankets, the same as soldiers who die in military hospitals. The people feel this very much, and the supply of coffins was obtained again as soon as possible.

The shop was very bare compared to others. The chief things noted were tinned salmon, men's shirts, women's skirts, concertinas, and cigarettes. The whole of Bethulie village and district is very short of supplies.

Mr. Deare, in reply to inquiry, said he thought at least four-fifths of the people in Bethulie Camp slept on the ground. We strongly and repeatedly urged on him the desirability of furnishing the camp with a larger supply of bedsteads, of however simple a description. He represented the difficulty of getting suitable material.

*Sanitation.*—On the trench system, and very rough. No proper seats (except in the school latrine) for men, women, or children, but simply logs thrown across trenches. The extent of the fouling of the ground in and around the camp involves serious danger to the health of the inmates. It is only fair to add that, with the exception of the school latrine, the latrine accommodation is so extremely bad that there is much excuse for fouling the ground.

All meat is supplied by contractor.

*Discipline and morals.*—Some men and women had been sent to gaol, and sentenced to hard labour.

★★★★★★

The people speak with the greatest contempt of the Ladies' Commission who came out They would, for instance, ask such a question as this: 'But has anyone in this camp been accustomed to such a thing as a bedstead in their homes?' The sanitary arrangements were certainly improved after they left, but then they had been simply indescribable before. During the days of their visit the people got beautiful beef, but before and after it has often been perfectly uneatable. The meat was kept in rooms where carbolic had been used, which so got into the meat that the smell was unbearable in lifting the lids off the pots while cooking.

I mostly came in contact with people from Dewetsdorp. They all tell the one tale of how their husbands and sons were ordered to the Magistrate's office to have their passes renewed, they might return home at once, instead of which they were sent off by rail to Cape Town for Green Point, and during their absence it was that the women were forced from their homes. 'You need take nothing, you will find everything in the camp,' that was the usual promise.

On their arrival there was not even a camp! They had no food along the way, and suffered dreadful privations. There were floods of rain. But the spirit of quiet endurance and resignation to God's will made me time and again thank God for such women. I felt proud of my race, and assured that they would come forth out of all this the better, the nobler, the stronger.

But their sufferings have been great, and still are; the tent-life, the constant worry of orders and counter-orders, the rumours, the constraint on a people accustomed to a free life, all this tells upon them. Whole families have died out. Mr. Venter has lost 26 of his children and grandchildren there. Mrs. Van der Heever has lost 18 relations in a little while. Mrs. Fourie has lost her

242

husband and eight children. 'The baby died 24 hours after its birth; the nurse (?) placed the baby next to the unconscious mother, and it died of cold that night, she said.

Another said, 'Do you suffer through the war in the Cape Colony?' I assured her of it 'I have lost,' she said, 'three little children, and my husband has been for eight months no one knows where, and I have nothing on earth left to me—everything gone, everything dead. But Christ is filling my empty arms and my empty heart as never before, and I can praise Him through my tears.'

Another, very ill in the hospital, such a pretty young woman: 'I feel how God has been dealing personally with me. In the days of our prosperity I forgot Him, but now He has taken everything from me and brought me back to Him; husband and seven children, all dead.'

Then we asked, 'And are you going to lead this new life in your own strength?'

'Oh no,' she replied; 'God has taken everything away—*emptied* me, and I shall just remain at His feet as a poor sinner, with nothing but His glorious strength.'

I sat with a good number making them tell me the stories of their deportation, etc. One said, 'You see, I was so totally unprepared to go, because I was so sure I would not be taken away. God's Word says, "If ye ask anything in My name, *I will do it.*" And I prayed God to spare us from being taken, and I felt that I wanted to honour Him by a perfect faith, trusting utterly that what I had asked in His name would be done to me. I laughed at the other women who were afraid, so sure was I.

Then, when it came, and I had to go at ten minutes' notice, I could not do anything. I only felt as if the foundations of the earth were giving way.' And then I asked, 'Did you lose faith?'

'Did I lose faith? Oh no; I had received the grace to see that I had asked unwisely, like a little child, and God could not answer me, but had something far better in store for me.'

That woman has lost *three* children; a fourth, formerly a strong young man, pining away in hospital for three months already; a fifth just sickening for fever while we were there; truly it was grand faith which could say 'God had something better in store' for her!

I made inquiries about Mrs. ——— and Mrs. ———; I could

not see them, as they with their families were in the wire enclosure—prison. They had gone to do some washing, and not having heard the new regulations, had washed in the usual spot in the river, which that day happened to be a forbidden place, and were punished thus. A large number of men, over one hundred, have already slipped away from the camp and joined the Boers, who have a *laager* not far off.

A young man who got away in that way has not been retaken, nor was any effort made to get him back, but his parents and brothers and sisters have been placed in the wire enclosure; the old father and brothers have to do convict's work from 6 in the morning till dusk (during summer), with quarter-hour meals three times during the day on *half-ration*. They are of our best people.

The children under six receive condensed milk, maizena and oatmeal, but less meat One sick woman told us she got butter and jam. But what of that, when they eat and drink in sorrow and sadness!

God help us and our people, we see no ray of light away from Him who makes no mistake. These camps are one huge 'mistake'; they cry aloud to God, and He will hearken; and these graves will stand as a monument of . . .

This extract gives a sad little reminder of the anxiety felt by prisoners of war about their homeless and often separated families, separated even in death. It is from Mr. H. J. J.

Heytmayer, prisoner of war, to Mr. Emous, Chairman of the Holland Committee—

Bermuda, Nov. 21, 1901.

Last Sunday I received a letter from my wife, informing me that on the 14th of September last she had been sent to Durban, so that she is now in a Refugee Camp at Merebank Station, Durban, Natal.

She further tells me: 'Our youngest child was left behind at Pretoria with the nurses of the Red Cross. It was then almost dead, and could not open its eyes any more. The officers, however, would not allow me to stay. I was forced to leave for Durban, and so our little one had to die in the hands of strangers.'

I need not tell you that my heart is broken. I cannot even give you an idea of what passes in my inmost soul. The said child was born about a month after I had been taken prisoner, and was about three months old when my wife had to leave it behind at Pretoria.

My wife has now three children left, the eldest being six years old. We have lost all our property.

About a month after the formation of the new camp at Merebank, Mrs. Dickenson visited and thus describes it :—

Oct. 12, 1901.

Yesterday I obtained a permit from the *commandant* to visit the so-called Refugee Camp at Merebank, about an hour's journey from Durban by the South Coast Railway. The site was selected by the P.M.O., Major M'Cormack, because it was supplied from the Durban main, and consequently pure water was ensured. The soil is sandy, but unfortunately a marsh lies in the depression between Camps 1 and 2. There is one medical man, who goes his rounds with an interpreter at present, but in view of the illness which already prevails another surgeon will shortly be appointed. This camp has been formed to contain ten thousand persons, but at present its inhabitants number two thousand. It has only been inhabited three weeks, and consequently is not in full working order. Merebank is a siding, with not even a railway station, and trains only stop there for the camp—Canvas Town, as it is called.

\*\*\*\*\*\*

Note:—
Ground which is waterlogged should not have been chosen.
*Recommendation,*—In spite of the great expense that has been incurred ... we strongly recommend that the camp should be shifted to a better place.—Cd. 893.
*N.B.*—This was not done.

\*\*\*\*\*\*

The day was showery (in Natal rainy weather has now set in), and the green tropical-looking foliage and thick rank grass glistened with moisture—a country much resembling Ceylon in its vegetation, which flourishes, but white humanity languishes. At Merebank I climbed from the train, which did not stop at a platform, and, picking my way through seas of mud, entered the camp, whose white tents stretched far away to the slope of a rising ground. They were arranged in rows, leaving a broad road down the centre.

Close to the entrance was the *commandant's* office, which was besieged by women, mostly dressed in black, with the '*kapje*' or sunbonnet generally used on Dutch farms, also of the same sombre colour. Barelegged children paddled through the mud and pools of water, carrying some a loaf of bread, others a bag of potatoes or a bundle of firewood.

Turning to the right, I passed up the principal street, if one may so term it, and came upon the store, which has been established to enable those refugees who have money to buy extra food and clothing. Of course things are dear; biscuits which I purchased costing double as much as in Durban. Still, it is a boon to those who can afford it.

The *commandant* of the camp, who wore no uniform, and looked quite unofficial, called after me to ask if I had a pass. I showed him the one I had. He offered to send a man round to show me everything, but I thanked him, and told him I would pursue my investigations alone, trusting to finding some people who spoke English to translate for those who did not.

From my experience of last year among the Dutch farmers of Cape Colony, I knew almost at once those who would be likely to be able to understand me. One of the first people I met was the doctor, going round with an interpreter. He was in the usual khaki uniform, his black gorgets alone distinguishing him from the combatant officers. Asking him as to illness, he told me the camp was, as he expressed it, 'riddled with a very bad form of measles.'

Soon sad evidence was brought before me. Four boys carrying a stretcher passed and stopped at a tent A woman, sobbing bitterly, stepped out and laid a little bundle wrapped in a railway rug on it. As the boys returned I met them, and saw that their burden was that of a young child, perhaps about five years old, who had just died—the second the poor mother had lost in a fortnight. There is no minister here, and no chance of any form of Christian burial.

A small grave is dug, and the tiny wasted body placed in it. By dint of inquiring amongst the women who seemed likely to give me information, I was directed to a tent of the larger description, occupied by the wife and daughter of the *landdrost*, *i.e.* chief magistrate of Pretoria, Mr. Schütter.

On explaining to the daughter, who spoke excellent English,

that I wanted to get a report on the camp to send to an Australian paper, they asked me to come inside. This was the only tent I saw which was in the least what one would call furnished. It was pathetic to see the remains of a pretty drawing-room—the Lares and Penates of a vanished home—in a squalid tent. The chairs were covered with velvet or morocco. A gilt clock ticked on a packing-case. A valuable old china vase, a cherished heirloom, stood in another corner.

Everything showed people accustomed to refined surroundings. Mrs. Schütter the elder spoke no English. She was a tall, dignified-looking woman, looking deeply depressed, and she hardly lifted her eyes. Her daughter-in-law, who had with her a baby of six months, talked freely, and told me that after the occupation of Pretoria they were allowed to live in their own house. Lord Roberts promising that they should not be molested.

Since Lord Kitchener's proclamation, however, they were suddenly told they must leave, being given only one night to make the necessary preparations. They have brought down all they could, but are daily finding out how much was left behind that might have been of the greatest use. An oil cooking-stove is one of their most valued possessions, as it obviates the hardship of cooking out of doors, which in the rainy weather is most trying work. The lot of the Schütters is that of the upper class of prisoners, and may be taken as typical. They have a certain amount of comfort purchased with their own money, but they feel the degradation of camp life more than the poorer people. For instance, they are watched by *Kaffir* police, and obliged to carry their rations and firewood in some cases three-quarters of a mile under the eyes of a lot of lazy blacks, who hugely enjoy seeing white people made to work while they idle. The sanitary arrangements are also of the roughest and most primitive kind, and at present quite insufficient for the requirements of the people. But building is going on, so it is hardly fair to judge what the completed condition of the camp will be.

The Misses Schütters and a Mrs. Erasmus and her daughters have organised a sort of 'district' of the most destitute families, and they took me to see some of them. The idea spread amongst these poor people that I could help them in some way with their sick children, and they crowded round, holding them in their arms and explaining their condition, which in many cases seemed hopeless.

One pale, haggard woman sat at the entrance of her bell-tent holding a child just at its last gasp, and wanted her photographed; but I told Mrs. Erasmus to explain how sorry I felt for her, but that the photograph would have been such a painful one she would never have liked to look at it. This woman had two sick boys lying on oil-cloth on the ground, with a blanket between them. One of her children died last week, and one the week before.

\*\*\*\*\*\*

The Commission feel very strongly that in this camp no one at all should sleep on the ground.—Cd. 893.

\*\*\*\*\*\*

A hospital is in course of erection, which will give the sick a better chance. This is a wooden shed, with galvanised iron roof; but some cubicles are partitioned off as a maternity ward. Mrs. Erasmus kindly interpreted my questions to the women of her 'district,' and their replies in all cases were much the same. Their rations in the camp were sufficient, though they would be thankful for a little treacle for the children, or something to eat with their bread. The firewood was not enough unless they picked some up or burned turf. They were not allowed to get through the barbed wire which surrounds the camp. If they did, their coffee was cut off for three days.

Asked if they came voluntarily, or if they were taken forcibly, all declared that they never asked for anything but to be left alone, and most had friends who would take care of them, were they allowed their liberty.

'Refugee Camp' is a misnomer; they are really prisons. A few of the prisoners are allowed out on parole once a week, but the monotony of the life must be terribly wearisome. The tents are so close together that sitting outside is impossible.

To visit No. 2 Camp, a walk through a brickfield and then a flounder of half a mile ankle deep in black slush are necessary. Once I lost my shoe, so thick and sticky was the mud; but I struggled on, and found this camp more unfinished than the first, and with a great many empty tents. Mrs. Schütter had advised me to find a Mrs. Kruger, a doctor's wife, which I did after some time. She was living in the same tent as a Mrs. Kleynaus, wife of the *landdrost* of Ermelo.

At first, they had another family put into their tent, but they remonstrated, and had them removed, as they had a boy of 16 who was supposed to occupy it with them as well as the Kleynaus' *Kaffir* servant-girl. This girl had remained with Mrs. Kleynaus through all their troubles. The latter, who looked very fragile, was taken out of a sickbed at Ermelo, and brought along in her nightdress, with her little boy.

She pleaded that one room might be left to her till she got better, but the officer said his orders were to burn the house. She saved two blankets and a box of clothes. While she lay in the waggon, she could see her piano and all her cherished possessions being smashed to pieces, and the house set fire to. Her jewellery was stolen from the waggon on the journey down. Mrs. Kruger said her husband was not fighting, but attending to the wounded. 'Your men as well as ours,' she added, 'so I don't see why I should be kept here.

Had it not been for the kindness of Mrs. Schütter, who asked me to have some luncheon, I should have fared badly, as there was no place to get refreshments at Merebank. Nothing was 'rations' but bread. It was their own coffee and fried fish, as it was not a meat day. The appointments of the table showed people of refined surroundings, good table linen and silver forks. I related my 'camping out' experiences in Australia, but, as they sadly remarked, 'you had a home, and were not a prisoner.'

The great want in the camp is blankets, boots, and underclothes for those who have no money. Miss Schütter suggested a bazaar, to which they could contribute work to be sold to the Durban people, for a fund to provide these things. The idea seems a very good one, and I hope they will succeed in carrying it out.

Mrs. Dickenson goes on to tell her readers about Maritzburg in the same simple fashion—

Pietermaritzburg, Oct. 24.

This camp differs from that of Merebank, described in my previous article, in several particulars. At the entrance is a sort of guard-house, and soldiers come out and demand a pass, whereas at Merebank there is no actual entrance into the camp at all. The tents at Maritzburg are mostly square, instead of the wretched, insanitary bell-tent. It is in a much drier and healthier situation also, on the slope of a hillside, overlooking the town. As before, the first people I met looked at me with doubt and suspicion, and only shook their heads uncomprehendingly when addressed.

Presently a minister of the Dutch Reformed Church passed, and I stopped him as he was entering a tent, and inquired if he could give me any information as to the health of the people, etc. 'No,' he replied very cautiously, 'I am sorry to say I cannot I am not allowed to give information.'

'At all events, you can tell me of some English-speaking people who will be able to answer my questions?' I inquired. He advised me to go to the little iron store (also a post-office) to ascertain the names of these people, so careful was the reverend gentleman to keep on the safe side. I inquired for a daughter-in-law of Mrs. Schütter whom I had met at Merebank, but found she had been removed to Howick Camp.

Mrs. Fourie, the storekeeper said, would give me information, as she spoke English well. She was a pleasant-looking person, busy ironing, but put her work aside and asked me to come in, and soon, in the hospitable way that reminds one of Australians, was preparing coffee for me.

The children had had measles and pneumonia, but, thank God, were now well. She had her man with her too, and all her boys, so she had no anxiety. Her boys went to the government school in Maritzburg, and were learning well. Her husband, too, was allowed out to work. When she knew the English were coming, she packed her waggon full of stores and locked it up, so they brought her and her family down in their own waggon. She had an oil cooking-stove, and they were not obliged to cook out of doors when it rained.

Mrs. Fourie seemed so cheerful and contented, that I began to think Maritzburg Camp must be singularly well managed; but it occurred to me to ask if she and her husband were taken prisoners or surrendered. 'Oh, I made my husband surrender,' she said. 'As we had to lose the home, we might as well take all we could.'

This was the secret. These people were actually refugees, but the first I had seen. There is, however, no doubt that the refugees or surrendered people constitute a very small minority in these camps. The next tent I visited belonged to a Mrs. Vanyder. It was beautifully clean, with a large pile of clothes freshly ironed in a corner. Her two daughters are working as dressmakers in Maritzburg. Her husband is on commando. The allowance of bread was too small, she said, and a little girl of 4½ years was supposed to live entirely on four tins of condensed milk a week, and to taste neither meat nor bread.

Afrikander children, like Australians, are brought up to eat a great deal of meat, so that they miss it much more than the English child would do. The ration card, showing exactly what each family receives, is hung up in each tent I noticed that Mrs. Vanyder's allowance was much less in proportion than the Fouries. Mrs. Fourie, who came in with me, explained this by saying that her family consisted of boys, and Mrs. Vanyder's were girls, who were not supposed to eat as much.

The prevalent disease now in this camp is enteric fever, but in August last 69 children died of measles. It must be remembered that these children are taken from farms where they lead the free, healthy life of Australian bush children, with any amount of good milk, eggs, and meat The change of diet alone, without the closeness and damp of the vile tents, would account for the mortality.

******

Deaths in August, 25.—Cd. 893. Report of Commission.

******

In the *Natal Witness* today I noticed a quotation from a letter by a nurse in Pretoria, attributing the death-rate among the children in the *burgher* camps to want of cleanliness. This I consider perfectly untrue. I was speaking only this morning to the wife of the English doctor of the Boer Camp here (Howick), and she tells me that her husband does not find them dirty. She has taken a girl as nursemaid, who, although she does not know a word of English, is very clean and tidy, and anxious to learn.

The next tent I visited was that of Mrs. Davis Van Niekirk, who was quite destitute. Her husband and sons were on commando, and she had six young children. All her bedding and furniture had been burnt, and they had very little ready money, which was now all spent There was nothing in the tent but two or three blankets and a packing-case.

A nice-looking young woman in deep mourning beckoned me to come into her tent She was a widow—a Mrs. Venter.

Her husband was commandeered early in the war, when they had only been married eleven months, and her baby just born. He was killed six months ago, and the baby died of croup three months after in this camp. However, she has a blind father-in-law, who took up much of her time. She was of English parentage, and spoke English fluently.

The old man could speak no English, so Mrs. Venter acted as interpreter. 'The old man says,' she began, 'that he wishes you to know how he was taken. He was in his farm with his sister, who was also blind, when the Khakis (*i.e.* the British) arrived; he begged them to leave him one cow and a pound of coffee, but they refused, and he was for a day and night without food, till some Boers passed, and took him to another farm. A few weeks after, that farm was burnt, and then he was taken along with the convoy, and finally reached this camp, when his daughter-in-law joined him.' The blind man's story I give *verbatim*, but cannot vouch for its actual truth.

His favourite dog had managed to follow the waggons in spite of all efforts to drive him back, and the faithful creature came up wagging his tail when he was mentioned. I inquired how they fed so large an animal, but Mrs. Venter told me he got the bones from ration meat, and the soldiers fed him too. The blind man was not at all satisfied with his treatment Only 19 lbs. of meat for five grown-up people weekly he considered too little. It certainly was not so much as the allowance to some other families. It was written on the card, so there was no doubt on this point. Firewood, also supposed to be 10 lbs. *per diem*, often did not amount to the same quantity per week, and they had to burn rags for fuel.

When people are fed by contract against their will, of course there is generally dissatisfaction; but I think a more varied diet without greater expenditure might be given. A little treacle and butter, instead of so much bread to be eaten dry, for instance. Mrs. Venter said she had to pay £1, 5s. for the coffin of her child (a mere infant), and in future the charge was to be £4 for each funeral Those who had no money are obliged to borrow from neighbours to make up the amount.

******

Provisions of Coffins, Shrouds, etc.—Everything is provided free of cost: £4, 10s. is paid for each adult's funeral.—Cd. 893.

I visited a good many other tents, and heard some pitiful stories. One young woman was on a farm with her old mother and two children, aged 4 and 5. When taken away by a convoy of soldiers about a couple of days' journey, the officer in command gave orders to leave the old mother at a farm in passing. The children cried to go with their grandmother, and they were left also. The mother, however, was forced to go on, and was promised she should see her children soon; but she has never done so, though seven months had elapsed, nor could she discover their whereabouts.

A young woman in the tent next to her had been brought down a week before the birth of her first baby. The husband had begged a Mrs. Bartmen to look after her when he was commandeered, but the latter lost sight of her, and only called down to find she had died in her confinement; but the baby was adopted by the woman, who had lost her own two.

Everyone here, especially military men, acknowledges that these camps were a mistake, and the money spent on them would have been far better applied in helping the British refugees.

Voluntary helpers write to the Cape Colony committees with the first note of improvement towards the end of the year—

Dec. 12.

At Maritzburg Camp there are about two thousand men, women, and children. In the Sunday school there are six hundred children. The health is now so good that during some weeks not even one death has taken place.

Howick, Dec. 1901.

At Howick the state of things is not so satisfactory. There are about four thousand people in the camp, and there is much sickness. Four to five funerals take place daily. The reason of all this sickness is the frequent arrival of newcomers from the Transvaal (Potchefstroom, Pretoria, etc.), who all bring diseases with them. Here, as at Maritzburg and Merebank, large schools are to be built. The military are going to take over all schools. It will be a great blessing when the hundreds of children who are now running about idle, because there is no room for them in the present schools, can be provided for.

Here follows one of the more cheerful letters, speaking of education, books, and trades. It is from Ds. Burger, Vereeniging. Letters like these, written by clergymen to relief committees, were composed with a recollection of the censor's eye—

Nov. 4.

The goods from Cape Town have come, and been received with great joy. A great work is going on amongst the children. The government has opened a day school, and makes more or less provision for its needs. The teaching is free. Three hundred and sixty children attend Sunday school. Twice a week we go to the banks of the Vaal River, about five hundred paces from the camp, and the children are taught to sing there. On such occasions, we divide the dates, etc., and everyone gets a share. The leather is most welcome. We have started shoemaking, and the young fellows are being taught the trade. We want also to give some young fellows instruction in carpentering and blacksmith's work. The camp superintendent gives his full approval A case of books was also sent; they were mostly old books, but have enabled us to begin a library.

### LIZZIE VAN ZŸL.

*The children and the sucklings swoon in the streets of the city. They say to their mothers, Where is corn and wine? when they swooned as the wounded in the streets of the city, when their soul was poured out into their mother's bosom.*—Lam. ii. 11, 12.

Lizzie Van Zÿl died in May 1901.

This little child has been made the subject of controversy painful to those who knew her and the circumstances under which she died.

It has been allied that her mother starved her. Mr. Chamberlain has alluded to her in the House of Commons, and Dr. Conan Doyle in his book on the war. Both gentlemen, from lack of accurate information, have misrepresented the facts.

Mrs. Van Zÿl and her family were amongst the earliest of those brought into Bloemfontein Camp in November 1900. Lizzie was seven years old and delicate. Being an "undesirable" child, she was amongst those receiving the lowest scale of rations. From the paper given me in the office at Bloemfontein I copy the scale for adults. I do not know if previous to the New Year children had less than grown people, though it is probable.

½ lb. meat

½ lb. either meal, rice, or samp.

½ oz. coffee.

1 oz. sugar.

1 oz. salt.

1/18 tin of condensed milk.

The child did not thrive on the diet, and, like many others, wasted rapidly in the great heat. Having no money to buy extra food for her children, and having a bare tent, without bed, mattress, chair, or table, Mrs. Van Zÿl strove hard, by washing for people of better means, to earn something to keep her family alive. Sufficient water was not brought into the camp for washing, so, like others, she had to take the linen to the dam, some half-mile distant In the stagnant water of this pool the clothes of the entire camp were washed for many months. While the mother thus worked, the younger children were left in the tent in charge of the eldest, a child of twelve or thirteen years of age. In December Lizzie was taken into the hospital. A lady, also a prisoner, who was brought into camp on December 14, saw her there at that date. Here she had such comfort as the rough little hospital possessed, under the immediate eye of the one *trained* nurse. Later the children's ward passed into untrained hands, and many mothers besides Mrs. Van Zÿl were anxious about the attention given to their children.

A neighbour, Mrs. Botha, tells me she was in the hospital one day when Lizzie began to cry very sadly, "Mother, mother, I want to go to mother." Mrs. Botha stepped to her to comfort her and try to stop her heartbroken wailing, and was just beginning to tell her she should soon see her mother, when a nurse in charge of that ward broke in very crossly, telling her not to trouble about the child, as she was a nuisance.

It was this tone prevalent in the camps in early months which gave the Boer women their horror of the hospitals; but their dislike passed away when nurses of good standing took the place of loyalist refugees.

Mrs. Van Zÿl felt it right to take her child away, and did so in the month of April. I used to see her in her bare tent, lying on a tiny mattress which had been given her, trying to get air from beneath the raised flap, gasping her life out in the heated tent. Her mother tended her, and I got some friends in town to make her a little muslin cap to keep the flies from her bare head.

I was arranging to get a little cart made to draw her into the air in the cooler hours, but before wood could be procured, the cold nights came on, and she died. She received no doctor's visit after her return to her tent, and the mother has since sent me word that she was never called up to give any account of her child's death. Dr. Doyle, though asked to do so, has not yet brought forward his "credible" informant who he says alleged that this mother was criminally tried for the ill-usage of her child. (See *The War: Its Cause and Conduct*, chap. vii. by A. Conan Doyle.)

It was in the end of January that I made acquaintance with Lizzie Van Zÿl, then in the hospital. She was a curiously winsome little thing, and she was able to sit up and play with the doll I brought her. She had as much attention as was possible under the supervision of the trained nurse. This nurse told me that the child's emaciation was caused by the carelessness and neglect of her mother, who "had starved her." I have no doubt the nurse believed this story, and it was not her business to inquire. But, feeling incredulous, I asked for proof of so serious an accusation, and was told that "the neighbours said so."

Beyond gossip there seemed no evidence. I determined to inquire into the case, as the accusation appeared to me one of a class and of a tone which had widely prevailed in speaking about the Boers, and which was painfully common amongst the officials of the camps at that time. I found nothing to show neglect on the mother's part; on the contrary, she was toiling to earn something for the support of her family.

The story against her, believed honestly enough, no doubt, by the doctor and the nurse, who did not visit her tent, rested solely on the word of the Swanepoel family, refugees and political enemies; other neighbours entirely denied it In addition, I found both in that camp and elsewhere numbers of children in every stage of emaciation.

The photograph allied by Mr. Chamberlain, (see his speech, *Times*, March 5, 1902), to have been taken by the doctor to show the condition in which children were brought into the camps, was not taken till after the child had been more than two months in camp, so of itself it establishes nothing as to her condition on entering. It was, I believe, taken by a Mr. De Klerk.

It does, however, exemplify, as I hoped it would when I sent it home, the effects of under-nourishment in the camps upon countless homeless children, and it did, I hope and believe, make some people realise where the brunt of the war was most heavily falling. In her short life Lizzie Van Zÿl had experienced its bitter hardships; she had been made homeless, and deprived of everything necessary for a delicate child, and she being dead yet speaketh in South Africa.

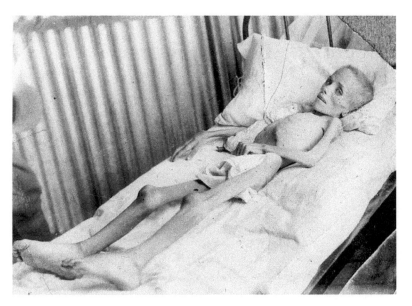

LIZZIE VAN ZŸL

# CHAPTER 5

# Women in 1901—Told by Themselves in Letters and Petitions

*They that be slain with the sword are better than they that be slain with hunger: for these pine away, stricken through for want of the fruits of the field.*—Lam. iv. 9.

*All her people sigh, they seek bread; they have given their pleasant things for meat to relieve the soul: see, O Lord, and consider; for I am become vile.*—Lam. i. 11.

*Arise, cry out in the night: in the beginning of the watches pour out thine heart like water before the face of the Lord: lift up thy hands toward Him for the life of thy young children, that faint for hunger in the top of every street.*—Lam. ii. 19.

*The tongue of the sucking child cleaveth to the roof of his mouth for thirst: the young children ask bread, and no man breaketh it unto them. They that did feed delicately are desolate in the streets: they that were brought up in scarlet embrace dunghills.*—Lam. iv. 4, 5.

This chapter must be read with the recollection that most of those who write do so under the shadow of the censor and martial law. Very few have dared to write at all, and even then only a little that has been felt dares find expression. In the days to come they will reveal the fullness of what they have experienced in mind and body. At present those who have not mingled with them must be content with the outline presented in these pages.

Letter from a Young Girl to her Former Teacher.

Translation.

Pietermaritzburg Camp, New Year's Day, 1901.

How strange to write to you the first evening of the New Year under these circumstances! Everyone tries to make the best of everything. I cannot tell how hard life is in a camp. Just imagine eleven people in one tent; it is very crammed. But I think this is just what we need, for if we should be here and have everything comfortable and nice, life would be unbearable; now we scarcely have time to think, for we have no sooner finished carrying water than we have to pull the ropes of the tents, or something is always to be done.

We are so many in tent, and yet each has a great deal to do, and when evening comes we are all just tired of the day's work, and so our days pass. I almost forgot to tell you that last night from 11 till 12 o'clock we went round the camp singing hymns (*gezangen*). Just at 12 o'clock we sang the *Nieuwjaar's* hymn in the middle of the camp; it was a quiet evening, and we could hold a candle as we went. It was a night never to be forgotten, for amid all our sorrow and trouble we sang '*Prys am Heer*' and many others. We were quite a multitude together.—Yours lovingly,

Maggie.

Early in the New Year the women of Klerksdorp drew up a petition to the President of the Worcester Congress, and forwarded it to him by the hand of Mr. J. L. Van der Merwe, who has embodied it in General De la Key's recent Report to Mr. Kruger, published in London and Holland. In February the women of Kimberley Camp signed a petition addressed to the Commandant, and in April the women of Johannesburg forwarded one to Lord Kitchener. It will probably be found some day that other camps did the same thing. The Klerksdorp petition differs from the others in that it deals principally with sufferings endured before entering the camp.

Klerksdorp, Women's Laager, Jan. 5, 1901.<br>
To the President of the Great Congress, held at Worcester, Cape Colony, on the 6th of December 1900.

Honoured Sir and Brother,—In the name of the undersigned sisters and of us all, resident in the South African Republic and the Orange Free State, we beg you and all those who took part in the Congress to accept our heartfelt thanks for all you have done in our most holy cause.

It was to us a great joy, comfort, and consolation to hear our brethren express themselves so freely against this unjust war. Be assured that all of us are still animated with undaunted courage, and that we are determined to fight to the bitter end, whatever happens. For ours is a just cause, and we know that the God of our fathers will not allow the triumph of Mammon. This conviction gives us the strength to bear whatever our enemy thinks fit to make us endure.

The sympathy which you have shown us gives us confidence in placing before you the facts which show the cruel and barbarous manner in which defenceless women and children are being treated by British officers and men. Wherever the enemy passed, destruction and misery followed in his steps. At first the enemy thought that this cruel oppression of women and children and the destruction of property would be sufficient to discourage our fighting *burghers*, and would force them to lay down their arms. But he soon found out his mistake.

The enemy commenced by burning down our homesteads and destroying other property. We were questioned by the officers in a rude manner as to our husbands and rifles. Rough soldiers visited our houses. All the necessaries of life were taken from us, and all the things which could not be conveniently carried away, such as flour, com, etc., were scattered over the *veld*. All vehicles of every kind which they could not take with them were also burnt Pictures, furniture, and household utensils were first broken to pieces and then set fire to, together with our homes. We were not even allowed to take some blankets and clothes with us for ourselves and our children. Everything was thrown into the flames. The clothes of our men were taken away for the British troops. In some cases even the children were left naked.

In this condition we stood under the bare sky, without shelter, without food, exposed to the rain, the cold, or burning heat This, however, did not yet satisfy the enemy. The crops, which, in the absence of the male population with the commandoes, we had sown ourselves, were to be destroyed or burnt. All the implements of agriculture, such as ploughs, harrows, and others, wherewith we could have again provided for our existence, were carried away or destroyed. All the poultry was killed and the cattle removed. In one word, the whole country was turned into a desert. Ah! we find no words to describe these horrors!

The barbarity of the enemy went further still: they carried the women and children off as prisoners. Even old, grey-haired, and impotent women did not escape from their ill-treatment We will state a few cases.

A certain number of women had been taken prisoners in and around Potchefstroom, and conducted to Welverdiend Station, a distance of about four hours' ride on horseback. The troops were accompanied on this march by some coloured women. The latter were allowed to sit on the waggons, but the Boer women had to go on foot, and were driven on by the *Kaffirs*. The consequence was that some fell down dead by the road, and that one woman gave birth to a child. On this occasion, *Kaffirs* were used, and they equalled the English soldiers in cruelty and barbarity.

The women knelt before these *Kaffirs* and begged for mercy, but they were roughly shaken off, and had to endure even more impudent language and rude behaviour. Their clothes were even torn from their bodies. In some cases, they had to suffer a harder lot still. The mothers were taken away from their children. The very small children were left behind, because some were ill in bed. The mothers were not even allowed to take leave of their dear treasures.

When they begged the soldiers to take pity on their children, the reply was, 'Get along; they must all come to an end.' Luckily, some women who were left behind took pity on the infants and nursed them. When the mothers were driven like cattle through the streets of Potchefstroom by the *Kaffirs*, the cries and lamentations of the children filled the air. The *Kaffirs* then jeered and cried, 'Move on: till now you were the masters; but now we will make your women our wives.' In this fearful state were the women obliged to march for four hours.

About six miles north of Potchefstroom lived the wife of Thomas Van Graan, who since February 1900 had been in exile with General Cronje. At first she had received permission to remain with her children on the farm. Quite unexpectedly, a British force arrived in the neighbourhood and at the farm. The soldiers kicked open the doors, and broke the furniture to pieces. In a violent thunderstorm, Mrs. Van Graan was placed with her little children in an uncovered waggon. These unwarranted proceedings were taken because it was supposed that Chief-Commandant De Wet had spent a night at the farm.

A great number of women along the Mooi River were also

victims of the cruelty of the English. A woman whose child was dying was removed by force, notwithstanding her heartrending entreaties. At a farm on the banks of the Vaal a woman refused to follow the soldiers. She was dragged along for a considerable distance over the *veld*, until at last they were obliged to leave her behind. Two young girls—this was also along the banks of the Vaal River—whose mother had already been carried away, were in danger of being violated, but managed to take shelter with a neighbour.

The soldiers followed in pursuit, but the girls refused to open the door. They were in great danger, but the saving hand of God protected them, and they escaped this ignominy; one of the girls made her escape, and walked a distance of six hours' ride. The sufferings of these women must have been excruciating: words are failing us to describe them.

On the Witwatersrand there was another fearful attempt at violation. In the struggle the woman's neck was twisted in such a manner that it will never come right again. Her daughter rushed to her assistance, but the ruffian drew his sabre and cut open her breast

We could add many other instances to these, but we think you will now have an idea of the cruel and barbarous manner in which the British officers and soldiers behave towards defenceless women and children.

We therefore implore your further assistance and your prayers for us to God.

Relying upon these, we remain, etc.,

(Here follow the signatures.)

## PETITION OF WOMEN TO MAJOR WRIGHT.

Kimberley Camp, Feb, 1901.

We, the undersigned, respectfully wish to address you with the following request:—

1. As we are separated from our husbands, and thus left without help, it is impossible, in the circumstances in which we are placed, to live.

2. On account of carelessness, bad management, and ill-treatment, it is now the second time that we are drenched through and through by rain, which caused our children, already sick with measles, whooping-cough, and fever, to become danger-

ously ill

3. Being without money, it is impossible for us to provide or obtain soap, candles, or other necessaries. It is now almost three weeks that most of us have been unable to do any washing. It is more than we can stand to be satisfied under all this. These are our griefs. This our humble request is—to look into our case with all reasonableness, and to have compassion on our position, and to give us our liberty by allowing us to return to our respective homes.

We hope and trust that you will take our humble request in favourable consideration, and meet us in this our request as soon as possible.—We are, dear sir, your humble servants,

| | |
|---|---|
| A. S. Earle. | C. E. Louw. |
| Annie Earle. | J. Van Niekerk. |
| J. M. Horak. | M. Britz. |
| R. Du Toit. | C. Roodt. |
| A. J. Brits. | C. Du Toit. |
| S. Botha. | Hermina Van Breda. |
| E. Botha. | R. Horak. |
| M. De Klerk. | M. Combrinck. |
| A. Serfontein. | S. Combrinck. |
| H. Brits. | A. Botha. |
| M. Brits. | C. Botha. |
| M. J. Roodt. | A. De Klerk. |
| E. M. Roodt. | W. Wessels. |
| A. C. Combrinck. | M. Serfontein. |
| A. Pienaar. | S. Brits. |
| S. Du Toit. | M. C. Roodt. |
| J. Horak. | J. J. Roodt. |
| M. Botha. | M. Herbst. |

J. C. Matthee.

Newton Refugee Camp, Kimberley.

*P.S.*—Major-*Commandant* and others in authority,—With God there is mercy. Is there, then, no mercy with you for us poor innocent women and children? Our request is to allow us to leave the 10th March 1901.

### WOMEN'S PETITION TO LORD KITCHENER.

Johannesburg (Racecourse), April 19, 1901.

The undersigned, all of whom are women and children, who

have been deported to and are at present kept in the racecourse, Johannesburg, respectfully submit—

1. That all of them are Afrikander women, whose husbands have either been killed or captured, or are still struggling for their beloved country.

2. That they have been forcibly taken from their farms and brought here against their will and desire by H.M.'s military authorities.

3. That in many instances the troops of H.M. have in a barbarous manner burnt and devastated their farms, and have stolen and destroyed other properties, so that we are now almost bereft of everything.

4. That since their arrival here they have been forced to live on the Racecourse crowded together, and only in a few cases were they allowed to live in houses in Johannesburg.

5. That in all cases without exception they have been deprived of the free, fresh, open air, and the healthy and sufficient nourishment to which they have been accustomed since the days of their birth.

6. That, in consequence of this overcrowding and this change in their surroundings and manner of life, their health has been greatly impaired. In proof hereof they can assure your Lordship that, up to the week ending on Monday, April 15, at 12 noon, fifteen (15) deaths have occurred in that one week, out of 2,789 souls on the Racecourse; whilst on the 16th and 17th of April ten (10) of us were buried.

7. That this rate of mortality exceeds by far that of the whole world or any portion thereof.

8. That, in short, this condition of things, as we have experienced the same since our arrival here, is indescribable and no longer to be tolerated.

Wherefore we request permission to return to our respective dwelling-places at the expense of H.M. Government, and that H.M. Government shall provide for our maintenance for at least the first six (6) months, we being of opinion that we have a right to demand this, because we have been brought hither against our will, and have never asked anyone for protection nor for maintenance. We have taken no active part in this war, but in spite of this we have been treated as prisoners of war ever since our banishment from our homes.—We are, etc.

Early in this year hundreds of families were going through the preliminary experiences which led to the Concentration Camps. Mrs. Uys of Braklaagte, District Bloemhof, says—

Colonel Milne came to my place and asked for Mr. Uys. I answered and said, 'My husband is on commando.'

On hearing this, he ordered his men to put paraffin on the furniture and things indoors, and told her to leave the house. She did not want to leave the house; he pulled her out into the dining-room while her bedroom was in a roaring fire, so she had to leave. When she got outside, she found her children on a waggon by order of the colonel, and then she was taken to Vryburg. She was kept in Vryburg for a month, and then sent to Kimberley Camp.

The widow, Mrs. Roodt, from Ebenezer District, Schweizer-Reyneke, states—

Lord Methuen came to my place on February 19, and took all my cattle and sheep. I told him I am a widow for three years, and asked why he does it. He told me to keep still, and get ready to get on the waggon. I was taken to Vryburg, and sent to Kimberley Camp. What became of my house is unknown to me.

Mrs. George Kalkenbrand, living at Lanstesta, District Bloemhof, Transvaal, states—

Lord Methuen came to our farm and asked me where the men are. I told him, 'On commando.' So he told me, 'I give you half an hour's time to leave the house, for it is to be burned down.' I cried, and could hardly do anything. I ran to the officers and pleaded for mercy; in turning round from them my house was all in a flame. I saved nothing but my clothes I had on. My nearest neighbour is Mrs. Dazel—where my children ran to, and where I also went—who gave clothes and food. The next morning the column came and took both Mrs. Dazel's and my stock, and sent us to Vryburg. What became of Mrs. Dazel's house, I can't say. I was sent to Kimberley Camp, and Mrs. Dazel is still in Vryburg.

Mrs. Abram Coetzee, living at Faurie's Graf, District Bloemhof,

Transvaal, says—

> My husband was on commando. When I saw the column com-
> ing, I got frightened, and fled into the garden with my children.
> They came to my house, and I saw them breaking the doors
> and windows, so I went home and pleaded for mercy. I told
> them that I got frightened, and that the officer must please
> have mercy on me. He told me to hold my tongue, and so
> they burned my house in my presence, and what has not been
> burned or destroyed they took, with live stock, and sent me
> to Vryburg, kept me there for a month, and then sent me to
> Kimberley Camp.

Mr. and Mrs. Snyman write—

> We lived in Jagersfontein, Orange Free State, formerly, and left
> for Bechuanaland in 1894, where we lived on the border of the
> Kalahari Desert, occupying some farms from a company in the
> Orange Free State, close to the grounds of which Captain O.
> R. Styles, Lee, and Gammon were agents and managers for a
> company in England. Through all the difficulties we struggled,
> made a home, took out water, and cultivated the ground. In
> 1899 we were so far on as to have a garden, and got to grow
> some vegetables. That was the first time, after all the long years
> of cultivating the ground, that we expected to reap something.
> In October 1899, the war broke out, and all the Cape Police
> left, so we were left without protection whatsoever. We re-
> mained on our farm, and some seven or nine families also on
> their farms, being over 100 miles from Vryburg. About a week
> before Christmas, one of our old boys, Aging, came to us and
> told us that the chief's son, Jantje Montchus, has gone to visit
> Major Baden-Powell in Mafeking, and has returned and given
> orders to loot the Dutch and take whatsoever they have, and if
> there is any opposition, to put out their eyes and take the Dutch
> women as spouses for the chiefs.
> We were all very frightened, as the natives did just as they
> pleased; every time they kept on stealing, and then sent word to
> the owners to follow them up if they dare. In the beginning of
> March they stole a lot of stock from Barend Breedenkamp from
> his place Dulfontein. The man being a haughty spirit, followed
> them up, when he was attacked by the thieves, who took his
> rifle and knocked his head full of holes. He walked home all

bleeding. His rifle, horse, saddle, and bridle were taken to the chief Montchus.

The next morning, on Sunday, my brother-in-law brought us the report that by all appearance the *Kaffirs* were intent on murder. We fled that day with just our clothes to the nearest neighbour, and left the house only locked, with everything in it At our neighbour's farm all the families came together, and we left for safety for Vryburg. About three weeks later we went back with a Boers' patrol to get the remainder of our goods left behind, but found nothing—everything taken out of the houses and the doors and windows destroyed.

In May the relief column came from Kimberley and Mafeking, and on a proclamation from Lord Roberts all the men at home gave up their weapons. In June I was imprisoned till September. During my imprisonment my wife bought some cattle, which the military under Colonel Galway took and sold for the Imperial Government, for which I sent in my claim for compensation, but was told that the rebels do not get any compensation, but they get disfranchisement for five years.

Having lost everything, I offered my services to the Municipal Council of Vryburg to deliver them a supply of flowing water, which will pass through a nine-inch pipe, so as to put the whole township under water, which was accepted on my terms: 'No water—no pay.' The military allowed me to work only to see the water ciphering a little, when I was stopped and sent as an undesirable to Kimberley Camp; after I defied Colonel Milne with the intelligence in a letter to bring any evidence against me, and why such steps are taken against me. From Vryburg we, with a batch of 120, were packed in cattle, coal, and sheep trucks for Kimberley.'

This narrative, supplied by a clergyman's wife, was taken down from her lips by an English lady in Cape Town. As my object is to put the case of the sufferings of the women generally before the world, and not to bring trouble or obloquy upon any individual concerned in their treatment, I purpose in this case to suppress names and even substitute false initials in order to avoid identification. By this means the story can be told with perfect freedom, which is desirable, as it presents a good picture of the life of the camps at that period, before the voice of public opinion had insisted on their reform, and a better class of persons formed the staff.

Mrs. Z. is Colonial born, and her parents live at a farm near Wellington. Her husband was the minister of the little town of X——, in the Orange Free State. Here they lived in great comfort until the occupation of Pretoria. For four months after this the British convoys were coming and going, and during this time Mrs. Z. showed many kindnesses to the British. She would send down loaves of nice white bread to the officers, and never turned away the poor hungry Tommies who came to her door begging for bread.

She once sent down some nice tarts she had baked to the officer who had arrived with a convoy, who said he almost went 'mad with joy' at the sight of pastry, for he had not seen it for months. Poultry the officers had, turkeys, ducks, and fowls, but white bread and pastry they never got. She often had them at her house and gave them tea. There was one officer who came through the town off and on, whom she particularly liked. He was Colonel R., of some Staffordshire Regiment; he would often drop in for a friendly chat She told a story to show how you could thoroughly depend upon his word.

A doctor had called, attached to one of the British convoys. 'I am sorry for you,' he said; 'the *burghers* have had a fine licking today. They actually tried to take one of our guns, but we gave them a drubbing, and they left forty dead on the field.'

This made their household very sad, and when Colonel R. came in and sat down by the fire for a chat, he noticed it, and said, 'What is the matter, Mrs. Z.? You don't look as bright as usual today.'

'Well,' she replied, 'I hear you have been fighting the *burghers*.'

'Yes,' he said, 'plucky fellows! They came on tremendously today, and as near as possible got our gun. They inflicted considerable loss, too, and suffered none themselves, except one man wounded. At least, I hear D—— is wounded, and he is a fellow worth removing.'

'There you had it,' said Mrs. Z. 'Out of one man's mouth came the truth, and out of another's a lie. If all the British officers were like Colonel R., this war would have been over long ago.'

At last the change came, and the clearing and farm-burning policy began, and reached quiet little X——. At once the whole tone of things changed. A permanent garrison was established in the town, and the old friendly relations ceased between the inhabitants and the troops. There was nothing but suspicion and tyranny. One day an order went forth that before 4 o'clock the people must take everything they wanted out of their gardens. They obeyed, but did not take much, not knowing what the order meant.

At 4 p.m. exactly the troops were let loose, pulling up and destroying everything in the gardens. Vegetables only just forming were pulled up, peach trees without a peach on them knocked about and shaken, and in a short time the flourishing and pretty gardens were a desert.

In future, whenever a convoy came through the town, the soldiers were so rude and overbearing that Mrs. Z. said she was generally ill for days afterwards. On one occasion an officer when going through the house actually made his way into her bedroom. 'Excuse me,' she said, 'these are my private quarters.'

'Private quarters?' he exclaimed; 'there are no private quarters now.' And indeed there was scarcely anything you could call your own.

They had a trap which the congregation had given to them, and which they therefore greatly valued. They had the greatest difficulty in keeping the trap. Three times it was commandeered by the military, and three times she had to exert her own personal influence to get it back. During these months of trial a certain Scotch chaplain, the Rev. Mr. McY., was a great help to her. He saved her ducks and fowls from the rapacity of the military, and interfered to prevent her husband from being sent away.

At last the blow fell which she had been dreading. Her house was searched by the military. The provost-marshal, Mr. Q., with four rough policemen, came to her house and said they were going over it to search for arms and ammunition.

She said, 'I will go round with you and show you everything. You will find nothing, because there is nothing to find.' So they all tramped into the house, and she opened everything for their inspection, and thereby saved her property in some measure from their rough handling.

Mr. Q. seemed satisfied. 'I see,' he said, 'you have no arms or ammunition—you're much too cool.'

'Mr. Q.,' said Mrs. Z., 'this time you've come as a tyrant; next time I hope you'll come as a friend.'

Far worse than this was the day when the final blow came, and the town of X—— was to be destroyed. Major W—— carried out the order, and in the roughest, harshest way imaginable.

This took place early in 1901. The people were told to get ready to be taken away to the camp, and their homes were then overrun by the military. Mr. Z. was made prisoner, and carried off to a tent on the top of a hill outside the town; his books, to the value of £500, were all burnt and destroyed; flooring, window-frames, doors, were all pulled out by the soldiers and burnt for firewood. The comfortable home was a desert. 'Where is your heart to do such things?' she exclaimed to Major W——. 'Heart!' he cried harshly, 'heart! we haven't got such a thing anymore.'

He went about the house like the Tommies, seeking for something to pick up for himself; but when she actually saw him opening her private drawer and taking the money which was now the sole barrier between herself and ruin, she snatched it out of his hand, and said, 'You thief! you shall not have that. That money is for me and my children!' She said he spoke to them all as if they were dirt, and before she left she had one more outburst. 'Some day or other,' she said, 'Major W——, you will see your name written in capital letters for all the world to see!'

'I know it,' he replied savagely, 'and that is why I'm treating you like this now.'

The journey to the camp was not so wretched as that which many others had to endure, seeing that they were allowed to take with them a certain amount of clothing and bedding and food for the journey. Still, it was a miserable time for the 140 people thus suddenly torn from their homes. One poor lady was very delicate, and the doctor said she could not stand the journey. He was justified in this opinion, for she died on her arrival in camp. They were travelling from Monday till Thursday, and it rained hard all the way. The sails of the waggon were all old and worn, and the rain came through, making them all sopping wet Mr. Z. tried to fix up his mackintosh to shelter them, but the holes were too many, and the only result was that he got wet himself without making them any better off. The last day they had no morsel of food after 11 o'clock.

On their arrival they found a few small bell-tents, but not half enough for the people to be accommodated. The consequence was that half of the people were thrown out on the bare *veld* for a fortnight, to fend for themselves as best they could. One lady, own cousin to the Rev. Mr. Steytler of Cape Town, had to do her best with two little babies on the damp ground. One of the forlorn party was an old gentleman of over eighty. These poor people had to make shelters of sticks and leaves, under which they crawled at night. It was wet on the top of them, wet at the bottom, wet all round.

After ten or twelve days Mrs. Z.'s husband was taken away from her. Her servants were being bribed to leave her; she herself lay sick, and there she was, left alone with her three little children, one of them an infant in arms. Her husband had no trial, nor was he treated like a gentleman, but abused and reviled. The only charge against him, apparently, was that he refused to take the oath of allegiance, or to ask the *burghers* to surrender. He had taken the oath of neutrality under Lord Robert's first proclamation, and had kept to it. But this was not enough, and he was condemned to be sent to India.

When Mrs. Z. heard this sentence, ill as she was she determined to protest She went to the quarters of the *commandant* and asked to see him. She was refused admittance, and told to go away. She asked again and yet again, and said that there she meant to stay until she saw the captain. Still they replied that she could not see him, until in a kind of desperation she cried out loud, 'But why then? Is he a kind of God, that he cannot see a woman asking about her own husband?'

At this she heard a voice say, 'Let her come in!' and she walked into the officer's presence.

'I want to know,' she began, 'why my husband is being sent away. He is a gentleman, why have you not treated him as such? What do your proclamations mean? You have not kept to one of them. No wonder we all laugh at them. My husband obeyed your proclamation. What did he get for it? He was abused, robbed, half starved, and now he is sent away.'

It was useless. The *commandant* threatened her subsequently with the guard-house if she said such bitter things. Her reply was ready: 'I'm not a bit afraid of your guard-house, and I'm any day ready for your gallows.'

The camp was not enclosed, and they were free to come and go; but this was not altogether an advantage, as it left the women exposed to the rudeness of the soldiers. They had to take care of themselves in every way. The tents were the ordinary bell-tents, and there were no huts or houses. The bell-tent, besides its confined space, has the great drawback that it entails constant stooping, the exact middle being the only place where you can stand upright. No bedsteads or mattresses were provided, and in some cases women expecting confinement from day to day were lying on the bare ground, with but one blanket under them.

The change of temperature was acutely felt in these small tents. In summer, you had to sit for hours with wet cloths on your head, while the babies lay gasping for breath. In winter, it was piercingly cold; one night in June the women sat up all night, as they were afraid to lie down for fear of being frozen to death. When Mrs. Z. first went to the camp she was placed in the line of 'undesirables.' The position of this line of tents was bad, and the rations served out to them were on a different scale. They only had mealie-meal to eat, with meal twice a week. This went on till the commotion was raised in England about differentiation of rations, and finally all were served alike.

But the quality of the food was never good. The flour was unfit to eat, the meat extremely poor, and the sugar a chocolate colour and very unpleasant to the taste. The military were not altogether to blame for the poor quality of the food, as the contractors were in some cases paid a good price. Some families arrived at the camp in so literally naked a condition that the military were forced to supply them with clothing. The contract was given to Messrs. Y—— & Y——, who supplied perfectly useless moth-eaten cloth, and then boasted openly that they had now 'cleared their store of all their old rubbish.'

The food contractors thought the women would blame the military and not them; but the women took the matter into their own hands. They took a quantity of flour, sifted it, made all the worms and weevils and creeping things into two neat packets, and sent one to 'Messrs. Y—— & Y——, contractors, with their compliments,' and another to the military.

After this the flour was better. The rations were served out weekly on a Monday; but there was often irregularity, and on one occasion the whole week went by till Friday, and still no rations. Then twelve women went in a body to complain to the general. His answer was, 'Well, it's lucky for you, you have any rations at all; if we had left you on your farms, you would all have been starved to death.' But after this the rations were given out more regularly. The women in this camp were both outspoken and fearless.

On one occasion, when Colonel R—— (Mrs. Z.'s friendly officer of former days) was passing through the town, he called to see Mrs. Z. in the camp. She gave him a cup of tea, or rather a little tin such as they used in the tents, and put into it a little white sugar which she kept by her for special occasions. The *commandant* was passing by, and she also invited him to come in and take a cup of tea. 'But,' she added maliciously, 'you shall not have any of that nice white sugar, but the same black stuff you give to us.' And she sweetened his tea with camp sugar.

On one occasion the camp was moved to a new site some distance away on the other side of the town. All the tents and goods were heaped on waggons, and such women and children as could not walk were told to clamber up and sit on the top of the piles of goods. The ladies felt themselves in a difficult and undignified position, for they had to hold on for dear life as the oxen rattled through the *sloots* and *dongas*.

One officer whom they met as they were crossing a *sloot* sang out, 'Rule Britannia, Britannia rules the waves.'

'But she will never rule the Boers,' sang back one of the women. As they passed through the town, three or four officers were on the *stoep* of the club and made fun of them perched upon the waggons. Mrs. Z. could not refrain from trying to make them ashamed of themselves. 'Yes, look well at your deeds of heroism,' she cried as they passed. 'You can't catch De Wet, you can't catch Steyn, so you catch us helpless women and drive us through the town on waggons. Look well at us, the result of your deeds of heroism!' The officers left the *stoep* and went inside.

The women had to defend themselves sometimes in other ways than with their tongues. Sometimes soldiers got into the tents at night and gave them much trouble. One night a Tommy got into the camp, and entered four or five tents in succession, frightening the women. At last some thirty of them joined together and chased him out, pinching him black and blue. On the following night several women felt very nervous, and Mrs. Z. herself thought it better to have her light burning. There was a sort of camp policeman, but he was only a 'hands-upper,' and had never been of much service as far as the women were concerned, and they held him in small regard.

That night, going the rounds, he saw her candle alight in the tent, and called out loudly, 'Put out that light.' She made no reply. 'Put out that light,' he called still louder, thumping on the ground.

At last she called back, 'I *shan't* put out my light It isn't safe here, with soldiers prowling about' '

Why, I'm here to protect you,' he said.

'You! what good are you?' she replied. 'Where were you last night when the Tommy got in?'

'Well, put out your light,' he said, 'or I'll report you to the captain.'

'Report if you please; but I shall not put out my light.'

She kept it alight, and the following day the guard reported the case to the captain. But the military were not much more favourable to the hands-uppers than the women, and the captain gave the man a snub for his pains. 'Would not put out her light, and treated you rudely, did she? Well, considering what happened the night before, I expect Mrs. Z. was nervous, and if I had been in her place I wouldn't have put out my light.'

This camp was much healthier than most, and comparatively few children died. But they all got earache with the damp and cold, and were always ailing more or less, and the women too. Mrs. Z. never felt really well all the time she was there, and at last the doctor said if she remained any longer she would die. It was by no means pleasant to be ill in camp. The first doctor who was there was extremely harsh and cruel to his patients. He would scarcely glance at them as he went his rounds; and then if he did stop to speak to them, overwhelmed them with taunts and abuse.

At last the women lodged a regular complaint against him, and asked him plainly, 'Do you think we're dirt, that you treat us like this?'

A single case will serve to illustrate the methods of doctor and nurses in the camp. An old Mrs. K., from the Free State, a wealthy old lady and much respected, had been torn away from a comfortable and beautiful home to come and live in the camp. The change in her whole manner of living was too sudden, and she was unable to bear up against it. She had been used to every comfort and even luxury, and now had to suffer every hardship. She took to her bed.

The nurse was summoned, but would not enter the tent, and would scarcely look at her. 'Oh, she's grumpy and full of pretence, like all old people,' she said, and walked on. The second and third day she never came near the tent. On the fourth day it was clear that unless something was done the old lady would die, and the nurse was summoned again. Both the nurses were dressed to attend an officers' tea-party, and were extremely angry that they could not go because old Mrs. K. was dying. However, they came to the tent, saw that the old lady was sinking fast, and ordered everybody to leave the tent. Her sister refused flatly to go.

'No,' she said; 'I've been nursing her all I could these days, when you would not come near her, and I am not going to leave her now.' That night she died. In the morning the nurse had said, when they asked her to call in the doctor, 'I'm not going to bother the doctor; she's just grumpy.'

As sometimes happens, the chief nurse, Nurse O., was more intent upon amusing herself abroad than attending to her duties at home. But, in addition to this drawback, her temper was so violent that everyone was in terror of her, and few dared ask her help. Even among the officers she was known as 'Little Tyrant,' 'Little Spitfire.' If you went to ask her for medicine, you must expect to get the door slammed in your face. On one occasion she left a little child of eight years old alone in the hospital tent all day, without food or medicine. Once, when Mrs. Z. herself went in, in the nurse's absence,—a daring thing to do,—all the patients started up in their beds and cried, 'Give us food! Give us food!'.....

Mrs. Z. could not speak too highly of the way in which the women bore up under the severe strain put upon them. The military gave them a chance of two months in which to write to their husbands to beg them to surrender. Not a single one wrote, though everyone knew what a difference it would make to their position. The hardships of the camp were so great that many times Mrs. Z. exclaimed, with tears in her eyes, 'If it had not been for the grace of God we could not have endured it' The arrogance and selfishness of the officers were severely commented on by her, and she constantly held up Colonel R. as her idea of a true gentleman, and as being the only one she met. One officer said to her, 'This war is not going to end yet; we're making too much money.'

Here is a little note I received from one of two sisters, who have been nearly two years prisoners of war. They had been several months in a camp, where they lived in great anxiety about their mother—

Feb. 15, 1901.

I could not answer your welcome note, which reached me safely, as I have been indisposed the last few days. Fancy, last Monday I sent in an application requesting to return home to my mother, who is so very lonely; and on Tuesday I received a letter from her stating that she too has been sent from home. She only lives half an hour from the village, and had of course to leave all her furniture and property unprotected, with only one native boy to look after it, and now has to live at her own expense in the village; otherwise she had to go to a Refugee Camp too.
Oh, what a disappointment the news was to me and my sister! for we both cherished the hope of receiving a favourable answer to our application. Oh, how this breaks my heart! Excuse me for being so forward as to mention home affairs, but this means so much to me that I cannot refrain from saying something about it
A new wash-bath was erected for the women, so that we have our bathing-place free again. Only two deaths occurred since you left.

One of the two ladies who give the following account of their eviction from their homes is known to me, and herself told me the whole story as it appears here, only with amplified detail. The other, Mrs. Bosman, is a great invalid, and her husband is a prisoner of war—
Mrs. Bosman said:

Our farm was six miles from S——. About the middle of last March 1901, British troops arrived. under the command of Colonel Hickman, and took away the greater part of our cattle.

For some time, previously my daughter and I—she is a child of fourteen—had been deserted by all save one *Kaffir* boy. As you see, I am rather a helpless person, having lost my right arm, and having sustained an injury to one leg that causes me constant suffering, and leaves me with the power only to move about with difficulty on a crutch. When Colonel Hickman and his men took away our cattle, they also took away our boy to look after them.

A few days later he returned to the farm, having escaped from the British. He and we lived in constant apprehension of another body of troops arriving to destroy our home. It was eight o'clock one morning when they came. I had not yet left my bedroom, but little Annie was working in the kitchen. When she saw the soldiers, she ran to the front door and tried to bar their progress, exclaiming that they should not come in. She was crying,—with anger, not fear,—and she said, 'You needn't think our men are so mean as to come in here and hide: they fight outside.' When the troops came into the house, she ran into my room, crying, 'Oh, mother, the English are here!'

In all, I suppose there must have been two hundred soldiers. They surrounded a lot of our fowls and ducks, threw great pieces of wood into the midst of them to break their legs, and then picked them up and twisted their necks. The pigs they killed by sticking them with their bayonets. They also got together some of the horses, oxen, and sheep that Colonel Hickman's party had failed to capture.

After wrecking everything inside the house, they began to smash up our carts. But two—a little fancy buggy that I used to drive about in, and a Cape cart—they set aside to take away. As a matter of fact I managed to save the cart. Just as they were moving off, the horses they had put in it proved obstinate. So I went up to the officer in command, Captain Robertson, and begged him to leave me the cart, as I was an invalid. He very kindly consented, so the horses were taken out and the cart was left

The boy fled to the hills on catching sight of the soldiers, and I saw no more of him. He was terribly afraid of what the British would do to him, because he had left them before.

In about an hour from their arrival the soldiers rode away. Captain Robertson politely saluting to me, and then my little girl and I were left alone in our ruined home.

We were obliged to walk over to my friend Miss Wessels' house. Just fancy! six miles and terribly hot, and I a cripple who can hardly hobble with my crutch, and have to spend most of my time lying down. The journey did not take much more than three hours. My little girl helped me along a good deal We had to rest pretty often. But the worst part of the experience was to see the veld strewn with dead horses, sheep, and other animals. Next day I was driven back to my wrecked farm by one of Miss Wessels' servants. He put mules in my cart, and I drove it back again. I have learnt to use the reins with my left hand. Before saying a final goodbye to my house, I picked up some photographs and other things that the soldiers had dropped as they marched away.

Miss Wessels, in whose house the invalid Mrs. Bosman had found shelter, said—

Our home was not broken up till some time afterwards. I lived in a house in S—— with my father—who is sixty years old and an invalid, and has been a member of the Volksraad for twenty years—and my sister. But passing columns of English soldiers had paid us occasional visits, but on each occasion they did little besides insist on receiving our grain, which they scattered on the road. When they had left, we used to go and sweep it up and sift it, and then it was fit for use. They visited all the houses for this purpose, and often they threw the grain down in places where it was spoilt. In some cases, they poured paraffin upon it, to be sure it would be useless.

One day they came and took away my beautiful bicycle, that had come all the way from London and had cost me £30. I made a great bother about having a receipt for it, and at last the officer gave me one for £7. A few days afterwards we had notice that we should all have to leave in three hours. By good luck we had ample provisions left in our house, and so we sent a message round to our neighbours, who had also had notice to quit, telling them to come and share our supplies.

For two and a half hours we were busy distributing our things among them. Then we asked them to go, and we spent the remaining half-hour in getting together bedding, clothes, a few cooking utensils, and other articles we proposed to take with us.

The soldiers had removed all our vehicles except a little American spider, which had been stored away in pieces, and which the English had not known how to put together. We had that and Mrs. Bosman's cart, and the commanding officer consented to our taking them with us, as we had two invalids—Mrs. Bosman and my father. The results were we were very much better off than our neighbours, many of whom started on their journey with next to nothing. We also had a great advantage in that my father had a sum of money to take with him.

At the end of the half-hour the soldiers came, our house was locked up, and we went off to the camp just outside the town, where we were to sleep that night At least, we didn't sleep. We all five lay on the ground under the waggon, and it was the first time I had passed a night in the open. Near us lay a poor old fellow, who kept muttering, being half-demented at what had occurred. At 3 a.m. I was up, and got permission to pay a last visit to my home to fetch something I had forgotten. When I drew near the place I saw three cows standing outside the gate. Those cows had twice been taken away by the English soldiers, but on both occasions, they escaped and came back, because their calves had been left behind in our yard.

I entered the house and struck a light, only to find that everything was smashed and topsy-turvy, the soldiers having ransacked the place since we left It was a touching last look at home—with the breakfast things still on the table amid the ruins, and the yeast on the stove. My sister came to call me back, as they were inspanning. We led the cows to the camp, and the *commandant* very kindly gave us permission to take them with us. The convoy started just at dawn.

But I must not forget to tell you about the two old ladies whom the English had decided to leave behind, because the ambulance doctor said they were too old and feeble to be moved.

When we heard they were not to be disturbed, we took some of our pictures and other valuables round to their house for safe custody. But what happened was this—just before the convoy started, their house was visited and ransacked, and the old ladies were carried out and put on one of the waggons.

Day was dawning when the convoy started from S——. There were about 250 carts and waggons, the former filled with

English infantry, the latter with our women and children. We five,—my father, my sister, Mrs. Bosman and her daughter and myself,—with two servants, shared a waggon with three other families, making twenty-two persons in all. We were all squeezed together, and of course horribly uncomfortable. We had no covering, and the sun soon became terribly hot Mrs. Bosman's cart, with our belongings, was tied behind. The bellowing of the cattle and the crying of the children made a never-ending din.

The sufferings of our two invalids became so intense that I made representations to Captain Robertson, who very kindly found us a waggon with a cover, and during the remainder of the journey we had it to ourselves. The Boers were in the neighbouring *kopjes*, and shots were heard every now and then. They were skirmishing about, and every now and then getting hold of some of the cattle that accompanied the convoy. At the river, that is seven miles from S——, we were delayed a long time by more serious fighting.

The Boers were firing from the opposite bank, and the little Tommies took up positions in front of the waggons, so that our people could not fire on them without endangering us. But I saw the dust thrown up by bullets that went into the ground a few yards off. A good few were killed and wounded, as we found afterwards when the convoy restarted, and additional ambulance waggons were wanted. One of the waggons selected for the purpose was that which contained the two old ladies I spoke about before. They afterwards told me how they were hoisted out and deposited in the road, where they feared they would be left. But at last some compassionate people came along, who lifted them into another waggon.

On the first day, we only got about ten miles. The fighting delayed us a lot, and, besides, it was very slow work getting along with a number of waggons going abreast Of course a formation in single file would have made a long line, and one very difficult to guard. I forgot to mention one very exciting moment in the fighting at the river. A *burgher* on the other bank rode right out into the open, killing several horses. Oh, such a lot of little Tommies fired at him, and I made sure he would be killed; but not one of them hit him, and he got away all right with the horses.

At night we had a very rough time; the soldiers weren't kept separate from us. As to food, our little party had nothing to complain of. You see, unlike most of the others, we had brought ample supplies in our cart. That night we cooked a fine turkey, and I made some coffee on an oil-stove included among our belongings. It was pitiful to see the sufferings of other people. Water and fuel were terribly difficult to get. We helped as far as we could; but of course, on occasions of that sort, every family has to look after itself, and we had two invalids on our hands. Rations were served out to all every day; but I don't know what they consisted of, as we never applied for any, having no need to.

Yes, we did have one thing—a little pot of jam that Mrs. Bosman managed to get! Seeing an officer with a pot of jam, Mrs. Bosman asked for it, and he said, 'All right; you shall have it.' I think he was sorry for her because she is a cripple. But none of us were allowed to retain our own meal. Officers kept riding along and asking the people in every waggon if they had meal, as it must be given up. One little girl begged very hard to be allowed to keep a cupful, to make her invalid grandmother some soup; but she wasn't allowed to.

After the first night, the camping arrangements were so far improved that the troops were kept apart from us. On the third day it rained in torrents, and you can imagine the sufferings of the poor creatures, huddled together, with no shelter overhead. There was a long halt at Orange River Bridge, where there were a lot of horrid men,—the scum of South Africa,—who jeered at us and said all the insulting things they could think of. We arrived at Aliwal North Camp on the fourth day. Here we had another stroke of good luck, as compared with our poor neighbours. A friend of ours who had been there for some time came to meet us, and gave us useful hints as to which was the healthiest part to pitch our tents, where we could obtain them, and so on. Aliwal, of course, is the best of all the Concentration Camps. But we saw an infinite amount of suffering there. Every night a lot of respectable people had to sleep in the open.

\*\*\*\*\*\*

Remarks from Ladies' Commission Report:

*Recommendation*—Remove the superintendent, and thoroughly reorganise the camp.—Cd. 893.

\*\*\*\*\*\*

It was pitiful to see them shivering in their blankets, which were often saturated with rain, and sometimes stiff with frost. We enjoyed the tremendous advantage of having money. It enabled us to procure a little house made of wood and canvas,—a great improvement as a sleeping apartment on the tents, which let the rain come streaming in upon you. The rations were very poor, and included coffee that made the children ill. Half a tin of condensed milk was supposed to last each person a week. We supplemented our rations by purchasing food at the store, where everything was about twice the usual price. We still had one of our cows to supply us with milk. We paid people to bake our bread and wash our clothes—so that they should have some money to buy food with. There was a great deal of sickness in the camp, and several deaths occurred every day.

\*\*\*\*\*\*

Cd. 893. See *Rations*.

The thriving and well stocked shops were also indicative of a fairly well-to-do population.

*Fuel.*—At the first interview with Mr. Greathead (Superintendent) he was asked what the fuel ration was. He replied, 'As much coal as they can consume, and some wood.' On investigation, this was found to be inaccurate. . . . . One loyal English woman said, 'You get very little coal, and no wood, unless you are cheeky.'

*Permission to leave Camp,*—No information.—Cd. 893.

\*\*\*\*\*\*

During the six weeks that I was in camp we received coal only twice, and then only enough to cook one meal.

When we went to the *commandant* and asked permission to go, he said we certainly might do so. But he made the condition that we should wire to the *commandant* of the place we were bound for and get his permission. We wired to Cape Town, but received no reply. This, we found, was the general experience. An answer was never sent, and so the people had to remain in the camp. But I took the matter energetically in hand, explaining that we wanted to get to Cape Town in order to sail for England; and at last, on the ground that Mrs. Bosman was an invalid, the *commandant* gave us a free railway pass to Cape Town—a pass, that is, for Mrs. Bosman, her daughter, and myself. We left little Annie at a school in Cape Town, and took the first ship to Southampton.

When we left, my father and sister were trying very hard to get permission to leave, but we have not yet learnt whether they have succeeded. By the by, my father nearly got into trouble with the authorities. He had been to hear the Dutch Reformed minister, and came away disgusted, remarking, 'Why, he talks nothing but politics.' This being reported to the officials, next day they sent for my father, who repeated that the minister's discourse was entirely political. The minister, who was present, said that was not true, whereupon my father replied, 'Well, surely I ought to know politics when I hear them, after all the years I have been in the Volksraad.'

'Then it is God's politics I am preaching,' the minister said; and they let my father off with a warning.

Most of our own ministers had been sent away as undesirables early in the war. Some people are led to suppose that the undesirables were bad characters. As a matter of fact they are some of our best and most influential people."

Miss Cameron's story of the long journey of her family and herself by convoy to Volksrust and Pietermaritzburg Camps is written in diary form—

*Amsterdam, New Scotland, Thursday, February 14,* 1901.—This morning, about eight o'clock, the cavalry of the enemy entered the town by the Glen Aggie road. They soon spread all over the town, the infantry following. In a short time every garden and tree was stripped of everything; not even a green peach remained. All the livestock was taken; the cattle and horses were collected by natives and driven off, while the poultry, pigs, etc., the soldiers made off with. We locked up all the doors and remained in the house, looking on. At about 11 a.m. two intelligence officers came to search the house; they went through every room searching for arms and ammunition, and took away a revolver and cartridges we had.

After some talk they left, saying another officer would come in the afternoon, from whom we would get our instructions. About 3 p.m. General Campbell arrived, with his staff; he was very abrupt, and the reverse of pleasant in his bearing. He said they, the English, had come to give us food and protection. Mother replied that he could not give us what we had not asked for, and that we were quite satisfied with the food and protection our own people afforded us. Then he said we were to be ready to leave the following day (Friday) at 10 a.m.; and after a deal of talk and argument he left, highly offended.

*Friday.*—Worse than ever. Another column has come through Sweede Poort, has just passed the house, and one can truly see the place is over-ridden. . . . At about 11 p.m. the provost-marshal. Captain Daniels, with four others, entered the house and began searching the place again. Mother was absent when they came. It would be impossible to describe how they rummaged and pulled everything about; the mattresses and pillows were felt, doubled up, and patted; every box, great or small, was thoroughly overhauled and searched to the very bottom; the fireplaces, bookshelf, kitchen, pantry, loft, every nook and corner was ransacked, and they took what they wanted—soap, candles, mealies, etc., even to white sewing cotton. When mother came in, an officer turned to her, and said, 'Those devils of Boers have been sniping at us again, and your two sons among them, I suppose. If I catch them they will hang.'

*Saturday, 16th.*—The place has been in a whirl all day. People never stop coming. A fight is going on out Swaziland way. We hear the cannon and saw the I.L.H. with large guns, and later another lot of troops go out to reinforce, we suppose.

*Sunday.*—At dawn Captain Ballantyne came, and said that a waggon would arrive in a few minutes, and we would be allowed a quarter of an hour to load, and only to take the most necessary things, as fifteen were to go on one waggon, and once in the English camps we would be supplied with everything that we required—food, medical comforts, etc. So we were one of three families in the waggon. The Mullers, from Middelburg district, living in Mrs. Davel's barn, sixteen in all, including an old woman over eighty years of age and a baby not three months old, were put on to a trolley, with a half tent fixed at the back. There was not even room for them all to sit.

We—that is, all the people—were taken across the *spruit* to the English camp, about half a mile out from the town. The waggons were drawn in rows, and each one thoroughly searched by a party of men, everything taken off, and each box and bag carefully looked through. Not a thing, however small, escaped inspection; even housewives' needle-cases were opened and looked through. What the men considered you did not need was taken. Feather beds, clothing, mattresses, chairs, chests, etc., odds and ends of all kinds, were piled in heaps and burnt

Foodstuff—flour, sugar, tea, etc.—was also taken.

In the afternoon at 2 o'clock we went on from there, the oxen never being outspanned, and trekked about twelve miles. There were over 400 waggons. We would trek a few yards, when there would be a block, and one would have to wait for the waggons to straighten out, so that most of the time was spent in waiting for a way to clear. It rained all day, and almost without exception every waggon leaked. Many people had not a dry thread in their waggons by the evening. No halt was made, no food partaken of since 6 a.m. At 9 p.m. we outspanned at the top of a *bult* in a hard rain; no food to eat, and not even a drink of water to be had. It was pitiful to hear the children crying all night in the wet waggons for water and food and not be able to get a thing for them. The oxen were just tied to the yoke in the mud—no grazing.

At dawn the next day the oxen were inspanned as they stood from the yoke, and we trekked past Volve Koppies and outspanned at about 9 a.m. Here we found out that we had to furnish the driver and leader of our waggon with food from what had been left us. We received no rations at all, no food of any kind, no wood or water. The driver had to walk fully a mile to fetch water, and we had some planks that we made fire of. It rained all day. This evening Lieutenant Pratt came and told mother he had had instructions to remove our waggon from the others, and that a guard was to be placed over us to prevent speaking to other people. So we were drawn away from our trek, and four armed soldiers were put by the waggon.

*Tuesday, 19th.*—We reached Piet Retief today. The English have a large troop of cattle and horses, which are driven into every mealie field or cultivated ground as we pass,—generally *Kaffir* lands,—and in a few minutes everything is totally destroyed. Also the cattle, goats, etc., are taken, as they might furnish food for the Boers. At Volve Koppies we saw a *Kaffir* hut on fire, and the troopers warming their hands in the blaze. This evening we received a leg of mutton, the first food of any kind supplied to us since leaving on Sunday morning. We are, of course, on one side with our guard.

The roads are bad beyond description—mud and slush everywhere; one is not able to obtain a clean standing-place. The ruts and holes are awful I did not think it possible for a waggon to go over such places, but we just bang in and out, over anywhere. If you capsize, stick fast, or come over, it is all right; every waggon must take its chance.

The drivers and leaders are natives, many *unfaans* who have never driven before, with a few white men as conductors. Our guard have pitched their tent beside the waggon; there is always one on guard at night During the day, while we trek, one is by the waggon, and at the outspan all four.

*Wednesday.*—Arrived at a mission station—Bergen, I think; Johannes the name of the clergyman in charge, a German. It is raining heavily, and has been wet all day. Surrounded by a ring of English camps.

*Sunday.*—We are on a very dirty spot. Heaps of sheep, the only food we get, are killed every day by the people and *Kaffirs*, and the skins and insides are left all over the place, just where the sheep are killed. The stench is almost unbearable. We have been here several days, and are in a ring of English camps. No convenience of any kind is put up for the women or children, and it is impossible to go out in the daytime without being seen. This morning there is no rain, so the people are taking the things out of the waggons. I saw a woman wring out her pillows and blankets and the corners of her mattress, all soaking wet, and she is but one of the many.

*Monday.*—We have moved on about two miles to a new camp.

*Wednesday.*—Came through a very bad drift today. Are still in Bergen, at Martin's farm.

*Thursday.*—Trekked all day long. The roads and drifts are something cruel—so bad, and the poor oxen are not allowed time enough to rest during the short outspan. At 7 p.m. we outspanned just by a river. At 11 p.m. came the order we were to go on. It was pitch dark. Our waggon was one of the front ones; so on we went in the dark over very bad roads, slippery with rain, and cut up with traffic. We crossed four dreadful drifts; and if our driver had not been a very good one, I do not know what would have happened. We outspanned at 2 a.m. Only a few waggons were with us. Several accidents happened, which blocked the road; a Mrs. Brodrick was hurt on her chest by a box falling on her when the waggon capsized.

*Friday.*—We have outspanned all day by the Pongola, waiting for the other waggons to come out On Saturday we took the whole day to make a short trek. This afternoon we started again in the pouring rain. At ten p.m. we stuck fast and almost overturned in the mud. As we were near the camp, the guard went for help; and we had 36 oxen on, and tried until 2 a.m. to get out, without success. Next morning we were pulled out

*Sunday.*—We trekked as far as the Red Paths, where we slept The Red Paths is one of the worst bits of road on one of the worst roads in the Transvaal Monday: We went up the Red Paths today. The waggon only had bedding and clothes on, and it took three spans to take our waggon up; the trek-tow broke four times; the mud is dreadful; it is all the oxen can do to drag themselves along. Outspanned other side of Bovian's River. Tuesday: Raining all day. Standing over waiting for the other waggons to come up. The road in front blocked by a convoy. Annie very sick. Must be the food, as we have only meat, and mealies when we can pick them; no bread, not even meal for porridge, and not able to get anything for love or money. Our guard was removed today by Captain MacStead, East Yorkshire Regiment. We have had men from the Suffolk Regiment, 5th Lancers, Dublin Fusiliers, East Yorkshire, and Gordon Highlanders. They were always willing to help in any way, and we had nothing at all to complain of from the men; they were good to us.

*Wednesday.*—Annie been very ill all day. A driving, misty rain. We are about 20 miles from Utrecht, unable to obtain anything in the shape of food, not even meat, as the sheep have been left behind on entering this district. There is a lot of sickness, owing to the wet weather and lack of food. The road is one mud-hole; waggons stick fast in the mud going downhill; it is worse than any we have yet come over. We have three spans of oxen on, and one ox fell down from exhaustion, and was beaten and dragged out of the road in a dying condition. Oxen with lung sickness are made to pull until they fall down in the yoke to die.

*Thursday.*—Cold, misty rain. Mother and Annie very ill. Nothing whatever to give them. Entered Utrecht today. Unable to buy bread, as the people have either given or sold what they had. Ordered to go through the town at 9 p.m.; raining, and very dark. Were kept over an hour at the office, then ordered to cross the river to the camp. Earlier in the evening a waggon capsized in crossing, but this did not prevent them taking all the remaining families over in the dark.

*Friday.*—Had to go at 3 a.m. for rations, the first we have received since leaving, February 17—flour 1 lb., sugar 1 oz., coffee 1 oz., salt ½ oz., per adult Made a very long trek until 4 p.m.; outspanned in the pouring rain; no fuel.

*Saturday.*—At the Umbana Camp; received three days' rations—3 lbs. mealie meal, 1½ oz. sugar, *ditto* coffee. Came on to Newcastle; sent the boy with money and note to buy bread. The guard refused to allow the boy to pass the bridge. It is raining, and we have no fuel.

*Sunday.*—Refused to allow boy to go over to the town to buy bread, though mother went down to the bridge and asked the guard to allow boy to get bread for us. Later a soldier volunteered to go and buy bread for us, which he did.

*Monday.*—Left Newcastle yesterday afternoon; arrived here (Volksrust) 9.30, in the rain. The station a sea of mud and slush. No provision of any kind made for the women and children, over 300. We bought what we required at the refreshment-room, but many had no money. The rooms formerly used by the Z.A.R. as customs offices were thrown open, and the women and children herded in until there was scarce standing-place. Those left out, ourselves among them, were loaded on to two trolleys and taken to what was formerly the Volksrust Hotel, where fourteen of us spent the night in a small single bedroom. It contained nothing but a table. One of our party brought two rugs with her, which we spread on the floor and sat down until morning.

*Monday.*—A pitiless downpour. Had to go to the station to see about our few possessions; we had not even a rug with us. The goods in the luggage vans had been off-loaded on to the station in a heap in the rain, and all the women and children in one struggling mass, each trying to separate their belongings from the heap. The trucks containing the bulk of the goods had been left behind at the reversing station at Majuba, or rather Boscobella. Our things were in the trucks, so we had to wait about in the rain and slush until that afternoon, late, when the trucks came in and were off-loaded, not on to the platform, but on to the bank on the other side, into pools of water and soft slush.

It would be impossible to describe the confusion of the scene—natives on the trucks off-loading, just pitching off everything pellmell. I saw a bag of meal burst open from end to end when it reached the ground, and the same with boxes—they stood in the water and mud until loaded on to a trolley. Everybody had to claim their goods as they came off the truck. The bank was lined with women, shouting and gesticulating as their things were tumbled off, so that the uproar was deafening.

*Sunday, March 17.*—A week of rain and misery. We are still at the Volksrust Hotel—eleven of us in a small verandah room; barely room to sleep; we eat and live outside. The camp is quite close to us in the town, among the houses. Many of the tents are standing in mud pools; the only concern of the *laager commandant* seems to be that the tents should be put up nicely in rows—where, does not matter; two bell-tents between three families. Mother would not take those shown to her, one single, one lined, standing in mud pools; the rain had washed right through, in one side, out at the other. She told Superintendent Nixon they were not fit for even a dog, and declined to move into them.

*Monday, 18th.*—Went today to receive rations. We have to stand in a lump in front of a window and give in the ration-ticket—1 lb. flour, 1 oz. sugar and coffee, ½ oz. salt per day, and 2 lb. meat per week for an adult; children under twelve, half-rations. The flour was all right; sugar and coffee very bad; the meat simply vile. The sheep killed are very poor; then the meat is piled up in a tent for the night, and very often, when served out next day, still quite warm and going sour.

*Friday, April 19th.*—At past eight last night, just as mother was going to bed, —— came with message that Major —— wanted to see her at once. Mother replied, 'Impossible; she would come in the morning.' The man said he did not dare to take such a message, mother must come; so eventually mother, Annie, and Polly Coltzer went with the policeman, who took them to the major's house, where they were shown into his bedroom. As mother passed through, the soldier put his arm across the door to prevent Annie from entering, but she lifted up his arm, saying, 'I am her daughter,' and with Polly entered the room.

The major was in a dreadful rage. 'You are Mrs. Cameron?'

'Yes.'

'You are a most dangerous woman. It has come to our ears that you have been speaking against the British Government. What do you think your puny personality can do against the mighty British Government? You will not be treated as a woman, but as a man. You are an Englishwoman.'

'All my sympathies are with the Boers.'

'Policeman, make a note of that.' When mother tried to speak, the major said, 'Silence; you are under our thumb, and we will keep you there.'

'That remains to be proved.'

'You dare to say that again! You will be taken to prison at once. You understand?'

'I understand.'

'All the concessions we intended making you will be withdrawn. You will not be allowed to receive any parcels. You hear?'

'Am I not to be allowed to defend myself?'

'Policeman, a guard is to be placed over this woman tonight, and she is to come up to the office tomorrow at 10 a.m., under escort'

'If you wish to see me tomorrow morning, I give you my word to appear. An escort will be unnecessary.'

'Your word!'

'Yes, my word. I refer you to the whole of Ermelo district and half of Piet Retief as to whether I keep my word or not.'

The major then repeated his former instructions to the policeman about the escort and guard. Mother bowed and said 'Thank you,' and walked out, and was escorted back by the policeman. A guard was posted at the room that night, and next morning mother and my sister were escorted by a policeman through the street to the office. Arrived there they were informed that the major was too unwell to attend his office, so had to return. Later on a policeman was sent to inform them to appear before the magistrate; they were again escorted to the office. The sum of what he said was that it had come to their knowledge that mother was stirring up the camp and encouraging the Boers in their resistance by saying that they would win, and if he had occasion to reprimand again, 'he would come down on her most severely.'

Some days later the two families in the room with us—Mrs. Strauss and Mrs. Coltzer—were removed to the new camp beyond the railway station, outside of the town. Mother, my sister, and self went to the office and inquired if we might not also go to the camp, as the superintendent told us he had received orders that we were to remain where we were. The major asked if we meant to live there. Mother said yes.

'Then,' he said, 'you will not be allowed to live in the camp. You are fortunate in having a room.' Mother said the room did not suit; she wished to change, if possible; and he replied she could do so.

*Thursday, April 25th.*—Late this afternoon we received the following:—

From Assistant District Commander to Mrs. Cameron.
Volksrust Hotel, Volksrust, April 25, 1901.

I beg to inform you that you are to proceed to Maritzburg to-morrow, 26th inst. by the 11 p.m. train. A waggon shall convey your luggage to the station.'

We did not leave until the following Sunday evening, as no waggon was sent to convey our luggage to the station until then. We arrived here on the 29th April, and are at present still here.              B. R. Cameron, Prisoner of War.

Green Point, Pietermaritzburg, Natal,
May 31, 1901.

From a Free State Girl, Daughter of a Colonist of Devonshire Birth.
April 16, 1901.

We were in the camp at Vredefort Road for two months, and we got let out at last at the request of an aunt who is a Jingo. We had suffered much anxiety at our home before we were taken prisoners. Still we did not want, as the Boer commandoes used to give us supplies of meat and meal. (This remark is interesting as showing that families were in some cases a drain upon the commandoes.)

When the British came to Vredefort, a trooper whom we questioned told us we should have to go as our name was on the list, but that we should be given plenty of time to prepare. We began at once to prepare; it was well we did, for at three o'clock we were told that we must leave in half an hour's time. Then there was a scene of great confusion. We worked as hard as we could, and some soldiers came in to help us, but as fast as they helped with one hand they stole with the other. The officers grumbled at the amount we got together, and the waggons were piled up high, for most of the inhabitants of Vredefort were turned out at the same time.

Our party consisted of my old grandfather, my mother, and a brother—a boy of eighteen. After we had started we soon stopped, and spent the night only about half an hour's distance from the town, in sight of our own homes. Here we were in the open waggons—no shelter—and many people without food. We had fortunately brought a good supply. The children kept on crying through the night.

The camp at the station is only three hours from Vredefort, but we took two days to reach it, because we made zigzags all the way to guard against surprise. The second night we also slept in the open, and we feared for grandfather's life in the bitter cold. When we reached the station towards evening, we were ordered to cross to the other side, then to recross, then to cross back again, and it was late into the night when we could settle down, and again the poor, hungry, tired children were crying and fretting.

Our camp was a real prison. There were entanglements all round it, and then fences, and sentries were placed at the entrances. The superintendent was nice, but the *commandant* was a terrible man, everyone, even the Tommies, trembled at the sound of his voice. He had a lock-up or guard-room for women who offended him. I have known women to be dragged from their beds at night to be put into this guard-room. A spirited woman, who hung her washing on the iron fence, was imprisoned because she said to the sentry who ordered her to take it off:

'Well, tell the, *commandant* then that he must make another wire fence for the washing, for we can't spread it on the bare ground.'

★★★★★★

*Discipline.*—No means of discipline except fining.—Cd. 893.

★★★★★★

Another woman got into trouble because the officer complained to her about the Boers pulling up railway lines. She replied:

'Well, it is their own railway; can they not do what they like with their own?'

She was ordered out of her bed and put into the guard-room, and asked for her two little children and a mattress. It was so draughty that she lay all night on the flap to keep the wind from the children on the mattress. Both these women were removed as undesirables; no one in the camp knew where they were taken.

Everyone received sufficient meal, but not meat. Those who had not money to buy food for themselves must have gone very short. The washing had to be done by themselves in a stagnant pool, which became very bad from constant use. The confinement and want of exercise was very much felt, for firewood was very scarce, and it was impossible to keep warm. Everyone slept on the floor, and the wind blew in at the sides of the tent.

★★★★★★

Meat ration is issued daily, and the usual difficulty arising out of the thinness of the meat has been experienced. Bully-beef had on two occasions to be issued instead of fresh meat, when the latter was too bad to eat. No reserve of rations is kept in the camp.—Cd. 893.

*Washing.*—Clothes are washed in shallow dams of dirty stagnant rain-water, half a mile from the camp. The women are only allowed to go out and wash their clothes at 7 a. m. in parties of from seventy to one hundred a day, with a police escort. The washing place is thoroughly unsuitable in every respect, but no other is available.—Cd. 893.

The lack of water makes cleanliness impossible.

*Fuel.*—At one time the people were dependent on 'mist,' which they collected, but owing to military regulations this had to be stopped.

*Beds and overcrowding.*—There is a great deal of unhealthy overcrowding. More tents are needed at once to abate serious overcrowding. More *kartels* are urgently required. One hundred and twenty-three tents are without any bed frames.

*Cemetery.*—Very roughly kept, and unenclosed.

*Mortuary.*—Very unsatisfactory; near the mule *kraal*. Very ragged bell-tent without trestles. Corpses wrapped in blankets only lay on stretchers on the ground. No means of keeping animals and idlers out. On the recommendation of the Committee it was removed at once to the hospital enclosure, and trestles provided. The superintendent also indented for calico for shrouds.—Ladies' Report.

See Mrs. Fawcett. Report of meeting and letter to the *Times*, March 24, 1902, where the need of calico for shrouds is characterised as 'foolishly sensational and wickedly misleading.' See also Bethulie Camp.

★★★★★★

The four of us shared a tent, and grandfather was ill all the while, and never got over the first two nights in the *veld*. One morning I said to him: 'Grandpa, you must get up, the sun is shining nice and warm outside.' He said: 'I cannot move a limb, I have gone stiff with the cold.' And it was true, he could not move at all. Then inflammation of the lungs came on, and he said we had better take him to the hospital. He had a bed to lie on at the hospital, but the doctor did not go near him until we asked him to look at him. Then he just glanced at him, and said: 'Oh! he's past my help!' and went away.

Next day grandpa died. He was a strong man before we were taken from our home. His body was put into a packing-case, and he was buried beside the railway line, where the many others who died were buried. Wood cannot be used to mark the graves, because it would be carried off for firewood. Every day there was one funeral, and sometimes there were as many as six. I never felt well all the time I was in the camp. It was very dull, for no one dared to speak much, as the camp was full of spies who carried the least word to the *commandant*. But none of the women wanted their husbands to give in. The *commandant* was very rude to us when we went away. When we were standing on the platform, he came up to us and said: 'What business have you to be going when your husbands and brothers and sons are still fighting? Why don't you tell them to give in?' Then he turned to me, and poked out his finger and thrust it into my face, and said: 'And what are you doing here? Writing, writing, always writing! What business have you to be complaining, and then leaving the camp?'

This story is told by a widow, who regards herself as an Englishwoman, though born in the Orange Free State—

On the 16th April 1901, a British column arrived at our village under General Elliot, on the afternoon of which day a large number of the inhabitants of the place got notice to get ready to proceed with the column to the railway camp, Vredefort Road. The people were allowed to take some clothing and bedding, which were packed in open waggons, on which they had to sit in the boiling heat in daytime.

Although the distance to be travelled was only sixteen miles, they had to submit to the torture of two days and nights on the *veld*. A start was made about four o'clock p.m., but the first halt was made within sight of the village. No tents were provided, and no other provision had been made for shelter against the cold nights, and they had to sleep on the open *veld*. The officers in charge of the convoy never troubled themselves about the people, and the women had to see how best to get on.

The second evening's halt was within sight of the camp and railway, and yet again they had to sleep in the open without shelter, old men and children suffering greatly.

The camp is surrounded by two barbed-wire fences, with wire entanglements between the fences, and a fort behind the camp; at each entrance sentries are placed to prevent escape.

But for that the women would soon be at large, the more as the Boers, notwithstanding the fort and searchlight, frequently approach the place, writing warnings on the water-tanks to the military to treat their women prisoners better and to give them better food. The food, as usual, is poor and scanty, without vegetables or variation.

★★★★★★

There is no fresh milk at all. The Commission found that the new rice ration was much appreciated.—Cd. 893. (Six months later.)

★★★★★★

Not infrequently the women are brought before the *commandant*, for the purpose of trying to extract information from them. A few instances will be given—

Mrs. Badenhorst, of the Farm Wit Koppies, Kroonstad District, was brought before the *commandant*, and was told to state where ammunition had been buried on her husband's farm. In reply, she stated that she was not aware that any ammunition had been buried there. Whereupon she was sentenced to twenty-four hours' solitary confinement in the guard tent, which is situated some distance away from the camp. At nightfall, she claimed to have her two youngest children with her, and some bedding. As the tent had no proper fastenings and pegs, she had to lie on the side of the tent's canvas to shelter her two little ones from cold.

The next day the poor woman was once more interrogated and cross-examined by this officer, with no better result, and another sentence of thirty-six hours' guard tent and solitary confinement. I should have mentioned that the day before the first charge was made, Mrs. Badenhorst committed the heinous crime of hanging her washed clothes on the inner barbed-wire fence to dry, and when told by one of the sentries to remove the same, she replied: 'You tell the *commandant* that if he objects to the washing being hung here to dry, he should provide some wire in the camp whereon we can dry our clothes. Surely he cannot expect the washing to dry on the dusty ground.'

This was too much for the dignified major, and hence the persecution that followed. Mrs. Badenhorst and her family were deported from this camp, no one knew where to. Her husband was at the time prisoner of war in Green Point, Cape Town, but now at Bermudas.

Mrs. Barend Pretorious, of Rietspruit District, Kroonstad, was similarly charged and sentenced, and deported no one knows where. Mr. Pretorious was confined in another guard-tent for the same offence of not being able to state where ammunition is buried, and when his sentence expired he found his wife and children deported; he is still inquiring in vain what had become of them.

Another woman had the audacity to tell the *commandant*, on being told by him to let their husbands know that they would be shot for tampering with the line of railway—'That she would not inform her husband not to do so, as the line had been built out of their pockets, and that they were at liberty again to destroy the same if they think fit to do so.' The sentence of guard-tent solitary confinement had no effect on her.

When she returned to the camp, she came with a smile on her face, in charge of the guard, and said aloud to her fellow-camp prisoners: 'I gladly suffered for the sake of our fighting men and brothers. I have done no wrong for which I need be ashamed. If I had been a man, I would not treat women and children as we are treated. Then I would hang my head and be ashamed. I glory in the suffering I have undergone.' Her boldness (it is presumed) will contaminate the camp; she was sent away.

The lady says that she was informed by one of the wounded soldiers that her house and everything in it, and several other houses of camp prisoners, were destroyed by fire after they left the village (that was the latter half of April). Her son is a prisoner of war, and was not there when the removal took place.

Mrs. Christian De Wet, wife of the well-known general, was captured sometime after her farm was burnt, and eventually taken with her family to Johannesburg. She was enabled to live without English help, owing to the charity of the German community. Her protest, which has since been followed by another, (see Part 3), was addressed to the *Daily News*, which paper had previously published her portrait

Johannesburg, April 24, 1901.

Sir,—Having been informed that besides the appearance of my portrait you also published that I was now living in Johannesburg "under the protection" of H.M. Government, I hereby wish most strongly to protest against the use of such expression. After our farm had been devastated by H.M. troops, and all our other possessions destroyed and taken, I roamed about with our children for some months, in order not to fall into the hands of the enemy of our nation, up to the 20th November 1900, when I was taken a prisoner and conveyed to Johannesburg in a cattle truck, notwithstanding they were well aware of the fact that I was the wife of General De Wet. Seeing that I was captured and conveyed hither against my wish and will, after having been robbed of everything, I demanded from the military authorities here sufficient food, and of good quality.

First this was promised me, but a few days later I was informed in writing that I would only be supplied with food in case I signed a document, and therein declared "that I was without means of subsistence and was entirely dependent on Her Majesty's Government." (The Queen of England was then still living.)

The authorities further reserved to themselves the right to publish such document. To have done this would have been very humiliating to me, and I could not expose myself to it, especially not to the enemy of our nation. I have asked no favour from the enemy, and I have no intention of ever doing so. It is true I live at Johannesburg, but against my will. From the English I receive nothing, and do not want anything from them. What I require I hope to receive through the intervention of humane friends, not from the English.—I am, etc.,

(Signed)                                    C. M. De Wet
                          (Wife of General De Wet).

Mrs. Roux writes:

I arrived at Winburg on the 3rd of May, and was first sent to the Refugee Camp. Afterwards I was transferred to the Show-yard camp, where the 'undesirables' were kept, and where I had to remain about a fortnight. In the Show-yard camp the number of men, women, and children varied between 400 and 275. I cannot exactly say how large its area is, but it is certainly under 200 paces by 300. It is surrounded by a fence of galvanised iron, 7 to 8 ft. high, so that no one can look over it. We were not allowed to leave the camp, and were treated as prisoners.

★★★★★★

*Extracts from Report of Ladies' Commission.*—Cd. 893.

A small number, called the undesirables, are living in the town Show-yard.

The Show-yard had forty-eight huts. The maximum number in the huts was eight.

*Show-yard Latrines.*—There is no special provision for children, and the large women's latrines should have more partitions.

*Meat.*—The people grumbled more about food and especially about meat than at any other place. The Segregation Camps had refused their meat on one occasion; it was taken back to the contractor and sold at once in the town. The ration-house in the Segregation Camp was very dirty and ill-kept.

*Coal* is issued (1 lb. per head per day only) weekly. The people need more fuel.

★★★★★★

In the camp are huts of galvanised iron, in which the women had to live. A watch was set over us, and there was but one gate, through which we were not allowed to pass. When I entered the camp it contained women and children who had been there for more than four months, without ever having been outside the gate. The doctor of the camp, Dr. Schneehagen, told me that he had drawn up a report about the sanitary condition of the camp, and would have sent it to the Board of Health at Bloemfontein, but he was not allowed to do so. He declared that all the ground was defiled, so that the camp was altogether unfit to live in. The sanitary arrangements are such as do not allow of discussion in public.

In a fortnight, there were seven deaths. Every one, without any exception, got meat, flour, and condensed milk, also sugar and coffee. We got ½ lb. of meat a day. The women, however, told me that before I entered the camp they had not had fresh meat for seventeen days. We got our water in carts, which are sent to the camp, but were not allowed to take as much water as we like. We also get firewood, but must make our fires outside, at a place appointed for it.

Sometimes it was raining, and though the place was slushy and dirty we still had to make our fires there. The children had nothing to do; as a rule, they would chop wood. They did not go to school, and had to remain inside the camp. Once a day they were allowed to play outside the camp. The play hour— only one hour was allowed them to be outside the camp in the playground, and only children under twelve were permitted to go outside the camp—was at three in the afternoon.

This hour, as a great favour, was allowed them, after they had been for four months inside the camp, by the advice of the doctor and Nurse Bakkes. The women in the tents were obliged to sleep on the ground, though some of them who had bedding were allowed to bring it with them. When Nurse Bakkes arrived, twenty-two patients in the hospital got only two bottles of milk a day. The condition in which she found the camp was such that she directly went to the commissioner, and begged him to go with her to the camp to see the children, who had not had proper food for three days, die with hunger, as the women had not received any firewood with which to prepare food for the children. He accompanied her, and sent three cart-loads of firewood to the camp.

Considering everything I have seen and heard, I cannot think but we are prisoners. There were two cases to prove this. One Mrs. Scot and seven children came to the camp. When there, one of her children, a girl, became ill, and was taken to the Show-yard hospital outside the camp, but the mother was not allowed to accompany her. When the child was dying, a permit was refused her to go to the hospital, and the child died without seeing her mother again. Afterwards two more children of hers fell ill, and were also taken to the hospital. In two months' time she lost four children, who died of fever; the latter she was allowed to visit. One Mrs. Esterhuizen, of Brandfort, repeatedly sent in a request to be allowed to stay at the village of Winburg at her own expense, which was refused her. She was taken ill with fever, and died while I was in the camp.

The commissioner at Winburg seems to be too young and inexperienced. When Nurse Bakkes begged him to send more articles to the camp and hospital, he answered that if they were to manage things in that way they would almost make England a bankrupt. The way in which the women are treated is not all that can be desired. They are removed from their farms by *Kaffirs* and taken to the camp. Sometimes these *Kaffirs* are most insolent A watch is set over the camp. Some of the Boers who surrendered—we call them 'hands uppers'—do the general work of the camps; fetch the water, carry the wood, and remove the dirt. Mr. Koenbrink told me to keep calm and quiet, or they would take me away from my children, and send me to another camp.

The women, too, were threatened with smaller rations if they would not keep calm and quiet They were not allowed to buy any food, though some of them had some money. I know Nurse Bakkes personally. She is like a ray of light for the camp, and does some noble work; she is heartily beloved by all the women and children in the camp. The nurses who have been sent to us by our friends we thank very much, they do the work of angels.

★★★★★★

Cd. 893:

*Opinion of Local Committee*—We would rather have an Englishman at the head of all departments in the camp."

Refugees can only buy foodstuffs in town by order of the magistrate.

Sister Bakkes (matron) knows her work, and is deservedly trusted by the doctors.

★★★★★★

Another lady, whose husband is too well known for her to give her name at present, writes her account of Winburg Showyard, which amplifies while it substantiates that of the last writer—

My sister and I lived quietly in Senekal Town to the end of April 1901. Up to that date everything had gone on as usual in that district. Women were living unmolested on their farms, and farming operations went on undisturbed though the men were away on commando. At times the British came through and occupied the place, and once a wounded British officer was left in my care. My sister and I nursed him tenderly for two months, and great was our pride and joy when at last he seemed on the mend and could get about a little with the aid of a stick. But the British came in again, and the officers occupied our house, and, greatly to our distress, insisted that the wounded officer must be sent to the military hospital to undergo an operation. We knew well what that would mean, and my sister bravely stood up before the English *commandant*, as he sat at table, and protested.

It was in vain, the officer was sent away, and in a day or two was dead. Our house was occupied by the military, we ourselves were sent away to Winburg Camp. This is really two camps, the ordinary Concentration Camp, and that for 'undesirables' on the racecourse. We were at first placed in the former, where the usual regulations prevailed. We were indeed allowed to walk into Winburg, but we were not allowed to add in any way to the rations, 'not by so much as a clove to flavour our soup.' (It will be remembered that the Commission visited this camp six months later.)

After a short time in this camp we were with some other women removed to that for 'undesirables.' It seemed in our case to be a punishment for holding the prayer meetings which are usual among the Dutch people at that particular season. In the racecourse camp there were at that time, during the month of May, about 400 people. These were veritable prisoners, surrounded by a high corrugated iron fence, and guarded night and day by armed sentries.

The huts or sheds were packed closely together, and the only view was that of the sky. The sanitary arrangements were very bad, being quite close on the tents, and the smell was horrible. Typhoid of course was rampant. The women were packed into long sheds, each family having a right to a space 8 ft. by 10 ft., but there were no partitions between, save the sheets or blankets that the women themselves might choose to rig up. You might have fever on the one side of you and fever on the other, for the air was common to all.

In spite of the terrible sickness, and the great monotony and confinement, the women were calm and cheerful. One poor woman had been brought to the camp with her seven children in an open waggon. It rained heavily, and for a day and a night the party sat huddled in mud and water. The consequence was that they arrived in a state which left them a prey to sickness, though they were strong children when they left home. One after another they died of typhoid. But the mother was quite calm; she said that death did not matter if only the country got its independence.

The children felt the imprisonment very severely; they moped and looked 'like little old men and women.' At last the military said they might go outside the camp to a certain space to play, but were threatened with punishment if they dared go beyond the bounds assigned them. The poor little things, instead of playing, sank down in a huddled heap together on the ground, and remained there till the play hour was over. Of course afterwards they made more use of their liberty, but were still sad-faced and grave.

Not so the women, who were all bright and cheerful, and

determined not to seem depressed, cowed, or down-trodden, whatever the pressure put upon them. Papers were brought them more than once to sign, in which their men on commando were to be implored to give in. Not one woman would sign, nor have anything to do with the 'Peace Commission.'

Later on a more subtle temptation was presented to them. They were asked simply to sign their names to a petition to leave that camp for a better place. The paper was apparently blank; merely the names were to be collected of such as wished to leave. The women were puzzled for a time, and wanted to know what to do. Finally, they all refused 'for fear the *burghers* should get to know.' One poor woman was sadly tempted by her little children, who clung to her skirts and cried and begged her to take them to a nicer place.

Mrs. Carstens tells us:

I had five minutes in April to pack up and get into the open waggon; two English farmers I knew were acting as guides to the column, and helped me to collect some bedding, etc., so I was better off than most When we got to the train, I refused to get into the open trucks, as I had my daughter's child with me, of three years old, just recovered from pneumonia, and the weather looked threatening. Then they got a carriage for me, in which I sheltered as many as could be crowded into it for the night. I was amongst those who were sent in from Springfontein to Bethulie, where I thought some provision would have been made for us; but when we arrived we remained again for two days in the train.

At the end of that time they said the train was needed, and we were all left on the platform, where some of us remained for three weeks waiting till our turn came to be removed to the camp as the tents arrived. We just slept on the open platform, cooking our food as well as we could, gathering sticks and mists. It was a sad night when we arrived there, all wet and cold, the poor children crying because they could not eat the hard biscuit and bully-beef. The doctors with the column were very kind and nice, but when we got to Bethulie, the doctor there, a German, was sent for to see two children who were dying.

My little one had a boil on its neck which needed to be lanced, so I took it to the doctor, and there were other mothers also

302

bringing their children to him, but he said very roughly, 'I was sent for to see two and I won't see a hundred,' and went off leaving many of the poor women in tears, most forlorn. The *commandant* of the camp, Mr. Deare, was a kind, considerate man, which was a great consolation to us in our trouble.

An anxious mother, with five children, writes pathetically to friends, when the camp life is still new and strange to her—

Potchefstroom Camp, May 22, 1901.
I was very much pleased to receive a letter from you, and thank you heartily for what you do for my dear husband, whom I love so much.

I did not receive a letter from my husband since April of last year, when in the month of June they said that he was dead. From other people I learned afterwards that my husband was a prisoner of war, and now, dear madam, they have taken me prisoner on the 12th of May. On Sunday morning, as we were breakfasting, we received notice to be ready to move by four in the afternoon.

I spoke to the general, but it was of no use. I said to him: 'Oh, I pray you shoot me dead now, for it is all the same whether I die here or in camp.' My children cried piteously. The officer came to me. He clasped his hands on seeing my beautiful house and the beautiful furniture, saying that it was a pity that I had to be taken prisoner. He kissed my children, and thought them so nice that he gave them some jam. May God grant me to keep them; so many grown-up people and children die here in the camp; sometimes seven in a day. The doctor says it is because the quantity of food is insufficient, and the quality of what is given is bad. If my husband knew all this he certainly could not live. I trust, my kind friends, that if you can be of any assistance to me you are willing to give it.

Is it possible that if I come to you at the Cape, either that you have got a room for me, or that you took a little house for me? I have got four bags of corn left, and other food to last me for some time.

It would be for me and my children, as well as for my husband, a terrible thing to die here. Oh! do take some trouble, please, before it is too late.

The parson's wife is going to the Cape too; it is impossible for her to stay here. I have been allowed to take with me some beds, bedsteads, and clothes. Do write an answer to this letter as soon as you can. I hope God will be with us. He alone can help. There is written in the Bible: '*Take a delight in the Lord: He shall give thee what thy heart desires*,' Oh! if we only relied on God at all times, and trusted in Him. I must finish now. I hope you will help me. May God bless you all.—Ever, your friend.

P.S.—I had already finished this letter, and we are now going to sleep. In a tent on one side, however, we hear a child coughing; in another, one or two groaning and wailing; then another again vomiting. Oh! I do fear so much for my dear children; they are accustomed to live in a new, well-built house, and now we must sleep in an open tent. Oh! do help me to get the Cape, I beseech you. My husband will afterwards repay you. Do exert yourselves in my behalf.

The tents have been pitched here side by side, and are bad for our health. I will do anything for you if you will help me. Once more, do send me an answer at your earliest convenience whether I can come, for I long so much for it now that I can stay no longer here.

Expecting your kind answer very soon.

★★★★★★

The superintendent has been issuing corned beef lately owing to the ordinary meat being so thin and poor.—Cd. 893.

Dr. Dixon's report for May shows that the health of the women and children was anything but satisfactory, and the mortality amongst children had been very great—due to a very severe epidemic of measles, accompanied with chest complaints, caused by a very cold wind from the south, together with exposure to cold by tent-living.

★★★★★★

Mrs. G.'s narrative was taken down from her lips in December last, the 16th. Being the wife of a prominent Free Stater, her name cannot be given without special permission, and it is not at present possible to communicate with her.

Mrs. G. and her husband lived on a beautiful farm at P. Mr. G. had been staying quietly on his farm as a prisoner on parole from March 1900 to January 1901, but in the latter month he was suddenly taken away and put in gaol, although he had in no way broken his parole, and had surrendered on the express understanding that he should live quietly on his farm. For four months longer Mrs. G. continued to live on the farm unmolested by the various columns which passed through the district, except that of course they took sheep as they wanted them.

On the 18th of June 1901, a large sweeping column, under Colonel Williams, was encamped at her sister's house, twenty minutes away. It was engaged in sweeping or clearing the district This was about the eighth column that had passed through the district since her husband had been taken away, and the one immediately previous to this, commanded by Colonel Williams, had started the practice of burning grain, forage, stores of food, etc., and had collected as much as it could in the way of cattle. Colonel Williams' column seemed to be sweeping the country bare in a circular fashion, round the central point of her sister's farm, where he lay encamped for a little over a week. It was the ninth day after his arrival, being the 1st of June, when the soldiers arrived at Mrs. G.'s farm. The women never minded the regular soldiers so much; it was the patrols of armed natives who were sent to do the worst sort of work, and it was these armed natives who gave the first alarm. It was a bitterly cold morning, the snow falling fast, and about sunrise, or 7 a.m., when they came. She was already up and dressed, had finished breakfast, and had got the dinner on the fire, when she saw armed natives had come, and were collecting stock, and behaving impudently to her servants.

They were driving away all the cows and calves, and one little servant boy in distress cried out; 'Leave me one cow with her calf, just one.' But the armed natives replied insolently. By this time the whole house was surrounded by armed khakis, and when she went out the verandah was full of them. By the deference paid him Mrs. G. soon discovered which was the captain of the troop. He had a pleasant face and spoke very politely to her. He said he regretted to say he had instructions to clear the country, and she must therefore get ready to leave home. She replied that she was not fit to travel.

Outside there was a whole convoy of waggons, full of other families of the district who had been turned out of their homes, and many of whom she knew. 'Oh, do make haste and pack,' cried many of these poor women. 'Yes, we know how you feel; we said we could not leave our homes. Look at our faces and see how we have cried. But it was no use; we had to go, and you'll have to go too. Oh, do begin to pack.'

'No,' said Mrs. G.; 'you can pack for me if you like, and you, and you; but as for me, I will lie on this sofa, and if they want me they will have to carry me away.'

'How would you live,' asked the captain, 'when you are all alone, and the country is devastated of food?'

'Oh,' she answered wildly, 'there are the doves. I have fifty doves flying about overhead; I can kill them one a day and live on them, and grow vegetables; I shall manage, I shall manage.'

Then, when she saw this was of no avail, she pleaded that her lungs were weak and she had hurt her side; but the army doctor came and examined her, and said that her heart was sound. Then she went almost frantic, fell down on her knees before the officer, and took hold of his hands, and cried: 'Oh, look at your soldiers carrying out my beautiful furniture. See what they are doing.' For they had made a big fire, and were heaping on to it her pillows and feather-beds; and out of the house the soldiers came running carrying her silver candlesticks, and all sorts of things—tables, chairs, clocks, etc. 'What are you doing?' she cried out; 'What are you doing with my things?'

'Oh! we are just taking away with us the things we want,' was the answer.

The officer was very distressed when she knelt before him and pleaded so hard to be allowed to remain in her own house, and said at last: 'Well, I'm awfully sorry, and I tell you what you had better do. Go to Colonel Williams, and plead your cause with him. He is on the next farm; just go with the convoy as far as that.' Mrs. G. again refused, and he said in despair to her little niece, 'Do go and speak to your mother and tell her she must come away at once.'

'Auntie,' said the little girl earnestly, 'do come, or the *Kaffirs* will come and carry you out; don't let the *Kaffirs* touch you, do come.'

'For God's sake,' replied Mrs. G., 'go away and leave me to myself, and leave everything to destruction.'

'Don't say that,' said the officer, distressed 'We won't destroy anything, only come away.'

She got up at last, and through the midst of her tears surveyed the waggon which stood ready to take her away. 'I can't get into that stinking thing,' she said, looking at the ill-smelling floor of the vehicle. But they forced her in, heartbroken as she was, and they moved slowly away, leaving the dinner cooking on the stove. They broke up the stove, they broke her husband's beautiful carpenter's shop, they smashed his ploughs and machinery brought lately from America, even down to the spades. The light furniture, also from America, the soldiers went on smashing before her very eyes.

Before she went away the two old *Kaffir* servant-girls, who had been with her for years and years, clung to her crying, and said, 'Oh, missis, missis, they've shot the baas's beautiful stallion in the stable!' This stallion had cost Mr. G. over £200. He was standing in the stable with an inflamed foot, so, as the soldiers could not take him away, they shot him dead. These two poor *Kaffir* women did not escape; their huts were burned, and they clung weeping and terrified to their mistress, crying '*Mÿn huis is verbrannt, mÿn huis is verbrannt.*'

The sad procession moved on. There were dozens of families filling up waggon after waggon. The wind was blowing gustily, cold and piercing, and the dust raised was so great that you could not see the wagons nor how far they extended. They were driven by *Kaffirs*, some of whom were very rude and insulting. Although her sister's farm was only twenty minutes distant, it was sundown when they got there. There was nothing but the bare ground to sleep upon. The house had been seized for the use of Colonel Williams and his staff, and there was no room for anyone else. They made a sort of camp out on the *veld*, trying to shelter near the waggons, but the snow was falling, the wind bitter cold, and the children were crying with misery. With Mrs. G. were her husband's aged parents, his mother of 75 and father of 77. She could bear their piteous looks no longer, and went indoors to find her sister. 'Look here, sister,' she said, 'old father and mother can't sleep out in the cold.' Her sister looked at her in a dazed, frightened way. 'What am I to do?' she said. 'I have not a bed in my own house; for a week I have lain in the pantry.'

Mrs. G. saw she was bewildered and broken, and on her own responsibility she brought in the old father to sit by the kitchen fire; he was starved and pinched with the cold, and every instant was coughing a hard, dry little cough. Colonel Williams appeared, and Mrs. G. obtained from him the concession that the old couple should sleep that night under the roof; but she could give them nothing to eat. The colonel had commandeered all the provisions in the house, and all that week the mistress of the farm had been rationed, scantily enough, out of her own food. At that moment, looking out of the window, Mrs. G. exclaimed, 'Oh, father, they are burning your carriage!' The soldiers outside were breaking it up for firewood. Then she went out to the rest of the party sitting in the snow in the gathering darkness of the *veld*. Her friends had, happily, packed a few things out of the house before she left, but the blankets and pillows were stored away in the waggons and hard to get at She managed to get out one or two, but the poor little party were almost frozen to death.

All night the children's incessant cry was, 'Oh, auntie, give us another blanket! Oh, auntie, give us something to eat!' until she was almost distracted, for she could do neither, and felt as if she were freezing to death herself. It was joy next morning to see the sun after that endless night of wind and darkness, cold and hunger.

The wind had fallen towards morning, and the snow ceased, and they were able to make a fire and cook some breakfast The order was soon given to move on, but a thought struck Mrs. G. She felt as if she and the old couple could not again stand the jolting of the dirty waggon, and there in the yard stood her own spider. She went to the colonel and asked permission to tie the spider behind the waggon. This was granted, and the old father and mother sat up in the spider and she sat with them. Thousands and thousands of sheep were driven along with the waggons on either side of the road, and they raised such a dust that there was no seeing the sun.

The whole of that day they jolted slowly, slowly in the clouds of dust, their vision bounded on either side by the toiling, frightened sheep, and in front and behind by the waggons full of women and children and household goods. All day long the old mother was murmuring, 'Oh, my child, it is the day of judgment, it is the day of judgment!'

Although the station was only one hour distant by ordinary travelling from Mr. G.'s farm, they did not get there till the evening. All the goods were then flung out of the waggons, and the people were left to shelter for the night as best they could.

They were just put down along the railway line, with no shelter provided of any sort whatever. The people huddled together behind the waggons, and now the dust was still, one could see hundreds of them. The soldiers made their rough jokes as they passed along the crouching, silent, huddled lines.

What a night! The cold was intense, and the icy wind blew round the waggons. As the sun set and the people realised that another winter night without food or fire was to be spent on the bare *veld*, some of them became terrified. Young girls took knives and began chopping bits of wood from the sides of the waggons to make a fire, but of course they were soon ordered to desist There was nothing else to make a fire of on all the wide *veld*, bare of tree or shrub or plant.

The children cried aloud from hunger, terror, and cold, but the women uttered no sound. They sat huddled up in the dumb patience of despair. What was most pitiful was to see the old people, sitting silent, without a word of complaint, with the tears rolling quietly down their worn cheeks. Mrs. G. looked at her old father with the icy wind blowing about him till she could bear it no longer. She went up to the guard and spoke to him sharply and decidedly: 'Guard, see here, you *must* find us food and you *must* find us fire. Can't you hear the children crying? Can't you hear the old men moaning? Are you going to let us die here on your hands?'

The guard was moved by this appeal, and brought her old candle-boxes, and things of that sort, with which the women made three little fires, enough each to boil a kettle and make a little cocoa, though what was that among so many? Still the very effort kept them going. At last the long night wore away, and the sun shone out again. Then the trucks began to come up in relays, and the people were carted off, some to Springfontein, some to Norval's Pont, and some elsewhere. Great was the noise and confusion over the luggage.

The people crowded round the trucks while the goods were being tossed in, and had to shout, 'That's mine, that's mine,' or, 'No, that's Mrs. So-and-So's, and she's on the other truck.' Mrs. G. got on to a dirty coal-truck with her party, her old father, mother, sister, nieces, nephew, the two old *Kaffir* girls, and two little orphan *Kaffirs*, and all their belongings. All along the servants had clung to her with desperate eagerness. 'Ah, missis, give me a bit of food,' they would say, as if she still had the household under her command.

But at Norval's Pont the little party was separated. The *Kaffirs* had to go into one camp and the white people into another. There was a strict rule against keeping any servants in the white camp, but they ventured to keep the two little orphan girls, as they had been brought up in the house and were like their own. However, they did not keep them long, for the police were sent to take away the two little girls, greatly to their distress.

Mrs. G. thereupon stated her case to the *commandant*, saying, 'They are orphans; I have had them ever since they were babies, and I am bringing them up as my own.' He was very kind, and said he would give her a permit As Mrs. G. said, he was a gentleman, and had some common sense. The only stipulation he made was that they should go back to the *Kaffir* camp at night. What became of the two old girls she never knew.

At Norval's Pont there was not the same misery at starting as in many other camps. There seemed plenty of tents for newcomers, and the *burghers* in the place brought these for the party and helped to put them up. Being a combination of three families, they at once applied for a marquee, which was granted. They then made the floor for themselves, got in their belongings, and settled for the night. It was sundown of the third day since they were torn from their farms.

Pitiful were the tales the neighbours told her of the way in which they had been driven into camp. Mrs. G.'s own two nieces, girls of about twenty, had been driven along in front of the soldiers' horses. They said they did not want to leave their home, and refused to climb into the waggons, for which they were told to run for their lives, and had to run for half an hour, panting and terrified at the coarse jokes of the soldiers, in front of the horses. A Mrs. Marais was marched for three hours in front of the horses.

A Mrs. Traichel was driven along by mounted natives for four hours, carrying her child. When at last she arrived at Philippolis with her three children, she was soaked to the skin by the rain and sleet. In this condition she was locked for the night into a room without food or fire. Mrs. G. said it was the use of the natives which all the people felt they could never forgive. She herself, a month or two before her deportation, had escaped to the mountains for four days in sheer dread of the native scouts. She had put the horses into the spider and driven off alone with her little niece; they walked their feet sore in the hills, and wore away her skirt into rags up to her knees among the rough stones, but this was preferable to facing a column with its native scouts, or being driven into a camp. Mrs. G. said she never dreaded the regular troops, it was the irregulars and the blacks who were so terrible.

About a fortnight after their arrival in camp, an old neighbour came in who described the present condition of her house. She told Mrs. G.: 'There is only one chair left. Your curtains, piano, tables, bedsteads, everything is gone. It is just a desolation.' This was not the last she heard of the beautiful home.

Mrs. G. never recovered those two terrible nights in the open. She got a cough and a weakness of the chest which camp life made ever worse and worse. The ground was incessantly damp; everything taken from the floor in the morning was heavy with cold damp. She worked, too, for the even greater sufferers around her, and the consequence was a severe illness and a complete breakdown of her health. Her husband heard of her state of health, and, being a prisoner on parole, he obtained with great difficulty permission to see her in the camp. It was a great shock, for he would scarcely have known her.

The doctor was kind and considerate, and made out a certificate to the effect that if she remained longer in camp she would certainly die. By this means, though with great difficulty, Mr. G. got his wife out of the camp after three months' residence there. From Norval's Pont they went up to Bloemfontein, and here she had her second chance of hearing about the state of her farm.

Two young nieces from that neighbourhood had lately been put in the camp, and, knowing that their aunt was passing by, obtained permission from the *commandant* to station themselves at a spot where they could have a few minutes' talk with her. At the sight of their aunt the girls burst into tears, and Betty said, 'Oh, auntie, your farm is burnt down to the ground, the trees are all cut down, the dam is blown up with dynamite, the walls are razed to the ground!'

Mrs. G. said the rations in camp were not sufficient They could never make them do. If you rolled two days' rations into one you could just manage to make it do for one day. She found camp an extremely expensive place, for you not only had to supply your own wants but you had to help along your poorer neighbours. For the poor who had no money it was veritable starvation diet.

The women were always busy from morning till night, baking, cooking, washing, and keeping their tents clean and tidy. Their spare time went in looking after the sick, of which there were always plenty, making poultices, sitting up at night, and so on. Mrs. G. shuddered at the thought of those dark times; the deathbed scenes in camp, she said, would remain with her to her dying day. The old father died shortly after he was brought in.

One night in the middle of May a patrol of British soldiers came to Tweefontein, the farm of Mrs. G. Jacobs. Her husband was at the time a prisoner of war in Green Point, and her sons either prisoners or on commando, she says:

I myself, with five children, the eldest a girl of eighteen, a Miss Rahl, and two other women, were taken by the soldiers to the British camp. I was in very delicate health, but as we had to proceed on foot we could not take anything with us. We started at eight o'clock p.m., and only reached the soldiers' camp at midnight. On the way, we had to wade through a *spruit*, so that we were wet up to our knees. Owing to fatigue, one of the children was not able to proceed farther, and was taken on horseback by one of the soldiers. Thoroughly knocked up and wet, we arrived at the camp, where we had to sit waiting till the next morning. Then we were put on a waggon and brought to the Refugee Camp at Springfontein.

Very touching is the translation given below of a letter asking for help. It was written to a lady, an acquaintance of mine, who happened to owe the prisoner some money—

Mrs. Bosman to Mrs. N.

Translation,

Bloemfontein Camp, June 1901.

Ah! what shall I say to you? We are all taken out of our beloved homes, which we now value rightly for the first time, and are placed in round tents in this camp. We came here on the 29th of May with a lot of others, nearly all our neighbours and ac-quaintance. Oh! it is wonderful to see what we have to endure. We women have to do more than what Basuto girls ever have to do at home with us. And yet we are satisfied and submissive. Each understands well that it is God's will that we should suffer for our dearly beloved country, and outside of His will can no great thing happen to us; the Lord has promised us in His holy word never to leave us or forsake us.

Dear madam, I must now share with you my bitter experience, that the dear Lord has thought well to take my dear—yes, my very dearest son; the 8th of February he was wounded, and on the 10th he died. Although the wound in my heart is deep and the place sore, I will bow and say what God does is well done. Oh, this time of proving has taught us much; dark clouds have gone over our heads, and still the end is not.

My son John is in Ceylon; my husband and son Pieter were in Simon's Town, but now I understand are sent to India. I have now only my three daughters and one son with me

Ah, dear madam, I am compelled to ask you to send me some money, and I trust with certainty that you will grant my re-quest if you understand the suffering we have. I shall be deeply obliged if you can send me £20. We get bare food here, no vegetables—nor anything else, so you can well understand that our need is great—for our very lives.

P.S.—It is bitterly cold in the tents, neither have we any proper place to write.

★★★★★★

*Insufficient Food Supply*—I think ½ lb. of meat for an adult not suf-ficient. Fresh milk and vegetables (even though compressed or pre-served) should be supplied two or three times a week. Etc.

Dr. Becker's Report.

Cd. 819.

*Bloemfontein Camp.*—It is unhealthy, and very bleak and much ex-posed to the cold winds.

Report of Superintendent.

Insufficient housing and covering, absence of warmth. The tents are not giving sufficient warmth to people who have been suddenly re-moved from houses. Some of the tents are useless as a covering.

Dr. Becker.

Cd. 819

★★★★★★

Mrs. Botha, who had applied many times during my stay in Bloemfontein to be released in order to join her relations in Cape Colony, was as often refused. I represented to the authorities that six months in camp had told seriously upon her, and that her strength was failing. If she was not allowed to go she would certainly be ill, and perhaps die.

Permission was refused; a long and serious illness was the result. Three months later she wrote to me—

### Mrs. Botha to Myself.

July 1901.

You will be surprised to receive a letter from me from the Cape. I would have written to you long ere this, but as our letters were censored at the camp one felt no inclination for writing. I daresay you will have heard that I was brought out of the camp last May. I took the fever, and was taken to Bloemfontein, to the Volks Hospital, where I was close upon two months. I had a complication with the fever. . . . The doctor gave a certificate that I was unable to return to the camp with such broken health, and advised me to go to the Cape, where I am once more enjoying home comfort after spending so many months of hardship in the camp, where I have lost my health entirely. . . . You have no idea how many deaths we have had since you visited the camps, so many of the old faces we will not see on earth again. The bathrooms have not been erected as yet, not through the fault of the military though, as they could not get the timber through.

We see in the newspapers that they are sending out a Commission from England to the camps. I am trying to go and meet them if I can get a chance, to tell them that I have just recently come from there, and tell them of all the good you have done to our people, and all the improvements, and ask them please to visit all the tents as you did and not the marquees alone.

The camp they have divided into four parts, the iron buildings they have turned into hospitals; removed all the lower tents up on to the opposite rise.

Miss F. asked me to ask you please to send more shoe-leather, as it is very much needed in the camp. We highly appreciate your statements and pleading for us women of the camps.

Well, the last but not the least that fills my heart and mind is to thank you and all the kind English friends for their great kindness in sending clothes, etc., to our poor women and children in trouble. It has comforted many a sorrowful heart and clothed many a naked body from the cold winter.

Every improvement that alleviated the hard life in camp, and every act of kindness that assuaged its bitterness, was noted and appreciated. Miss Ferreira writes:—

Bloemfontein, July 18.

I am glad to say our room-mates are all well still.

We have so much sickness in camp, over five hundred people have died since December.

A new hospital has been erected since you left; it is fitted up well with stoves. All the measles, pneumonia, and bronchitis patients are nursed there. Miss M'Leod, an American lady, is matron, she is a *dear, dear* person, she is liked by all patients. I have learned to know her well, as I have been sixteen days in hospital nursing my aunt, Mrs. Van Rooyen. I am sorry to inform you that Mrs. Van Rooyen died 6th inst. of pneumonia. She will be missed by many in camp.

My time is very occupied in giving out candles, barley, soap, etc., to the sick, and taking up names of the poor for clothing.

I must thank you most heartily for what you have done to my fellow-sufferers. I can assure you it was a sweet drop in the bitter cup that we have to empty. Every kind act or word from someone is very much appreciated nowadays.

I will always be happy to hear that you are well.

But sickness and death were the prevailing themes throughout the year, and from every tent-home of which we have a glimpse—

Letter to a Friend in Cape Town.

Howick Camp, June 6, 1901.

Poor Fanie is ill with fever. I feel so sad and downhearted sometimes, and think why must I have so much trouble? The Rev. Mr. Rousseau preached for us here this afternoon from the text in Job, ' Shall we receive good at the hand of God, and shall we not receive evil? '

It has greatly consoled me, I must say, and I find that amidst all my trouble I have much to be thankful for still. The doctor says it is not enteric that Janie and Fanie have, so he has left them in the tent for me to nurse, for which I am thankful. The R.'s have gone into another tent, so I have plenty of room for them here. Isabel has also returned home from the hospital, so you see I have them all together again. She is getting strong already, but Janie remains so weak she can with difficulty walk from her bed to a chair, and she is up almost a week now. Fanie is still very ill, and his fever runs as high as 103° but he looks strong, and I hope he will soon be over it too.

The 'hands uppers' here in the camp, with the exception of three, have turned British subjects now by promising to take the oath of allegiance; I always bore an ill-feeling towards them, but now I simply loathe them. They all have sons, brothers, and fathers still fighting, and how can they face them after this? But I believe the women here gave them a good bit of their mind, and the result is that they shun us, and simply stick to their tents. Mr. C. and two other Heidelbergers have also taken the oath, and *have returned to Heidelberg*, I hear several others at Ladysmith are taking the same oath, and then they are allowed to go home. But one can hardly expect anything better of 'hands uppers'!

Another prisoner in Howick, one who has spent her time in helping the poor amongst her people there, says—

Howick, Sept. 29.
The washhouse, which has till now been our church, is by far too small, and will not seat a quarter of us. . . . Most of the new arrivals are in a very poor condition, some really in rags, and such a lot of sickness amongst them; the little ones so pinched and hungry looking; they are an advertisement for the camps whence they came! We have taken up names of those who are most needy, and from tomorrow (D. V.) we intend to commence distributing. The authorities are also making a move to supply clothing. But some of the poor are afraid to go in for this; they are supposed to pay some day, and they say they do not like to accumulate debts.

With the new arrivals measles and whooping-cough made their appearance. In making the rounds of the tents last week, we came across sad things; in nearly every third tent there is sickness, measles, measles and measles again; in two tents we found all laid up except the mother. . . . they seem to get through the measles better here, I think. A lot depends on the medical treatment.

Letters from women in Irene Camp have been very scarce. Yet one was received which says—

July 1, 1901,

There have been as many as eleven sick with measles in one tent in K.'s ward. Two and three have died in one tent within twenty-four hours. Last week the deaths at Irene were forty-six, mostly in two wards. Nearly all measles and debility. And yet new arrivals are added daily to the sick wards—I mean healthy people from other districts are brought in. The consequence is in less than a week they are all down. Whooping-cough has made an appearance also. There will be no chance for the convalescent measles patients. Food they have not to give the poor hungry sick ones.

The mothers say: 'My children are getting better, but they are so hungry, and if I give them the only thing I have—bread and black coffee—they will not have it.' You must remember for many. months they have had nothing but bread. Children under eight (it used to be under twelve about three weeks ago) still receive half rations—½ lb. of flour per day, no meat—and you know the Boer children live on meat from infancy, good bread, meat, and milk. The flour is better now, but the meat is unfit to be eaten even by a dog. I have seen it with my own eyes, and was told that the sheep were carried to be slaughtered—they could not walk.

★★★★★★

The whole camp (Sept. 23) is served with 1½ lbs. of meat per adult, and 1 lb. each child under twelve years) twice a week. This ration includes bone. The meat was extremely thin (the sheep only weighed 15 and 16 lbs. each) and the ration certainly looked very scanty."—Cd. 893.

Shrouds and coffins had invariably been provided for all corpses."—Cd. 893. (Whether by Government or charity is not indicated.—E.H.)

The task of inspection was rendered additionally troublesome and perplexing by the impossibility of obtaining accurate statements as to matters of fact from the superintendent." See also description of Mortuary requirements at Vredefort Road and Bethulie. I can from my own experience confirm the accuracy of the particular need alluded to in this letter.

Deaths for month of July, 403.—Cd. 819. Medical Report

Deaths for July, 413.—Cd:893.

★★★★★★

A lady writes:

Middelburg Camp, July 7, 1901.
It was very pleasant, to receive letters from you, and then, too, such a sum of money. I did not think you could in these bad times get so much together. It was a pleasant surprise. The money is in the hands of Mrs. Burger. She knows the needy ones better than I do. Please thank the charitable givers, and tell them the poor in camp thank them too.

Candles were very scarce, so that an invalid had frequently to be attended to by the light of a match. Now many a mother will have a bit of calico again in which to wrap the corpse of her little child."

In four days' time, there were fifty-two burials. Sad, is it not? Now whooping-cough is raging, so that many a child recovered from measles now dies of this terrible cough.

Vegetables we seldom see here. For the animals there is nothing in the *veld*, and with great trouble do we now and again get a bag of mealies for £1. 7s. The Lord holds His hand over us, otherwise we had long ago perished When shall there be peace? At night when I sit lonely, then the tears roll down my cheeks. Boys' suits are scarce, so I make everything myself, and am always busy.

Much the same account of the sorrow of Middelburg Camp is given in the following short diary written by one or another of a large family to friends in Europe. There was the mother, grandmother, and six children:—

*9th of July.*—All of us suffer much from a severe cold The number of deaths is very large. Seventeen or more a day. Oh! the misery suffered is indescribable. We may not write letters, but one day everything will be disclosed Henry Vanden Berg, his wife, and their last child, are now dead, so are a great many others of our acquaintances and neighbours.

★★★★★★

It (the camp) is one of the most unsatisfactory we have seen. . . . There is complete want of order, method, and organisation, and there is hardly one department of camp life which can be reported on as being in a satisfactory condition.—Cd. 893,

★★★★★★

*16th of July* (by the same).—There is much news to write, but we dare not to do so. Oh! the misery that is suffered in the camps is so great. But I am not shaken in my belief that we shall regain our independence. Oh dear! how much there will be then to tell each other. On Sunday I was in a tent. Two of our old people were lying there, the old father, 77 years of age, was on the point of death, the old mother of 79 years was so weak that she could turn round no more. They were lying together on the ground on a blanket

The day before yesterday a new cemetery was laid out. Yesterday thirty people were buried there, and this morning there are another twenty people lying in the hospital, and how many more in the camp I do not know. God, however, comes at last when we think He is farthest off, and I believe that relief and deliverance are at hand

*17th of July* (by the mother).—Our men who are with their commandoes were put hard to it of late. The English about us say that they have got no clothes left. That some wear trousers made of skins. And are, then, our husbands and sons better than our ancestors, who succeeded though they wore trousers made of skins, had no expensive clothes, but made us free?

*24th of July* (by the same).—Oh, God be thanked, our men in the field are doing well They look well Our Heavenly Father takes care of them. We dare not write everything, but are full of hope.

24th of July (by the daughter).—I have just come from the hospital. Five of our *burghers* who were wounded have been left behind there. One of them is a young *burgher* of fourteen. He had ridden up against the barbed wire, and was then carried to the hospital.

*25th of July* (by the mother).—Another batch of women from Utrecht have arrived here, escorted by a strong column of English soldiers. They were in carts on the road during sixteen days.

Nurse Jacobs is again here. She has been carried all about the world. To Carolina, Ermelo, Standerton. Back again to Barberton, and then to Middelburg. Ah, who can believe it! The misery we suffer in these camps is so great. Yesterday 570 people had died here since March. What will be the end of all these sufferings?

*25th of July* (by the grandmother, aged 79).—Dear child, it is a sad thing to see and hear everything. But everything is kept a secret from us, and we dare not write the truth. But the day is near when the curtain will be drawn aside and everything will come to light My children are dispersed to different parts. Those of Johannes are here, so are Annie and her children. Oh, my dear child, so many people die here, 20, 22, 39, and even more in one day.

*30th of July* (by the mother).—I am under the necessity of sending you sad news. Brother Stefenus has been brought in here a prisoner. He told us that brother Piet had died of an illness. We have learned that their wives are at Balmoral Great is the distress suffered here by women and children. The mothers themselves are obliged to carry their children to the cemetery if others do not do it for them. Sometimes they themselves draw the cart in which the body had been placed, to the cemetery, which is at an hour's distance from the camp. There is a hearse, but if they wish to employ it they have to pay £3 for the use of it. And we have even no money to buy food for our children.

Old Mrs. Janson of Suikerboschkop is also with her children in one of those dreadful tents. The youngest boy has already died with misery.

This place Middelburg ought to be given another name and be called '*Weenen*,' for people weep and shed tears here by day and by night; there is nothing else but weeping and shedding of tears.

————————

From Norval's Pont, where comparatively there was much to bring alleviation, a well-born woman writes to ask temporary help from the clergyman of the parish, a stranger known only to her by name—

Translation,

July 1, 1901.

You will certainly wonder at receiving a letter from such an unknown person; I must introduce myself. I am the wife of P. Faure who lived once at Stellenbosch. He, my husband, entreated me to write to you to ask you to get for us a little vegetable such as potatoes or onions, and also butter or lard, and to send them here to us; we will make it all right, with you after the war. Forgive me for being so presumptuous, but believe me, dear Sir, that it goes hard here in the camp. I am quite sickly with all my children, and I believe you feel for us.

Vegetables we never see here. Oh, it is bitter to have had every good thing and now to possess nothing. The tents are so frightfully cold in the nights, and so warm in the day. There is a terrible amount of sickness here, such as inflammation, measles, and also fever; many die also.

Pardon, dear Sir, once more for my presumption, but the need is great.

P.S.—Should anything be sent to Norval's Pont Camp, forget me not, even in such things as clothes.

We have a worthy minister here in Mr. Van der Merwe of Beaufort West; it is certain that his work will bear much fruit Pardon my writing, but I write on a packing-case, and the wind blows terribly.

★★★★★★

*Ladies' Report*—The superintendent's remark was, 'They want vegetables badly,' and scurvy would come unless they got them. He also would like everyone to sleep on bedsteads, not as a matter of luxury, but of health.—Cd. 893.

★★★★★★

One of the difficulties experienced by the nurses was how to keep the children patients amused, especially in the convalescent stages. Passing through the wards, I myself used to see one child's head after another look up from the pillow, and the word "*poppie*" would echo down the row of beds, when I had only perhaps one doll amongst twenty or thirty applicants. So, a kind-hearted woman, Nurse Strachan of Kroonstad Hospital, writes—

July 14.

Your generosity gives me courage to apply to you for 'dolls.' You may think my request a strange one, but to me it is heartbreaking to hear a wee dying girlie craving for a doll and not have one to give her. I have girlies of my own and have to keep them at school, or I could myself supply, but under circumstances, and being a war refugee myself, I cannot afford to buy, much as I would like to. I think I will manage to dress, if you can manage to supply the artificial baby. Poor wee girlies! lots of them have lost father and mother too; to me it is hard to bear the cry for a '*poppie*.'

If you can send something to amuse my wee boys, I shall be doubly grateful. You yourself must think of what would be best for them.

From Mrs. Isaak Meyer to her Mother.

Valkyrs, July 26.

I had no chance of writing before, poor wee Memory (daughter) was so dangerously ill. She has the measles.

Measles are raging in this camp.

You will be very sorry to hear that Jannie's little Marthe is so ill from inflammation of the lungs. The doctor has no hope of her recovery. Mrs. B. Lombardo's youngest sonnie is also ill of inflammation.

Yesterday, Mrs. Bothusa died, Mrs. Frans van Deventer's baby of about two summers died last week. Today, Mrs. Brijtenbach's girl of about seventeen died.

The camp has been enlarged, and we are (on this corner) very close to the British fortresses. There is hardly a tent that there is not a sick child or woman in, and goodness alone knows what the end will be.

Letter to her Sister, Mrs. Louis Botha. From Mrs. Meyer.

Volksrust, Aug, 1901.

I can never describe the life we had in camp, bitter was not the name for it.

The most essential was our food, which, though the British supplied us, was so little, that we often and often retired with an empty stomach. Shall I ever forget the death scenes, they are so depicted on my mind; never in all my life have I seen such hardships, heard so much wailing, as in the segregation camp of Volksrust; daily 10, 12, 14, 16 and even 20 children and people died, daily that same number of coffins carried out to be rested for ever in the paupers' graves; no wonder my head is like that of an old woman of 50, so grey; for who, that had a spark of sympathy, could be otherwise, to see friends carted away on buck-waggons, one day used for bringing rations, the next for bearing the dead to their resting-places.

The food we got was *bad*; flour, coffee, and sugar for the week which only lasted about two days, and the meat was so dreadful because they killed brand-sick sheep and rams for us.

So many of our people have died in camp; during the four months I was in the Volksrust Camp 587 people died. Is that not a terrible number in four months? This I was told by our superintendent, Mr. Carter.)

★★★★★★

*Recommendation.*—We urge that this camp ought to be reduced in numbers. The present camping ground is not sufficiently large for the numbers congregated upon it.—Cd. 893. Nov. 25.

The refugees, as a rule, observe clean habits. . . . As a general rule, it is not presumed that their life in tents is a very great hardship.—Cd. 819, Supt. Report.

The smallest meat ration which we have seen in any camp. Recommendation vii. Bring up the meat ration to the level of other camps.—Cd. 893, Ladies' Report.

In this camp, as in many others, the real numbers of deaths are very hard to obtain. This lady, writing in August, gives 587 as the number that died in 4 months on the word of the superintendent. The Blue Book, Cd. 819) gives 4 months: May, 30; June, 39; July, 49; August, 248—Total, 366. It will be observed that no returns of deaths in the Transvaal are given earlier than May. The Ladies' Commission elect to omit also the deaths of May and June, and begin with July. Consequently, their figures are valueless. The full tale of deaths is never likely to be known.

★★★★★★

Letter from Mrs. Klazinga, taken to Mafeking Camp.

Aug. 1901.

. . . I will tell you all from the beginning, but solely what I personally have seen and undergone.

On the 1st of August I was made prisoner at Welverdiend, District Wolmaransstad. In the morning of that day the English under Colonel H—— approached my house. The first thing they did was to capture and slaughter all the poultry (about a hundred fowls) and the pigs. They even took a small monkey which had belonged to my little boy who had died a short time before, and to which I therefore told them I was much attached. When they had looted all outside, they went to the house—but I would not let them in, because the head officer was not yet with them. I locked all the doors, and went to the verandah with the children and the servants. There were hundreds of soldiers round the house.

Suddenly I heard a great noise inside: they had broken the window of my husband's surgery, and were there, looting. Well, when the commanding officer arrived, they had searched the whole house. The first officer who came was a respectable and polite man, and he said I should be allowed to remain in my

323

house; but the second was stern and rough, and only said: 'Pack up your things and get ready to go, the waggon will be here directiy.'

And so it was, they hardly left me ten minutes to get my things together. Though I cried, and told them my husband was a Hollander and had remained neutral, and had an appointment as medical helper to the Boers, it availed nothing. I was obliged to go. (Her husband had left a signed document to be shown to every column that passed. It is appended.)

The chief officer himself promised to give me a cheque for the medicines out of my husband's well-filled shop, but I have never heard any more about it since, and I never received the cheque. The officers took all my plate and smashed all that was breakable before my eyes, and burned the very valuable books (mostly medical works, and in costly bindings) belonging to my husband. They also took away more than three hundred sheep and silk-goats, and beat them to death with sticks. They took possession of the shepherd with a couple of mules and a horse, and armed our *Kaffir* boy.

In the evening, as we were encamped at an hour's distance from my house, this *Kaffir* came to me, and said: 'Oh! my dear missis, now I must shoot my own master, or the English will shoot me down.' I asked him what he had been told to do. He answered that at night he was to be a spy with the English, and search for and capture Boers.

When we left the house they had poured paraffin oil all over it and the other houses in the place, and had set fire to them and burned them with all they contained.

They pull down the churches and burn the pastors' houses.

We were transported to Taungs through District Bloemhof, and wherever the convoy passed, the English burned, destroyed, and captured all and everything; they even took the *Kaffirs* and servants and burned their straw huts. The food on our road to Taungs was scarce. Sometimes we were left without food or drink for twenty-four hours. They halted in the evenings at places where neither wood nor water was to be had, and left before daybreak next morning, to drive on till late in the afternoon. In this way we and the children suffered from privation, and the poor dumb animals died of hunger and fatigue. All along the road we saw them lying about, dead or dying.

Wherever the English pass they burn the grass, hoping by so doing to starve the Boer horses; but the Lord is a righteous God, and suffereth no unrighteousness, for when the grass is burned up, He sends rain, and in a few days the grass is high enough for the horses and the sheep.

Altogether the treatment we receive is far from what it should be. Our escorts act in an arbitrary way. They who laugh and joke with them receive their rations, but those who will not, often have to wait three days for a little meal and coffee. Our escort was named Hamilton (a Colonial), a boy of nineteen or twenty, who lorded it over us. When we arrived at Taungs, our luggage, consisting of bedding and a few clothes, was simply thrown out of the waggons on to the dirty soil, and had to be left there till the afternoon, when each had to get their own things on the railway trucks.

These were exceedingly foul, some covered with coal-dust, others with manure, none of them had even been swept. But for us poor women they were good enough. The dirtier they make us, the truer their reports about us seem to be. But the fact is that no Boer or Boer woman is naturally dirty; they always are glad to clean themselves if they have the opportunity—and soap! But the Tommies are careful that this should not be the case. We had not even sufficient water for drinking! In that way we had to spend three nights and two and a half days. On some of the trucks were more than fifty women, children, and old men. There was no space for sleeping; some had stiffened legs when they arrived at Mafeking, and all were ill from the wind, the sun, and the cold. My eldest child was two years, the youngest two months old; you can understand the state I was in. Happily, I nursed the baby, or it would have died from privation; the eldest sometimes cried for some hard biscuit, so-called 'stomach-bombs,' saltless things made of coarse meal and as hard as stone. But the English consider them fit for food.

As the train left Taungs, we were told not to speak to the *Kaffirs* along the line; later on, we understood why; wherever we came, they called us names and threw dirt at us—which seemed rather to amuse the Khakis.

A few of the English pitied us heartily, and gave us as much help as they could, as for instance getting us some boiling water from the engine to make coffee, but most of them enjoyed the sight of us, and laughed all the time. When we reached Mafeking, after eleven at night, and the little children were sound asleep, warmly wrapped up on our knees, we begged to be allowed to remain where we were till morning, to prevent the little ones from getting cold and ill. But we were not listened to; our things were again thrown out of the trucks, and we were forced to sit and wait till we should be taken to the camp.

At last a donkey-cart came for us, and I was conveyed to the camp at 2 o'clock a.m. The children cried with misery; at home, they had been accustomed to soft warm beds—my mother's heart bleeds to think of such a treatment. When we reached the camp, we were set down in front of the so-called schoolroom without a roof over our heads, and had to wait till the gentlemen were pleased to provide us with a tent. Some have lain out there two whole days in sunshine and rain.

✶✶✶✶✶✶

The superintendent attributed the introduction of the sickness to the arrival of a large number of people on 15th August. They were brought in by the military from Taungs District in the middle of the night, and in consequence were neither examined nor isolated on their arrival; they were temporarily housed in the school and in waggons.—Cd. 893.

It will need a sustained strong effort to pull this camp out of the deplorable condition into which it has been allowed to sink.

A request to headquarters for an assistant doctor, sent 22nd July, had been quickly attended to, and Dr. Limpert arrived on 6th August. He was found to be useless, . . . Medicine is deplorably deficient. Much anaemia among women and children, and no iron. Much diarrhoea, yet no bismuth nor chalk nor catechu with which to cure it. Many deaths and no mortuary. One of the cemeteries only 20 feet from the camp boundary, and graves only 3½ feet deep. We saw little children engaged in filling them in.—Ladies' Report.

During the last two months, weeks have passed with only a rare ration! of fresh meat at intervals, and now a sufficiency for the hospital and staff only is obtainable. 'Bully-beef' and bread form a quite unsuitable diet for children, who will certainly die in numbers if so fed.—Ladies' Report.

The Commission are unanimously of opinion that the superintendent and the former medical officer are greatly to blame.

Two Boer women said separately that if English ladies sent gifts they ought to distribute them themselves; if left to local committees of the camp people, they gave to their own friends rather than those most in want.

★★★★★★

All our things were soon too much soiled to touch. Those women in the camp who had been there for some time, and were acquainted with all the horrors, brought us bread and coffee now and again. Some of them had been treated in the same way, and some even more inhumanly.

As for the camp life, it is, in a word, 'slow starvation and defilement.' I cannot thank God enough for having been enabled to leave it so soon, and come out alive with my two children.

Medical assistance is to be had in the camp. There is one Dr. Limpert, and another whose name I have forgotten. There also are a couple of nurses; but this is far too little for a population of 6,000 people, and sickness in every tent. Consequently the mortality was very great. It has happened that mothers with small children have had to wait three days before being able to speak to the doctor; and when at last their turn came, simply were told to go away, for 'Did they not know all children *under the age of five must die?*' Such a one would return to her tent with tears in her eyes, and an undying and implacable hatred towards the enemy in her heart.

★★★★★★

Note:—"*Alle kinder onder fÿf moet firek.*" "*Frek*" is used of the death of animals. It is quite probable that the overworked and under-staffed doctor meant by this that he could not, had not, the means to keep them alive, while to people unfamiliar with English it would sound deliberate.

★★★★★★

The rations are very small. In six weeks I was three times given a pound and a half of almost uneatable meat. The doctor himself said, 'You can eat, but don't come to me for medicine then!' Luckily, I possessed some money of my own, and was able to buy myself some food; but most of the women either had nothing when they were captured, or were robbed of what they possessed by the troops, and these are obliged to live solely on the scant rations provided.

The day after I arrived they received meat, but when they wished to go and complain about the quality to the colonel at Mafeking, and show him that the meat was not fit for food,

327

the camp superintendent, MacCowat, would not grant them a pass. This made the women so furious that they took hold of him and pushed the raw meat into his mouth, saying, 'Eat that yourself; we are used to better meat.'

I have been in the camp for six weeks. During that time clothes have been distributed once. But just those women whose husbands, sons, or brothers have taken the oath of loyalty were given any; those whose husbands are still fighting receive nothing, and some of them with their children go barefoot.

It is not true that the Boer women beg to be taken to the camp—all of them would rather have stayed in their own house and their own place, even though they were not amply provided with stores.

I, for instance, need never have gone; my house was filled with corn, meal, and clothes, and I have always had plenty to give away to the needy in our village. I was carried off illegally, since my husband is 'volunteer' or '*dilettant*' doctor with the Boers, has a certificate as such, and moreover is neutral, and both of us are Hollanders.

... You must know that in the camp we may not show our true colours, or our rations are decreased. The wisest is to suffer in silence. ...

PAPER LEFT BY MR. KLAZINGA AS A PROTECTION FOR HIS WIFE.

The Hon. Officer in Command of His Majesty's Forces acting in the District of Wolmaransstad, and visiting this farm Welverdiend.

Herewith I take the liberty to bring to your knowledge the following facts and circumstances about me and my family:—

1. *That I am an Uitlander*, staying in the Transvaal for about two years and a half before the war; *no burgher of the South African Republic*, but still a subject of a neutral State (Holland).

2. *That I am the acting chief of the Wolmaransstad field-ambulance* since the beginning of the war, in which position I had already in several cases the pleasure to render important services to the British forces in taking care and giving every help needed to wounded, or on the battlefield follow officers and troops from His Majesty's army, or otherwise.

Considering in this way to be in a quite neutral position, as well by my being a certificated Red Cross officer, as my being a subject of Her Majesty Wilhelmina, Queen of the Netherlands; I request humbly, but most determinately,

(*a*) That my wife and children will be left in this house, if there should be any intention on your side to take them away.

(*b*) That my family may be kept safe from any molestation, as well as the few properties I possess here. No guns or cartridges will be found in my house.

(*c*) So that I am treated just as, for example, the neutral Uitlander storekeepers in this and other districts, whose persons, families, and possessions are fully respected in every way.

Further, I beg you to assist my wife, if possible, with some corn flour, coffee, etc., and a pair of cows, as I am informed has been granted at other places to women wanting these articles.
Giving my hearty thanks for all the kindness and help you will grant to my family, believe me to remain, Honourable Sir, yours most faithfully,

A. H. Klazinga,
Acting-Chief, Wolmaransstad Ambulance.

Welverdiend, March 1901.

A woman who ran away from Mafeking Camp told her story on oath before General Celliers: it agrees with all which comes from other sources—

On this day, the 16th of November 1901, appeared before me at Vergenoegd, District Zeerust, South African Republic, Petronella Jehanna Van Staden, who declares on oath, (see Report of General De la Rey):—

I am the wife of Adriaan Van Staden, a resident of this place. On the 11th of June last, I was taken prisoner here, together with other women, and conducted to Mafeking. On arrival there we were placed in the women's camp in tents. We received the following daily rations: meat, rice, flour, and jam; also coffee and sugar. We were satisfied with our food. This lasted for two months.

First our meat rations were reduced to 2 lbs. per week. Later on the coffee and sugar; and so it went on until the first of this month, when I escaped, and our rations were then for eight days as follows: a plateful of flour, 2 lbs. of rice, ¼ lb. of coffee, and 1 lb. of sugar; meat, 2 lbs. per week for every adult Children under 12 years of age got half rations.

The doctors treated us very roughly. Sometimes they assaulted us when we applied for medicines. Many a time we were told: 'If all those in camp perished it would not matter.' As for firewood, they allowed us 30 lbs. of green wood per week. We were obliged to dig for roots in order to enable us to make fires. They did not give us any clothes, unless we were in the direst want of them, *viz.*, when we were almost naked. Clothes that had been collected for us by our minister. Rev. Van der Spuy, in Cape Colony, were not given to us, but to the families of those *burghers* who had surrendered to the enemy.

The same happened with the victuals sent for us. By 'us' I mean the wives of those *burghers* who are still in the field. The cases of mortality in the camp were very numerous. Last month we had 580 deaths, mostly children. I have these statistics from my brother, Johannes Smit, who has assisted in making the coffins. The British authorities supply the coffins, and cause the graves to be dug, but we ourselves must attend to the funeral. The cases of mortality varied from 20 to 30 a day. With the exception of the distribution of clothes, no distinction is made between us and the wives of the 'hands-uppers.' Whenever we go to make a complaint, we are roughly treated, and most of the time we are told to go to H——.

Our complaints were never investigated. We were told that the women that had escaped had been murdered by the *Kaffirs*, and further that our own officers did not want us anymore, and also that General De la Rey had said that he would shoot all women that ever escaped. Before I escaped, several other women had done so, and it was reported that they had been murdered by *Kaffirs*.

However, I decided to run away. Myself and Aletta Smart escaped from the camp on the 7th inst. at night. We arrived here after wandering about for two nights and two days. But for the reports that are being circulated, as to the murdering of escaped women by *Kaffirs*, many more women would try to escape.

All of them are very dissatisfied as to their treatment. We got nothing but tinned meat. At first it was good, but afterwards it was very bad. Once we were warned not to eat the meat, as the animals had died from lung disease. The tinned meat is very unhealthy, and causes diarrhoea. Before I escaped, two women from Lichtenburg ran away, who were, however, arrested and brought back by *Kaffirs*. They were then punished, with eight days' rice-water. They got no other food, and were moreover put in a separate camp. I had a child when I was taken a prisoner; it died in camp.

Most of the children die of measles. The food is supplied and distributed in camp. Many a time we have to wait from early in the morning till late in the afternoon before they give us anything, and many a time they tell us that we are no better than ——.

P. J. Van Staden.

Sworn before me on the date and at the place aforesaid.

J. G. Celliers,<br>Fighting General for Lichtenburg and Marico.

******

Going carefully through the camp, we could not but feel that little or nothing had been done by the superintendent to carry out our recommendations. On the contrary, the conditions had in some respects deteriorated since our visit, and it was plain that until the arrival of Dr. Morrow no real effort had been made to prevent or to cope with the sickness. This had steadily increased, until 2,000 cases of disease were registered at one time: 29 deaths had occurred in one day, and over 500 lives had been lost during the ten weeks since we had left.—Cd. 893. Ladies' Report.

******

Terrible as Mrs. Klazinga's description is, every word is endorsed by the various official reports relating to Mafeking Camp.

A young girl also wrote from there—

Your letter and £5 note to hand, for which accept my heartiest thanks. I also received the same amount from Miss Monkhouse, so bought thirteen boxes of soap and candles, and distributed it among the needy, for which they were very thankful. Here are over 5,000 people now, and we expect 400 more today. Miss Monkhouse and Mellor did not reach here yet. I hope they'll turn up one of these days. Here were six other ladies, (namely, the Ladies' Commission), but I haven't had the pleasure of meeting them. Nurse Crawfurd was ill for a time, but am glad to say she is enjoying good health again; there are about four nurses besides her now. Two of my sisters are laid up; one has fever, I think.

331

A member of the Cape Town Committee writes—

Jan, 28, 1902.

A girl called to see me who has been let out of one of the camps. She was so ill that they consented to let her go to save her life. She has been a month in bed, and is still very pale and shaky. Her spirit is extraordinary. She is bound by a sort of promise not to detail stories about the camps, on pain of being had up before a court-martial and 'dealt with like a man, without respect of age or sex.' She could therefore only speak quite generally, but she is on fire with suppressed fury. She is pretty, slight, and graceful, of the highly-organised, nervous, dark-haired type of Transvaal woman, not like the calm, slow-spoken Cape Dutch.

She says, speaking of the Natal camps in 1901, that these have been fairly healthy, but will be so no longer, for they are being crowded with thousands of new-comers from the north, who arrive wretched in the last degree, and bring disease with them. Howick has now a high mortality, though death was infrequent there before. She described the advent of some hundreds of poor people lately from Klerksdorp. They had been travelling for many days, but had no food whatever by the way. They arrived at the camp like wild animals raging with hunger—a pitiful sight—the children and women alike worn down to literal skin and bone.

The children were screaming in an appalling way, and when at last hot porridge was put before them, they fell upon it and literally devoured it, though it was scalding hot A man who saw the sight felt as if years had been added to his life. The poor creatures looked scarcely like human beings at all. They had not been allowed out of the vehicles in which they were conveyed, even for ordinary needs.

One baby had died of starvation on the way; the mother had to hand the little body down to be buried. At night they were guarded by bayonetted soldiers, and could not move. Their torments were unspeakable.

Mrs. Strassheim, likewise a distributor of relief in her camp, writes gratefully from Klerksdorp—

To the Honorary Secretary, Relief Committee, Cape Town.

Sept. 5, 1901.

It is with great pleasure that I acknowledge the goods received by us for the relief of women and children in the camp here.

I need hardly tell you how welcome your gift is: we have very many needy ones to whom all this will come as a God-send. I shall try and do what I can in connection with the distribution. It is a great pleasure for me to be able to do anything for our poor people, and I hope I shall be worthy of the confidence you have placed in me.

What pleases us very much are the boxes with contributions from friends who, it seems, have personally prepared the work. It is touching to notice how lovingly the little garments have been got up. Will you tell the donors how much we appreciate their thoughtfulness and kindness? I want also specially to mention the boots, stockings, and also the leather, which will go a long way in supplying a great need.

There are 1,733 women over sixty-two years in the camp, and 2,352 children, so you can understand that everything will come in very handy, and that many hearts will be made glad.

We have had an epidemic of measles here, which I am sorry to say has carried off many of the children. There is still a good deal of sickness, but much is being done to alleviate the suffering. They are fortunate in having in the superintendent a real friend—one who feels for them, and who has their welfare at heart

The rice, maizena, peas, etc., will be used for soups for the sick, I just want to say that only three out of the eight bags of rice have reached us. . . .

This lady, whose husband was a chaplain with the Boer forces, was amongst those exiled to Natal, ten days after writing the above. On 15th September 1901, the deportation was described by General De la Rey—

In virtue of Lord Kitchener's proclamation, on the evening of 15th September 1901, at Klerksdorp, 500 women and children of *burghers* still on commando were driven in open cattle trucks; the night was rough and stormy. Among the women was the wife of General Liebenberg with her children, the wife of Mr. Pienaar (Mining Commissioner), the wife of the Rev.

Strassheim, and many others of the prominent inhabitants of Klerksdorp and the neighbourhood, with their children.

Next morning the train started; the whole company, including the people who had come to bid them goodbye, first sang a psalm, whereupon the eldest daughter of General Liebenberg displayed a Transvaal flag, which she herself had made. An English officer advanced and tore the flag from her hands, amid loud protests of the women. As soon as the train had started, the same young lady brought out another flag, which she waved, while all the women and children in the cattle trucks sang the National Anthem, until the station of Klerksdorp was lost to sight. (See Report of De la Rey and Smuts.)

### On the Death of a Brother.

A young teacher wrote:

Winburg Camp, Nov. 16.

Many thanks, for your most welcome letter of condolence. I was indeed very pleased to hear from you, for I did not know what had become of you. It is very hard to have parted with such a dear brother. He was indeed so much to us—a dear brother and a father to us. I can't tell you how terribly I miss him. But we have a very great comfort: he was prepared to meet his God, and what more do we want! We can only submit and say, '*Thy will be done.*' And how beautiful to know God has done it all out of love to us, for those He loveth He chasteneth. Poor Mary is at Harrismith Camp with Mrs. L. The camp is large now; there are about 3,000 people. There were up to eight corpses a day. Several school friends are here. Sarah, Maria, Maggie, Stinie, and others. We have a school here: I am helping in it. We have about 300 children that attend. I should be glad if you could send me a few nice stories that would do for my Sunday-school class.

In the same quiet tone writes another to Miss Murray—

Bloemfontein Camp, Dec. 10.

I was so glad to hear from you again. It is such a comfort to hear from friends in this miserable camp. I do wish you could stand on the *randje* and watch it for a few minutes. Your thoughts seem to overwhelm you, and you have to turn away. What is God's will? For what purpose has He brought us so far? These are thoughts which often puzzle us. Of our treatment we cannot complain, although the heat is sometimes so bad that we cannot endure it, yet God gives us strength even in this. We do miss our comfortable homes, our butter and milk, and vegetables and fruit gardens; we can only sing, '*Oh wait and murmur not.*'

What I have experienced since I saw you last cannot be written on paper. We have gone through deep waters and many trials, and even had shells over our heads. I speak of home, but in reality we have no homes now, only farms. My piano and harmonium are utterly destroyed.

The death-angel has also entered our home and taken away our blessed brother. He had no illness, but fell on the battlefield. Particulars are not known to us, for he fell since we are in camp. I know he is safe, for his life showed plainly Whose he was and Whom he served. I am also longing to lead such a life. My aunt also died here in camp, and her little orphans were left to our care. The hospitals are quite crowded with sick people; so many deaths I never heard of in my life.

Schoolchildren at Irene, Nov. 1901

CHAPTER 1

# January to June—Further Homes Destroyed and Proclamation of Peace

*Did we think Victory great?*
*So it is—but now it seems to me,*
*When it cannot be helped, that defeat is great.*
*And that death and dismay are great.*—Walt Whitman.

The year 1902 opened in anxiety for watchers over the welfare of the camps, and small relief came with the publication of the December death-rate. It was lower than the previous months, but still stood at 261.09 for camps in the aggregate. The two first Blue Books, (Cd. 89 and Cd. 853, 1901), had revealed a state of things far worse and more widespread in ill effects than the little Report, which had occasioned such indignation six months earlier.

But in spite of Blue Books, debates, and publication of facts, ignorance still prevailed about the Boer women and children, only it was now a wilful ignorance. The women of England seemed in the state described by Ruskin, they "shut out the death cries, and are happy and talk wittily among themselves. That is the utter literal fact of what our ladies do in their pleasant lives." They are reached, he goes on to say, "only at intervals by a half-heard cry and a murmur as of the wind's sighing when myriads of souls expire." (*Crown of Wild Olive.*)

In a word, the majority did not heed or did not care, while others were glad to avail themselves of the new reasons given for the origin of the camps by Mr. Chamberlain in the House of Commons. (Jan. 19, 1902.) He assured the country that the "whole responsibility for such misery as has been caused rested upon the shoulders of the Boer *commandant*." (*Times*, Jan. 20, 1902.) He referred the House to the correspondence between Lord Kitchener and General Botha, which is given elsewhere, and which he affirmed was the origin of the camps. (Part 1. chap. 1, and Part 2 chap. 1.)

If Mr. Chamberlain's plea had been in accordance with facts, it could only have served to strengthen the case against the concentration system. It entirely cut the ground from under the argument that concentration was a work of unparalleled humanity undertaken to save women and children from starvation, and turned it into a mere act of reprisal No ingenuity could call an act of reprisal humane which caused 20,000 deaths, chiefly among children. But Mr. Chamberlain's plea was not in accordance with facts. We have seen already that the correspondence on which he rested his case was vitiated by a misquotation on a vital point, and that the documents referred to by Lord Kitchener contain no evidence that the burning of farms was adopted as a method of punishment by the Boer Generals, but rather prove the contrary.

It must be added that the correspondence between Lord Kitchener and General Botha did not take place until many camps had been in existence for many months—and already contained thousands of people. Mr. Chamberlain, however, thought, and doubtless many were glad to think with him, that with "a humanity absolutely unprecedented in the history of war, we, upon whom these women and children have been forced, have executed the duty and responsibility in the name of humanity." (*Times*, Jan. 20.) Further, the Colonial Secretary thought there had been "gross exaggeration" as to the deaths in the camps. There is, he said, an enormous child mortality in normal times, and that mortality must be deducted. "With such a people the death-rate could not be expected to fall below 100 per 1,000." (*Times*, Jan. 20.) During this last May (1902) we have seen, since Mr. Chamberlain's thorough reforms, the rate fall to 20!

Every week telegrams now appeared announcing some improvement in the camp system. New schemes for supplying water in Bloemfontein, Kroonstad, and Winburg—new arrangements for housing in huts instead of tents—the issue of vegetables, and so forth. Particularly pleasing was it to learn that 200 boys were learning woodwork in Irene Camp, and that Miss Pughe Jones is teaching knitting at Kroonstad, and Miss Wilson, sister of the Secretary to the Administration, is teaching knitting and the making of point and Flemish lace to the girls in the Bloemfontein Camp. Her labours have been so successful that teachers from other camps are coming to learn the work during their holidays.

The total number of children in the Government schools of the Orange River Colony is now 13,409, as compared with a total of 8,900 in the Government and private schools under the old regime. (Laffan, *Manchester Guardian,* April 1, 1902; Cd. 1163 (1902).)

Indeed, the work of the Education Department advanced rapidly as sickness decreased, and a hundred teachers were selected by the English and Scotch Education Departments for South Africa. Mr. Sargant wrote, (Cd. 1163 (1902), Report of Mr. E. B. Sargant):

It has been most gratifying to observe how quickly friendly relations were established between the old teachers and the new. . . . The English teachers report that they find the children intelligent, docile, and eager to learn. They speak highly also of the results the Dutch teachers had achieved before their arrival.

By these and other means the life of the camps was made bearable, and for the children, even interesting, while the greater suffering passed to those families who, it will be seen, were still in the various districts where military operations continued.

On March 4 1902, Mr. Humphreys Owen moved the following amendment—

This House deplores the great mortality in the Concentration Camps formed in the execution of the policy of clearing the country.

To his remarks Mr. Chamberlain replied in a speech which showed he had been misinformed on many points. He denied that farm-burning was the origin of the camps, for he believed only some 600 were burnt, and that figure multiplied by five, taking five as an average family, would not account for the large number in the camps. (See *Times,* March 5, 1902.) This shows that Mr. Chamberlain still believed that the handful of farms returned as burnt in Cd. 524 was the sum-total destroyed. He went on to say that when the guerilla warfare began "it was found that from one cause or another vast numbers of Boer women and children would be. left unprotected on the *veld.* As a Christian nation, we could not leave them there." (See end of chapter.)

One I does not know what date Mr. Chamberlain fixes as the beginning of guerilla warfare, but the eviction by our troops of Boer families, and their deportation, exile, and concentration, began, as we have seen, many months before Lord Roberts left South Africa. The remark is puzzling, because inconsistent with his previous explanation. Mr. Chamberlain does not offer any reason why British columns "captured" women and children living quietly in towns, and also those who were not unprotected, but had been placed in *laagers* by the Boers, who supplied them with food, and left them in the care of old men past fighting. He repudiated the complaint that there had been delay in making improvements in the camps after attention had been called to the need of it; yet, if Mr. Chamberlain had done in June what he did in December, thousands of lives might have been spared.

The Colonial Secretary's figures were arrived at by quoting infantile mortality against a child mortality, which was reckoned to twelve years in the Transvaal, and to fifteen years in the Orange River Colony. Finally, he said he did not know that the women were unwilling to come into the camps, though "it is fair to say they were brought in." He thought very few wanted to go to friends, and the people were allowed to go when it was quite certain they would be well taken care of.

This statement does not agree with facts which have repeatedly come before public notice. A well-known instance is that of Mrs. De Wet, who had written openly to Mr. Brodrick about her detention, and about whom the War Secretary was questioned as recently as May. (*Manchester Guardian*, May 14, 1902.) Mr. MacNeill extracted the information on that occasion that Mrs. De Wet might only leave the camp to go out of South Africa, and that in the opinion of the Secretary for War exaggerated importance had been attached to the lady. Consequently, Mrs. De Wet was kept a prisoner in Pietermaritzburg Camp till the cessation of hostilities. Mrs. Neethling, who died in Balmoral Camp, is another instance, and a very sad one. Repeated applications by her relations failed to secure her release. These cases could be easily multiplied.

The Report of the Ladies' Commission was issued in February. To comment upon it in detail would be outside the scope of this book, but a few words may be usefully said. The book is divided into two parts, the General Report, and reports on separate camps. Considerable care has been shown in dealing with some of the twenty-two points examined in each camp, especially the Sanitary and Hospital

Departments, and the issue of rations. Other important branches, such as the orphans, the local helpers, applications to leave, and the mortality lists, received scant attention. The whole was, of course, a rather superficial view, as the Commission rarely spent more than the inside of two days in a camp. This precluded them from entering at all into the life of the camps as felt by the people, for the Boers are not a race inclined to open their hearts to strangers of a day's acquaintance.

The Commission reiterated the facts, and urged the recommendations made months before, and made some useful improvements which they had power to do. One of their best pieces of work was securing the appointment as Inspector, of Mr. Cole Bowen, an idea proposed months previously. The mortality figures given by the Commission are unreliable. They disagree with the Blue Books, and are misleading, as they begin and end according to fancy. Neither are the dates given for the establishment of camps always correct For instance, February 1901 is given as the commencement of Johannesburg Camp, whereas it was a large camp in November 1900. (See Part 1, chap. 2.)

The regrettable feature of the book is the tone of the General Report, which does not bear out the separate reports. Particularly unfortunate is the endeavour to cast a large part of the responsibility for their children's deaths upon the Boer mothers. However constantly and unchivalrously ministers, hard up for excuses, have sheltered themselves behind the supposed stupidity and carelessness of Boer mothers, one hoped that Englishwomen would have been above such accusations. They have only succeeded in collecting a few isolated cases—such as one woman who used green oil paint—one who used vermilion paint—one who used varnish— one who ate a poultice. These are not many out of some 40,000 or 50,000 women.

For the rest, their error seems to have been the use of old-fashioned remedies, many of a like kind to which can be studied in Nicholas Culpeper, and all can be capped in English villages in the twentieth century, with parish doctors everywhere. Today one hears of mouse-pie in certain parts of England, of snails to cure consumption, those found creeping *up* a churchyard wall, those crawling *down* are of no avail, and in a northern county blacklead is used to anoint wounds in sore legs. A jelly of black slugs, stewed in water, is mentioned by a recent writer in the *Spectator* as obtaining still in villages known to him, and we are all familiar with a potato carried in the pocket for rheumatism, and a dead spider tied in a bag for measles. But does one ever hear of deaths arising from these remedies?

The case of the green oil paint seems to have occurred in Krugers-dorp Camp. It was said to have been used externally by one mother, and two children died from its effects, or perhaps from the ailments from which they were suffering. Dr. Kendal Franks tells us the name of these children was 'Smith.' (Cd. 819.) This instance, like the story of the raw carrot, was bandied from camp to camp, published far and wide, quoted in Parliament and Press, till people believed it was a common usage of the Boer mothers. The American leather, spoken of as being a medical trophy brought home by the Commission, is, doc-tors tell me, quite a common and not a bad foundation for a plaster in South Africa.

The vermilion oil paint, which so alarmed a nurse, is doubtless *Rooie poeder* or *Rooie minie*, which is a preparation of red lead. A doc-tor, with twenty years' practice behind him in the Free State, says it is constantly used by Boer women, in the same way as we use iodine, to paint externally where there is some inflammation. He says it is *abso-lutely* harmless. Sometimes they mix it with linseed poultices, but it is never used to paint sores or open wounds. Mrs. Louis Botha told me she has used it with success on her children.

Apart from traditional remedies, the Dutch medicines were pro-hibited by the Commission, who believed that to them "many a child has fallen victim." (Cd. 893.) They are prepared by a Cape Town firm, in a convenient little case called a '*Huis Apothek.*' There is hardly a country house in the whole extent of South Africa which does not possess one of these little boxes. The doctor previously mentioned told me that every one of the medicines in this little chest is absolutely harmless, and that one might take the whole lot at once without being any the worse. They are, he said, a kind of homoeopathic medicine, quite innocuous; and during his long experience he has never known any harm accruing from their use, though his patients frequently took them, while following also his prescriptions. Mrs. Dickenson, before quoted, noted also that the women much prefer their own medicines, she says:

> Some of which are made of herbs gathered on the *veld*, others are what we generally use under different names. I endeavoured to reconcile them to the use of ours, as the Dutch medicines are forbidden, and a doctor (one of the prisoners) was arrested at Bethulie and sent to Bloemfontein for prescribing them!

Individual acts of carelessness or stupidity or ignorance, which result in death, are to be met with daily in every community, and these only mar the impartial character of an official report. One feels sorry at this raking up of trivialities, calculated to transfer to the sufferers the blame for our ineffectual carrying out of our self-made responsibilities. The Commission stand on firmer ground when they deal with the two other reasons they assign for the high mortality, *viz.* the unhealthy state of the country consequent on the war, and causes within the control of the Administration.

But, leaving the General Report, the Commission in the various camps make admissions, and conduct sweeping reforms, which are the more significant considering the spirit in which they write about the women. They do not shrink from condemning ill-chosen sites, dismissing incompetent superintendents, reforming entire hospitals, urging various improvements in food, fuel, and water, recommending beds and ameliorating sanitation.

But nowhere do we find in the pages of this Report any condemnation of the custom of detaining women well able to leave, or orphans to whom welcome is offered in Cape Colony, or of the punishments meted out to women of good character—such as wired enclosures and solitary guard tents for breaking petty rules not clearly understood, or perhaps simply because pride was expressed in the persistence of their husbands in the field. The Commission glide over these things with some short paragraphs on "discipline and morals."

Meanwhile, during the last months of the war, after the camps had been improved, the condition of the families not brought in called for the greatest pity. Speaking on March 4, Mr. Chamberlain had said that as a Christian nation we could not leave numbers of Boer women and children unprotected on the *veld.* (*Times,* March 5, 1902.) Yet during the last five months of the war that was what was done.

In December 1901, Lord Kitchener had said he had given orders that "no more women and children were to be brought into the camps unless it was clear that they must starve upon the *veld.*" Side by side with this order it appears that destruction of houses continued. General Lukas Meyer stated that in February of this year (1902) he saw the smoke of burning houses rise in the Pretoria district between White Nek and Rhenoster Kop, and Generals Hertzog and Smuts say also that the destruction of houses and foodstuffs was persisted in after the order was issued to bring no more women into the camps. Indeed, the destruction of homes continued right up to the beginnings of peace, and I learn on high authority that even during the negotiations

COOKING IN CAMP, 1901

a house was burnt in the district of Heilbron.

It must not be forgotten that not merely solitary farms had been burnt, but whole villages laid waste, in many cases even to the churches. The villages of Piet Retief, Bethel, Ermelo, Dullstroom, Amsterdam, Paul-Pietersberg, Roos Senekal, Bloemhof, Schweizer-Reineke, Hartebeestfontein, Wolmaransstad, Lindley, Ventersburg, and Bothaville were thus demolished, together with parts of Reitz, Frankfort, Dewetsdorp, Jacobsdal, Fouriesberg and others. It was just at the period when at length the camps had been properly organised and supplied with necessaries that women were refused admittance, unless they brought their husbands with them, while at the same time suffering loss of their own shelter and means of subsistence. The number of people thus suffering, and the full facts concerning them, were not known until the *Burghers'* Conference took place at Vereeniging, and each *commandant* laid the report of affairs in his district before the Assembly.

The following information was given to a Cape lady by some of the generals:—

> The Conference discovered that there were still 10,000 women and children who were not in camps. These women were in a shocking condition—their homes and all food supplies were destroyed. Their men were able to supply them with food, but the British sent out at once to rob them of these fresh supplies, and did this by means of bodies of armed natives, who took away all food and clothing, and broke up the women's cooking utensils. The women were then entirely at the mercy of these natives, with results that one dare not dwell upon. . . . Many women were almost naked when their men arrived, some had on only blouses. Many of the women were found in *Kaffir* huts.

This description is supported by General Hertzog, who, writes Mr. Drew:

> . . . tells me the necessity for surrendering came upon the Free State *burghers* as an unexpected shock. It was the state of things which Louis Botha disclosed in the Eastern Transvaal, which left no option but to give in. Some 10,000 Boer women and children were being fed principally in that district, but only enough provision remained for another six weeks. The British had for many months stopped the practice of gathering families

into the Concentration Camps, though the work of destroying both the houses and the food-stuffs was still persisted in. Families would be left in the bare *veld* by the side of the blackened, roofless walls of their houses, and with not so much as a peck of flour left them for bread. The meal would be either removed or emptied out on the ground, and anything else fit for food would also be destroyed. 'Twas useless to appeal to the general to receive into the camps the women and children thus left to starve, and admission was even refused to the families of surrendered burghers, who were already prisoners in Ceylon or elsewhere. To worsen matters, *Kaffirs* were being armed by the thousand and sent forth over the country, sometimes in separate corps, and sometimes attached as scouts to the British columns. . . . The natural consequences of rape and murder did not fail to ensue.

The account given me by General Lukas Meyer of the women's condition coincided with the above.

Finding remonstrance was useless, the Boer generals felt they must review the whole position, and the sufferings of the women outside the camps, together with the mortality in the camps, and the arming of the *Kaffirs*, which endangered life and honour, were embodied in the first three resolutions drawn up at the Vereeniging Conference, and form the main reasons for the surrender which followed. It was a surrender as fine as the struggle so long persevered in; the object of that struggle was manfully set aside when it was clear that the price in innocent life would be so terrible. The three first reasons given in the document handed to Lord Milner and Lord Kitchener ran as follows, (Cd. 1163—slightly varying translation):—

1. That the plan of campaign followed by the British military authorities has led to the utter devastation of the territory of both Republics, and the burning of farms and villages, and the destruction of means of subsistence has exhausted all sources of food supply necessary for the maintenance of our families and the existence of our army.

2. That the placing of our captured families in Concentration Camps has led to an unparalleled condition of suffering and sickness, so that in a comparatively brief period about 20,000 of our near and dear ones have died in the camps, and we have to face the terrible prospect that by the further prolongation of

the war our people may die out altogether.

3. That the *Kaffir* tribes within and outside the borders of the Republics are almost all armed and take part in the war against us (by the committal of murders and other atrocities), thus causing an intolerable state of things in many districts of both Republics—as, for example, in the district of Vryheid, where fifty-six *burghers* were cruelly murdered and mutilated by natives, etc. etc.

Thus Peace was brought about and proclaimed, and the news came to the women whose spirit had never failed. As their lot had been far harder than that of the men prisoners of war, so the measure of their relief is greater.

Strange scenes were witnessed at the Irene Concentration Camp yesterday when the conclusion of peace was announced. The occupants assembled and gave expression to their joy by praying and singing psalms. Many of the people shed tears.—June 1, Press Association.

Bloemfontein Camp, June 3.

This morning a party of Boer representatives arrived from Vereeniging. They were followed by a great crowd, but there was no cheering or other demonstration. Later, several of them rode into the Refugee Camp, where they were received with an extravagant demonstration of joy, men and women weeping and laughing at the same time. Crowds of refugees surrounded the horsemen, talking together and all asking for news of relatives and friends.

A CAMP GARDEN BORDERED WITH MILK TINS

# Chapter 2

# Women in 1902

*Oh cease! must hate and death return?*
*Cease! must men kill and die?*
*Cease! drain not to its dregs the urn*
*Of bitter prophecy!*
*The world is weary of the past,*
*Oh might it die or rest at last!*—Shelley.

Letter from the Clergyman's Wife.

Harrismith Camp, Jan. 3, 1902.

I am afraid we will all die of fever if we remain much longer in this crowded and closed camp. The wire fencing is quite close to the tents, and there is no chance for a walk in order to get a little fresh air; we can't even go into town any more. Measles, whooping-cough, and fever have been raging most furiously among old and young. Oh! to see the dear little children wasting away like tender plants before the hot rays of the sun. Every day there are two, three, up to eight, to be buried. We cannot live in these single bell-shaped tents; they are too hot in the daytime; even though the lower part is rolled it is so hot on the beds that Mr. T. and I have often left our parasols over the head of a sick baby to give it a little more shade.

All of a sudden a thick cloud comes from the Natal mountains; it rains, and you turn in for the night with a very cold and damp wind playing on you all night. Often these tents leak, for some of them are old and thin. Many a measles patient gets wet all over, and consequently dies of inflammation in the lungs. And even though they don't leak, still your bed and clothes, everything, get quite damp on rainy nights. We have to fasten up the

349

openings on rainy days and creep underneath through the mud. Oh, it is a horrid life; there are broken hearts in almost every tent. '*Rachel weeping for her children, and would not be comforted, because they are not.*'

Poor Mrs. L. is no more. She got measles; her tent was near mine, so I watched over her and brought her food She did not seem bad at first, but her tent got wet, and she got inflammation of the lungs. I went immediately for the doctor, but he had his hands so full that he could only come three days later; he took her to the hospital, where she died the same day. They are well cared for in the hospital, and the superintendent does everything to keep the camp healthy. Today we got some onions and potatoes, a present; but I don't know how we will live through the summer without vegetables and fruit When I see the dear, innocent little children passing away, it reminds me of a children's sermon your father had on the text, '*The streets of the city shall be filled with boys and girls playing in them.*'

We have had very hot weather and great scarcity of water for the last three days. We cannot wash our clothes or take our baths; we can scarcely cook our food. We are hard up for fuel, and often have to go without dinner because we have no firewood. Everything is done by our Commissioner to improve the health and comfort of our camp. The sweets and cakes sent by our friends from the Colony arrived here in time to give the children a treat on New Year's Day.

Even should peace be declared and people allowed to go back to their homes, they will have no houses to live in and no food. The only consolation is that our future is in God's hands. I should be glad to see my children safe in the Colony, but prefer staying here myself to be a help to Mr. T. and to my fellow-suffering people. May the coming year bring us together again, to work with fresh courage. May we be enabled to sing 'Peace on earth,' for now it is hell in South Africa, and oh, I can't stand it any longer.—With much love to all inquiring friends, your loving friend,

C T.

P.S.—Mrs. de L. and family have all had measles, and so has Mrs. du P. The latter has lost her dear little baby, with its pretty little dove's eyes. When whooping-cough and measles come together they can't pull through, and even when they get through the measles they seem to get a sort of consumption, which puts an end to their life. When you have once seen them cry, you can never forget their pitiful little faces.

A second letter says—

Jan. 24.

There is no news here, only that the people all die of the fever. It is a wonder when one recovers, and such a one resembles a skeleton more than anything else.

Another point of view is presented by a young prisoner who writes from his gaol, where he says he is allowed cigarettes, which help pass the time, to Miss Martha Meyer, his cousin—

Central Gaol, Jan. 9.

My brother and sister are with Aunt Pretorius for their holidays. Poor little Lenie had a rough time of it with this war. She has faced what I have not, namely, a sword. I suppose if I were to say much about the matter this letter would never reach you. Lettie and Hattie came down to see us two weeks ago. We had a jolly time together. Aunt Engela is in the so-called Refugee Camp. They were well drenched through and through by a thunderstorm which passed over the unlucky prison camp. Their tent was blown all to pieces. She was captured after being shelled the whole day. Oh, Martha! how can we forgive? . . . I have not much to write about, as the *lex loci* does not permit the use of facts, but I have volumes to talk about . . .

A young girl with patriotic fervour still unquenched writes:—

Howick Camp, Jan.

We have just had a wire saying that my father and eldest brother (19 years) have been captured. It is difficult for me under the circumstances to write fully. But it is too painful even to think about, that after not having seen them for twenty months, now they have to be sent across the waters and we not even allowed to greet them. Do pray for my youngest brother (17 years), who is still on commando, that he may not only be spared, but be also kept from taking any wrong step as regards surrendering. Mother and we two sisters are trying to make the best of this life in exile; and only wish to be fully sanctified through this sore affliction. We do sometimes long so intensely to go back to our homes and be with our dear ones again; but we do not wish to return if thereby our independence shall be forfeited. We women in the camp still keep up courage and are in no way desponding.

The sickness described by Mrs. Dickenson at Merebank and prophesied by the Ladies' Commission did not fail to gain ground. A woman experienced in camp life wrote thence on January 7—

At Howick, they say, the death-rate is slightly decreasing. Here I am afraid it is still on the increase.... Opposite my small canvas room I can see the workshop where the coffins are being made daily. It is too saddening to see the little coffins being carried out continually. Last night four little ones died in« our immediate neighbourhood.

From other parts, as January advanced, reassuring news began to arrive, and it was clear that improved conditions were bringing improved health. Rev. W. p. Rousseau, Pietermaritzburg, to Committee at Amsterdam.

Jan. 8, 1902.

...... I have great satisfaction in informing you that the mortality in the camps (in this country at least) has greatly decreased. There are but few sick here in the camp. Some are ill with enteric in hospital. At Howick also, where some time ago as many as four or five were buried in a day, it is much less now. The military always help with clothes, etc., but there are many complaints that the help is not timely and often not as was desired. In all urgent cases the Committee help.

Again, Mr. W. F. Hollard to Committee at Amsterdam—

Pretoria, Jan, 9.

I have much pleasure in informing you that I have heard that the mortality in general, and in particular amongst the children, has greatly decreased as the hospital arrangements have been improved.

We have in most cases been able to provide the women and children with stretchers, so that they are no longer obliged to lie on the ground, and we were able to provide restoratives. I believe I need hardly remark that, notwithstanding all our efforts added to the important aid we have received from friends, such as you in Holland, Paris, Germany, etc. etc., want is still very great, which you will understand when I say that the camps are daily enlarged and still more women and children are brought in.

With the decrease of sickness and death, the monotony and weariness the life became more apparent It pressed sadly upon the old, as appears from what is written to her daughter in Cape Town by an old Dutch lady—

Volksrust, Jan. 27, 1902.

I must do everything for myself and for ———. We can get no assistance. In our tents we sit on the bare ground. During continuous winds, we are enveloped in a whirlwind of black dust, and during the continuous rains we have now, it is a mess of mud. I cannot possibly describe our life in the tents and in the camp, but since the New Year it has proved too much for me; with my last remaining strength I have also lost my courage. . . . Ah, may this sad war speedily draw to a close! I am at this moment sitting in T———'s tent, for she is lucky enough to have a table and a seat, which I have not.

For night-table I have two boxes placed on the top of each other. My bed was only the frame of an iron bedstead laid on a couple of chests. B——— and the child slept for months on the bare ground, but now at last they have got an iron bedstead. You cannot possibly realise how we have suffered, at first from the cold and wet, and now from the heat and heavy thunderstorms. God alone knows what is still in store for us. T——— has been ill since the 5th of December.

When the heat gets too great in her tent, she comes over to mine, for since my illness I have got an over-tent, as I could not stand the wet and the cold. It is not possible to write about everything as I should wish, for one does not know if the letters will be passed, if one gives too exact a description of our position. . . . I could write no further, being over-tired, and I trembled so that writing was out of the question. B——— has been eight days in the hospital with enteric fever; he is now getting better, but many have died from it.—Now I will tell you something about H———'s wounds.

One bullet entered his chin and stuck in his jaw. This had to be extracted. Another shot went clean through his knee. A third bullet passed over his foot through his big toe. Besides, he has many small wounds about the face, probably from the bursting of a shell.

We do not know where we shall see each other again. All we possessed has been destroyed and swept from the face of the earth. Send us some money, for without it we can get absolutely nothing. There are four of us, and these are our weekly rations: sufficient flour and rice, a little coffee, scarcely any sugar, this lasts us about three days. Once a week we get some meat, mostly bones; and every fortnight every person a piece of soap the length of my hand to do all our washing with. On this we are supposed to keep alive and well.

No time was lost by those who began to experience the improvements now really being effected in some camps, in giving expression to their relief. The two next letters are full of appreciation. The first is from the clergyman's wife who had written so despondingly a few weeks previously—

Ladysmith Camp, Feb, 17, 1902.
I am happy to say your prayers for us are heard: sickness and death have decreased to a great extent in all the camps. We arrived here on the 8th; about 900 of our camp have been removed to this place. It is so glorious to live in a house again. They are large iron buildings, lined with wood, boarded floors, and big windows, and though we are five or six families in one building, with only blankets for partition walls, still we consider it a great comfort compared to the horrid little round tents.

When we see the dust-storms and rain coming we need not run to fasten up our tents and fix down the pins, nor need we crawl on all-fours through the mud through the small openings of our tents in order to get backwards and forwards to our wooden kitchens. For the present we still cook outside here, but they intend giving us sheds later. . . . The water and bathrooms are nearby. We also get our drinking water boiled in big tanks. The meat is beautifully fresh, and we may buy vegetables and fruit . . . Though our camp is closed, still we are allowed to go into town with passes three times a week. We have a nice comfortable hospital, good nurse, and old Dr. —— for camp doctor. So you see how much there is to be thankful for. . . . Lottie seems to feel the heat and the rough camp life more than any of us. She is always complaining of weakness, and has grown thin. My brother-in-law has sent her journey money to Cape Town, but hitherto we could not get her a pass.

M. F. is in Winburg Camp, and has lost her four youngest children, including her only little girl; she has only the two eldest living. Mr. P. T. is in Bloemfontein Camp, and has lost his wife and youngest child. He has three little children to care for with him, and only one hand to fulfil a mother's duties. The histories of some people are too sad to relate.

★★★★★★

No one is allowed to leave who has relatives still on commando.—Cd. 893.

★★★★★★

From a Young Girl to a Former Teacher—

Tin Town, Ladysmith, Feb. 17.

You'll doubtless be surprised to see that we have again been moved.

We arrived at this place on the 2nd of February. I suppose the whole of the Harrismith Camp is to be sent here, but as yet there are many of our friends there still.

We have certainly made a great change for the better, inasmuch as we are now in nice comfortable houses, with decent windows and floors. One feels quite another being since one can walk and sit straight again in a nice high room.

Some of the Harrismith townspeople have been sent here too. Here are quite a number of our old Seminary girls in camp. Bessie and Helena are both in Harrismith Hospital with fever. The death-rate in that camp was frightful during the last month of our stay there. . . . Five of us were confirmed the day before we left the camp at Harrismith. There were more than forty '*catechisanten*,' and so the little building used as a church being too small, Ds. Theron had the service in the open air. It certainly was the most imposing scene I had ever been present at It was a beautiful afternoon, and nearly the whole camp was assembled there. Mr. Theron said he thought it certainly was the first time since the days of the '*Voortrekkers*' that confirmation was held in the open air.

It is with something of a shock that I realised I am really and truly eighteen years already, and oh! how very far I am still from that rung of the ladder where I've always determined to stand at that age. However, God knows it's through no fault of mine. It is so very hard to understand why I should have been so completely checked in the course of my studies just when it was all growing so immensely interesting. However, I have not at all given up hope yet, and am going to apply again. I suppose you know that Lottie also wishes to go to Stellenbosch. Perhaps we may be allowed to go together. The last answer I had from the 'Powers that be' was that they have nothing against my going, but only could not allow me to go at present . . . You'll answer me soon, won't you?

From Miss Lottie Rossouw to a Friend—

Refugee Camp, Kroonstad, Fed. 2. 1902.
A few weeks ago, I received your kind letter and parcel Mother is very glad to have the papers to read, for we get no reading of any kind unless it is an old newspaper. . . . I had a disappointment about your letter; when I had just opened it, a whirlwind came through our tent and carried away the first half and I have been unable to find it again. . . . We are all still in very good health and daily picking up lost strength. The heat is unlike anything we have ever felt even in Natal, and it is responsible for much of the illness and debility of the people.

We have been able to fare pretty well lately, for grandfather sent us two large cases of vegetables with a promise of more, and we shall soon be able to have potatoes and beans from papa's wee garden. Our Choral Union has changed conductors, and last night we gave a very successful entertainment, which was thoroughly enjoyed by all, including several townspeople and the whole hospital staff not on duty.

I have not been teaching since the Christmas holidays, and I think several other teachers will have to leave now, because four or five teachers arrived from England yesterday to take charge of the Camp School I am quite anxious to hear how they will get on with these children. One of our teachers is dangerously ill with enteric fever. . . .

Here there is hardly any grass and no flowers; on all sides, you have nothing but tents in long rows; all is so monotonous and every street just like the other, strangers seldom find their way. The streets, and even the tents, are numbered, ours being E. 18

and 19, Section V. Some name their tents, and one of our neighbours called theirs Bellevue Tent, so Ella promptly christened
ours Bell-Tent View!

They have sisters and nurses now for the out-patients, and the
hospital accommodation is very large. Altogether there have
been various small improvements and some fresh restrictions.
Last Monday, two girls, sisters, were drowned whilst bathing,
and now no one except grown-up men is allowed to bathe at
all. This is very awkward, for very few people have baths, and
the banks of the river being terribly steep it is no joke to carry
up sufficient water for a bath. No bathing arrangement is made,
and I pity too the women who have to do their washing outside in the sun, and carry the wet linen up the banks to dry. . . .

A Colonial lady's picture of the improvements in Bethulie *after* Mr.
Cole Bowen's visit and reforms cannot fail to interest—

We visited Springfontein Camp on the 25th of February. The
even streets, the clean tents, the whitewashed stones placed to
mark different squares and streets, made the impression on the
stranger of order and prosperity. Now I can understand how a
stranger coming for a peep at the camps can leave well satisfied
with all that is done in such a place for its inmates. He naturally
does not see behind the scenes, the heartache, the oppression,
the indignities often heaped upon these patient, silent Boers.
On the 27th we were in Bethulie, and during that and the
following weeks saw something of what happens there in the
camp with its 5,000 inmates.

A pleasing sight was the soup-kitchen, with its rows of huge
soup-pots. Mrs. Du Preez, the matron, told us that she received
150 lbs. of meat every day, and from that made soup for 3,000
persons. Every school-child was entitled to a cupful of soup
with a little piece of meat in it The soups were as varied as possible from day to day. They were busy erecting baking-ovens
for people to bake their bread. This, we believe, will save much
labour and trouble. We went at different times to the so-called
Orphanage.

It broke my heart to see the state of those 40 children there;
the others at that time were ill in hospital. Ill-kept, ill-clad, a
disgrace to the Christian (?) nation who will not let them be
given over to us, who would at least treat them with love and

pity. The hospitals are, I daresay, as good as possible under such circumstances; I am not able to say much about them. But the feeling is that if the people had been properly fed there would have been much less need of such places.

Shortly before this Mrs. Dickenson had been writing from Bethulie Camp—

The Inspector of *Burgher* Camps, Mr. Bowen, has been here for a fortnight, trying to ascertain the cause of the terrible mortality in Bethulie Camp. On his arrival he at once dismissed the superintendent, who seemed to have been entirely unfitted for his position. In fact, I was told that his qualifications for the post consisted in being a great sportsman, and having been the means of recovering some offices valuable dog which had been lost. He was supposed to live in the camp, but spent his time at the hotel, while the 4,000 people under his charge died by hundreds (1,200 in six or seven months).

The overworked doctors either fell ill, and sometimes died themselves, or resigned their hopeless task. The camp had every fault possible, Mr. Bowen told me—overcrowding, tents too near together, and never moved for months; bad sanitary arrangements, insufficient water supply, and a poor, scanty dietary. Under his direction, the tents are being spread out so as to cover a much larger area on the new ground, the dietary is improved, and already the death-rate is lowered.

Epidemics of measles and whooping-cough are responsible for many deaths, but at present debility and atrophy among the mothers, and a sort of marasmus among the children, are what the doctors have to contend with. Some of the people are really mere skeletons. 'Only a course of port wine, jelly, and change of air would be ordered for them,' as the superintendent quietly remarked to me, 'were they in a position to get either.' He says he has just obtained from the government permission to allow tinned milk for young children, which has hitherto not been given except in case of sickness.

Bethulie, which has always been a most healthy little village, has a good deal of enteric,—a disease unknown here before the war,—and this is the case all over the Orange River Colony. The cause is the contamination of water supplies by the presence of large bodies of troops, or those hotbeds of disease, the

Concentration Camps. The thousands of slaughtered cattle lying all over the farms add to the insanitary condition of the country, and I strongly suspect that cholera will break out when the farms are again inhabited.

Of Bethulie, a Mr. Grant, of whom I asked the question, replied, 'Undoubtedly their owners will be allowed to return to them, whether they are in Ceylon, St Helena, or India. They will be sent back, and allowed to resume possession of their land English law recognises the right of private individuals to their own property, even in a conquered country.' The first question I am asked by the women in the Concentration Camps is, 'When will this terrible war be over, and we be able to return to our homes?'

I have met none of that belligerent spirit I was led to expect among them.—Extract from *Advertiser* of South Australia.

Mrs. Dickenson informs me that a good deal of this letter was cut out before it reached the Australian *Advertiser*,

She had mentioned that the sub-superintendent had been getting tobacco from government at 1*s*. 6*d*. and selling the same to the men in camp at 4*s*. per pound. Also, that the people complained that their letters posted in camp were never received by their friends unless they were registered, and that people making complaints in letters were forbidden to *write at all* These items the censor deemed dangerous to the military position if published in Australia, and they were suppressed.

I was about three weeks in Bethulie and during that time (after the reforms of the Inspector, Mr. Bowen) the health of the people improved, and the death-rate lessened considerably. Speaking to the medical men and dispensers, they told me about September and October, when things were at their worst, the death-rate averaged about 120 a week out of 4,000 people! One day 27 funerals took place (they are always buried on the day of death).

About August some very bad meat was sent into the camp, and the doctors condemned it as being the flesh of cattle that had died of disease. A dispenser told me it was full of yellowish spots. However, the meat was returned, and the superintendent was told that they must make it do. After this, dysentery and enteric broke out. When I was there, the deaths were mostly owing to debility and prostration. Children, who reminded one of the famine-stricken people of India, and who were gradually wasting away. Women, whose only chance would be sea air and a generous diet But most of the patients had gone too far for any human aid.

Mrs. De Wet, who had on previous occasions expostulated on our methods of treating a general's wife, now wrote direct to Mr. Brodrick. She had been supported in the town of Johannesburg without expense to the English Government, but when her husband did not surrender she was exiled to Natal, and placed in the camp at Pietermaritzburg, though able and willing to support herself elsewhere.

March 13, 1902.

Sir,—This is to acquaint you that I protest against the treatment accorded me by the British Government.

I was living in Johannesburg, in a comfortable house, at my own expense, and was deported from there against my expressed wish and inclination by order of the military authorities, July 26, 1901, and put in the Concentration Camp here, into a canvas house consisting of two rooms, with my family, eight souls in all. One of the rooms had been occupied by an enteric patient until within a few days of my arrival. The floors are so wet after heavy rains as to be positively unhealthy.

I was told when I was sent from Johannesburg that a furnished house would be given me at Pietermaritzburg, and that I and my family would be both well treated and provided for; instead of which I was put into a two-roomed canvas house, without furniture or conveniences of any kind, not even a kitchen, so had to cook outside in all weathers, until friends kindly put up a verandah and shelter for me to cook in. The ordinary rations are served to me, upon which no one can live unless supplemented by vegetables, fruit, milk, butter, and eggs. The fuel allowed is insufficient to cook the food, the soap is also insufficient for washing and cleanliness, and three and a half candles per week are not enough to light one room, let alone more.

Shortly after my arrival here I applied to return to Johannesburg, at my own expense. Reply received: 'Your husband is fighting.' I have made applications at different times to leave the camp and live elsewhere, but that has been denied me. I also asked the British Government to provide me with a furnished house and funds to live in Pietermaritzburg, as my application to go to Vredefort Weg was refused.

On receiving answer from the authorities here that I was receiving the same good treatment in the camp as the other *commandants'* wives, my request for a furnished house in Pietermaritzburg could not be entertained, I then wrote to Lord Kitchener, asking him to allow me to leave the camp and to reside in Pietermaritzburg at my own expense. Up to the present time I have received no answer.

I fail to understand where the good treatment comes in, as I have been treated with scant courtesy. The British have destroyed my home and property, placed me in a Concentration Camp in a shanty such as my servants on my farm would have scorned to occupy.

C. M. De Wet.

The mental suffering of the people, all along more intense than their physical sufferings, became more prominent as these last were alleviated. A lady who has laboured for months among the camps has entered fully into this, and her views are expressed in the following letter:—

She says that literally it is now a case of no money being spared to make the camp life as healthy as possible. But though now food and clothing are supplied, she says the deadly monotony of the life remains, and she thinks that now the suffering is more mental than physical, and that suffering she never can forget. . . . She thinks that many are so wretched, have suffered so much, and lost so many of their relatives, that when illness attacks them they make no great fight to live. Even many young girls die because they are broken-hearted at having lost their lovers. The little she said gave me a more awful impression of the substratum of agony on which these camps rest than anything else I have heard.

A people are being tortured to death. Of course one knows it all, but the talk with her brought it all very vividly before one. . . . The women are convinced that their cause will ultimately triumph. She says she tells them that if the camps were to last ten years longer England will continue the war for that length of time, so that to continue to fight is absolutely useless as far as the Republicans are concerned. She assures them that they will never get back their country. But the suffering and agony weigh her down, and her eyes are always full of tears, as it were, and she looks as if they had shed floods of tears. It is awful to meet so compassionate a woman and to find her at bottom determined on victory for her country, whatever it may cost to those who are to be conquered.

The following little note from a minister, with its application for books, gives a timely hint of the large sums that will be required to replace the endless losses of so many families—things which the Government fund is not likely to provide. Every household article, from a saucepan to a piano, will be lacking:—

From Rev. C G. Jooste.
Translation.

Brandfort Camp, April 2, 1902.
Send me, if you please, three Dutch Bibles and three hymn-books. They must not be very dear, nor very large, but the usual convenient size. They are for old people in the Refugee Camp who have lost almost everything. Elderly people who are more than 60 or 70 years of age, so that a good clear print is needed. The hymn-books as soon as possible, with full notes, that is, with notes to each verse.

The people are so poor in this camp, they have lost so much, that it would be difficult for them to pay anything out even for books. Our Colonial people at the camp may be assured that they are really needed. They are so very poor here, but they must at least have Bibles. May the Lord bless us in this work. I have written to Dominie Marguard about these books, but have not yet heard from him. I must have these books for the camp.

The improvements are nowhere more gladly recognised than by the President's wife, who had suffered deeply in sympathy with her people. Mrs. Steyn writes to Lady Farrer—

Bloemfontein, March 3, 1902.
You will no doubt be surprised to hear from me, but as you are Treasurer of the 'Women and Children's Distress Fund,' and one who has done so much for our women and children, I feel as if I would like to write and tell you how our hearts have been gladdened lately by the very marked improvement which has

taken place in the different camps.

I will, of course, write more particularly about the one here, as I am in a position to judge a little for myself. In December I was as a favour allowed to drive out to visit the camp hospital, and the sight was indeed most touching. To see ward after ward crowded with sick women and children could not but make one feel very sad. I went from bed to bed, spoke a few words to those who were well enough, and they all seemed delighted to see me.

One woman in particular, a wealthy farmer's wife, and a very good creature, I found very, very ill; her big strapping daughter of about nineteen stood beside the bed. I said to her: 'Whisper to your mother, "Mrs. Steyn is here."' The girl (did so; the poor woman opened her eyes, stretched out her hand for mine, pressed it to her heart for some minutes, and all she could say was: 'Thank you, thank you.' My eyes were dim with tears. I turned and left the bedside, with the fervent prayer that God would restore her to health—but—both she and her daughter are 'no more.' It was an afternoon of many touching incidents, and I shall never forget it.

The wards, I must confess, looked very neat, and the patients clean and comfortable, and I could not understand why our women, one and all, so strongly objected to the hospitals, when to my mind they were infinitely preferable to the hot tents. On inquiry afterwards, I found the food, and in many cases the young inexperienced nurses taken to assist the trained nurses, were the great objections. Just passing through the hospital, it was difficult for me to judge about these matters. The death-rate at that time was high, and I felt very cast down. I knew, however, that the authorities were doing everything in their power to improve things, and that was a great comfort.

In January the soup kitchens were started, better meat was supplied, the rations increased, and in addition a fair amount of vegetables allowed for each family. We had lovely rains, cooler weather set in, and in a marvellously short time the improvement was so great it seemed almost incredible. The health of the camp improved with rapid strides, and the death-rate decreased accordingly, so that just lately for four days the mortuary was empty.

You may imagine how great our rejoicings were, and how

many prayers of thanksgiving were offered up to God.

Only this morning I had a woman with me, an old inhabitant of the camp, she had lost two children last year, and once before called to see me; wept so bitterly then, and said: 'Oh, Mrs. Steyn, how I hate the hospital, and how hard it is to have our loved ones taken to it!' Last month her only surviving child took ill, and soon after herself also. She begged not to have either of them removed, but the doctor spoke kindly, and at last she consented. Her words to me were: 'Mrs. Steyn, I am so thankful I went, both my child and self recovered in no time. We were treated very well, had plenty of good food, and the improvement in the hospital is very great' She spoke so nicely, and I most earnestly hope the improvement may continue; I have such confidence myself that it will.

You must understand, to very many of our people, even under the most favourable circumstances, the life in a camp and a tent is a hard one; but they are all more satisfied and contented with their treatment, and that is a very great comfort to me. I daresay you will have heard that I was all packed and ready to leave for Europe in November, and at the eleventh hour my departure was cancelled. It was a terrible thought to me to have to leave South Africa while my husband was still exposed to so many dangers, and I was delighted when unforeseen circumstances arose which prevented my departure.

Mrs. Blignaut, though not visiting the camp, still does a great deal for our people, and is often kept very busy. We gratefully remember our kind friends, and will always deeply appreciate what is being done for us . . .

Letter from Mrs. Geldenhuis to myself—

Bloemfontein Camp, April 12, 1902.
I am glad to say, through the merciful grace of Providence, myself and mine have so far been all spared, all enjoying fairly good health. My little Sarah has been in hospital some time, but is quite well again, and has grown to quite a big young lady since you saw her.

Our life in camp has greatly improved of late. Medical arrangements too are on a far better scale than some time back. Our hospitals are almost empty; last month there were only 28 deaths, while this month up to date only three.

I am sorry to say, after you left, for some or other small reason, I was placed in the prisoners' camp, where I had been, so to say, forgotten by everyone outside. I cannot now give you full details of how I have been kept in the dark.

I am making up a little parcel of curios I intend to send you with a friend of mine. Hoping the time is near when we can correspond more freely.

Quite recently a friend of mine sent to the *New Age* these few lines, the substance of her conversation with a Dutch woman, a relative of General De la Rey—

April 29, 1902.

My acquaintance with their language, and expressions of sympathy for the sufferings of the women in the camps, soon gained their confidence. The principal speaker was a very tall, finely-built woman, with eyes that were capable of a great variety of expression; generally they were only half opened, while the speaker's soul veiled itself under an appearance of calm and indifference—very typical of this land of peace and basking sunshine and violent and tremendous storm.

I inquired as to whether there was an improvement in the general condition of things in the camp she had just come from. Most assuredly there was—the food was better, the aged and infirm and delicate were dead. She attributed the terribly high death-rate of the past to the way in which the people had been dragged from their homes, and exposed without food or shelter to the inclement weather.

On arrival, there was, as a rule, neither shelter nor food, and the continued exposure and exhaustion led to severe outbreaks of sickness, with the result that numbers died. 'Are the women losing heart?—are they willing that their husbands should surrender?' I asked. A light spread over her face, and welled up in her eyes, as she said:

'There are some Afrikanders—hounds I call them—that have given in; but there are numbers of women in our camp that will never give in; that will never bid their husbands give in. I say my husband must fight to the last; if only two men are left, he must fight on; if he is left alone, while he can hold a gun he must fight on. It is a sore thing to part with your husband—to know that he is fighting; but I would rather he lay dead on the battlefield than gave in.'

'And what about the women themselves—about their sufferings?' I asked.

She threw back her fine head and said: 'I have never had anything the matter with me; the harder I get it, the stronger I seem to get—strength comes as you need it. It is true I have seen whole families die out in camp; but there are also others who have lost none, who are still all together. But if I die—I die—it matters not; never, never will I give in. It is my light,' she continued, 'that everyone must do what they can for their own land. I cannot do otherwise. I cannot understand those who do give in. I do not hate the British. I have no hate in my heart, but I can never forget nor forgive what we have gone through. We have had it too bitter. We have suffered too much—too many have died—too many tears have been shed. I can't cry any more—there are no more tears left in me. I have to laugh sometimes. There is no one to help us, so we have to keep each other's spirits up.

'But the poor "Tommies,"' she went on—'I will always do all I can for a Tommy. They get it too bitter—they get it as we do. It was awful to see them when they first came into our town. They were starving. They crowded round our ovens when the bread came out, to get a morsel. They ate all the green fruit off the trees. One poor "Tommy" was found dead at his post. His body was opened—he had filled himself with green mealies.'

I asked whether the negotiations that were going on would lead to peace. She replied: 'There will be no peace unless we get what we want—unless we get what is right' Then the same strange, beautiful light again spread over her face, and filled her eyes, as she said: 'We may get it still more bitter, still more hard; I may be without a petticoat at last But if everything is gone— that day that we get our independence I will dance and play like a little child.'

Nothing can more fitly close this slight outline of the tale of the women's sufferings than the passages which follow, culled from the Report of General J. C. Smuts, late State Attorney, (New Report of General J. C. Smuts to Mr. Kruger)—

Never can pen describe what the heroines of our people have suffered and endured since the spring of 1900. Fleeing before the enemy into the woods and mountains of Rustenburg, Waterburg, Loutpansburg, Lydenburg, Swaziland, and Zululand, where skeletons now cry to Heaven against the barbarous Kaffir . . . hiding with their little ones knee-deep in water in the reeds of Schoonspruit and Mooi River, where they were fired at by the enemy with Lee-Metfords and Maxims and driven into towns; then after months of useless fleeing dumped at last into the prison camps of the enemy, where, sick unto death themselves, they saw their children buried, and where they went hungry because they could not eat the bad meat and the still worse meal, and had no firewood for cooking—week after week, month after month, year after year, they sit meditating and longing and brooding over their husbands and sons who have perhaps already been shot. Has such a picture of suffering ever been unfolded to the world before? The life of the man on the *veld*, although hard, is comfortable compared with the slow death of their imprisoned loved ones.

And still the women keep up marvellously; nearly all the letters which are smuggled out of these prison camps encourage the men to hold out to the death and never to bring shame on their name and family by surrender. . .. I do not believe that there was ever a more noble spectacle among men, and one of which humanity may more rightly be proud, than that of the Boer wife. Her quiet suffering points out the way to our independence; her noble and heroic character is the guarantee for the greatness of our future.

The terms signed on the 1st of June will not alter or quench this fine spirit The question remains: Will it, under the guidance of a wise and understanding statesmanship, be incorporated with the best English feeling, or will it smoulder beneath repression, petty tyranny, and narrow intolerance till it kindle anew the abandoned resistance of the men?

It is there, and it is a factor to be dealt with in the problem of the South African future.

# CHAPTER 3

# The Boer Women

*"The Lord gave, and the Lord hath taken away: blessed be the name of the Lord."*— Job 1. 22.

To draw in outline the character and disposition of the Boer women would have been comparatively easy, if they had not been so systematically reviled. Imputations made in heated moments have come to be widely believed, and must be stripped off to judge them impartially. The Boers themselves, formerly brutal brigands, marauders, robbers, murderers, and rebels, are now better understood as brave and gallant men, dignified and sensible, with very proper views of self-defence.

It may be found that their wives, those dirty, lazy, lying women, so heedless of their children as to neglect or even to poison them deliberately, are after all a civilised, industrious set of people, as truthful as the rest of the world, and capable of bringing up large families with love and care. It may come to be acknowledged that they are more than this: that they are capable of unflinching loyalty at whatever personal cost; that they understand self-restraint, endurance, and other fine qualities which belong to high breeding.

To stigmatise them as dirty, is both unfair and untrue. It is unfair, because we had placed them in conditions where all the things that go to help cleanliness were scarce or altogether lacking. Water, soap, towels, brooms, utensils, all were hard to obtain or unobtainable in camp. For many months, there was *no soap at all*, except what the women made from the fat of their rations. It is untrue, because, in spite of these drawbacks, the bulk of the women were quite wonderfully neat and clean.

I remember Mr. Selous, who perhaps knows the Boer people more intimately than any other Englishman, telling me that he did not consider them a dirty people in normal times. He has stayed with them on their farms continually during many years. Two doctors who have worked in the late Free State, one for twenty, the other for ten years, both supported this view, the older man saying he thought it would be hard to find a cleaner community. Probably the back *veld* Transvaalers ranked lower in this respect In the abnormal circumstances in which they were living, their cleanliness was striking. There were in each camp, as would be found in every town of equal size in all countries, a few thriftless and dirty families. These have been quoted as if their habits were universal.

This view is endorsed by Mrs. Dickenson, who has been already quoted. She remarks—

> Having last year stayed at farms and visited others occupied by Cape Colonial Dutch, I was able to judge of the way they lived, and their habits and modes of thought. In the first place, I am often asked, 'Are they not so extremely dirty, that sitting in a tent with them would be most unpleasant?' To this I can certainly emphatically answer, 'No; they are as clean as any average Australian or English working-woman would be under the same circumstances.' There are, of course, great differences in education and position among the families in the various camps. From the back *veld* Boer, who is really a peasant farmer, to the wealthy inhabitant of the luxurious and beautiful homes in Pretoria, there is a great gulf. Of course, it is the actual Boer of the remote country districts of whom it has been said that the mortality amongst their children is caused by their dirty habits. All I can say is, that had their tents been infested with insect life, I should certainly have carried away some specimens, as I have often done in visiting cottages in England!

The Boer view of English cleanliness would be dangerous to depict. Their horror at the frightful sanitary arrangements of many of the camps, and at the ill-kept condition of latrines in other camps, was very real. Above all did they shrink from the habit which frequently prevailed, of packing men, women, and children into trucks and carriages, and absolutely forbidding them to leave these *for any purpose whatever.*

Of the carelessness of their children of which they are accused, I saw nothing, for there was no sign of it. The accusation resolves itself into this, that, mother-like, they thought they knew and understood better how to deal with their children than strangers, who for long months had but the very roughest hospitals, doctoring, and nursing to offer in place of the mother's care.

The *preliminary* state of those hospitals and that nursing was such as wholly to justify the people in retaining their sick. They had no right to send their little ones where the wants they expressed could not even be understood. With the improvement of the hospitals and staff, and the certainty that their sick would have personal attention, the objection to the hospitals gradually waned. It was fatal to their success that many nurses, generally half trained, were deliberately chosen from the political enemies of the people, and supplemented by wholly untrained Boer girls, most of whom were drawn from the surrendered and distrusted class amongst *themselves*. Had the authorities been able to take a large view of the situation, and to be guided by common sense and humanity only, instead of politics, these added difficulties need never have arisen.

Lord Milner has complained of the want of personnel. Of this there was never any lack. What he meant was of *political* personnel. Abundant persons were forthcoming who would voluntarily have nursed in, and reorganised the camps, and have stemmed the great tide of distress; but they were refused. Kindness was what was wanted. Everyone was too ill to care for politics. Such kindness, given unstintingly by people who had a wider grasp than that possessed by half-educated loyalist refugees, of the real breadth of English generosity and humanity, would have had an indirect but wholesome political effect.

It would be hard to find a people more true or more reliable in their dealings with those who have won their respect and their trust But it must first be won. Towards all others they maintain an attitude of uncertainty and suspicion. Lately their position was fraught with difficulty, for they were made rebels in their own country. Unfortunately, those with whom English officials were mostly brought in contact, were those weaker vessels, the surrendered *burghers*, who generally obtained the plums of the camps, in the shape of paid employments. Men who are untrue to their own kith and kin, as some of these had been, are likely to be found untrue also in other relations of life.

Stripping off these and other accusations, and approaching the Boer women with unbiased mind, we find a very simple womanhood, calm and composed in manner, but always brimming over with hospitable impulses. They possess shrewdness and mother-wit in abundance, and they are wrapped in suspicion like a coat of mail. Once succeed in piercing that armour, and the trustfulness below is complete as a child's. Betray that trust, and it will never be forgotten; win it, and you will be accepted and confided in as a friend. The women have a natural and homely dignity, which becomes them well, and commands respect. Beneath all, one is conscious of underlying depths stored with reserved power, which will one day express itself in various ways. In these dark days that reserve has been largely drawn upon to furnish endurance for their own trials, and endless encouragement for their men in the field. Now and again strange flashes light up the calm, unruffled surface, and reveal those hidden depths with their reserve of unknown power. They love their country passionately.

Of their conduct since they have been massed together in camps or scattered in exile over many lands, it is difficult to speak, for there is no comparison at hand to help in forming a judgment. Their experience is unique. Never before has the entire womanhood of a white nation been uprooted and placed in circumstances of such difficulty. We do not know how we should have stood the test of such a trial We can only ask in what spirit and temper it is borne by them, and what its effect upon their character. Should not a nation be judged by its best rather than by its worst? Because the few have been outspoken and bitter; because the few have been dirty, thriftless, or unruly, therefore the whole people have been libelled.

The great mass have borne their unprecedented trials with a silent heroism which has astonished many who have witnessed it Two things have united to produce this endurance. First, the depth of their religious feeling, which took all as from a Higher Power, refusing to blame the human instrument; and secondly, that proper pride which forbade any exhibition of feeling before their enemy. Thus, often they welcomed with hymns of praise every opportunity of suffering for their country. Their quiet endurance is an intimation of strength of character and resolution with which we shall have to reckon.

"The people do not complain," "There are no complaints," "They are satisfied and happy," are remarks reiterated from the camps. It was often just there where no complaint issued that the suffering was keenest Endurance, theirs by inheritance, developed with the demand made upon it, and their idealism increased under the influence of an enforced detachment from all material advantages. Their minds were set free to dwell upon the spiritual and immaterial, and centred upon the longing for freedom, independence, and the right of self-development In a very practical way they had learnt that life consisteth not in the abundance of the things possessed. The effect of their attitude was to nerve their men to greater efforts. De Wet told a lady now in exile, that where ten men had encouraged him by their conduct, twenty-five women had done so.

It will probably be found when the women come to speak or write their own tale of the camps, and never yet have we heard *their* side, that harder to them than the physical suffering were the punishments and political treatment meted out to them. Official curtness and rudeness, borne outwardly in silence, was resented inwardly by women of good positions. Punishments were inflicted, without due investigation, on the accusation of some ignorant or embittered spy; women of high character were shut into wired-enclosed prisons for trivial or imagined offences; solitary guard-tents, denied passes, docked rations, all kinds of irritating and humiliating treatment, reserved chiefly for the women who were regarded as rebels, because husband or son was on com-mando. This was the sole reason advanced in numerous cases for refusal to such women to leave the unhealthy camps and maintain themselves elsewhere. This policy accentuated resistance and created an abhor-rence of English rule, which wiser methods might have obviated.

To Mr. E. B. Sargant the country owes its gratitude for creating what has been the redeeming feature of camp life—the schools—where already many children have learnt a higher side of English character and thought than that which the war seemed to have taught them. Much, very much, may develop from the beginning made in these camp schools.

It is true that some of the people have sunk; the more ignorant, deprived of all those outward trappings which help to maintain self-respect, even of sufficient clothing, abandoned hope and courage, and fell an easy prey to the peculiar temptations of the life.

There have been many dark spots in the fate that has befallen some of the women during the two years and eight months of the war, barely touched upon in these pages, because not yet investigated, but which would look black even against the sombre background of this book. Maybe such things occur in every war. If that is so, there is all the strong-er reason for abolishing war, and adopting International Arbitration.

As a whole, the great body of Boer women have come finely out of the ordeal to which we have subjected them. But that is no justi-fication of their having been so subjected. Never before have women and children been so warred against England, by the hands of Lord Roberts and Lord Kitchener, adopted the policy of Spain, while improving upon her methods. She has placed her seal upon an odious system. Is it to be a precedent for future wars, or is it to be denounced not merely by one party, but by every humane person of every creed and every tongue, denounced as a 'method of barbarism' which must never be resorted to again—the whole cruel sequence of the burning, the eviction, the rendering destitute, the deporting, and finally the re-concentrating of the non-combatants of the country, with no previous preparation for their sustenance?

It ought to become a fixed principle with the English people that no general acting in their name should ever again resort to measures of such a nature. Lord Ripon wrote, (*Times*, June 19, 1901):

> It is a question of the fair fame of our country, and of the repu-
> tation for manliness, to say nothing of chivalry of our people .
> . . . for the system no condemnation is too strong. It is cruel in
> the present, and inconceivably foolish in regard to the future. . .
> . . If we allow it to continue, the full responsibility will be ours.
> One strong word from the British people will sweep the whole
> thing away. Have we the courage to speak it?

But the British people had not the courage to speak that noble word. The camps went on and the graves filled till 16,000 children, (up to twelve years in the Transvaal, and up to fifteen years in the O.R.C.), perished, and over 4000 adults. These are official figures, and they do not account for all

Now the time is drawing near when these women shall gradually be released and drafted back to their desolate homes. The three mil-lion provided under the terms of settlement may give them shelter and some stock, and implements of labour, but how far will that go? That sum cannot cover the great extent of the loss, which the generals estimate at 50 million. Each house will be empty of furniture. One way of confessing the great mistake that we have made is humbly to help them to begin their simple lives again. Thank-offerings that the war is over, and peace-offerings too, can be fitly made for this object It will take many thousands of such offerings to meet the needs of a homeless and ruined people. One woman writes:

We are paupers now, and it is terrible."

And another:

"Can you form an idea of what it is to have nothing—literally *nothing?*"

# Appendix A

## I.

## EARLY SCALE OF RATIONS IN O. R. C. FOR REFUGEES AND UNDESIRABLES

Undated, but before January 16, 1901. Handed to me in the office at Bloemfontein.

| *Refugees.* | *Undesirables.* |
|---|---|
| $\frac{1}{2}$ lb. Fresh Meat. | $\frac{1}{2}$ lb. Fresh Meat. |
| $\frac{1}{2}$ lb. either Meal, Rice, Samp, or Potatoes. | $\frac{1}{2}$ lb. either Meal, Rice, or Samp. |
| $1\frac{1}{2}$ oz. Coffee. | $\frac{1}{2}$ oz. Coffee. |
| 3 oz. Sugar. | 1 oz. Sugar. |
| 1 oz. Salt. | 1 oz. Salt. |
| $\frac{1}{12}$ tin of Condensed Milk. | $\frac{1}{18}$ tin of Condensed Milk. |

CAPTAIN

*Assistant Provost-Marshal,*

O. R. C.

## II.

*"Economy is as essential in the management of your camp as the welfare of your charges."* [1]

# LINE OF COMMUNICATION ORDERS

L. of C. No. 129.

By Lieut.-General Sir A. HUNTER, K.C.B., D.S.O., Commanding
L. of C. from Norval's Pont to Wolverhoek.

BLOEMFONTEIN, *Wednesday, January* 16, 1901.

## SCALE OF RATIONS FOR REFUGEES.

ADULTS, AND CHILDREN OVER SIX YEARS OF AGE.

|  | Refugees. | | Families who have Members on Commando. | |
|---|---|---|---|---|
| Flour or Meal | 1 lb. daily. | Mealie Meal | 3 lb. daily. |
| Meat | $\frac{3}{4}$ lb. „ | Meat | 1 lb. twice weekly. |
| Coffee | 1 oz. „ | Coffee | 1 oz. daily. |
| Sugar | 2 oz. „ | Sugar | 2 oz. „ |
| Salt | $\frac{1}{2}$ oz. „ | Salt | $\frac{1}{2}$ oz. „ |

### CHILDREN UNDER SIX YEARS OF AGE.

|  | | | | |
|---|---|---|---|---|
| Flour or Meal | $\frac{1}{2}$ lb. daily. | Meal | $\frac{1}{2}$ lb. daily. |
| Meat | $\frac{1}{2}$ lb. „ | Meat | $\frac{1}{2}$ lb. twice weekly. |
| Milk | $\frac{1}{4}$ tin „ | Milk | $\frac{1}{4}$ tin daily. |
| Sugar | 1 oz. „ | Sugar | 1 oz. „ |
| Salt | $\frac{1}{2}$ oz. „ | Salt | $\frac{1}{2}$ oz. „ |

[1] Cd. 819, p. 9, General Instructions.

## III.

## AMENDED SCALE OF RATIONS,[1] O. R. C.

*March* 8, 1901.

### To all White Refugees.

$\frac{1}{2}$ lb. Fresh Meat (or tinned when fresh unobtainable).
$\frac{3}{4}$ lb. either Meal or Rice, Samp or Potatoes, upon due
notice being given.
1 oz. Coffee.
1 oz. Salt.
2 oz. Sugar.
$\frac{1}{12}$ part of tin of Condensed Milk.

## IV.

This scale continued till September, when $\frac{1}{3}$ lb. Rice daily
was added, on the recommendation of the Ladies' Commission.

## V.

## REVISED RATION SCALE [2]

*January* 1902.

### Children of Five Years and under.

| | |
|---|---|
| 44.7 oz. Meal. | $\frac{1}{4}$ oz. Coffee. |
| 44.7 oz. Oatmeal or Rolled Oats. | 2 oz. Sugar (white). |
| | $\frac{1}{2}$ oz. Salt. |
| 44.7 oz. Rice and Maizena. | 1.7 tin Jam. |
| 2.7 tin Milk (Condensed). | 1.7 of 1 oz. Lime Juice. |

In addition, one plate of Soup (of Meat, Vegetables, and
Pearl Barley) per head per diem to all children.

[1] Cd. 819, p. 37.
[2] Cd. 934, p. 98.

½ lb. Meat.
¾ lb. Meal.
1 oz. Coffee.
2 oz. Sugar.
1 oz. Salt.
$\frac{1}{12}$ tin Milk (Condensed).

1 oz. Butterine per diem.
½ lb. Rice per week.
4 oz. Lime Juice per week.
1 lb. Jam per fortnight.
Fresh Vegetables, as obtainable.

---

# I.

## TRANSVAAL RATION SCALE [1]

PRETORIA, *December* 1, 1900.

### *Refugees.*

7 lb. Meal or Flour weekly.
1 lb. Meat twice a week.
4 oz. Salt    weekly.
6 oz. Coffee    ,,
12 oz. Sugar    ,,

#### *Refugee Children under Twelve.*

$3\frac{1}{2}$ lb. Meal or Flour weekly.
½ lb. Meat twice a week.
2 oz. Salt    weekly.
3 oz. Coffee    ,,
12 oz. Sugar    ,,

### *Undesirables.*

7 lb. Flour weekly.
*No Meat.*
4 oz. Salt    weekly.
4 oz. Coffee    ,,
8 oz. Sugar    ,,

#### *Undesirable Children under Twelve.*

$3\frac{1}{2}$ lb. Meal or Flour weekly.
*No Meat.*
2   oz. Salt    weekly.
2   oz. Coffee    ,,
8   oz. Sugar    ,,

# II.

Scale raised,[2] February 27, 1901. All indigent **Refugees** to receive, in future, *Meat* rations, in terms of Class I.

[1] Cd. 819, p. 21.
[2] Cd. 819, p. 21.

377

# III.

## REVISED RATION SCALE [1]

### January 13, 1902, after Visit of Commission.

#### CHILDREN UNDER TWO YEARS. WEEKLY.

14 quarts Milk.
2½ lb. Flour or Boer Meal.
6 oz. Sugar.
6 oz. Syrup.
4 oz. Butter.

2 oz. Salt.
8 oz. Soap.
Soup and Vegetables as supplied by Matron.

#### CHILDREN OVER TWO AND UNDER FIVE YEARS. [2]
#### WEEKLY.

14 quarts Milk.
6 oz. Syrup.
3½ lb. Flour, Boer Meal, or Oatmeal.
6 oz. Sugar.

4 oz. Butter.
2 oz. Salt.
8 oz. Soap.
2 lb. Meat and Soup.

#### CHILDREN OVER FIVE AND UNDER TWELVE YEARS.
#### WEEKLY.

7 quarts Milk.
5 lb. Flour, Boer Meal, or Oatmeal.
6 oz. Sugar.
6 oz. Syrup.
8 oz. Rice, Beans, or Samp.

4 oz. Salt.
4 oz. Butter.
4 oz. Coffee.
3 lb. Meat.
8 oz. Soap.
24 oz. Vegetables.

[1] Cd. 934 (1902), p. 96.
[2] Cd. 934 (1902), p. 96.

ADULTS.

| | |
|---|---|
| 7 lb. Flour or Boer Meal. | 1 tin Milk. |
| 12 oz. Sugar. | 8 oz. Soap. |
| 7 oz. Coffee. | 1 lb. Samp, Rice, or Beans. |
| 4 lb. Meat. | 24 oz. Vegetables. |
| 4 oz. Salt. | |

I am indebted to Mr. Alfred Marks for the subjoined Table, in which he has worked out the cost of food per head per diem in the year 1901.

' I may add that in the camps with which I was familiar, the supply often came short of the notified allowance. Mafeking stood alone at the date of my visit in having a more generous scale than other camps.

## COST OF THE RATION IN THE TRANSVAAL CAMPS

For the months of May, June, July, October, and November 1901, calculated from the Government Returns (these are the only months for which full data for each Camp are given). The cost of "Rations Issued" is alone taken, all other charges, "Medical Comforts, Wages, Clothing," etc., are excluded.

For the TRANSVAAL CAMPS, generally, the figures given in the Returns (including all charges) are as follows ; the corrected figures (excluding all but rations) are given where data exist. All sums are stated in pence :—

| 1901. | Feb. | Mar. | April. | May. | June. | July. | Aug. | Sept. | Oct. | Nov. |
|---|---|---|---|---|---|---|---|---|---|---|
| Figures of Return | 6.46 | 4.84 | 4.42 | 4.37[1] | 4.44 | 4.25 | 4.70 | 5.45 | 5.70 | 6.23 |
| Corrected Figures | ... | ... | ... | 2.36[1] | 2.04 | 2.06 | 2.04 | 2.19 | 3.01 | 3.41 |

| | May. | June. | July. | Oct. | Nov. |
|---|---|---|---|---|---|
| Balmoral . . . . | ... | ... | ... | 3.04 | 3.65 |
| Barberton . . . . | 2.92[1] | 2.58 | 2.32 | 2.82 | 3.21 |
| Belfast . . . . | ... | 1.63 | 1.95 | 2.63 | 2.83 |
| Heidelberg . . . | 1.72 | 2.07 | 1.62 | 2.75 | 3.20 |
| Irene . . . . | 1.44 | 1.62 | 2.05 | 4.04 | 3.39 |
| Johannesburg Town . | 1.48 | 1.42 | 1.41 | 2.38 | 2.85 |
| Do. Camp . . | ... | 1.50 | 1.84 | 3.52 | 4.23 |
| Klerksdorp . . . | 1.25 | 0.34[2] | 1.68 | 2.61 | 3.36 |
| Krugersdorp . . . | 1.37 | 1.39 | 1.54 | 2.66 | 3.53 |
| Mafeking . . . . | ... | 14.92 | 15.90 | 3.56 | 4.14 |
| Middelburg . . . | 3.97 | 3.62 | 3.08 | 3.32 | 3.39 |
| Nylstroom . . . | ... | 1.30 | 1.16 | 3.03 | 3.00 |
| Pietersburg . . . | 1.72 | 2.03 | 2.04 | 2.93 | 2.88 |
| Potchefstroom . . | 1.44 | 1.52 | 1.81 | 2.83 | 3.13 |
| Standerton . . . | 1.47 | 1.63 | 1.91 | 3.91 | 3.26 |
| Vereeniging . . . | 1.45 | 1.50 | 1.49 | 1.66 | 2.07 |
| Volksrust . . . . | 1.33 | 1.87 | 1.81 | 2.70 | 2.97 |
| Vryheid . . . | ... | ... | 1.55 | ... | ... |
| Waterval, North . . | ... | ... | 1.62 | ... | ... |
| Vryburg . . . . | ... | ... | ... | ... | 3.33 |
| V. D. Hoven's Drift . . | ... | ... | ... | ... | 3.25 |
| Pretoria Relief . . . | 6.22 | 4.15 | 3.97 | 2.93 | 5.11 |

[1] May 4, 4.37d. Excluding a sum wrongly brought into the Barberton account for this month (Cd. 819, p. 175) the amount is 4.00d. The corresponding correction is made in "Corrected Figures," and in the Barberton amount.

[2] The lowest amount to be found in the Table is that for Klerksdorp for June, viz. 0.34d. The cost of the ration at Port Elizabeth has been 13.50d. (1s. 1½d.).

# COST OF THE RATION ELSEWHERE THAN IN THE TRANSVAAL CAMPS

## ORANGE FREE STATE.

| | | | | | |
|---|---|---|---|---|---|
| March | 1901 | 9.00 pence. | Cd. 819, p. 36. | For food only by contract. |
| June | ,, | 8.83 ,, | ,, p. 109. | |
| July | ,, | 8.50 ,, | ,, p. 211. | |
| August | ,, | 7.02 ,, | ,, p. 294. | |
| September | ,, | 12.81 ,, | Cd. 853, p. 20. | No definite statement. |
| October | ,, | 10.57 ,, | ,, p. 127. | |
| November | ,, | 12.53 ,, | Cd. 934, p. 36. | |
| December | ,, | 11.21 ,, | Cd. 936, p. 5. | |

## NATAL.

| | | | | |
|---|---|---|---|---|
| March | 1901 | 8.71 pence. | Cd. 819, p. 40. | Apparently for food only. |
| December | ,, | 5.57 ,, | Cd. 902, p. 129. | For food only. |

## PORT ELIZABETH.

March 1901    13.50 pence.    Cd. 819, p. 42.    For food only.

This camp has been spoken of by Mrs. Fawcett as "a show camp."

# Appendix B

## Rates of Mortality

In these Tables, wherever practicable, the mean population has been taken. Therefore the population at the end of the month will not be found in agreement with that on which the death-rate is calculated. Summary I. shows the actual population; Summaries II. and III. the mean, when this could be ascertained.

No two persons working on the returns would bring out precisely the same results; but, as near as possible, this is a correct presentation of the facts, so far as revealed. The references cited make it easy to consult the returns. To get the mean, the population is taken on the first of the month, adding half the arrivals and births, and deducting half the departures. For the sake of clearness the rates are stated in dark figures.

Summary III. and Table I. relate to children's deaths. The highest general death-rate for children is in the O. R. C. Camps. The highest single rate for children for one month is that at Brandfort, in October, 1891, of 1,951 per thousand *per annum.*

There is grave reason to fear that many more deaths have taken place than appear in these official returns.

## SUMMARY I.—POPULATION (IN FULL), AND DEATHS IN ALL CAMPS.

| Date. | Population. | | | | | Deaths. | | | | |
|---|---|---|---|---|---|---|---|---|---|---|
| | Transvaal. | O. F. S. | Natal. | C. Cy. | Total. | Transvaal. | O. F. S. | Natal. | C. Cy. | Total. |
| **1901.** | | | | | | | | | | |
| January | ... | ... | ... | ... | ... | ... | 40 | ... | ... | 40 |
| February | 21,105 | 11,563 | 2,524 | ... | ... | ... | 62 | ... | ... | 62 |
| March | 23,812 | ... | ... | ... | ... | ... | 119 | ... | ... | 119 |
| April | 37,939 | ... | ... | ... | ... | 240 | 155 | ... | ... | 395 |
| May | 45,659 | 31,694 | 2,614 | 372 | 102,651 | 338 | 335 | ... | ... | 673 |
| June | 62,479 | 37,049 | 2,751 | 370 | 111,540 | 750 | 395 | 104[1] | 12[2] | 1261 |
| July | 65,500 | 42,822 | 2,848 | 295 | 116,225 | 1067 | 642 | 6 | 1 | 1716 |
| August | 65,314 | 44,572 | 6,044 | 283 | 118,408 | 1477 | 1164 | 24 | 1 | 2666 |
| September | 63,707 | 45,306 | 9,112 | 278 | 117,871 | 1369 | 1127 | 76 | ... | 2572 |
| October | 62,325 | 45,083 | 10,185 | 280 | 117,125 | 1616 | 1514 | 75 | ... | 3205 |
| November | 61,961 | 43,755 | 11,129 | ... | ... | 1521 | 1331 | 74 | ... | 2926 |
| December | ... | ... | ... | ... | ... | 1040 | 1250 | 147 | ... | 2437 |
| **1902.** | | | | | | | | | | |
| January | 60,151 | 42,404 | 12,206 | 276 | 115,037 | 639 | 755 | 83 | ... | 1477 |
| February | 53,724 | 41,138 | 19,045 | 274 | 114,181 | 287 | 289 | 52 | ... | 628 |
| | ... | ... | ... | ... | ... | 10,344 | 9178 | 641 | 14 | 20,177 |

[1] Appears to be a total for several months.  [2] Total from October 1900.

### NOTES ON ABOVE SUMMARY.

The number of deaths here shown is . . . . 20,177

UNRECORDED DEATHS.

To this number have to be added—

*Transvaal.*—Deaths occurring prior to April 1901.

*Orange Free State.*—Deaths occurring prior to January 1901.

*Transvaal.*—Finally, deaths of the population in the "Relief and Military Posts" (Cd. 939, p. s) from July 1901 to February 1902, both inclusive; this population averaged over 8000.

# SUMMARY II. (MAY 1902).

POPULATION (CORRECTED), DEATHS AND DEATH-RATES [in *dark figures*] (PER 1000 PER ANNUM) OF THE CAMPS, IN GROUPS AND IN THE AGGREGATE.

As far as practicable, the mean population for each month has been taken. The totals do not therefore agree with those in another Summary, showing the totals at the end of each month. Further, there is a large difference in the Transvaal totals, due to the omission here of the population of "Relief and Military Posts," where no record of deaths has been kept. This difference for the months of July to February (both inclusive) averages over 6000

| Date. | TRANSVAAL. | | | ORANGE FREE STATE. | | | NATAL. | | | ALL CAMPS. | | |
|---|---|---|---|---|---|---|---|---|---|---|---|---|
| | Population. | Deaths. | Death-Rate. | Population. | Deaths. | Death-Rate. | Population. | Deaths. | Death-Rate. | Population.[1] | Deaths.[2] | Death-Rate. |
| **1901.** | | | | | | | | | | | | |
| July | 50,111 | 1067 | 255 | 37,049 | 642 | 206 | 2,681 | 6 | 27 | 90,213 | 1716 | 228 |
| August | 57,530 | 1477 | 306 | 42,107 | 1164 | 331 | 2,813 | 24 | 102 | 102,820 | 2666 | 311 |
| September | 58,182 | 1369 | 283 | 44,572 | 1127 | 303 | 4,433 | 76 | 206 | 107,482 | 2572 | 287 |
| October | 59,523 | 1616 | 326 | 45,306 | 1514 | 401 | 6,752 | 75 | 133 | 111,864 | 3205 | 344 |
| November | 56,883 | 1521 | 321 | 45,083 | 1331 | 354 | 9,865 | 74 | 90 | 112,109 | 2926 | 313 |
| December | 56,821 | 1040 | 219 | 43,755 | 1250 | 343 | 11,129 | 147 | 157 | 111,985 | 2437 | 261 |
| **1902.** | | | | | | | | | | | | |
| January | 55,297 | 639 | 139 | 42,404 | 755 | 213 | 12,206 | 83 | 81 | 110,183 | 1477 | 160 |
| February | 48,728 | 287 | 71 | 41,138 | 289 | 84 | 19,175 | 52 | 33 | 109,315 | 628 | 60 |

1 Including Cape Colony, not here tabulated.
2 Two deaths in Cape Colony (July and August) are in this total.

## SUMMARY III.—NUMBER OF CHILDREN IN CAMPS. NUMBER OF DEATHS AND DEATH-RATE (in *black figures*) PER 1000 PER ANNUM (MAY 1902).

| | TRANSVAAL. | | | | | ORANGE FREE STATE. | | | |
| Date. | Official Returns. | Number of Children. | Deaths. | Death-rate. | Date. | Official Returns. | Number of Children. | Deaths. | Death-rate. |
|---|---|---|---|---|---|---|---|---|---|
| **1901.** | | | | | **1901.** | | | | |
| May | Cd. 819, 51 | 16,257 | 252 | **186** | January to April | Cd. 853, 121 | ... | 253 | ... |
| June | Cd. 819, 113 | 19,595 | 584 | **358** | May | Cd. 853, 121 | ... | 218 | ... |
| July | Cd. 819, 223 | 22,974 | 860 | **449** | June | Cd. 819, 105; 853, 121 | 17,349 | 238 | **164** |
| August | Cd. 819, 311 | 26,226 | 1190 | **544** | July | Cd. 819, 208; 853, 121 | 20,580 | 482 | **281** |
| September | Cd. 853, 34 | 26,750 | 1124 | **504** | August | Cd. 819, 290; 853, 121 | 23,500 | 944 | **482** |
| October | Cd. 902, 44 | 26,589 | 1295 | **585** | September | Cd. 853, 17, 121 | 24,654 | 924 | **449** |
| November | Cd. 934, 54 | 24,611 | 1201 | **586** | October | Cd. 853, 130, 121 | 25,170 | 1319 | **629** |
| December | Cd. 936, 17 | 24,375 | 780 | **384** | November | Cd. 853, 131; 934, 36 | 24,709 | 1089 | **529** |
| | | | | | December | Cd. 936, 2, 3 | 23,542 | 910 | **464** |
| **1902.** | | | | | **1902.** | | | | |
| January | Cd. 939, 5 | 23,734 | 429 | **217** | January | Cd. 939, 3; 934, 103 | 18,784 | 407 | **260** |
| February | Cd. 939, 6 | 20,404 | 190 | **111** | February | Cd. 939, 4; 936, 32 | 18,179 | 154 | **102** |

## SUMMARY III.—Continued.

| Date. | NATAL | | | | Date. | CAPE COLONY | | |
|---|---|---|---|---|---|---|---|---|
| | Official Returns. | Number of Children. | Deaths. | Death-rate. | | Official Returns. | Number of Children. | Deaths. |
| **1901.** | | | | | **1901.** | | | |
| Prior to July | Cd. 608 | ... | 84 | ... | Prior to July | Cd. 819, 183 | ... | 10 |
| June | Cd. 819, 188/9 | 1457 | ... | ... | ... | ... | ... | ... |
| July | Cd. 819, 203/5 ; 694 | 1494 | 6 | 48 | July | Cd. 819, 207 | 257 | ... |
| August | Cd. 819, 28/5 ; 789 | 1557 | 21 | 162 | August | Cd. 819, 287 | 257 | ... |
| September | Cd. 853, 27/9 ; 793 | 2386 | 65 | 327 | September | Cd. 853, 8 | 204 | ... |
| October | Cd. 853, 130 | 3570 | 62 | 208 | October | Cd. 853, 130 | 197 | ... |
| November | Cd. 853, 131 | 5182 | 71 | 164 | December | Cd. 853, 131 | 197 | ... |
| December | Cd. 902, 134 | 5382 | 120 | 267 | November | Cd. 934, 93 | 198 | ... |
| **1902.** | | | | | **1902.** | | | |
| January | Cd. 934, 103 | 5855 | 60 | 123 | January | Cd. 936, 24 | 197 | ... |
| February | Cd. 936, 32 | 8867 | 36 | 49 | February | Cd. 939 | 197 | ... |

### NOTES ON ABOVE SUMMARY OF CHILDREN'S DEATHS, ETC.

#### NUMBER OF CHILDREN.

Where practicable, the mean for the month has been taken. The Table is, as far as practicable, compiled from the more detailed Returns. Children were counted as such up to twelve years in the Transvaal, and up to fifteen years in the Orange River Colony. At the close of 1901, the twelve years limit was adopted also in the Orange River Colony.

#### DEATHS.

The deaths in this Table are — *Transvaal*, **7305** ; *Orange Free State*, **6986** ; *Natal*, **525** ; *Cape Colony*, 10 ; total, **15,378.**

#### UNRECORDED DEATHS.

*Transvaal.*—No deaths recorded prior to May 1901.
*Orange Free State.*—No deaths recorded prior to January 1901.
*Transvaal.*—Finally, there are the unrecorded deaths of Children in the "Relief and Military Posts" (see, for example, Cd. 939, p. 3). From July 1901 to February 1902, the number of Children coming under this head averages over 3000.

# TABLE I.

## HIGHEST RATES OF MORTALITY AMONG CHILDREN IN THE CONCENTRATION CAMPS (WHITES).

| Date. | Camp. | Number of Children (Mean). | Number of Children (end of Month). | Number of Deaths. | Rate of Mortality per 1000 per Annum. |
|---|---|---|---|---|---|
| 1901. July . . | Middelburg . | 3567 | ... | 342 | 1150 |
| August . | Kroonstad . | ... | 1727 | 270 | 1878 |
| ,, . | Nylstroom . | 804 | ... | 95 | 1418 |
| ,, . | Pietersburg . | 1475 | ... | 149 | 1212 |
| October . | Brandfort . | ... | 2122 | 345 | 1951 |
| ,, . | Heilbron . | ... | 1727 | 212 | 1474 |
| ,, . | Mafeking . | 2419 | ... | 350 | 1737 |
| ,, . | Standerton . | 1326 | ... | 205 | 1855 |
| ,, . | Vryburg . . | 449 | ... | 45 | 1202 |
| November | Klerksdorp . | ... | 1833 | 161 | 1054 |
| ,, | Nylstroom . | ... | 683 | 67 | 1178 |
| ,, | Mafeking . | ... | 1853 | 197 | 1277 |
| December | Bethulie . . | ... | 2278 | 197 | 1038 |

# TABLE II.

## Transvaal Camps.

| Date. | Off. Ret. | Men. | Women. | Children. | Total. | Men. | Women. | Children. | Total. |
|---|---|---|---|---|---|---|---|---|---|
| | | POPULATION. | | | | DEATHS. | | | |
| 1901.<br>Mar. 22 | Cd. 819, 16 | 8,214 | ... | 12,091 | 21,105[1] | | | ... | ... |
| | | | 800 | | | | | | |
| Apr. 30 | Cd. 819, 47 | 3,593 | 7,505 | 12,714 | 23,812 | | | ... | 240 |
| May 31 | Cd. 819, 51 | 6,842 | 12,263 | 18,834 | 37,939 | 39 | 47 | 252 | 338 |
| June 30 | Cd. 819, 113 | 8,596 | 16,111 | 20,952 | 45,659 | 55 | | 584 | 750 |
| July 31 | Cd. 819, 223 | 10,481 | 23,261 | 28,737 | 62,479 | 66 | 141 | 860 | 1067 |
| Aug. 31 | Cd. 819, 311 | 10,808 | 24,645 | 30,047 | 65,500 | 83 | 204 | 1190 | 1477 |
| Sept. 30 | Cd. 853, 34 | 11,156 | 24,732 | 29,786 | 65,314 | 74 | 171 | 1124 | 1369 |
| Oct. 31 | Cd. 902, 44 | 11,073 | 24,078 | 28,556 | 63,707 | 85 | 236 | 1295 | 1616 |
| Nov. 30 | Cd. 934, 54 | 10,907 | 23,780 | 27,638 | 62,325 | 94 | 226 | 1201 | 1521 |
| Dec. 31 | Cd. 936, 17 | 10,884 | 23,827 | 27,250 | 61,961 | 73 | 187 | 780 | 1040 |
| 1902.<br>Jan. 31 | Cd. 939 | 10,304 | 23,391 | 26,456 | 60,151 | 51 | 59 | 429 | 639 |
| Feb. 28 | Cd. 939 | 10,246 | 20,516 | 23,162 | 53,924 | 29 | 68 | 190 | 287 |

[1] Division into Adults (all over 12) and Children ; 800 not classified.

## TABLE III.—ORANGE FREE STATE CAMPS.

| Date. | Official Returns. | Population. | | | | Deaths. | | | |
|---|---|---|---|---|---|---|---|---|---|
| | | Men. | Women. | Children. | Total. | Men. | Women. | Children. | Total. |
| **1901.** | | | | | | | | | |
| January | Cd. 853, 121 | ... | ... | ... | ... | ... | ... | 28 | 40 |
| February | Cd. 853, 121 | ... | ... | ... | ... | ... | ... | 37 | 62 |
| March | Cd. 819, 36 / Cd. 853, 121 | ... | ... | ... | 11,563 | ... | ... | 86 | 119 |
| April | Cd. 853, 121 | ... | ... | ... | ... | ... | ... | 102 | 155 |
| May | Cd. 853, 121 | ... | ... | ... | ... | ... | ... | 218 | 335 |
| June 30 | Cd. 819, 105 / Cd. 853, 121 | 4991 | 9,354 | 17,349 | 31,694 | | | 238 | 395 |
| July 31 | Cd. 819, 208 | 5318 | 11,151 | 20,580 | 37,049 | | | 482 | 642 |
| August 31 | Cd. 819, 290 / Cd. 853, 121 | 5677 | 12,930 | 23,500 | 42,107 }[1] 715 } | Returned as Adults | | 944 | 1164 |
| September 30 | Cd. 853, 17 | 5995 | 13,923 | 24,654 | 44,572 | | | 924 | 1127 |
| October 31 | Cd. 853, 123/4 and 121 | 5906 | 14,471 | 24,929 | 45,306 | | | 1319 | 1514 |
| November 30 | Cd. 934, 32 / Cd. 853, 131 | 6636 | 14,608 | 24,439 | 45,083 | 59 | 183 | 1089 | 1331 |
| December 31 | Cd. 936, 2 / Cd. 902, 134 | 5676 | 14,537 | 23,542 | 43,755 | 85 | 255 | 910 | 1250 |
| **1902.** | | | | | | | | | |
| January | Cd. 939, 3 / Cd. 934, 103 | 7232 | 16,388 | 18,784 | 42,404 | 96[2] | 252[2] | 407[2] | 755[2] |
| February | Cd. 939, 4 / Cd. 936, 32 | 7006 | 15,953 | 18,179 | 41,138 | 36 | 99 | 154 | 289 |

[1] 715 from Heilbron "arrived too late to be classified."

[2] Covers a longer period, apparently four days over calendar month; correction made here.

389

## TABLE IV.—NATAL CAMPS.

| Date. | Official Returns. | Population. | | | | Deaths. | | | |
|---|---|---|---|---|---|---|---|---|---|
| | | Men. | Women. | Children. | Total. | Men. | Women. | Children. | Total. |
| **1901.** | | | | | | | | | |
| March 21 | Cd. 819, 38 | 236 | 826 | 1462 | 2,524 | ... | ... | ... | ... |
| June 30 | { Cd. 819, 188/9 } Cd. 608 | 273 | 863 | 1478 | 2,614 | 5 | 15 | 84 | 104[1] |
| July 31 | { Cd. 819, 203/5 } Cd. 694 | 319 | 908 | 1524 | 2,751 | ... | ... | 6 | 6 |
| August 31 | { Cd. 819, 283/5 } Cd. 789 | 337 | 932 | 1579 | 2,848 | ... | 3 | 21 | 24 |
| September 30 | { Cd. 853, 27/9 } Cd. 793 | 578 | 2251 | 3215 | 6,044 | 1 | 10 | 65 | 76 |
| October 31 | Cd. 853, 130 | 915 | 3434 | 4763 | 9,112 | ... | 13 | 62 | 75 |
| November 30 | Cd. 853, 131 | 1028 | 3909 | 5248 | 10,185 | ... | 3 | 71 | 74 |
| December 31 | Cd. 902, 134 | 1266 | 4481 | 5832 | 11,129 | 5 | 22 | 120 | 147 |
| **1902.** January 31 | Cd. 934, 103 | 1386 | 4965 | 5855 | 12,206 | 5[2] | 18[2] | 60[2] | 83[2] |
| February 28 | Cd. 936, 32 | 2624 | 7554 | 8867 | 19,045 | 2 | 14 | 36 | 52 |

[1] This is, no doubt, the total for several months.
[2] Return covers, apparently, four days more than calendar month; allowance made here.

## TABLE V.—CAPE COLONY (PORT ELIZABETH) CAMP.

| Date. | Official Returns. | Population. | | | | Deaths. | | | |
|---|---|---|---|---|---|---|---|---|---|
| | | Men. | Women. | Children. | Total. | Men. | Women. | Children. | Total. |
| July 15 1901. | Cd. 819, 183/4 | 32 | 83 | 257 | 372[1] | ... | ... | ... | ... |
| Deaths to date | { Cd. 819, 183/4 / Cd. 608 } | ... | ... | ... | ... | 1 | 1 | 10 | 12 |
| July 31 | Cd. 819, 207 | 32 | 83 | 257 | 372 | ... | 1 | ... | 1 |
| August 31 | Cd. 819, 287 | 31 | 82 | 257 | 370 | ... | 1 | ... | 1 |
| September 30 | Cd. 853, 8 | 28 | 63 | 204 | 295 | ... | ... | ... | ... |
| October 31 | Cd. 853, 130 | 27 | 59 | 197 | 283 | ... | ... | ... | ... |
| November 30 | Cd. 853, 131 | 23 | 58 | 197 | 278 | ... | ... | ... | ... |
| December 31 | Cd. 934, 93 | 24 | 58 | 198 | 280 | ... | ... | ... | ... |
| January 31 1902. | Cd. 936, 24 | 22 | 57 | 197 | 276 | ... | ... | ... | ... |
| February 28 | Cd. 936, 32 | 21 | 57 | 196 | 274 | ... | ... | ... | ... |

1 " Exiles," exclusive of 16 " Refugees."

# TABLE VI.

## CONCENTRATION CAMPS OF THE TRANSVAAL.

TABLE showing (so far as recorded) the POPULATION of each Camp at the end of each month, DEATHS and DEATH-RATE (in *black figures*) per 1,000 per annum. Where data exist for its calculation, the mean Population for the month is shown in *italic figures*, and the Death-Rate is calculated on this mean. (JUNE 1902.)

| 1901 | APRIL. | | | MAY. | | | JUNE. | | |
|---|---|---|---|---|---|---|---|---|---|
| | Pop'n. | Deaths | Rate. | Pop'n. | Deaths | Rate. | Pop'n. | Deaths | Rate. |
| Barberton . . | 445 | 4 | **108** | 576 *353* | 1 | **38** | 870 *725* | 3 | **49** |
| Balmoral . . | .. | .. | .. | .. | .. | .. | .. | .. | .. |
| Belfast . . . | .. | .. | .. | .. | .. | .. | 823 *575* | 3 | **62** |
| Heidelberg . | 1086 | 2 | **22** | 1434 *1086* | 17 | **188** | 1579 *1512* | 11 | **84** |
| Irene . . . | 3703 | 49 | **188** | 4319 *4011* | 70 | **209** | 4716 *4597* | 131 | **342** |
| Johannesburg | 3170 | 90 | **347** | 3379 *3274* | 80 | **293** | 3428 *3351* | 41 | **147** |
| Klerksdorp . | 991 | 2 | **27** | 1963 *1477* | 8 | **65** | 2560 *2270* | 15 | **71** |
| Krugersdorp . | 1088 | .. | .. | 1531 *1354* | 2 | **18** | 2602 *2085* | 8 | **47** |
| Meintjes-Kop. | .. | .. | .. | .. | .. | .. | .. | .. | .. |
| Middelburg . | 1292 | 9 | **83** | 6637 *4881* | 30 | **74** | 7425 *7114* | 166 | **280** |
| Mafeking . . | 765 | 4 | **63** | 1046 *905* | 5 | **66** | 1842 *1446* | 3 | **25** |
| Nylstroom . . | .. | .. | .. | .. | .. | .. | 1087 *919* | 8 | **105** |
| Pietersburg . | .. | .. | .. | 2301 *1707* | 7 | **49** | 3145 *2671* | 54 | **242** |
| Potchefstroom | 5724 | 24 | **50** | 6149 *5936* | 44 | **89** | 6065 *6223* | 235 | **453** |
| Standerton . | 1237 | 25 | **243** | 2983 *2110* | 34 | **193** | 3154 *3095* | 32 | **124** |
| Vereeniging . | 733 | 5 | **82** | 811 *772* | 5 | **77** | 806 *809* | 6 | **88** |
| Volksrust . . | 3578 | 26 | **87** | 4810 *4194* | 35 | **100** | 5324 *5086* | 34 | **80** |
| Vryburg . . | .. | .. | .. | .. | .. | .. | .. | .. | .. |
| V. D. Hoven's Drift . . . | .. | .. | .. | .. | .. | .. | .. | .. | .. |
| Relief and Military Posts . | .. | .. | .. | .. | .. | .. | 233 | .. | -- |
| | 23,812 | 240 | .. | 37,939 | 338 | .. | 45,659 | 750 | .. |

## TABLE VI.—*Continued.*

| 1901 | JULY | | | AUGUST | | | SEPTEMBER | | |
|---|---|---|---|---|---|---|---|---|---|
| | Pop'n. | Deaths | Rate. | Pop'n. | Deaths | Rate. | Pop'n. | Deaths | Rate. |
| Barberton . . | 1994 *1458* | 17 | 142 | 1938 *2005* | 75 | 449 | 1928 *1984* | 56 | 338 |
| Balmoral . . | .. | .. | .. | 1660 *1716* | 16 | 112 | 2262 *1976* | 37 | 199 |
| Belfast . . . | 1214 *1024* | 13 | 152 | 1407 *1383* | 25 | 226 | 1566 *1516* | 50 | 338 |
| Heidelberg . | 1996 *1759* | 18 | 123 | 2222 *2149* | 81 | 452 | 2241 *2252* | 50 | 266 |
| Irene . . . | 4409 *4635* | 147 | 381 | 4655 *4562* | 57 | 149 | 4277 *4491* | 80 | 214 |
| Johannesburg | 3666 *3567* | 38 | 126 | 3506 *3626* | 82 | 271 | 3175 *3359* | 39 | 130 |
| Klerksdorp . | 3552 *3075* | 38 | 148 | 4588 *4160* | 179 | 517 | 4512 *4624* | 147 | 361 |
| Krugersdorp . | 4152 *3383* | 12 | 42 | 4853 *4565* | 125 | 326 | 5299 *5139* | 135 | 302 |
| Meintjes-Kop | .. | .. | .. | .. | .. | .. | .. | .. | .. |
| Middelburg . | 7751 *7790* | 404 | 622 | 6523 *7196* | 119 | 199 | 6208 *6417* | 102 | 196 |
| Mafeking . . | 3515 *2693* | 9 | 40 | 4676 *4111* | 31 | 90 | 5245 *4038* | 155 | 400 |
| Nylstroom . | 1521 *1321* | 36 | 327 | 1475 *1553* | 111 | 857 | 1851 *1688* | 54 | 384 |
| Pietersburg . | 3307 *3383* | 113 | 413 | 3713 *3603* | 184 | 613 | 3612 *3706* | 86 | 278 |
| Potchefstroom | 7144 *6671* | 133 | 229 | 7355 *7283* | 64 | 105 | 7598 *7524* | 94 | 150 |
| Standerton . | 2996 *3093* | 36 | 189 | 3297 *3161* | 30 | 113 | 3049 *3236* | 125 | 463 |
| Vereeniging . | 1038 *924* | 4 | 52 | 976 *1031* | 50 | 582 | 970 *993* | 40 | 484 |
| Velksrust . . | 5462 *5455* | 49 | 108 | 5271 *5490* | 248 | 568 | 5090 *5240* | 129 | 300 |
| Vryburg . . | .. | .. | .. | .. | .. | .. | .. | .. | .. |
| V. D. Hoven's Drift . . . | .. | .. | .. | .. | .. | .. | .. | .. | .. |
| Relief and Military Posts . | 8762 | .. | .. | 7386 | .. | .. | 6431 | .. | .. |
| | 62,479 | 1007 | .. | 65,500 | 1477 | .. | 65,314 | 1360 | .. |

TABLE VI.—*Continued.*

| 1901. . . . | October. | | | November. | | | December. | | |
|---|---|---|---|---|---|---|---|---|---|
| | Pop'n. | Deaths | Rate. | Pop'n. | Deaths | Rate. | Pop'n. | Deaths | Rate. |
| Barberton. . | 1904 *1923* | 12 | 75 | 1720 | 10 | 64 | 1631 | 7 | 51 |
| Balmoral . . | 2577 *2454* | 68 | 333 | 2488 | 90 | 434 | 2685 | 75 | 308 |
| Belfast . . . | 1390 *1492* | 29 | 233 | 1374 | 31 | 271 | 1876 | 41 | 358 |
| Heidelberg . | 2196 *2240* | 43 | 230 | 2213 | 67 | 309 | 2212 | 37 | 207 |
| Irene . . . | 3985 *4180* | 100 | 287 | 4027 | 90 | 268 | 4116 | 39 | 113 |
| Johannesburg | 2936 *3069* | 27 | 105 | 2821 | 14 | 59 | 2797 | 28 | 120 |
| Klerksdorp . | 3825 *4248* | 159 | 449 | 3889 | 194 | 600 | 4073 | 159 | 468 |
| Krugersdorp . | 5488 *5442* | 92 | 203 | 5385 | 178 | 397 | 5345 | 105 | 235 |
| Meintjes-Kop | .. | .. | .. | .. | .. | .. | .. | .. | .. |
| Middelburg . | 5593 *5970* | 139 | 279 | 5223 | 208 | 477 | 5113 | 115 | 269 |
| Mafeking . . | 4778 *5215* | 406 | 934 | 4496 | 231 | 616 | 4373 | 90 | 247 |
| Nylstroom . | 1812 *1861* | 59 | 380 | 1618 | 91 | 675 | 1731 | 55 | 381 |
| Pietersburg . | 3593 *3627* | 48 | 159 | 3583 | 46 | 154 | 3170 | 64 | 242 |
| Potchefstroom | 7438 *7561* | 85 | 135 | 7247 | 74 | 122 | 7177 | 70 | 117 |
| Standerton . | 2946 *3115* | 240 | 925 | 3092 | 82 | 318 | 3355 | 64 | 229 |
| Vereeniging . | 906 *941* | 8 | 102 | 925 | 6 | 78 | 950 | 15 | 189 |
| Volksrust . . | 5234 *5210* | 46 | 106 | 5286 | 60 | 136 | 5239 | 45 | 103 |
| Vryburg . . | 1255 *976* | 55 | 676 | 1191 | 51 | 514 | 1266 | 24 | 227 |
| V. D. Hoven's Drift . . . | .. | .. | .. | 305 | 8 | 315 | 212 | 7 | 396 |
| Relief and Military Posts . | 5802 | .. | .. | 5442 | .. | .. | 5140 | .. | .. |
| | 63,707 | 1616 | .. | 62,325 | 1521 | .. | 61,961 | 1040 | .. |

TABLE VI.—*Continued.*

| 1902 . . . . | JANUARY. | | | FEBRUARY. | | | MARCH. | | |
|---|---|---|---|---|---|---|---|---|---|
| | Pop'n. | Deaths | Rate. | Pop'n. | Deaths | Rate. | Pop'n. | Deaths | Rate. |
| Barberton . . | 1577 | 9 | 68 | 1533 | 5 | 38 | 1508 | 2 | 16 |
| Balmoral . . | 2703 | 84 | 373 | 2433 | 24 | 118 | 2331 | 14 | 72 |
| Belfast . . . | 1345 | 15 | 134 | 1474 | 12 | 97 | 1380 | 7 | 61 |
| Heidelberg . | 2247 | 13 | 69 | 2202 | 12 | 65 | 2164 | 6 | 33 |
| Irene . . . | 4067 | 19 | 56 | 4062 | 15 | 44 | 4154 | 11 | 31 |
| Johannesburg | 2557 | 13 | 61 | 2211 | 8 | 43 | 1732 | 9 | 63 |
| Klerksdorp . | 3979 | 86 | 259 | 3983 | 46 | 138 | 3532 | 40 | 136 |
| Krugersdorp . | 4629 | 63 | 163 | 3848 | 22 | 68 | 3943 | 6 | 18 |
| Meintjes-Kop | .. | .. | .. | 326 | .. | .. | 427 | .. | .. |
| Middelburg . | 5058 | 51 | 121 | 5171 | 16 | 37 | 4996 | 6 | 14 |
| Mafeking . . | 4312 | 35 | 97 | 4328 | 21 | 58 | 4347 | 5 | 14 |
| Nylstroom . | 1650 | 31 | 225 | 1623 | 8 | 59 | 1474 | 7 | 57 |
| Pietersburg . | 2883 | 29 | 120 | .. | .. | .. | .. | .. | .. |
| Potchefstroom | 7126 | 35 | 59 | 5786 | 25 | 52 | 5263 | 11 | 25 |
| Standerton . | 3454 | 65 | 226 | 3429 | 37 | 130 | 3395 | 23 | 81 |
| Vereeniging . | 937 | 13 | 166 | 955 | 3 | 37 | 944 | 3 | 38 |
| Volksrust . . | 5173 | 56 | 130 | 3788 | 25 | 79 | 3553 | 15 | 50 |
| Vryburg . . | 1600 | 20 | 150 | 1776 | 8 | 54 | 1878 | 9 | 57 |
| V. D. Hoven's Drift . . . | .. | 2 | .. | .. | .. | .. | .. | .. | .. |
| Relief and Military Posts . | 4854 | .. | .. | 4996 | .. | .. | 4477 | .. | .. |
| | 60,151 | 639 | .. | 1 53,924 | 287 | .. | 51,498 | 174 | .. |

1 In the Government Return, Cd. 939, 6, there is a wrong addition.

# TABLE VII.

## CONCENTRATION CAMPS OF THE ORANGE FREE STATE.

TABLE showing (so far as recorded) the POPULATION of each Camp at the end of each month, DEATHS and DEATH-RATE (in *dark figures*) per 1,000 per annum.

| 1901 . . . | MAY. | | | JUNE. | | | JULY. | | |
|---|---|---|---|---|---|---|---|---|---|
| | Pop'n. | Deaths | Rate. | Pop'n. | Deaths | Rate. | Pop'n. | Deaths | Rate. |
| Aliwal North | .. | 13 | .. | 4428 | 33 | **39** | 4451 | 63 | **169** |
| Bloemfontein | 1297 | 168 | **1554** | 4753 | 157 | **396** | 5118 | 102 | **239** |
| Brandfort . . | .. | 7 | .. | 1815 | 11 | **73** | 1865 | 13 | **84** |
| Bethulie  . . | .. | 7 | .. | 3440 | 9 | **31** | 4280 | 31 | **87** |
| Heilbron .  . | .. | 4 | .. | 2077 | 15 | **87** | 2364 | 22 | **111** |
| Harrismith  . | .. | .. | .. | 656 | 1 | **18** | 927 | 3 | **38** |
| Kroonstad  . | .. | 41 | .. | 3797 | 47 | **148** | 3855 | 157 | **489** |
| Kimberley  . | .. | 13 | .. | 2186 | 17 | **93** | 3613 | 63 | **209** |
| Ladybrand  . | .. | .. | .. | .. | .. | .. | .. | .. | .. |
| Norval's Pont | .. | 12 | .. | 2772 | 35 | **151** | 3391 | 60 | **212** |
| Springfontein | .. | 37 | .. | 2667 | 42 | **189** | 2645 | 101 | **458** |
| Vredefort Road | .. | 19 | .. | 1365 | 18 | **158** | 1421 | 14 | **118** |
| Winburg . . | .. | 14 | .. | 1738 | 10 | **69** | 2216 | 13 | **70** |
| Orange River | .. | .. | .. | .. | .. | .. | .. | .. | .. |
| Kromelleboog | .. | .. | .. | .. | .. | .. | .. | .. | .. |
| | .. | 335 | .. | 31,694 | 395 | .. | 36,146 | 642 | .. |

For July to October the Population is given from Cd. 853, 119.  It will be found that the totals do not agree with those given in Summaries I., II., and III., and the Table from which those Summaries are compiled.  In those cases the Returns of Population taken are those given in Cd. 819, 209 and 290 ; Cd. 853, 17 and 130.  There is no apparent reason for attributing greater weight to either set of Returns.

*June* 1902.

TABLE VII.—*Continued.*

| 1901 . . . | August. | | | September. | | | October. | | |
|---|---|---|---|---|---|---|---|---|---|
| | Pop'n. | Deaths | Rate. | Pop'n. | Deaths | Rate. | Pop'n. | Deaths | Rate. |
| Aliwal North | 4437 | 209 | 565 | 4651 | 41 | 106 | 4712 | 19 | 48 |
| Bloemfontein | 6586 | 96 | 175 | 6429 | 107 | 199 | 6424 | 204 | 381 |
| Brandfort . . | 3404 | 22 | 77 | 3867 | 138 | 428 | 3555 | 372 | 1256 |
| Bethulie . . | 4707 | 175 | 440 | 4811 | 230 | 588 | 4771 | 154 | 387 |
| Heilbron . . | 2799 | 23 | 98 | 3391 | 144 | 509 | 3063 | 238 | 933 |
| Harrismith . | 1134 | 5 | 52 | 1304 | 2 | 18 | 1596 | 5 | 37 |
| Kroonstad . | 3326 | 326 | 1173 | 3405 | 171 | 603 | 3674 | 93 | 379 |
| Kimberley . | 3701 | 160 | 519 | 3739 | 53 | 170 | 3767 | 45 | 143 |
| Ladybrand . | .. | .. | .. | .. | .. | .. | .. | .. | .. |
| Norval's Pont | 3215 | 50 | 186 | 3284 | 54 | 197 | 3294 | 52 | 189 |
| Springfontein | 2893 | 52 | 216 | 2693 | 33 | 147 | 2849 | 114 | 480 |
| Vredefort Road | 1714 | 21 | 147 | 1911 | 101 | 634 | 2110 | 91 | 518 |
| Winburg . . | 2624 | 18 | 81 | 3268 | 30 | 110 | 3144 | 72 | 275 |
| Orange River | 1507 | 7 | 56 | 1522 | 17 | 134 | 1500 | 55 | 440 |
| Kromelleboog | .. | .. | .. | 1.. | .. | .. | .. | .. | .. |
| | 42,107 | 1164 | .. | 44,275 | 1127 | .. | 44,459 | 1514 | .. |

[1] Cd. 853, 17, States Pop., 19.

TABLE VII.—*Continued.*

| 1901 . . . | NOVEMBER. | | | DECEMBER. | | | 1902. JANUARY. | | |
|---|---|---|---|---|---|---|---|---|---|
| | Pop'n. | Deaths | Rate. | Pop'n. | Deaths | Rate. | Pop'n. | Deaths | Rate. |
| Aliwal North | 4613 | 80 | 208 | 4555 | 54 | 142 | 4514 | 23 | 61 |
| Bloemfontein | 6322 | 178 | 338 | 6049 | 184 | 365 | 5949 | 127 | 256 |
| Brandfort . . | 3981 | 158 | 476 | 4221 | 130 | 369 | 4143 | 100 | 290 |
| Bethulie . . | 4531 | 236 | 625 | 4255 | 276 | 779 | 4088 | 139 | 408 |
| Heilbron . . | 3081 | 155 | 603 | 3072 | 124 | 485 | 2878 | 82 | 342 |
| Harrismith . | 1650 | 13 | 94 | 1623 | 63 | 761 | 1470 | 32 | 261 |
| Kroonstad . | 3768 | 128 | 408 | 3673 | 153 | 500 | 3545 | 95 | 321 |
| Kimberley . | 3806 | 34 | 107 | 3867 | 12 | 37 | 3469 | 13 | 45 |
| Ladybrand . | 696 | .. | .. | .. | .. | .. | .. | .. | .. |
| Norval's Pont | 3269 | 47 | 172 | 3228 | 35 | 130 | 3185 | 19 | 71 |
| Springfontein | 2678 | 101 | 452 | 2593 | 69 | 319 | 2592 | 31 | 143 |
| Vredefort Road | 1983 | 62 | 375 | 1967 | 60 | 366 | 1887 | 41 | 260 |
| Winburg . . | 3127 | 92 | 353 | 2995 | 81 | 324 | 2978 | 42 | 169 |
| Orange River | 1575 | 56 | 427 | 1657 | 9 | 65 | 1706 | 11 | 77 |
| Kromelleboog | 3 | .. | .. | .. | .. | .. | .. | .. | .. |
| | 45,083 | 1340 | .. | 43,755 | 1250 | .. | 42,404 | 755 | .. |

## TABLE VII.—*Continued.*

| 1902 . . . | FEBRUARY. | | | MARCH. | | |
|---|---|---|---|---|---|---|
| | Pop'n. | Deaths | Rate. | Pop'n. | Deaths | Rate. |
| Aliwal North | 4472 | 16 | 41 | 4484 | 10 | 27 |
| Bloemfontein | 5880 | 50 | 102 | 5694 | 28 | 59 |
| Brandfort . . | 4090 | 40 | 117 | 3901 | 24 | 74 |
| Bethulie . . | 4043 | 33 | 98 | 4047 | 11 | 32 |
| Heilbron . . | 2850 | 19 | 79 | 921 | 18 | 234 |
| Harrismith . | 608 | 4 | 79 | 348 | 1 | 34 |
| Kroonstad . | 3500 | 31 | 106 | 3528 | 13 | 44 |
| Kimberley . | 3503 | 12 | 41 | 2885 | 12 | 50 |
| Ladybrand . | .. | .. | .. | .. | .. | .. |
| Norval's Pont | 3479 | 2 | 7 | 3476 | 6 | 20 |
| Springfontein | 2573 | 24 | 112 | 2564 | 13 | 61 |
| Vredefort Road | 1871 | 14 | 89 | 1806 | 7 | 45 |
| Winburg . . | 2561 | 31 | 145 | 2537 | 22 | 104 |
| Orange River | 1699 | 13 | 92 | 1688 | 14 | 99 |
| Kromelleboog | .. | .. | .. | .. | .. | .. |
| | 41,138 | 289 | .. | 37,939 | 179 | .. |

# TABLE VIII.

## CONCENTRATION CAMPS OF NATAL.

TABLE showing for each Camp (so far as recorded) the POPULATION at the end of each month, DEATHS and DEATH-RATE (in *dark figures*) per 1,000 per annum. Where data exist for its calculation, the mean Population for the month is shown in *italic figures*, and the Death-Rate is calculated on this mean.

| 1901 | MARCH. | | | JUNE. | | | JULY. | | |
|---|---|---|---|---|---|---|---|---|---|
| | Pop'n. | Deaths | Rate. | Pop'n. | Deaths | Rate. | Pop'n. | Deaths | Rate. |
| Ladysmith . | .. | .. | .. | .. | .. | .. | .. | .. | .. |
| Colenso . . | .. | .. | .. | .. | .. | .. | .. | .. | .. |
| Howick . . | 705 | .. | . | 649 *658* | 1 | 18 | 678 *663* | .. | .. |
| P'termaritzb'rg | 1819 | .. | .. | 1965 *1913* | 6 | 37 | 2073 *2018* | 6 | 35 |
| Jacobs . . . | .. | .. | .. | .. | .. | .. | .. | .. | .. |
| Wentworth . | .. | .. | .. | .. | .. | .. | .. | .. | .. |
| Merebank . . | .. | .. | .. | .. | .. | .. | .. | .. | .. |
| Eshowe . . | .. | .. | .. | .. | .. | .. | .. | .. | .. |
| | 2524 | .. | .. | 2614 | 7 | .. | 2751 | 6 | .. |

| 1901 | AUGUST. | | | SEPTEMBER. | | | OCTOBER. | | |
|---|---|---|---|---|---|---|---|---|---|
| | Pop'n. | Deaths | Rate. | Pop'n. | Deaths | Rate. | Pop'n. | Deaths | Rate. |
| Ladysmith . | .. | .. | .. | .. | .. | .. | | | |
| Colenso . . | .. | .. | .. | .. | .. | .. | | | |
| Howick . . | 674 *679* | 2 | 35 | 2323 *1499* | 1 | 8 | | | |
| P'termaritzb'rg | 2174 *2134* | 22 | 124 | 2161 *2155* | 45 | 251 | 9112 | 75 | .. |
| Jacobs . . . | .. | .. | .. | .. | .. | .. | | | |
| Wentworth . | .. | .. | .. | .. | .. | .. | | | |
| Merebank . . | .. | .. | .. | 1560 *779* | 6 | 92 | | | |
| Eshowe . . | .. | .. | .. | .. | .. | .. | | | |
| | 2848 | 24 | .. | 6044 | 52 | .. | | | |

**TABLE VIII.—*Continued.***

| 1901 | November. | | | December. | | | 1902. January. | | |
|---|---|---|---|---|---|---|---|---|---|
| | Pop'n. | Deaths | Rate. | Pop'n. | Deaths | Rate. | Pop'n. | Deaths | Rate. |
| Ladysmith . | | | | | | | .. | .. | .. |
| Colenso . . | | | | | | | .. | .. | .. |
| Howick . . | | | | | | | 3323 | 13 | 47 |
| P'termaritzb'rg | 10,185 | 74 | .. | 11,129 | 147 | .. | 2266 | 2 | 10 |
| Jacobs . . . | | | | | | | .. | .. | .. |
| Wentworth . | | | | | | | .. | .. | .. |
| Merebank . . | | | | | | | 6364 | 70 | 132 |
| Eshowe . . | | | | | | | 253 | .. | .. |
| | | | | | | | 12,206 | 85 | .. |

| 1902 | February. | | | March. | | |
|---|---|---|---|---|---|---|
| | Pop'n. | Deaths | Rate. | Pop'n. | Deaths | Rate. |
| Ladysmith . | 1044 | 1 | 11 | 1043 | .. | .. |
| Colenso . . | 2371 | 3 | 12 | 2384 | 10 | 40 |
| Howick . . | 3330 | 5 | 18 | 3305 | 2 | 7 |
| P'termaritzb'rg | 2263 | 5 | 26 | 2326 | 4 | 20 |
| Jacobs . . . | 1094 | 1 | 11 | 2587 | 11 | 51 |
| Wentworth . | .. | .. | .. | 33 | .. | .. |
| Merebank . . | 8342 | 36 | 51 | 8305 | 43 | 62 |
| Eshowe . . | 231 | 1 | 52 | 232 | .. | .. |
| | 19,175 | 52 | .. | 20,715 | 70 | .. |

# Appendix C

## LIST OF FARMS

| | |
|---|---|
| S. W., A. W., and H. A. C. Meintjes . . | Dansfontein. |
| J. P. Meintjes . . . . . | Minverdrag. |
| G. C. Erasmus . . . . . | Populuefontein. |
| M. and P. J. Meintjes . . . | Bundput. |
| S. W. Meintjes . . . . . | Randfontein. |
| H. A. Meintjes . . . . . | Uitzecht. |
| P. J. Meintjes . . . . . | Langlaagte. |
| A. W. Meintjes . . . . . | Karrookan. |
| J. A. Meintjes . . . . . | Boschkopje. |
| A. Labuschagne . . . . | Grootvlei. |
| O. Botha . . . . . . | „ |
| C. Labuschagne . . . . | „ |
| — Lotter . . . . . . | „ |
| A. Keeve . . . . . . | Palin. |
| P. Delport . . . . . . | Kroonbloem. |
| W. Botha . . . . . . | Gast Vryheid. |
| C. F. Le Roux . . . . . | Langkuil. |
| E. P. Serfontein . . . . | Tochgekregen. |
| —————— . . . . . | Eerste Geluk. |
| A. Meyer and H. Serfontein . . | Roodewal. |
| M. S. W. Combrinck . . . . | Rietgat. |
| E. P. Serfontein . . . . | Graspan. |
| Prinsloo (several) . . . . | Doornland. |
| B. J. Van Niekerk . . . . | Klipkraal. |
| H. Klopper and others . . . | „ |
| D. Kleynhaus . . . . . | Doornkop. |
| G. Vosloo . . . . . . | Loskop. |
| H. Vosloo . . . . . . | Boschpoort. |
| (H.) Steyn . . . . . . | Doorndraai. |
| (H.) Loggenberg . . . . | Kopje Alleen. |
| — Labuschagne . . . . . | ... |
| D. C., H. P., and W. Serfontein . . | { Liverpool and Schwirepoort. |
| J. Besters (several) . . . . | Uitenhage. |

The following is a list of some farms burned and destroyed by British troops, during September and part of October 1901; the families have been brought into Irene Camp—10th October 1901—and affidavits were taken there :—

### SEPTEMBER 1901.

| Names. | Destroyed or Burned. | Officer. | Farm. | |
|---|---|---|---|---|
| Michael Adriaan v. d. Berg. | House. | Broadwood. | Buffelsfontein, | Pretoria. |
| Piet. Gert. Labuschagne. | ,, | ,, | ,, | ,, |
| W. J. A. van Schalkwyk. | 3 houses. | ,, | ,, | ,, |
| T. J. Barnard. | 1 house. | ,, | ,, | ,, |
| J. G. Erasmus. | 2 houses. | Clements. | Leeuwfontein, | Rustenberg. |
| J. J. H. Engelbrecht. | 7 houses. | ,, | Groenkloof, | ,, |
| J. H. du Plessis. | 1 house. | Broadwood. | Elandskraal, | ,, |
| L. A. S. van Wyk. | ,, | ,, | ,, | ,, |
| W. J. Jacobs. | 2 houses. | ,, | Buffelshoek, | ,, |
| J. C. Barnard. | 2 ,, | ,, | ,, | ,, |
| W. C. Barnard. | 4 ,, | ,, | ,, | ,, |
| D. J. C. Riekert. | 1 house. | Paget. | Rietfontein, | Pretoria. |
| S. C. le Roux. | ,, | ,, | ,, | ,, |
| A. G. Riekert (widow). | ,, | ,, | ,, | ,, |
| P. J. Viljoen. | 4 houses. | ,, | Witkopjes, | ,, |
| J. Coetzee. | 3 ,, | Colenbrander. | Boschfontein, | ,, |
| M. W. Jacobse. | ... | ,, | Nylstroom, | ,, |
| J. J. Uys. | 1 house. | ,, | Zeebrandkloof, | ,, |
| A. J. Kleinsmit. | 3 houses. | ... | Rooiplatz, | ,, |
| C. C. Minnaar (widow). | 1 house. | English at Eerste Fabr. | Elandsfontein, | ,, |
| J. A. Bosman. | 1 house. | ,, | ,, | ,, |
| W. B. Prinsloo. | 2 houses. | ,, | Crocodilspruit | ,, |
| C. J. de Waal. | ,, | ,, | Dykkop, | ,, |
| J. A. Liedenberg. | 1 house. | ,, | Rooiplatz, | ,, |
| M. Opperman. | 3 houses. | ,, | Bopsfontein, | ,, |
| D. J. Steenkamp. | 2 ,, | ,, | Klipfontein, | ,, |
| J. F. P. Erasmus. | ,, | ,, | Klipspruit, | ,, |

| Names. | Destroyed or Burned. | Officer. | Farm. | |
|---|---|---|---|---|
| M. J. Jacobs. | 2 houses. | English at Eerste Fabr. | Buffelshoek. | |
| J. J. Maret. | ,, | ,, | V. Dykspruit, | Pretoria. |
| M. C. M. Fourie (widow). | 3 ,, | ,, | De Kroonspruit, | ,, |
| P. J. L. de Beer. | ,, | ,, | Rooitplaat, | ,, |
| J. H. Botha (widow). | 1 house. | Kitchener. | Derdepoot, | ,, |
| W. J. J. Buckley (widow). | 3 houses. | ,, | Rooiplatt, | ,, |
| H. J. Botha. | 1 house. | ,, | ,, | ,, |
| J. A. Benkes. | 4 houses. | Plumer. | Zusterhoek, | ,, |
| J. H. Botha. | 2 ,, | ,, | Doornfontein, | ,, |
| S. S. Dreyer. | 1 house. | Kekewich. | V. Dykspruit, | ,, |
| J. L. J. Erasmus. | 4 houses. | ,, | Hartebeestspruit, | ,, |
| L. J. Erasmus. | 2 ,, | English. | V. Dykspruit, | ,, |
| B. J. Geldenhuis. | 2 ,, | Plumer. | Klipkkopje, | ,, |
| S. J. C. Jansen (widow). | 1 house. | Kitchener. | Tweepoort, | ,, |
| R. J. van Jaarsveld. | 3 houses. | English. | V. Dykspruit, | ,, |
| G. S. Koekemoer. | 4 ,, | ,, | Zusterhoek, | ,, |
| E. Gesyn (unmarried). | 3 ,, | ,, | Witfontein, | ,, |
| M. J. J. Minnaar (widow). | 1 house. | Kitchener. | Tweespruit, | ,, |
| A. L. Oosthuysen (widow). | 3 ,, | ,, | V. Dykspruit, | ,, |
| J. J. Pieterse. | ... | Plumer. | Zustershoek, | ,, |
| M. J. Prinsloo (widow). | 2 houses. | Kitchener. | V. Dykspruit, | ,, |
| S. J. L. Prinsloo. | ,, | ... | Crocodilspruit, | ,, |
| C. J. H. Steenkamp. | 3 ,, | Plumer. | Klipfontein, | ,, |
| W. L. Steenkamp. | 2 ,, | ... | ,, | ,, |
| C. J. S. Vermaak (orphans). | 1 house. | Kitchener. | Tweespruit, | ,, |
| S. J. de Wet (spinster). | 1 ,, | ... | Cameelfontein | ,, |
| M. J. J. de Waal (widow). | ,, | Kitchener. | Tweespruit, | ,, |
| F. J. Wolmarans. | ... | ,, | Derdepoort, | ,, |
| M. C. v. d. Westhuisen (widow). | 3 houses. | ... | Rooikopjes, | ,, |
| C. M. de Waal (orphans). | 2 ,, | Kitchener. | Tweespruit, | ,, |
| P. J. J. Swarts (surrendered). | 7 ,, | Kekewich. | Klipkop, | |

# Appendix D

Unable myself, from lack of time and strength, to investigate the conditions or personally carry relief to the native camps, I confidently expected that the Ladies' Commission would have made it part of their work to do so. After the issue of their Report, which showed that they had not touched this important branch of the concentration system, I called upon Mr. Fox Bourne, and laid before him facts which had come to my knowledge when in South Africa. Clergymen, who worked among the coloured people in these camps, and others, told me sad tales of the sickness and mortality, which was then very high. Beyond giving a little relief for the sick, I was not able to do anything. Subsequently, Mr. Fox Bourne addressed the following letter to Mr. Chamberlain, whose reply is appended. The mortality list, compiled from official sources, is obviously incomplete, and only commences in June. To my knowledge, deaths had been numerous during the previous months.

Mr. Fox Bourne to Mr. Chamberlain.

Broadway Chambers, Westminster, S.W.

Sir,—I have the honour, by direction of the Committee of the Aborigines Protection Society, to address you with reference to the native refuge camps in South Africa.

From the very scanty information as to these camps which is incidentally furnished in the papers relating to the working of the refuge camps which have been laid before Parliament (Cd. 789, 793, 853, 854, 902 and 936), it appears that, in addition to the white refugees, there were under government control, in August 1901, 32,272 coloured persons, about five-sixths of whom were women and children, and all but about a sixteenth in the Orange River Colony; and that the number had risen to

43,594 in the Orange River Colony alone on 15th November last, with which date the information as regards that Colony ceases. It further appears that the death-rate in the Orange River Colony native camps, which, according to the returns, was about 170 per 1,000 in August, and about 91 per 1,000 in September, rose from 137 per 1,000 in the first fortnight of October to 363 per 1,000 in the first fortnight of November.

In the Transvaal, moreover, it is shown by the returns that the number of natives in the refuge camps had risen from 1,829 in August to 39,323 in November, the latest month accounted for, and the death-rate, which was about 242 per 1,000 in August, exceeded 291 in November.

If statements that have reached our Committee from private sources are accurate, the death-rate at some of the native camps, including those at Bloemfontein, Edenberg, Springfontein, and Klerksdorp, greatly exceeds those appalling figures; and though the diet appointed and paid for by the authorities may be adequate, the actual supply of food is often very unsatisfactory, especially in the case of young children.

Our Committee is aware that the conditions of native life inevitably render the concentration of large numbers within limited areas extremely insanitary, and it offers no opinion as to the policy of thus disposing of the wives and children of male natives employed for the most part in services connected with the war. But it asks that such inquiries may be instituted by His Majesty's Government as should secure for the natives who are detained no less care and humanity than are now prescribed for the Boer refuge camps.

As a preliminary to any further steps that may be deemed proper, I am to suggest the expediency of a report being called for, giving much fuller information as to the condition of these camps, the accommodation and treatment provided in each, and other details, than are contained in the Parliamentary papers; also to ask that this information, while including reference to the earlier state of affairs in the Transvaal, Cape Colony, and Natal, as well as in the Orange River Colony, shall be continued for the period subsequent to November, when the increased death-rate was so startling.

I am also to respectfully suggest to you the appointment of a Ladies' Committee, the members of which might be satisfactorily selected from residents in South Africa, to be entrusted with a mission for the benefit of the natives, similar to that which has been so useful in the case of the Boer women and children.

I have the honour to be, Sir, your obedient Servant,

H. R. Fox Bourne.

March 24, 1902.

Mr. Chamberlain's reply, dated May 2, contained the following passages, and enclosed the report of the Superintendent of the Department:—

2. I enclose a copy of the latest report on the working of the native camps in the Orange River Colony which has been received in this Department It has since been ascertained by telegraph that in the native camps in the Transvaal, with a population of 40,000, the deaths in January were about 880, in February 550, and in March 400.

3. In the Orange River Colony, with a population of about 45,000 in native locations, the deaths were in January about 1400, in February about 800, and in March about 470.

4. The figures given above appear to show that the conditions of life in the native camps have improved considerably, and Mr. Chamberlain has no doubt that Lord Milner will not fail to exercise all proper care in dealing with the natives who are dependent on the government.

I am, Sir, your obedient servant,

Fred. Graham.

The Secretary to the Aborigines Protection Society.

Native Refugee Department,
Bloemfontein, 2nd January 1902.

Sir,—I have the honour to forward herewith a copy of the November return for the native refugee camps in the Orange River Colony. . . .

The several reports by the camp superintendent have been of a very satisfactory nature.

Discipline in the camps has been uniformly good, and the natives seem generally contented, and are readily turning out for work both with the government and on the lands round the camps, which are being cultivated for their own benefit. The death-rate appears high, but, under the circumstances, I think it can scarcely be called excessive.

Food has been scarce, and in many cases the natives have had to put up with considerable privations before they were brought into the camps, and, in addition, must be taken into consideration the invariable increase in the death-rate in this country during the hot weather before the breaking of the rains, especially so in the case of young children. Every effort is being made to deal with this matter. Large supplies of comforts, such as milk, sugar, medicine, etc., are being distributed, and I am glad to say that at present there is every sign of a steady decrease of the sick list . . .

To sum up, I consider the report to show a very satisfactory state of affairs generally. The Department is now organised on a sound footing, and the natives themselves appear to thoroughly understand the present condition of things, and to appreciate the efforts that are being made by His Majesty's Government on their behalf.

I have, etc.,

(Sd.)                                         F. Wilson Fox, Capt.,
                        Supt. Native Refugee Department, O. R. C.

TABLE I.—POPULATION AND DEATHS IN NATIVE CAMPS.

| Date. | Official Return. | Camps. | Population. | | | | Deaths. | | | |
|---|---|---|---|---|---|---|---|---|---|---|
| | | | Men. | Women. | Children. | Total. | Men. | W'm'n. | Ch'n. | Total. |
| **1901**<br>June | Cd. 608 | Natal | 7 | 2 | 11 | 20 | … | … | … | Nil. |
| | " | O. R. C. | 2076 | 7313 | 11,201 | 20,590 | … | … | … | " |
| | " | Transvaal | 244 | 800 | 1,835 | 2,879 | … | … | … | 5 |
| | | | | | | 23,489 | | | | |
| July | Cd. 694 | Natal | 7 | 6 | 17 | 30 | … | … | … | Nil. |
| | " | O. R. C. | 2622 | 7947 | 12,431 | 23,000 | 43 | 49 | 164 | 256 |
| | " | Transvaal | 517 | 309 | 598 | 1,424[1] | … | … | … | 7 |
| | | | | | | 24,454 | | | | |
| August | Cd. 789 | Natal | 18 | 28 | 35 | 81 | … | … | … | Nil. |
| | " | O. R. C. | 3495 | 9724 | 17,140 | 30,359 | 40 | 57 | 333 | 430 |
| | " | Transvaal | 695 | 394 | 740 | 1,829 | … | … | … | 37 |
| | Cd. 819, 313 | Do. N.L.D. | 2278 | 3639 | 8,822 | 16,739 | … | … | … | … |
| | | | | 2000[3] | | 49,008 | | | | |

| Month | Cd. No. | Province | | | | | | | | |
|---|---|---|---|---|---|---|---|---|---|---|
| September | Cd. 793 | Natal | 1 | 1 | 22 | 24 | … | … | 2 | 2 |
| | ,, | O. R. C. | 4453 | 11,136 | 20,893 | 36,482 | … | … | … | 277 |
| | | Transvaal | 737 | 503 | 801 | 2,041 | … | … | … | 22 |
| | Cd.'' 853, 35 | Do. N. L. D. | 3942 | 5,763 | 13,090 | 22,795 | … | … | … | … |
| | | | | | | 61,342 | | | | |
| October | Cd. 853, 130 | Natal | … | … | … | 33 | … | … | … | Nil. |
| | ,, | O. R. C. | 6000 | 13,574 | 22,253 | 41,827 | 57 | 85 | 556 | 698 |
| | ,, | Transvaal | 755 | 451 | 747 | 1,953 | … | … | … | 37 |
| | Cd.'' 934. 75³ | Do. N. L. D. | 6032 | 8,165 | 17,890 | 32,006 | … | … | … | … |
| | | | | | | 75,819 | | | | |
| November | Cd. 853, 131 | Natal | 5968 | No Return. | 23,671 | 43,594 | 38 | 63 | 473 | 574⁴ |
| | ,, | O. R. C. | … | 13,955 | … | … | … | … | … | … |
| | ,, | Transvaal | … | No Return. | … | … | … | … | … | … |
| | ,, | Do. N. L. D. | | | | | | | | |
| December | … | Natal | … | … | … | … | … | … | … | … |
| | | O. R. C. | … | … | … | … | … | … | … | … |
| | Cd. 936, 31 | Transvaal | 7472 | 10,591 | 21,260 | 39,323 | 39 | 83 | 834 | 956 |

[1] Cd. 819, 225, "This does not include Returns of Native Refugee Camps, under the control of the Native Labour Depôt."
[2] "Refugees at Klerksdorp not yet classified."
[3] The Return gives a list of twenty camps and a depôt.
[4] These are the deaths for a fortnight only.

# Appendix E

It has been difficult in some cases to ascertain the exact month of the establishment of camps, and where doubt exists, if the camp actually began in 1900 or 1901, the name is asterisked.

|  | Red 1900. | Blue 1901. | Green 1902. |
|---|---|---|---|
| TRANSVAAL. | Johannesburg. | Balmoral. | |
| | Krugersdorp. | Middelburg. | |
| | Klerksdorp. | Barberton. | |
| | Vereeniging. | Volksrust. | |
| | Standerton. | Pietersburg. | |
| | Heidelberg. | Nylstroom. | |
| | Potchefstroom. | Belfast. | |
| | Irene.* | | |
| | Mafeking. | | |
| O. R. C. | Heilbron. | Harrismith. | |
| | Vredefort Road.* | Vryburg. | |
| | Kroonstad. | Winburg.* | |
| | Bloemfontein. | Orange River. | |
| | Norval's Pont. | Brandfort.* | |
| | | Kimberley. | |
| | | Springfontein. | |
| | | Bethulie. | |
| | | Aliwal North. | |
| NATAL. | Pietermaritzburg. | Merebank. | Ladysmith. |
| | Howick.* | | Mooi River. |
| | | | Colenso. |
| | | | Eshowe. |
| | | | Jacobs and |
| | | | Wentworth. |
| | | | Uitenhage. |
| CAPE COLONY. | Port Elizabeth. | | East London. |

**LEONAUR**

# ALSO FROM LEONAUR

### AVAILABLE IN SOFTCOVER OR HARDCOVER WITH DUST JACKET

**THE FALL OF THE MOGHUL EMPIRE OF HINDUSTAN** *by H. G. Keene*—By the beginning of the nineteenth century, as British and Indian armies under Lake and Wellesley dominated the scene, a little over half a century of conflict brought the Moghul Empire to its knees.

**LADY SALE'S AFGHANISTAN** *by Florentia Sale*—An Indomitable Victorian Lady's Account of the Retreat from Kabul During the First Afghan War.

**THE CAMPAIGN OF MAGENTA AND SOLFERINO 1859** *by Harold Carmichael Wylly*—The Decisive Conflict for the Unification of Italy.

**FRENCH'S CAVALRY CAMPAIGN** *by J. G. Maydon*—A Special Correspondent's View of British Army Mounted Troops During the Boer War.

**CAVALRY AT WATERLOO** *by Sir Evelyn Wood*—British Mounted Troops During the Campaign of 1815.

**THE SUBALTERN** *by George Robert Gleig*—The Experiences of an Officer of the 85th Light Infantry During the Peninsular War.

**NAPOLEON AT BAY, 1814** *by F. Loraine Petre*—The Campaigns to the Fall of the First Empire.

**NAPOLEON AND THE CAMPAIGN OF 1806** *by Colonel Vachée*—The Napoleonic Method of Organisation and Command to the Battles of Jena & Auerstädt.

**THE COMPLETE ADVENTURES IN THE CONNAUGHT RANGERS** *by William Grattan*—The 88th Regiment during the Napoleonic Wars by a Serving Officer.

**BUGLER AND OFFICER OF THE RIFLES** *by William Green & Harry Smith*—With the 95th (Rifles) during the Peninsular & Waterloo Campaigns of the Napoleonic Wars.

**NAPOLEONIC WAR STORIES** *by Sir Arthur Quiller-Couch*—Tales of soldiers, spies, battles & sieges from the Peninsular & Waterloo campaingns.

**CAPTAIN OF THE 95TH (RIFLES)** *by Jonathan Leach*—An officer of Wellington's sharpshooters during the Peninsular, South of France and Waterloo campaigns of the Napoleonic wars.

**RIFLEMAN COSTELLO** *by Edward Costello*—The adventures of a soldier of the 95th (Rifles) in the Peninsular & Waterloo Campaigns of the Napoleonic wars.

LEONAUR

# ALSO FROM LEONAUR
## AVAILABLE IN SOFTCOVER OR HARDCOVER WITH DUST JACKET

**ZULU:1879** *by D.C.F. Moodie & the Leonaur Editors*—The Anglo-Zulu War of 1879 from contemporary sources: First Hand Accounts, Interviews, Dispatches, Official Documents & Newspaper Reports.

**THE RED DRAGOON** *by W.J. Adams*—With the 7th Dragoon Guards in the Cape of Good Hope against the Boers & the Kaffir tribes during the 'war of the axe' 1843-48'.

**THE RECOLLECTIONS OF SKINNER OF SKINNER'S HORSE** *by James Skinner*—James Skinner and his 'Yellow Boys' Irregular cavalry in the wars of India between the British, Mahratta, Rajput, Mogul, Sikh & Pindarree Forces.

**A CAVALRY OFFICER DURING THE SEPOY REVOLT** *by A. R. D. Mackenzie*—Experiences with the 3rd Bengal Light Cavalry, the Guides and Sikh Irregular Cavalry from the outbreak to Delhi and Lucknow.

**A NORFOLK SOLDIER IN THE FIRST SIKH WAR** *by J W Baldwin*—Experiences of a private of H.M. 9th Regiment of Foot in the battles for the Punjab, India 1845-6.

**TOMMY ATKINS' WAR STORIES: 14 FIRST HAND ACCOUNTS**—Fourteen first hand accounts from the ranks of the British Army during Queen Victoria's Empire.

**THE WATERLOO LETTERS** *by H. T. Siborne*—Accounts of the Battle by British Officers for its Foremost Historian.

**NEY: GENERAL OF CAVALRY VOLUME 1—1769-1799** *by Antoine Bulos*—The Early Career of a Marshal of the First Empire.

**NEY: MARSHAL OF FRANCE VOLUME 2—1799-1805** *by Antoine Bulos*—The Early Career of a Marshal of the First Empire.

**AIDE-DE-CAMP TO NAPOLEON** *by Philippe-Paul de Ségur*—For anyone interested in the Napoleonic Wars this book, written by one who was intimate with the strategies and machinations of the Emperor, will be essential reading.

**TWILIGHT OF EMPIRE** *by Sir Thomas Ussher & Sir George Cockburn*—Two accounts of Napoleon's Journeys in Exile to Elba and St. Helena: Narrative of Events by Sir Thomas Ussher & Napoleon's Last Voyage: Extract of a diary by Sir George Cockburn.

**PRIVATE WHEELER** *by William Wheeler*—The letters of a soldier of the 51st Light Infantry during the Peninsular War & at Waterloo.

LEONAUR

# ALSO FROM LEONAUR
## AVAILABLE IN SOFTCOVER OR HARDCOVER WITH DUST JACKET

**ESCAPE FROM THE FRENCH** *by Edward Boys*—A Young Royal Navy Midshipman's Adventures During the Napoleonic War.

**THE VOYAGE OF H.M.S. PANDORA** *by Edward Edwards R. N. & George Hamilton, edited by Basil Thomson*—In Pursuit of the Mutineers of the Bounty in the South Seas—1790-1791.

**MEDUSA** *by J. B. Henry Savigny and Alexander Correard and Charlotte-Adélaïde Dard* —Narrative of a Voyage to Senegal in 1816 & The Sufferings of the Picard Family After the Shipwreck of the Medusa.

**THE SEA WAR OF 1812 VOLUME 1** *by A. T. Mahan*—A History of the Maritime Conflict.

**THE SEA WAR OF 1812 VOLUME 2** *by A. T. Mahan*—A History of the Maritime Conflict.

**WETHERELL OF H. M. S. HUSSAR** *by John Wetherell*—The Recollections of an Ordinary Seaman of the Royal Navy During the Napoleonic Wars.

**THE NAVAL BRIGADE IN NATAL** *by C. R. N. Burne*—With the Guns of H. M. S. Terrible & H. M. S. Tartar during the Boer War 1899-1900.

**THE VOYAGE OF H. M. S. BOUNTY** *by William Bligh*—The True Story of an 18th Century Voyage of Exploration and Mutiny.

**SHIPWRECK!** *by William Gilly*—The Royal Navy's Disasters at Sea 1793-1849.

**KING'S CUTTERS AND SMUGGLERS: 1700-1855** *by E. Keble Chatterton*—A unique period of maritime history-from the beginning of the eighteenth to the middle of the nineteenth century when British seamen risked all to smuggle valuable goods from wool to tea and spirits from and to the Continent.

**CONFEDERATE BLOCKADE RUNNER** *by John Wilkinson*—The Personal Recollections of an Officer of the Confederate Navy.

**NAVAL BATTLES OF THE NAPOLEONIC WARS** *by W. H. Fitchett*—Cape St. Vincent, the Nile, Cadiz, Copenhagen, Trafalgar & Others.

**PRISONERS OF THE RED DESERT** *by R. S. Gwatkin-Williams*—The Adventures of the Crew of the Tara During the First World War.

**U-BOAT WAR 1914-1918** *by James B. Connolly/Karl von Schenk*—Two Contrasting Accounts from Both Sides of the Conflict at Sea D uring the Great War.

Ingram Content Group UK Ltd.
Milton Keynes UK
UKHW042339030523
421181UK00001B/151